Feedback on Rational Spirituality

'I think Ian Lawton deserves more attention than he is getting. *The Little Book of the Soul* is well written, clear, logical, honest. He isn't making a bid to be your next guru. He's just contributing, I think quite effectively, to what he perceives to be an important next step in human development, namely bringing science and reason to bear on issues of spirituality. The book captured me, because Lawton offers an interesting and original idea that seems to me a plausible explanation for an important paradox in spirituality. One can experience in mystical vision that one's identity is not different from that of God. At the same time, near-death and regression research offers much evidence for an afterlife or reincarnation, and some of that evidence is presented in this book. But who are you really? Are you an individuated soul that passes from body to body? Or are you identified with the Godhead who does not know limitation or passage through time? He proposes that this paradox can be understood by regarding our souls as holographic.'

Margaret Magnus, amazon.com

'*The Book of the Soul* is a triumph. I bought it twice so that I could read it with both eyes! It's not as thick as *Genesis Unveiled* – another stunning masterpiece – but the content is twice as meaty. It shows the interlife in such vivid detail that I can't wait to die! I love the book so much that I have taken to stalking Ian Lawton in an attempt to pressure him into writing more. Rock on Rational Spirituality!'

Ashley Bradbury, personal correspondence

'Are you ready for a life-changing book? *The Book of the Soul* is the most amazing book I have ever read, and one which I know has already changed my life for the better. I'm an analyst by profession, so it's in my nature to have all the facts in front of me, and from those facts make rational judgment calls backed up by evidence of why I chose that path.

I was brought up in a family who considered themselves faith healers, looked after by spirit guides etc. So as a child I was always being told stories of miracles or tales of what their guides had told them about life and death. To me this was simply an opportunity to be told another story and I didn't really buy any of it. As I have grown up, as we all have, I have come to feel that religion is a control mechanism to provide people with power and authority over mankind, and that people believe because they can't face up to not having something to believe in. But it's depressing to believe that this really is it, and this had left me rather despondent. I did believe in the power of the mind and that we are somehow not living to our full potential, but I have no interest in new age religion, and can't fully accept concepts that aren't backed up by scientific fact. However, directed by a friend, in Rational Spiritualists I have finally found like-minded people who aren't just flying along on a belief system because they can't handle not having a god of some kind to believe in. I ordered the book straight away and within the first chapter I was blown away by what I was reading. Ian Lawton does not push his views, he researches and analyses all alternatives and then presents his conclusions based on facts.

Now my outlook on life and death is somewhat different. My character is changing too. I feel that I have more patience with people, and have started to be more positive about human nature and the individuals on this planet. Instead of judging people for their actions, I try to understand why they acted like they did. I also have started to become aware of how I handle certain situations. In times of stress or grief, it's how you handle those emotions and learn from the experience that is key. And that skill, once learned, will be with you forever. These are just some of the many lessons I have learned from this book.

You know that every once in a while you are asked 'who, dead or alive, would you most like to meet?' For me, Ian Lawton is top of my list. I'm not a writer, so I find it hard to put words together to do justice to him and his book, but somehow he manages to make a potentially complicated subject incredibly easy to understand. He is not aggressive in his beliefs, and his research and knowledge have no end! He has that ability to make you think and consider alternatives regardless of your beliefs. The fact that he has struggled to even get this book published makes him seem more genuine, and in turn makes the concepts in the book more real. Ian's peace, patience and insight make him sound like one of the most incredible individuals on the planet, and I'm incredibly grateful that I've had the opportunity to read this book and to discover Rational Spirituality.'

Anita Newman, amazon.co.uk

'My spiritual quest of the past six years has come to an end. Rational Spirituality is the only alternative to the intellectual suicide of orthodox religion and some of the New Age movements, as well as to the spiritual void of materialist atheism.'

Shereen Schouw, personal correspondence

'Rational Spirituality is something that the western world is in need of, and hopefully can help people become aware of their true natures. Thank you for the opportunity that it offers.'

Gina Chartier, personal correspondence

'I am a clinical hypnotherapist and actively practice past-life work. Much of my work has involved trying to demystify and ground clients and, over the years, myself. I am for anything non hocus-pocus.'

Simon Hartley, personal correspondence

'I've believed in reincarnation for many years, but have not found a religion that contains all the things I feel to be true. After reading *The Book of the Soul* I think that Rational Spirituality makes the most sense.'

Lynn Voedisch, personal correspondence

'Your book was a revelation. It affected me at the deepest level. I think it one of the most extraordinary pieces of spiritual research I have come across. Congratulations and many thanks.'

Anita Woolf, personal correspondence

'I've spent several hours with your book, focusing on sections of particular interest. Really nice work, Ian. I find myself repeatedly agreeing with your assessment of persons and issues. Lots of good, hard-hitting, uncommon common sense. Much appreciated.'

Chris Bache, Professor of Religious Studies at Youngstown State University, personal correspondence

'There is a vast difference between religion and spirituality. Religion divides us, spirituality unites us. It's time each and every one of us awoke to the fact that we are all one and the same. We are of the same eternal Source and we are all in this for the same end. Ian Lawton has tapped this source and come closer than anyone I've witnessed in making it accessible to all. With love and admiration I wish to be a part of this awakening.'

James Gobrecht, personal correspondence

'I think *The Book of the Soul* is one of the best books I have ever read on these topics.'

Rowland Bowker, personal correspondence

'I had the pleasure recently of reading *The Book of the Soul*. Here we have a very unusual book; a book that fills a void in the literature concerning spirituality. This book will appeal to those who question things of faith because there is no scientific evidence, no way to methodically prove it is a reality. I highly recommend that anyone who wishes to educate as well as help heal souls invest in this book.'

Lou Siron, Journal of Regression Therapy

'I have now finished reading your excellent *Book of the Soul*, which I have found insightful, mentally provocative and inspirational. I just want to personally thank you for writing it. As I completed the last pages I knew that I must begin to reread it straight away.'

Adam Donaldson Powell, personal correspondence

'I've read many similar books on the various subjects in your outstanding book, but yours is the best.'

Richard Hartnett, personal correspondence

'Lawton is an exhaustive researcher, and goes to great lengths to present the detail behind an often glossed-over subject. A far better offering than the vast majority of so-called spiritual books out there.'

Greg Taylor, Daily Grail website

'Roger Bacon saw that one day science and religion would merge. *The Book of the Soul* fulfills such a purpose. I cannot say enough good things about it. It is the only book I know of that combines all of the latest and past research on nde's, past-life regression, childhood memories of past lives and between-life experiences. It is scientific yet eminently readable. The author lays out an impressive case for the continuation of the soul.'

William House, Reverse Spins website

'This book is so far removed from the usual lightweight, New Age tosh and drivel pumped out by well-meaning but useless authors that it's not only not in the same room, it's on a different continent. Quite simply this is the most comprehensive, objective, well-researched and fascinating book on reincarnation to have been written in the English language. Really, it is that good.'

David Southwell, amazon.co.uk

THE BIG BOOK OF THE SOUL

RATIONAL SPIRITUALITY FOR THE TWENTY-FIRST CENTURY

IAN LAWTON

Rational Spirituality Press

First published in 2008 by Rational Spirituality Press.
Second Edition 2010.

All enquiries to be directed to www.rspress.org.

A CIP catalogue record for this title is available from the British Library.

ISBN 978-0-9549176-3-0

Cover design by Ian Lawton.
Cover image by Jason Waskey (www.jasonwaskey.com).
Author photograph by James Franklin (www.jamesfranklin.com).

holographic soul, *hol'ögraf'ik söl, n.*

Soul consciousness is holographic. We are both individual aspects of Source, and full holographic representations of it, all at the same time. However this does not mean that soul individuality is in itself an illusion. The principle of the hologram is that the part contains the whole, and yet is clearly distinguishable from it.

The primary aim of Source, in diversifying into all the billions of holographic soul aspects of itself that operate in the various realms throughout the universe, is to experience all that is and can be. So as individualized aspects of Source who have chosen to reincarnate on this planet, we are merely fulfilling a small part of that objective by gaining a balance of the experiences available via this route.

this book is dedicated to the memory of...
my sister Sheila, a true child of nature if ever there was one
my mother Beryl, the most selfless woman I have ever known
and my father Syd, a brilliant role model and true friend

CONTENTS

ACKNOWLEDGMENTS

First of all the following correspondents kindly pointed me towards detailed information in various sources I might otherwise have overlooked: Denise Arvidson, Chris Bebbington, Rowland Bowker, Ashley Bradbury, Mike Davies, Jean Galbraith, Michael Hayes, Beverly Heiss, Ian McFerran, Robert Olson, John Ratcliff, Dave Ward and Michael Willshire-Keen. In particular I would like to single out Gaia Martinez and David Stollar, who rectified my shameful ignorance of what I have come to regard as two of the most important and profound spiritual outlooks ever made available to humanity – those of Sri Aurobindo and the Pathwork Guide.

On a more prosaic level a number of people were good enough to help with obtaining various information: Marion, Janet and Brenda Coffman and Jim Parkman with a video recording of Peter Ramster's rarely seen 1980s documentary about past lives; Veronique Lindholm, Susan Bories and Chris Bright with a French translation of part of this documentary; Stephen Gawtry with sources describing the trial of the Essex witch Agnes Waterhouse; Laila Bergmann about notes and correspondence belonging to her late mother, the past-life regression therapist Linda Tarazi; Thelma Freedman with her studies into past-life therapy; and Michael Newton with an explanation of his historical involvement in interlife regression.

More generally, over the past few years a great many correspondents have generously taken the trouble to write in with positive feedback on Rational Spirituality and on the various *Books of the Soul*, a selection of which is reproduced in the first few pages. Meanwhile David Southwell, Stephen Gawtry, Andy Tomlinson and Judy Hall took the time to provide immensely useful feedback on specific chapters in the current book. Judy also pointed out certain obscure sources of information, as did Hans TenDam; and Hans in turn was gracious enough to provide a quote for the cover, as were Edith Fiore and Jim Tucker.

I am thoroughly indebted to all of the above. But my special thanks go to Mark Goodman, whose long-term support for my work has been so humbly given; to Ian Allen, whose editing remains second to none; and to former partners Sarah Axford and Liz Swanson, for putting me on this path and keeping me on it respectively.

PREFACE

To understand the context of this book we need to delve, at least a little, into the history of humanity's attitude to religious, spiritual and metaphysical ideas. First of all, although we cannot be certain what approaches may have been taken in the mists of prehistory, I have written elsewhere that there is good reason to suppose early humanity's spiritual worldview was rather more sophisticated than is normally assumed. Indeed once we wash away the clutter and noise that repeated misinterpretation has imposed we find many esoteric yet simple treasures buried in the earliest texts and traditions from all around the globe, and almost certainly these did not emerge when they were first written down, but long beforehand.

Then around five thousand years ago the first major civilizations of recorded history, those of Ancient Mesopotamia and Egypt, began to introduce the idea of organized, state-sponsored religion that has provided the pretext for countless wars, suppressions and conquests ever since. Moreover, although religious belief has clearly provided strength, hope and courage to millions of individuals, no longer can anyone sensibly deny that for millennia the main religions of the world have used fear and intimidation to impose entirely subjective moral codes on their followers, primarily to keep them under political control. The concept of eternal damnation in hell is a fine case in point.

It is this, coupled with the demonstrably illogical and faith-based nature of traditional religious belief, that has provided such a fertile hunting ground for modern atheism. Indeed, we can hardly disagree with the disgust of its transatlantic figureheads, Daniel Dennett and Richard Dawkins, that the advance of secular science in recent centuries has done little to affect humanity's ability to tear itself apart by masquerading behind the mask of different religions. They are intelligent men who seem to care deeply about our planet, about humanity and its future, and especially about making sure that future generations are sufficiently educated to break out of this repeating pattern. For all this they are to be applauded.

But I would beg to differ with them over their assumption that *all* spiritual belief is inherently irrational. This is why for many years I have been developing and refining 'Rational Spirituality' – a spiritual approach that relies primarily on *evidence*, not *faith*; and the choice of battleground is key to this. Dennett and Dawkins deliberately concentrate on the issue of

1

evolution versus creationism or intelligent design. But this is really only a sideshow because metaphysically inclined scientists are increasingly accepting that the key question is not whether evolution happens – it clearly does – but how and why a universe was created in which it even *could* happen.

By contrast other atheist-skeptics like James Randi, of 'million-dollar challenge' fame, concentrate their attacks on the typical spiritualist areas of clairvoyance, mediumship, telepathy and so on. There are undoubtedly many gifted psychics in existence, but some are not averse to using pure psychological trickery to fake supposedly paranormal abilities when they are in the spotlight, especially if this forms the main source of their reputation and living. The damage this causes is enormous, however, because by giving skeptics such an easy target they encourage the natural tendency to 'throw the baby out with the bathwater'.

So what sort of evidence does Rational Spirituality adduce? The prime areas of research are into near-death and out-of-body experiences, spontaneous past-life memories in both children and adults, and past-life and interlife regression – each of which we will discuss in detail in the main chapters. In all these areas we find cases in which subjects recall incredibly obscure information that is subsequently verified, although sometimes only with great difficulty, providing compelling evidence for a spiritual worldview. That this view is also the most *rational* interpretation is evinced by the largely reductionist and indeed irrational dismissals of materialists and skeptics, as we will see. Moreover it is because sometimes-new evidence emerges, or new analysis is required, that this book is a complete rewrite of the original *Book of the Soul*.

So Rational Spirituality is deliberately designed to provide a new way forward in what has now become a somewhat stagnant debate between atheists and believers. Its motto 'evidence not faith' emphasizes that is has its roots firmly planted in the fertile soil of modern evidence, in contrast to traditional religions that tend to rely heavily on faith in ancient scripture and modern interpretations of it. But that is not to say that faith, or perhaps better trust, does not have its place. Total trust in the behind-the-scenes dynamics of the universe is fundamental to a Rational Spiritual worldview. Nor does it underestimate the power and majesty of transformative spiritual experiences, or underplay the ultimate spiritual message of universal, unconditional love.

Which leads us neatly onto the fact that evolution-versus-creation is by no means the only spiritual debate of crucial significance in the modern world. The last half-century has witnessed a marked movement away from traditional Western religions towards the mysticism of the East. To begin with a Hindu-style approach to the reincarnation of the individual soul and its cycle of karma came to the fore. But gradually a more Buddhist flavor has crept in, with modern spiritual seekers increasingly attracted to the idea of a divine universal energy or consciousness of which we all form part. This idea of 'the unity of everything' has always formed the basis of transcendental experiences achieved either via prolonged meditation or, for the lucky few, spontaneously. In recent decades it has been strengthened by increasing numbers of people having, or at least reading about, similar experiences induced by hallucinogens. And there has been one final impetus for this more unity-oriented approach, and that is the relatively recent emergence of a number of scientists and metaphysicians, who have used theoretical physics and other research to argue that everything in the universe, both seen and unseen, is fundamentally interconnected. But this approach can also foster 'illusionism' – that is the assumption that either the physical world, or even any notion of soul individuality, is illusory. The implication under either view tends to be that our main purpose is to 'see through' the illusion, and these ideas seem to be increasingly attracting those of a more intellectual spiritual persuasion.

So where does the truth lie? Do our individual souls reincarnate repeatedly to fulfill some sort of purpose? Or do they do so only as long as we fail to see through the illusion of the physical world? Or is the whole notion of individuality so illusory that as soon as we die our soul consciousness again merges with Source? The option that we favor is surely of crucial importance, because it must have a huge bearing on the context within which we view our everyday lives in the physical world. Or is there another way of looking at all this? Many approaches tend to concentrate *either* on the evidence for individual soul reincarnation, *or* on the evidence for a universal soul consciousness. Yet it seems clear that there is strong evidence in support of both. So is there a way of understanding how both propositions might be true at the same time? And is there a framework under which the supposed illusion can in fact be seen as a deliberate part of the overall plan – indeed part of the very reason why Source bothers to manifest the universe in the first place?

When I wrote the original *Book of the Soul* in 2004 I was dimly aware that both individual and universal soul consciousness must be recognized:[1] 'There is a dualistic element to any intelligent spiritual worldview that accepts we are individual souls, but also merely parts of the ultimate

3

oversoul, all at the same time.' However I said little else about this idea, and was only forced to give it more consideration by several correspondents of a more universalist persuasion. Over time my thoughts crystallized until in 2005 I realized that the concept of the hologram was crucial. Of course I knew that eminent thinkers such as Karl Pribram and David Bohm had been at the forefront of developing the idea that the brain and indeed the entire universe operate holographically, but ironically this had led them and many others to adopt a primarily universalist standpoint. Whereas it seemed to me that, if a spiritual theory was going to accommodate *both* the individual *and* universal aspects of the evidence, the holographic principle needed to be applied to soul consciousness itself. So finally, when writing *The Wisdom of the Soul* in 2006, I formulated and defined the concept of the 'holographic soul'.

Despite this hopeful improvement, up until now the emphasis of my books and papers has still tended to be on the individual rather than universal. This has been because I felt it was important that people should be able to use the Rational Spiritual framework to inform their approach to their everyday lives, and I still think that is vital. But more recent correspondence and discussion has made me realize just how much I have fallen short by failing to emphasize that, at the same time as being individual souls on our own paths, we are indeed all One. The simple realization, that when we hurt someone or something else or our planet we are ultimately hurting ourselves, is obvious but also incredibly powerful.

On top of that I have undertaken a great deal of further research in the last four years, and have found much in the original book that needed to be updated or revised. For all these reasons this retitled book is a complete rewrite, which will hopefully go some way towards presenting a more accurate and balanced view.

Ian Lawton
October 2008

Apart from the cover change, the updates to this second edition are relatively minor. They include the addition of a few newly unearthed cases of spontaneous recall, and some changes in emphasis in the final chapter. For more details see www.ianlawton.com.

February 2010

1

NEAR-DEATH AND OUT-OF-BODY EXPERIENCES

Common Characteristics

In the 1970s Elizabeth Kübler-Ross and Raymond Moody captured the American public's imagination with their reports of near-death experiences, with Moody's classic 1975 book *Life After Life* quickly becoming a bestseller. Since then a number of their compatriots, in particular psychologist Kenneth Ring, cardiologist Michael Sabom and psychiatrist Bruce Greyson, have all made rather more scholarly contributions to the further understanding of the phenomenon, while important additional research has been conducted in Britain by psychiatrist Peter Fenwick and medical doctor Sam Parnia. So there are now literally thousands of documented near-death experiences on file from various studies.

One of the most celebrated cases is that of thirty-five-year-old musician Pam Reynolds, documented as part of Sabom's 'Atlanta Study' in his 1998 book *Light and Death*. In 1991 her doctors diagnosed a massive aneurism – a weakness in the wall of an artery that causes it to balloon out – at the base of her brain. Its size and awkward location meant that it was not just life threatening, but also virtually inoperable. Yet she had one last chance. She had been referred to Robert Spetzler, a leading neurosurgeon in the Barrow Neurological Institute in Phoenix, Arizona, who had pioneered a new form of surgery known as hypothermic cardiac arrest. Nicknamed 'standstill' by his team, the procedure involved the blood in her body being cooled from its normal ninety-eight degrees Fahrenheit down to a mere sixty degrees, during which time her heart went into deliberate cardiac arrest and stopped beating. Once cooling was complete, her body was inclined on the

5

operating table and her blood allowed to drain out so that the incredibly delicate and complex procedure of excising the aneurism could take place. At this lower temperature her brain could cope with the lack of blood supply for longer than normal without sustaining permanent damage, but Spetzler still had only a maximum of thirty minutes to work his magic.

Fortunately Pam survived to tell the tale, but the tale itself was rather more than might have been expected. This is how she describes what happened to her:[1]

There was a sensation like being pulled, but not against your will. I was going of my own accord because I wanted to go. I have different metaphors to try to explain this. It was like the Wizard of Oz – being taken up in a tornado vortex, only you're not spinning around like you've got vertigo. You're very focused and you have a place to go. The feeling was like going up in an elevator real fast. And there was a sensation, but it wasn't a bodily, physical sensation. It was like a tunnel but it wasn't a tunnel.

At some point very early in the tunnel vortex I became aware of my grandmother calling me. But I didn't hear her calling me with my ears. It was a clearer hearing than with my ears. I trust that sense more than I trust my own ears. The feeling was that she wanted me to come to her, so I continued with no fear down the shaft. It's a dark shaft that I went through, and at the very end there was this very little tiny pinpoint of light that kept getting bigger and bigger and bigger.

The light was incredibly bright, like sitting in the middle of a light bulb. It was so bright I put my hands in front of my face fully expecting to see them and I could not. But I knew they were there. Not from a sense of touch. Again, it's terribly hard to explain, but I knew they were there.

I noticed that as I began to discern different figures in the light – and they were all covered with light, they *were* light, and had light permeating all around them – they began to form shapes I could recognize and understand. I could see that one of them was my grandmother. I don't know if it was reality or projection, but I would know my grandmother, the sound of her, anytime, anywhere.

Everyone I saw, looking back on it, fits perfectly into my understanding of what that person looked like at their best during their lives.

I recognized a lot of people. My uncle Gene was there. So was my great-great-Aunt Maggie, who was really a cousin. On Papa's side of the family, my grandfather was there. They were specifically taking care of me, looking after me.

They would not permit me to go further. It was communicated to me – that's the best way I know how to say it, because they didn't speak like I'm speaking – that if I went all the way into the light something would happen to me physically. They would be unable to put this me back into the body me, like I had gone too far and they couldn't reconnect. So they wouldn't let me go anywhere or do anything.

I wanted to go into the light, but I also wanted to come back. I had children to be reared. It was like watching a movie on fast-forward on your VCR: you get the general idea, but the individual freeze-frames are not slow enough to get detail.

Then they were feeding me. They were not doing this through my mouth, like with food, but they were nourishing me with something. The only way I know how to put it is something sparkly. Sparkles is the image that I get. I definitely recall the feeling of being nurtured and being fed and being made strong. I know it sounds funny, because obviously it wasn't a physical thing, but inside the experience I felt physically strong, ready for whatever.

My grandmother didn't take me back through the tunnel, or even send me back or ask me to go. She just looked up at me. I expected to go with her, but it was communicated to me that she just didn't think she would do that. My uncle said he would do it. He's the one who took me back through the end of the tunnel. Everything was fine. I did want to go.

But then I got to the end of it and saw the thing, my body. I didn't want to get into it. It looked terrible, like a train wreck. It looked like what it was: dead. I believe it was covered. It scared me and I didn't want to look at it.

It was communicated to me that it was like jumping into a swimming pool. No problem, just jump right into the swimming pool. I didn't want to, but I guess I was late or something because he pushed me. I felt a definite repelling and at the same time a pulling from the body. The body was pulling and the tunnel was pushing. It was like diving into a pool of ice water. It hurt!

This account has most of the hallmarks of the typical near-death experience.[2] First, the journey through what is often described as a dark tunnel and out into the brilliant light, accompanied by a sense of tranquility and euphoria. Second, the meeting with a 'welcoming party' made up of one or more light or energy beings who emanate unconditional love and compassion – usually identified as deceased family members, or as the personal 'spirit guides' or guardian angels who watch over our earthly lives and provide advice and support. Third, the telepathic communication and instant rapport with these beings. Fourth, the sense of a point of no return or 'barrier' that must not be crossed. Fifth, the somewhat reluctant but nevertheless accepted decision to come back through the tunnel and return to the physical body, more often than not because of some sort of unfinished business.

It is fair to say that subjects' descriptions of the realms they enter do vary. Whereas Pam describes a place of pure light and love without apparent physical detail, many see beautiful green fields or gardens and vivid blue skies; and while she is aware that the people she meets are light or energy beings, she also gradually perceives them taking a simulation of physical form that corresponds to her best and most comfortable memories of them. So it seems that everyone forms their own constructs of what these realms look like, at least during such initial encounters. And whereas some might be comfortable with the purely energetic nature of the environment, others impose a degree of familiar, quasi-physical detail on their surroundings. However, the basic elements of the experience stand as highly consistent and universal features across all studies.

Normal Explanations

Such reports from near-death subjects may have much to tell us about what initially happens after death that will be corroborated by other research in chapter 6. But if we are to place any reliance on them we must first deal with the various materialistic or 'normal' – as opposed to 'paranormal' – explanations put forward to account for them. These are all thoroughly described in the 1993 book *Dying to Live* by the British psychologist Susan Blackmore, who is also a member of the preeminent body of the skeptic community, the Committee for Skeptical Inquiry or CSI.[3] But the leading researchers in the near-death field have all put forward what are arguably convincing counter-arguments.[4] So let us look at each alternative and see how well it stands up to close scrutiny.

The first is, of course, that these experiences are nothing more than dreams or imagination. Yet there are clear differences because, although they sometimes feel extremely real at the time, we normally recognize dreams for what they are as soon as we wake up. They do not display the sort of lucidity and consistency that is so characteristic of the near-death experience, and nor do they have the same lasting and profound impact on the subject – which is typically the elimination of any fear of death and a tendency towards a more spiritual path.[5]

The next argument is that medical drugs are the cause, because certain drug-induced hallucinations share many similarities with the typical near-death experience. But studies show that no drugs of any kind are involved in the majority of these; indeed in his 1982 book *Life at Death* Ring quotes studies that suggest the presence of medical drugs may even impair them or reduce their likelihood.[6] By contrast, of course, non-medical hallucinogens have been deliberately used throughout the ages to induce an altered state of consciousness in which enlightenment may be attained. So while the phenomenon may be *similar* to certain drug-induced hallucinations, which is only what we would expect, these drugs tend *not* to be of the medical type and, even if they were, in no way could they be offered as a universal *cause* of the phenomena.

What about the idea that people facing death attempt a 'psychological shutdown'? Psychiatry recognizes conditions known as 'dissociated states' that are triggered to protect the person from extremely painful emotions. On the one hand, 'derealization' involves shutting out the outside world so that it becomes unreal, as if a dream; by contrast, 'depersonalization' allows people to become detached, as if looking at themselves from outside.[7] But both of these states are completely at odds with the typical description of the near-death experience, in which heightened perceptions are backed up by an overwhelming sense of a *genuine reality* in which whatever is released from the physical body is the 'real me', while the nonphysical realms encountered are 'far more real' than the physical world.[8] Indeed in many cases we find subjects reporting that they have 'total knowledge or wisdom', both about themselves and about the universe as a whole, even though this is usually lost on their return. Of course skeptics scoff at this latter aspect and ask why 'returnees' are not allowed to bring even snippets of such information back with them, but we will see in chapter 6 that this fits in well with the general idea of a 'veil of amnesia'.

If we now turn to physiological or neurological explanations, the first is that oxygen starvation of the brain, or hypoxia, might cause such experiences because the temporal lobe of the brain responds by generating strong feelings of emotion and often euphoria. But huge numbers of deliberate studies of hypoxia conducted with, for example, mountain climbers, pilots and medical students, reveal that it also produces increasing confusion and loss of perception before the subject lapses into unconsciousness. This is the complete antithesis of the lucid near-death experience. Nor do any of the thousands of subjects in these experiments tend to report anything similar in terms of detail.

Blackmore in particular has also advocated the idea that hypoxia can produce the 'tunnel and light vision' so typical of near-death experiences. The 'neural-noise' theory proposes that as oxygen levels reduce, because more eye cells are devoted to the centre of the visual field than to the periphery, random cell activity causes lots of bright lights to flash at the centre, making the outside seem dark; and, as the condition worsens, this central light becomes larger and larger.[9] This is ingenious, but it is also typical of the arguments skeptics put forward. They claim to have explained away one aspect, while conveniently ignoring numerous others.

Nevertheless, what about endorphins or endogenous morphine? Skeptics argue that the brain automatically produces these in response to severe pain or emotional stress, and as with all opiates they have a calming and euphoric effect, similar in some ways to aspects of the typical near-death experience. But many such cases result from circumstances so swift that the body has no time to produce endorphins, while euphoria too is only one aspect of the phenomenon. So again we have a putative scientific cause that does not stand up to close scrutiny as a *complete* explanation for the broad spectrum of contextual circumstances in which the near-death experiences now on record have occurred, nor for the full range of their typical components.

Skeptics also tend to focus on their supposed subjectivity by arguing that, because consistent reports of such experiences have now gained widespread exposure, people are culturally conditioned to have them. This modern exposure cannot be denied, but there is strong evidence that it did not play a significant role in many of the cases that formed the basis of the original, pioneering studies. For example, let us consider Fenwick's research. He was instrumental in setting up the British branch of the International Association of Near-Death Studies in 1987, and after appearing on various radio and television shows he received a huge number of replies to his request for first-hand accounts of such experiences. From these he selected five hundred people to whom he sent a detailed and standardized questionnaire, to which three hundred and fifty responded. One of the key questions was whether they had been aware of the phenomenon before they had their own experience and, despite the modern exposure, a mere two percent answered in the affirmative.[10] Reading through the multitude of cases reported in his 1995 book *The Truth in the Light*, one of the major reasons for this appears to have been the advanced age of many of the respondents, and the fact that their experience occurred many decades before. They universally express their delight that at last they could share it with someone who would understand, whereas they had always been too afraid of ridicule beforehand, even in many cases from their nearest and dearest.[11]

Sabom had similar feedback from his first study, documented in his 1981 book *Recollections of Death*, reporting that only twelve percent of these subjects claimed to have heard of the phenomenon before. Ring even found that prior knowledge seemed to *lessen* the likelihood of having a near-death experience.[12] Meanwhile Fenwick also points out that a significant number of very young children have reported experiences that are essentially the same as that of adults, and that the chances of these arising from cultural preconditioning are particularly remote.[13]

Notwithstanding this, are subjects merely imposing their existing religious or spiritual beliefs on whatever experience they are having – and, when faced with the daunting prospect of death, conjuring up a psychological safety net from a combination of these beliefs and their imagination? There can be little doubt that broad cultural factors do have a part to play because when, for example, Fenwick compared cases in America, Britain, India and China he found there were clear differences of emphasis.[14] Nevertheless his own British study shows some surprising results. A massive eighty-two percent of his respondents indicated they were of a Christian denomination of one form or another, and when asked about their commitment to their religion a still significant thirty-nine percent reported that it was important to them.[15] Yet an incredibly small number suggest that they met with an identifiable religious figure such as Jesus during their experience; and although a larger number use the broad terminology of meeting with 'God' or 'their Maker', even these subjects described the experience as involving a broad spirituality that had little or nothing to do with their exposure to orthodox religion and its associated dogma.[16] Indeed, Ring and others have suggested that subjects' spiritual horizons are considerably widened, although as a committed Christian Sabom argues against these findings.[17] Above all, near-death experiences seem to share the same common elements irrespective of the subject's religious belief or lack thereof.[18] So, again, this surely cannot be regarded as the underlying *cause*, even if it can have a degree of influence – especially on how a subject *interprets* their experience.

In 1980 Ring made the following observation:[19]

It is not difficult – in fact it is easy – to propose naturalistic interpretations that could conceivably explain some aspect of the core experience. Such explanations, however, sometimes seem merely glib and are usually of the 'this-is-nothing-but-an-instance-of' variety; rarely do they seem to be seriously considered attempts to come to grips with a very puzzling phenomenon. A neurological interpretation, to be acceptable, should be able to provide a *comprehensive* explanation of *all* the various aspects of the core experience. Indeed, I am tempted to argue that the burden of proof has now shifted to those who wish to explain near-death experiences in this way. In the meantime, I think it is fair to conclude that physiological or neurological interpretations of near-death experiences are so far inadequate and unacceptable.

Several decades later, and after plenty of new research effort on both sides, arguably this conclusion still holds true.

Four Veridical Cases

If any doubt remains about this shift in the burden of proof, we can turn to the *veridical* elements of near-death experiences to see if they swing the debate one way or the other. These are aspects of recall that are not only subsequently verified but also sufficiently obscure that the subject is extremely unlikely to have just made a lucky guess. We have four cases of this nature to examine, which we will do at some length because of their crucial importance.

Pam Reynolds and the Saw

The first involves Pam Reynolds again. Here is her description of what happened at the very beginning of her experience:[20]

> The next thing I recall was the sound: it was a natural 'd'. As I listened to the sound, I felt it was pulling me out of the top of my head. The further out of my body I got, the more clear the tone became. I had the impression it was like a road, a frequency that you go on. I remember seeing several things in the operating room when I was looking down. It was the most aware that I think that I have ever been in my entire life. I was metaphorically sitting on Dr Spetzler's shoulder. It was not like normal vision. It was brighter and more focused and clearer than normal vision. There was so much in the operating room that I didn't recognize, and so many people.
>
> I thought the way they had my head shaved was very peculiar. I expected them to take all of the hair, but they did not...
>
> Someone said something about my veins and arteries being very small. I believe it was a female voice and that it was Dr Murray, but I'm not sure.

Do these memories reflect what actually happened? Certainly the conversation concerning the size of her veins was confirmed by the surgical team. At the time they were readying the femoral arteries in her groin for attachment via tubes to the cardiopulmonary bypass machine that would cool her blood – and when the right artery was found to be too small to do the job alone, the left one was also prepared.[21] This seems pretty impressive. But are there nevertheless any natural explanations for Pam's recall?

When this case was featured in a BBC *Horizon* documentary in 2003, entitled 'The Day I Died', viewers were given the clear impression that Pam was clinically dead when this veridical aspect of her experience took place. But Sabom's account indicates that the whole operation took in excess of five hours, so we need to be careful about our timings. In fact at this point Spetzler was opening her skull in order to perform a preliminary investigation of the aneurism, which he would achieve by threading a flexible tubular microscope between the various lobes down to the base of her brain. It was only when he established some two hours later that it was 'extremely large and extended up into the brain' that the need for standstill was proved beyond doubt, and the blood-cooling procedure initiated. So at the time of this veridical experience she was heavily anesthetized, and had already been totally unconscious for nearly an hour and a half while her body was prepared for surgery, but she was *not* clinically dead.

Another veridical aspect of Pam's experience came towards the end of the operation. She somewhat comically describes the moment she returned to her body as follows:

> When I came back, they were playing 'Hotel California' and the line was 'You can check out any time you like, but you can never leave'. I mentioned [later] to Dr Brown that that was incredibly insensitive.

Again Sabom was able to confirm that the junior members of the surgical team involved in the closing procedures were playing this song.[22] But this too was once the operation was complete and her brain, heart and lungs were returning to full function.

The most intelligent skeptic dismissal of this case, an article in *The Skeptic* in 2005 by Dutch anesthetist Gerald Woerlee, focuses on these timings. He insists that at the two points of her veridical recall Pam was not only clinically alive but her levels of anesthetic may have dropped sufficiently to render her semi-conscious – while other drugs would still have been numbing any pain.[23] Sabom indicates that small speakers had been fitted into each of her ears to emit regular pulses checking her brainstem reaction, and insists they would 'altogether eliminate the possibility of physical hearing'. But Woerlee counters with some apparent justification that she may still have been able to hear through these, just as we can when wearing earphones.

We can see from all this why discussion of near-death experiences, either generally or in relation to particular cases such as Pam's, so often revolves around detailed arguments about whether or not the subject was clinically dead, merely unconscious or even semi-conscious at the time. These arguments then move on to what we really mean by 'dead', whether someone who is unconscious can make coherent mental models *and remember them*, and so on.[24] But there is one factor in Pam's case that arguably renders all such discussion redundant – because while there might be valid, normal explanations for those veridical aspects that involved her *hearing* things, there is another that unquestionably involved *sight*. This is an additional recollection from the start of her experience that was omitted from the quote above:

> The saw thing that I hated the sound of looked like an electric toothbrush and it had a dent in it, a groove at the top where the saw appeared to go into the handle, but it didn't. And the saw had interchangeable blades, too, but these blades were in what looked like a socket wrench case. I heard the saw crank up. I didn't see them use it on my head, but I think I heard it being used on something. It was humming at a relatively high pitch and then all of a sudden it went *Brrrrrrrr!* like that.

Of course most near-death subjects have their eyes shut during the experience because they are either unconscious or deeply comatose, so sight will always be the key factor. But in this case we have the further authentication that Pam's eyes had been lubricated and taped shut right at the start of the operation. So how could she 'see' so accurately when she undoubtedly did not have the normal use of her eyes?

Woerlee attempts to explain this by suggesting that Pam would have been well acquainted with the drills used by dentists – which are not dissimilar in looks, and make a similar noise – and that she would have used her imagination to fabricate a visual narrative from the sound. But then why would she not have done the same with the other two veridical aspects of her recall, rather than remaining quite content to describe merely hearing them? More damning still, although drills are usually pointed, as a layperson Pam was clearly expecting – and indeed describes the instrument as – a saw, not a drill. So why would she fabricate a narrative about it being pointed, or like an electric toothbrush?

Another argument picks up on her description of the saw having 'a groove or dent at the top where it appeared to go into the handle', which even according to Sabom himself is supposedly a little puzzling.[25] In his internet-based paper *Hallucinatory Near-Death Experiences* skeptic Keith Augustine seizes on this to argue that it was inaccurate in the one aspect that she could not have merely imagined.[26] Of course we might simply argue that this is so fine a detail that its being wrong would not invalidate Pam's still-unlikely identification of a pointed, toothbrush-like saw. But in fact on a different interpretation the picture reproduced in Sabom's book does show a groove exactly where the bit goes into the handle.[27]

The Dutchman and the Teeth

Cardiologist Pim van Lommel performed an extensive thirteen-year study of near-death experiences in ten Dutch hospitals, publishing his results in the prestigious medical journal *The Lancet* in 2001. One particularly striking case was reported and verified by a nurse:[28]

> During a night shift an ambulance brings a 44-year-old, cyanotic, comatose man into the coronary care unit. He had been found about an hour before in a meadow by passers-by. After admission, he receives artificial respiration without intubation, while heart massage and defibrillation are also applied. When we want to intubate the patient, he turns out to have dentures in his mouth. I remove these upper dentures and put them onto the 'crash cart'. Meanwhile, we continue extensive CPR. After about an hour and a half the patient has sufficient heart rhythm and blood pressure, but he is still ventilated and intubated, and he is still comatose. He is transferred to the intensive care unit to continue the necessary artificial respiration.
>
> Only after more than a week do I meet again with the patient, who is by now back on the cardiac ward. I distribute his medication. The moment he sees me he says: 'Oh, that nurse knows where my dentures are.' I am very surprised. Then he elucidates: 'Yes, you were there when I was brought into hospital and you took my dentures out of my mouth and put them onto that cart, it had all these bottles on it and there was this sliding drawer underneath and there you put my teeth.' I was especially amazed because I remembered this happening while the man was in deep coma and in the process of CPR. When I asked further, it appeared the man had seen himself lying in bed, that he had perceived from above how nurses and doctors had been busy with CPR. He was also able to describe correctly and in detail the small room in which he had been resuscitated as well as the appearance of those present like myself. At the time that he observed the situation he had been very much afraid that we would stop CPR and that he would die. And it is true that we had been very negative about the patient's prognosis due to his very poor medical condition when admitted. The patient tells me that he desperately and unsuccessfully tried to make it clear to us that he was still alive and that we should continue CPR. He is deeply impressed by his experience and says he is no longer afraid of death. Four weeks later he left hospital as a healthy man.

Apart from the impressive veridical element, this case also reinforces the suggestion that near-death subjects tend to lose any fear of death.

George Rodonaia and the Baby

Our next case is documented by two researchers, Phyllis Atwater – herself a near-death survivor – and Phillip Berman in their books *Beyond the Light* and *The Journey Home*, published in 1994 and 1996 respectively; and it reinforces the suggestion that survivors often develop a more spiritual outlook on life as well, because George Rodonaia's experience transformed him from a gifted young Soviet scientist and staunch atheist into a highly respected church minister in Texas. He was only eighteen when, in 1974, he was invited to study at Yale. He was delighted at the opportunities this would open up, but the KGB had other ideas. As a neuropathologist he was researching the way certain chemicals acted on the human brain, and they found this useful for interrogations. If they could not keep him, they did not want the Americans to have him either.

Over the next two years they put various obstacles in his way but, when he got married and had a child, it finally appeared they would let him leave. Then on the day of his departure, as he stood on the pavement in Tbilisi waiting for a taxi to the airport, he was mown down by a car and pronounced dead at the scene. Bystanders confirmed that, having already sent George flying, the driver even reversed back to run over him again. His body lay in a morgue for *three days*. But as the autopsy began his eyelids flickered, and he was rushed to surgery.

Given his total commitment to science and avowed atheism, George's family were amazed when, three days into his lengthy recovery, he began to describe what had happened to him while he was 'dead'. His is a fascinating experience in that it was of a more transcendental nature and did not encompass all the standard elements, and as such we will return to it in the final chapter.[29] But for our current purposes the key aspect was his claim that while 'out-of-body' he could travel anywhere he liked. At one point he found himself drawn to the newborn daughter of a neighbor, who remained in the hospital in which his body lay because she would not stop crying, and doctors had been unable to diagnose the problem. Much to his surprise he found that he was able to communicate with her telepathically, even though the surrounding adults remained blissfully unaware of his presence. What is more, he was somehow able to scan her body and establish that her hip had been broken at birth. Incredibly, as soon as George was able to pass on this information, the doctors x-rayed the baby

16

and found that she did indeed have a fractured hip.[30] But how could he have made such an accurate diagnosis while his physical body was lying in a mortuary cabinet? Moreover, as with Pam, if this veridical element of his experience was not imaginary, what about all the rest?

Maria and the Shoe

Our final case comes from another near-death survivor, Kimberly Clark, who went on to become a social worker and counselor working with similar patients in the Harborview Medical Center in Seattle. She describes what happened to one of them, a migrant worker called Maria, when she went into cardiac arrest at the hospital in 1977:[31]

> Maria proceeded to describe being further distracted [while in her out-of-body state] by an object on the third floor ledge of the north end of the building. She 'thought her way' up there and found herself 'eyeball to shoelace' with a tennis shoe, which she asked me to try and find for her. She needed someone else to know that the tennis shoe was really there to validate her out-of-body experience.
>
> With mixed emotions I went outside and looked up at the ledges but could not see much at all. I went up to the third floor and began going in and out of patients' rooms and looking out their windows, which were so narrow that I had to press my face to the screen just to see the ledge at all. Finally, I found a room where I pressed my face to the glass and saw a tennis shoe! My vantage point was very different from what Maria's had to have been for her to notice that the little toe had worn a place in the shoe and that the lace was stuck under the heel and other details about the side of the shoe not visible to me. The only way she would have had such a perspective was if she had been floating right outside and at very close range to the tennis shoe. I retrieved the shoe and brought it back to Maria; it was very concrete evidence for me.

Like that of George Rodonaia, this case has attracted the attention of the skeptic community. In a 1996 article in the CSI's journal, *The Skeptical Inquirer*, biopsychologist Barry Bayerstein and two of his undergraduates from the Simon Fraser University in British Columbia attempted to debunk it on the basis that it was supposedly considered the best case of veridical recall within a near-death experience at the time.[32] So we in turn should spend a little time examining their attempt, not least because it provides another excellent example of the skeptic's art.

First of all they use the 'scatter gun' approach, commencing with a discussion of Maria's apparent recall of details of her room, and of the hospital entrance and driveway outside its window, which are so insignificant in the general scheme of this case that they are not even worth reporting. When finally they do turn their attention to the shoe we should give them credit that at least they actually visited the hospital and placed another one in roughly the same location. From this they deduced that it was generally visible from the ground, although they do not bother to remind us that the finer details about the worn toe and so on would still have remained undetectable from this location. They also suggest that, instead of having to press their heads against the window to see it on the ledge, it was visible from only a few paces inside the room – and that when their heads were pressed up against the window they could see any details of its 'supposedly hidden outer side'.

Given that apparently they did not know the exact position of the original shoe, we can counter that it would surely have been possible to place it further away on the ledge until the far side was no longer visible. But in any case this issue pales into insignificance when we come to their main argument:

> It is not a far-fetched notion to assume that anyone who might have noticed the shoe back in 1977 would have commented on it because of the novelty of its location. Thus, during the three days prior to her NDE, Maria could have overheard such a conversation among any of the doctors, nurses, patients, visitors, or other hospital staff who frequented this busy area... It is apparent that many people inside as well as outside the hospital would have had the opportunity to notice the now-famous shoe, making it even more likely that Maria could have overheard some mention of it.

This is a wonderful piece of conjecture but, when it is posing as a supposedly rational and impartial argument, it leaves something to be desired. It seems highly debatable whether the existence of a shoe on a window ledge would have become such a talking point throughout the entire hospital, but even if it did Clark reported Maria's experience to other staff soon after it happened, causing widespread interest. So, as the American novelist Michael Prescott notes in his amusingly succinct rebuttal of this article, how come no one pointed out her error:[33] 'What's the big deal? Everybody's seen that shoe. We've been talking about it among ourselves for weeks. It's the most exciting thing to happen to this hospital since I started working here!' He adds that it is even more far-fetched to suppose that any conversations about the shoe would have included the finer details: 'Did you see how the shoelace was tucked under the shoe? How about that? A tucked-in shoelace. Wow!'

Of course skeptics tend also to dismiss such cases as 'purely anecdotal' and scientifically non-repeatable. But even this is something that future studies hope to rectify – for example by placing cards with numbers on them on top of tall cupboards and other places that would normally be visually inaccessible in hospital rooms, in the hope that some cardiac patients may confirm them.[34] Meanwhile, even in the absence of such formalized research, we are entitled to ask: at what point does dismissing a growing core of veridical cases as merely anecdotal become an excuse for evading what seem to be, for some, uncomfortable or even unthinkable implications?

The only other normal explanation for these veridical cases would, of course, be deliberate fraud. But even most skeptics accept that this is highly unlikely to have been committed by professionals like Sabom or van Lommel. As for the subjects themselves, Pam, George and Maria had all just had narrow escapes from death, and would presumably have had rather more important things on their mind than the perpetration of an elaborate hoax.

Unpleasant Experiences

Another important issue is whether near-death subjects ever have unpleasant or even hellish experiences. Pioneering researchers such as Ring, Sabom, Greyson and Fenwick mention very few cases of this type.[35] However there may be a question mark over how receptive they were to such reports. Certainly Greyson felt he needed to redress the balance and by 1992, after a decade of further research, he and a colleague had collated some fifty hellish cases on which they reported in *Psychiatry* magazine.[36] Yet this is still not a significant proportion.

There are really only two researchers who insist that unpleasant experiences are commonplace. The first is Atwater, who claims that fifteen percent of the subjects in the study recorded in her 1994 book *Beyond the Light* had had hellish experiences.[37] Far more controversial is cardiologist Maurice Rawlings who, in his 1978 book *Beyond Death's Door*, suggests that hellish experiences are far more common – perhaps occurring as much as fifty percent of the time. However this appears to derive from a relatively arbitrary extrapolation of his assumption that subjects tend to forget negative aspects of a near-death experience after a short period. Nor can there be any question that he is an unashamedly fervent Christian whose aim is to persuade people that if they do not change their ways they will go to hell.[38]

As biased as Rawlings' testimony might be, and as much as they might not be especially commonplace, it is clear that unpleasant experiences do occur and cannot be summarily dismissed. Although they do not conform to a standardized pattern, one of the most renowned and in some senses typical cases is that of Howard Storm, again documented by Berman.[39] As a professor of art at the University of North Kentucky Howard seemed to 'have it all', but was inwardly deeply sad and a control freak. One afternoon in 1985, while on a trip to Europe, he was suddenly taken ill with a perforated small intestine and rushed to a hospital in Paris. As he awaited an operation the following morning he was in such intense pain that he felt he could not survive. Then, drifting in and out of consciousness, he suddenly found himself standing by the side of the bed looking at his own body.

His utter confusion at this point was at least partly due to his avowed atheism, but he was also angry and upset. So when he realized his wife could not hear him screaming at her, and then heard voices saying they could help him, he reluctantly followed them out of the door and into a 'hazy fog'. He had the impression of walking for a very long time, while the silhouetted figures with him became increasingly aggressive. When he tried to turn back they pushed and shoved him, and then started clawing and biting him. As fast as he pushed them off more arrived, all of them wanting to hurt him and cause him pain, seeming to feed off his misery.

In the midst of all this fear and turmoil an inner voice told Howard to pray and, despite the reluctance of his still 'rational' mind, he started to chant the Lord's Prayer. His tormentors went into a frenzy, screaming and yelling but at least backing off, until he found himself alone. Yet he still felt utterly hopeless until, in his desperation, he cried out to Jesus to save him. At this point a small dot of light began to approach, growing and growing until it surrounded him with an incredibly radiant love, compassion and healing, and then took him off into the light itself.

There are a number of observations to be made about Howard's unpleasant experience. The first is that he was extremely confused and angry when it started, and the fact that this acted as a magnet for his tormentors seems to be a common theme of such near-death experiences. So it seems that thoughts, emotions, intentions and expectations are all-important in these other realms, and that 'like attracts like'. Of course Howard did not expect to find *anything*, let alone loving beings or any sense of the light, and this coupled with his anger and strength of negative emotions seems to have kept him trapped in a somewhat denser realm inhabited by spirits who were clearly tormented themselves. It is also conceivable that a devout Christian who felt they had transgressed badly *might* have a similarly unpleasant, hellish experience because that is what they were expecting, although by no means would this be guaranteed.

The other common theme demonstrated by Howard's account is that the unpleasant element was only a temporary interlude, and most subjects of such an experience seem able to turn it into a pleasant one at some point.[40] As with Howard this is usually achieved via some expression of love or prayer or by asking for help, but it seems that just surrendering physical emotions and concerns, relaxing and 'letting go' can also be effective.

Atwater seems to take the view that these are merely 'inverted' experiences, which actually share the same characteristics as pleasant ones but are perceived differently by the subject.[41] However similar accounts from other areas of research that we will examine in chapter 6 seem to indicate that instead it is crucial to *differentiate* between the two 'places' reported in the different types of experience. Even in the simplest model we can identify three different realms or planes, albeit that they might have different 'vibratory levels' or, better still, 'aspects'.[42] There is the physical plane, of course, which is the densest or lowest in terms of energy and vibrations. There is the 'light' plane, which is what most near-death subjects describe as being at the end of the tunnel – albeit that they are not allowed to enter it properly – which is the lightest or highest plane. Then somewhere in-between these two in terms of energy and vibrations there is what we might refer to as the 'intermediate' plane.[43] This is the one in which spirits can become trapped if they remain strongly attracted to the physical and retain intense unresolved emotions – of fear, anger, jealousy, hatred, revenge and so on – or a general sense of unfinished business. Moreover it seems that they stay in this plane as long as they continue with such preoccupations, either failing to realize or refusing to accept they are dead, or at least remaining oblivious to the light or any attempts to repatriate them to it. Although we will return to this topic in chapter 6, for now it seems most likely that historical reports of near-death experiences of this nature have played a significant part in reinforcing religious ideas of a hellish realm.[44]

If all this sounds somewhat daunting, we should remember that relatively few near-death subjects have such an experience, perhaps because the tunnel phenomenon protects them in some way.[45] In addition unlike the fiery and permanent hell of Christian tradition, for example, it is only temporary and can be transformed in an instant. Better still when we consider the fact that one day we will all have to face death, it seems likely that the intermediate plane can be avoided altogether with just a little understanding and preparation during life. All of these are subjects to which we will return in chapters 6 and 7. But as for those near-death subjects who have had an unpleasant experience, Atwater rather than Rawlings seems closest to the mark when she observes that most of them seem able to learn something important from it – and that in many cases it is probably more useful to them, for example in confronting repressed emotions or fears, than a positive one would have been.[46]

Out-of-Body Experiences

Let us now turn to the related topic of out-of-body experiences. These are obviously a key element of many near-death reports, but they can also occur spontaneously to people who are nowhere near death. In fact they are reckoned by some to be extremely common. However for many the ultimate goal is to be able to make them happen at will.

One of the first people to research them in any detail was Sylvan Muldoon, an American who first experienced what he called 'astral projection' aged twelve. In 1929 he teamed up with paranormal researcher Hereward Carrington to write their first book, *The Projection of the Astral Body*, which contained details of Muldoon's own experiences and the techniques he developed to instigate them. They followed this up with several others, including *The Phenomena of Astral Projection* in 1951, which was the first major survey of other people's largely spontaneous experiences and which attempted to classify them in terms of triggers. Another major figure was Robert Crookall, a respected British geologist who devoted his retirement to the investigation of the phenomenon. His first contribution came in 1961 with *The Study and Practice of Astral Projection*, and he went on to write a number of follow-ups.

However probably the most influential researcher of modern times is Robert Monroe. A highly successful businessman from Virginia, he had his first spontaneous experience in 1958 while in his forties, and when it happened several more times he increasingly devoted himself to exploring the phenomenon. He wrote several books, the first and most celebrated being *Journeys Out of the Body* in 1971. This appears to corroborate his reputation as a highly intelligent man with widespread interests who was fastidious in his approach to his research, and in particular to the documentation and analysis of nearly six hundred out-of-body journeys in those first twelve years. He secured his legacy by founding his own institute in 1972, where important research continues to this day. Like others, Monroe devoted considerable time to experimenting with various techniques to induce out-of-body experiences; and, although this is not our main concern here, many books and videos on this topic are now available for those who are interested.

The first major aspect of his research that is of relevance to us is his efforts to have experiences from which certain elements might be subsequently verified. In particular he found that attempting to visit close friends by focusing on them worked reasonably well. So on one occasion, for example, he deliberately concentrated on a psychologist friend who was ill on the assumption that he would be lying in his bedroom, which Monroe had never seen before and might be able to subsequently describe. The projection to the house was successful but, when he arrived, his friend and his wife were walking out to the car. Monroe was surprised but made a careful mental note of their clothes – he in a light overcoat and hat, she in a dark coat and all dark clothes underneath. Then he returned to his body, reentered it and made careful notes, including of the timings. That evening he phoned his friend, whose wife answered, and said nothing else other than to ask where they had been between four and five that afternoon. She confirmed that she had needed to drive to the post office, and her husband had decided that some air might do him some good. The clothes and timings all matched too.[47]

On another occasion Monroe focused on a female friend who he knew was holidaying somewhere on the New Jersey coast. He quickly found himself in a kitchen, with his friend seated on the right and two young girls in their late teens, one blonde, the other brunette, on the left. All three had glasses in their hands. He then decided to see if he could pinch his friend in her side, just to see what would happen, although he knew that normal physical rules did not usually apply to his out-of-body state. To his astonishment she jumped and let out an exclamation. He left and again recorded the details and time. Several days later he checked with his friend on her return as to what she had been doing that day in the afternoon. After giving it some thought she remembered that this had been one of the few times there was not a crowd of people at the beach hut she had been staying in, and that she had been sitting in the kitchen sharing drinks and chatting with her niece and a friend – who were both in their late teens, and dark and blonde respectively. But then Monroe asked if she remembered anything else, and when she repeatedly said no he finally gave in and asked if she recalled being pinched. A look of complete astonishment crossed her face. 'Was that you?' she asked as she lifted her jumper at the side to reveal two clear bruises. She said it had hurt, and Monroe apologized.[48]

The second aspect of his research that interests us is his categorization of the types of experience he had according to the locations he visited. This is because he did not only find himself exploring the earth plane, which he referred to as 'Locale I', but also a 'Locale II' that appears to provide some excellent corroboration of both the light and intermediate planes that we discussed previously. He suggests that time in this locale is effectively nonexistent, even though events do occur in sequence, and that it is 'a state of being where thought is the wellspring of existence... as you think, so you are... like attracts like'.[49] He also supports our earlier suggestion that quasi-physical attributes can be adopted in this environment, at least partly to 'reduce the trauma and shock for newcomers'. He goes on to provide a brief report of his more pleasant trips to this locale:[50]

> On one visit I ended up in a park-like surrounding, with carefully tended flowers, trees, and grass, much like a large mall with paths crisscrossing the area. There were benches along the paths, and there were hundreds of men and women strolling by, or sitting on the benches. Some were quite calm, others a little apprehensive, and many had a dazed or shocked look of disorientation. They appeared uncertain, unknowing of what to do or what was to take place next. Somehow I knew that this was a meeting place, where the newly arrived waited for friends or relatives. From this place of meeting, these friends would take each newcomer to the proper place where he or she 'belonged'.

This seems to suggest an area of the light realms just beyond the barrier that near-death subjects cannot cross. But on several other occasions Monroe appears to have traveled rather further into the light:[51]

> Three times I have gone to a place that I cannot find words to describe accurately... To me it was a place or condition of pure peace, yet exquisite emotion... You are Home. You are where you belong. Where you always should have been. Most important, you are not alone. With you, beside you, interlocked in you are others. They do not have names, nor are you aware of them as shapes, but you know them and you are bonded to them with a great single knowledge. They are exactly like you, they are you, and like you, they are Home. You feel with them, like gentle waves of electricity passing between you, a completeness of love, of which all the facets you have experienced are but segments and incomplete portions. Only here, the emotion is without need of intense display or demonstration.

But by way of contrast Monroe reports that Locale II can also incorporate unpleasant experiences:[52]

> The areas of Locale II nearest to the physical world in vibratory frequency are peopled for the most part with insane or near insane, emotionally driven beings... They include those both alive but asleep or drugged and out in their Second Bodies, and quite probably those who are dead but still emotionally driven... This near area, quite understandably, is not a pleasant place to be.

This seems to be very reminiscent of the intermediate plane as discussed earlier, and again it seems likely that historical reports of this type of out-of-body experience have reinforced religious ideas of a hellish realm. Moreover, people who use hallucinogens to achieve altered states and to aid astral traveling also describe both pleasant and unpleasant experiences. Rather concerning, though, is Monroe's contention that regular astral travelers are likely to encounter this 'near plane' at some point, and that there is no special way of avoiding it that he could deduce, other than to tread carefully and quietly:[53]

> It is a grey-black hungry ocean where the slightest motion attracts nibbling and tormenting beings. It is as if you are the bait dangling in this vast sea. If you move slowly and do not react to the curious 'fish' who come to investigate, you pass through without much incident. Move violently and fight back, then more excited denizens come rushing in to bite, pull, push, shove.

This exactly brings to mind Howard's highly emotional state at the outset of his near-death experience, and how it attracted his tormentors. So it seems that the trick for those who have just died, or who are experimenting with astral projection, is to keep their emotions in check as far as possible, with the aim of passing straight through the intermediate into the light realms – or, in Monroe's terms, the more pleasant areas of Locale II. From this we can see that, as much as they may be somewhat simplistic, our distinctions between the light and intermediate planes are extremely important. This is especially because many commentators on near-death and out-of-body experiences, and on altered states of consciousness more generally, do not make them – leading to much potential confusion.

Monroe's research has of course attracted some criticism from skeptics, most notably from Blackmore in her 1982 book *Beyond the Body*.[54] The most serious is, again, that his reports are purely anecdotal and have no

25

independent corroboration; and this time, at least in respect of the specifics that interest us, the criticism has more foundation. But let us be clear that the general thread of our argument does not rely on his research as primary evidence. The suggestion is merely that *if* it has any validity then it does seem to corroborate certain findings from other primary areas of research.

The Seat of Consciousness

Another leading skeptic is the philosopher Paul Edwards, who taught at the New School for Social Research in New York and whose 1996 book *Reincarnation: A Critical Examination* is widely praised as a landmark in the field – and as such clearly deserves our close attention. At the outset we cannot help but point out that a substantial proportion of the book is devoted to *ad hominem* jibing, which is clearly supposed to come across as erudite and witty – although many will surely regard it as at best padding of a somewhat crass nature, and at worst indicative of a paucity of genuine argument.

More specifically it does include a number of chapters dealing with near-death experiences and related topics, with considerable time devoted to personal attacks on the integrity of Kübler-Ross and to a lesser extent Moody.[55] But, while their early research did much to publicize the phenomenon, their books were never meant to be the most scholarly of contributions. Moreover, even if Kübler-Ross did go somewhat off the rails in later years, is Edwards' lengthy exposition really germane to the more important arguments concerning near-death research? In fact, even when he does finally mention a more scholarly researcher like Ring, again he ridicules him for supporting certain rather dubious predictions about the future, which were apparently made by some of his near-death subjects.[56] But this too is a mere sideshow. In fact if Edwards had wanted to go further he could have mentioned that by the mid-1980s Ring, who was by now the president of the International Association of Near-Death Studies, had somewhat abandoned his earlier objective stance and was attempting to set up a new, more universal world religion with a decidedly Eastern flavor.[57] But whether or not one supports such a move, can anyone sensibly argue that it invalidates his earlier meticulous research?

A further fine example of Edwards' sophistication is his dismissal of all near-death experiences as the fantasies of the ignorant:[58] 'It is not clear how Moody selected his sample. What is clear is that his subjects... are totally uneducated and devoid of the slightest capacity for self-criticism.' It would have been fascinating if Edwards and, for example, George Rodonaia were both still alive to discuss this proposition.

Rather more substantial is the fact that the mainstays of Edwards' arguments are so strictly materialist that even many skeptics probably find them somewhat embarrassing. As far as near-death experiences go, one of his main targets is to ridicule the idea of the 'astral body'.[59] But without apparent irony he concerns himself with weighty questions such as 'where are astral clothes manufactured?' He also insists that, because the astral body must be the exact double of the physical body, they must die simultaneously. Such exaggeratedly literal interpretations seem hardly deserving of further discussion.

Arguably the only issue of relevance here about which Edwards has something useful to say is the million-dollar question: is the brain itself the source of consciousness?[60] Here he is on prime territory because this question has exercised philosophers for centuries, but let us steer clear of the sort of contortions of logic so beloved of most such contributors to this debate, Edwards included. Instead we will keep it simple. At the outset we can clearly state that materialists insist the physical brain is entirely responsible for all thought, indeed for all consciousness, and that as soon as it dies all consciousness expires with it. By contrast non-materialists insist that the brain is merely the *instrument* through which our essentially non-material consciousness operates in the physical world.

One of the main examples used by Edwards is Alzheimer's. According to him the cause of this disease has been narrowed down to 'a dramatic loss of neurons from the nucleus basalis' in the brain, which in turn reduces the production of an enzyme essential to the production of neurotransmitters. He continues:

> While still alive, an Alzheimer's patient's brain is severely damaged and most of his mind has disappeared. After his death his brain is not merely damaged but completely destroyed. It is surely logical to conclude that now his mind is also gone. It seems preposterous to assert that, when the brain is completely destroyed, the mind suddenly returns intact, with its emotional and intellectual capacities, including its memory, restored.

This is surely a ridiculously simplistic analysis. We all know that, while Alzheimer's might produce a general and progressive reduction in the sufferer's intellectual capabilities, they can also have intermittent periods of great lucidity. Moreover it is certainly not the entirety of the memory that is affected because, while their short-term awareness of people's names and of their surroundings might be badly impaired, their longer-term memory

27

can remain as sharp as ever.[61] Edwards also talks about an acquaintance who suffered from Alzheimer's who became increasingly aggressive and even violent, and compares this with her previous 'normal' personality. But again we all know that drugs or even alcohol can produce chemical changes in the brain that significantly alter moods or behavior – which are nevertheless only temporary as long as the imbibing is not excessive or too prolonged. He then attempts to apply similar logic to what he calls 'irreversible comas'. But what is his real point? There are plenty of documented cases of long-term coma patients who have amazed their doctors by reviving with their faculties completely intact.

Superficially more impressive is the argument put forward by Edwards and others that memory can be badly affected by brain damage. But in fact, as we will discover in the final chapter, there is strong evidence to suggest that memory and indeed the brain itself operates holographically. Similarly, brain-scanning experiments show that certain sets of cells in various areas become chemically active in response to the stimuli of different thoughts or feelings, but in no sense does this prove that these cells are responsible for *producing* the thoughts or feelings in the first place. It is equally possible that they originate quite separately in the nonphysical mind and the brain is merely *responding* to them.

However it is undoubtedly true that modern consciousness research is a hotbed of controversy, with an almighty battle being waged between those who insist on operating within an ever more limited, materialist framework and those who regard consciousness as the driving force of modern metaphysics. In the former camp we have the leading atheist campaigner Daniel Dennett, and he has been joined by a number of other prominent researchers – not least Blackmore, who has been extremely vocal on this topic, as perhaps befits a 'convert' who was originally drawn to paranormal research but decided there was no firm evidence to be found. In fact in her 2005 book *Consciousness* she takes the materialist argument to the extreme, insisting that all apparent thought and action is so much the result of neural activity that consciousness itself is an illusion, and that we have absolutely no free will. But for most people this is totally counterintuitive and unrepresentative of actual experience.

As yet none of these philosophical and scientific arguments have conclusively falsified the non-materialist 'brain-as-instrument-only' hypothesis, and nor have they succeeded in sufficiently proving the 'brain-equals-mind' hypothesis to justify a prima facie rejection of the survival of consciousness after death. So if there is other strong evidence for this –

such as a not insignificant number of persuasive, veridical, near-death cases, let alone the other areas of research we will discuss in due course – then the former hypothesis receives significant support.

Let us close with a wonderfully perceptive quote from the hallucinogenic explorer Aldous Huxley. It comes from *The Doors of Perception*, first published in 1954:[62]

> Reflecting on my experience, I find myself agreeing with the eminent Cambridge philosopher, Dr C D Broad, 'that we should do well to consider much more seriously... the suggestion that the function of the brain... is in the main *eliminative* and not productive. Each person is at each moment capable of remembering all that has ever happened to him and of perceiving everything that is happening everywhere in the universe. The function of the brain and nervous system is to protect us from being overwhelmed and confused by this mass of largely useless and irrelevant knowledge, by shutting out most of what we should otherwise perceive or remember at any moment, and leaving only that very small and special selection which is likely to be practically useful.' According to such a theory, each one of us is potentially Mind at Large. But in so far as we are animals, our business is at all costs to survive. To make biological survival possible, Mind at Large has to be funneled through the reducing valve of the brain and nervous system. What comes out at the other end is a measly trickle of the kind of consciousness which will help us to stay alive on the surface of this particular planet.

But if we have a consciousness – or perhaps now we can dare to call it a 'soul' – that survives physical death, what happens to it? In particular is there any evidence that, rather than just having one life, our souls reincarnate repeatedly?

2

CHILDREN WHO REMEMBER PAST LIVES

Two Strong Cases

James Leininger and James Huston

The past-life recall of James Leininger of Lafayette, Louisiana, made the headlines when he featured on ABC News in April 2004. But the full details that follow were only revealed in an in-depth article in the local *Acadiana Profile* magazine in December of that year.[1]

From the earliest age James had been fascinated with aircraft. He spent hours playing with toy planes, and always pointed and yelled when he saw a real aircraft in the sky. His parents Bruce and Andrea, a well-educated and grounded couple, were both satisfied that this was just typical childhood behavior – even when James became obsessed with crashing his planes into the living room table that served as his landing strip. But in the spring of 2000, as he approached his second birthday, vivid nightmares began. He would regularly thrash around in his sleep, especially kicking out with his legs up in the air; and it was the words he uttered while writhing that really shook his parents: 'Airplane crash, on fire, little man can't get out.'

They began to fear that his obsession might not be so harmless after all. Why on earth did he keep replaying the actions of a pilot desperately trying to kick out his cockpit window? It was at this point that Andrea's mother, having read a book about similar cases, suggested that these might be memories of a past life. Andrea contacted the author, Carol Bowman, and followed her suggestion that she and Bruce should take the nightmares seriously and discuss them with James. This did reduce their regularity. But as a result James also started to come up with startling details, usually when being comforted after a nightmare. Over that summer and into the autumn he revealed that the pilot of the plane was also called James; that he had been shot down by the Japanese; that he had flown Corsairs; and that one of his fellow pilots went by the name of Jack Larsen. He also mysteriously mentioned the single word *Natoma*.

Bruce remained dubious about any sort of spiritual explanation, but his curiosity simply would not allow him to ignore the level of detail James was reporting. He knew that neither he nor any other member of their family had any particular interest in aircraft or the war. Nor did he feel that the information could have come from such a young child, who could not even read at this point, watching documentaries without anyone else being aware of it. So, still with the primary intention of somehow proving that there was a perfectly rational explanation for James' memories, he began to research them.

His first port of call was to search for the word *Natoma* on the internet. This quickly established that an aircraft carrier called the USS *Natoma Bay* had been stationed in the Pacific during the latter part of World War II and, among other things, had taken part in the notorious battle for the Japanese island of Iwo Jima early in 1945. Coincidentally his book club catalogue included one all about this battle, so he ordered it, even though at this point he still felt the whole thing was pure coincidence. But not long afterwards he was really shell-shocked for the first time. One day he was flicking through the book when James came over to sit on his lap, and it happened to be open at a map. Immediately James pointed to the island of Chichi Jima to the north of Iwo Jima and said, 'Daddy, that is where my plane was shot down.' His interest now well and truly piqued, Bruce continued his internet research and came across a 'Natoma Bay Association', by which means he was able to contact a radioman who had been involved in the Iwo Jima conflict. Although he reported that their squadron had flown only Avengers and Wildcats, not Corsairs, he did confirm that a Jack Larsen had been one of the pilots. This was starting to look like more than just coincidence.

For the next eighteen months Bruce searched military records trying to find out more details about Larsen, but in vain. Indeed he was close to giving up when he attended a reunion of the Natoma Bay Association in the autumn of 2002. Without disclosing his real interest, he was able to establish that Larsen was not dead as he had assumed, but alive and living in Arkansas. Even more revealing, he found out that while a total of twenty-one men had been lost from the *Natoma Bay* during the campaign in the Pacific, only one pilot had been lost at Chichi Jima – and coincidentally his name was Lt *James* M Huston Jr. Aged only twenty-one, he had volunteered to fly that one last mission on 3 March 1945 before he was due to return to the US. Bruce immediately arranged to visit Larsen in Arkansas, and he confirmed he had been Huston's wingman that day. But neither he nor any other members of the squadron had actually seen what happened to Huston's plane in the heat of battle. Nevertheless, something else now slotted into place for the increasingly stunned Bruce. His son had always signed his drawings of aircraft 'James 3'. Was this his way of recognizing that his former personality had been James Huston *Junior*, and his father in turn James Huston *Senior*?

At this point the investigation switched to tracking down any surviving members of the deceased's family, and at the beginning of 2003 Bruce made contact with Huston's elderly sister, Anne Barron, in California. Without telling her his true interest they became friendly, and she kindly sent him a number of packages of photos of her long-departed brother. By this time the only major statement that James had made that did not ring true was his insistence that his former personality had flown Corsairs. Bruce knew that Huston had been flying a Wildcat on that fateful day, and this gave him some sort of faint hope that James' memories might still turn out to be just coincidental. That was until he examined the photographs – because in amongst them was a clear shot of Huston standing proudly next to a Corsair. Bruce subsequently confirmed from military records that, before he was posted to the *Natoma Bay*, Huston had been part of an elite special squadron of only twenty pilots, the 'Devil's Disciples', who test-flew Corsairs for carrier use. At this point he finally submitted to what his wife and others had long accepted – that his son James really was the reincarnation of a pilot who had died nearly sixty years before.

But even this was not all, because James made a number of other detailed and obscure statements that turned out to be true. For example, he insisted that Corsairs often suffered with tire punctures, which was confirmed by an aircraft museum. He also said that his former personality's plane had been shot in the engine, which set it on fire before it hit the sea; and eventually Bruce made contact with several members of a bomber squadron that had also been attacking Chichi Jima that day, who all confirmed that they had seen the engine on Huston's plane explode into flames.

As if his detailed recall of names, places and other obscure information were not enough, perhaps the most impressive part of James' recall related to three 'GI Joe' dolls that he called Leon, Walter and Billie. Again military records confirmed that three of the pilots from Huston's squadron who had been killed in other *Natoma Bay* engagements were Lt *Leon* S Conner, Ensign *Walter* J Devlin and Ensign *Billie* R Peeler. In fact when James was asked why he named the dolls that way he replied, 'because they greeted me when I went to heaven'; the records also showed that all three had died before Huston. And in an entirely fitting conclusion James is now, once again, in possession of two of his former personality's most treasured belongings, forwarded on by the military after Huston's death and in turn by his sister Anne when she heard the rest of the story: a bust of George Washington, and a model of a Corsair aircraft.

The media coverage ensured this case attracted plenty of attention from skeptics. Typical of their reaction was that of Paul Kurtz, a professor of philosophy at New York State University who is also the head of the CSI. He confidently declared to ABC that James' parents were 'self-deceived' and 'so fascinated by the mysterious that they build up a fairy tale'.[2] Given the full details, such a dismissive reaction was surely ill-considered for anyone expecting to be taken seriously as a commentator on the case. By contrast at least Richard Rockley attempted a more detailed analysis in his *Skeptico* internet blog in 2005.[3] Moreover to his credit he is generally highly critical of the reductionist and simplistic response to any paranormal research adopted by many of the most renowned skeptics. So how well does his contribution stand up?

One of Rockley's problems is that he does not seem to have read the full *Acadiana Profile* account of this case, and instead has obtained his information from the shorter ABC News report and from a brief contemporary article in the *Pittsburgh Daily Courier*.[4] His first argument centers on Bruce taking a twenty-month-old James to a local aircraft museum, where a Corsair with drop tanks was on display. He makes great play of this detail being omitted from the ABC News report, although there was no attempt to hide it in either of the other two – because, it appears, James had shown an interest in planes even before this event. Nonetheless, let us pretend that Rockley is right when he assumes that this is what triggered James' memories. He continues as follows:

> However, although he was excited by the planes, the images of WWII battles also frightened him, and they soon began to give him nightmares about being trapped in a plane on fire. This is when the real problem starts. The child's grandmother, for no obvious rational reason I can think of,

suggests he is remembering a past life. She brings in Carol Bowman (an author of several books on reincarnation), to 'affirm' James' nightmares. (Bowman is said to have been influenced by Ian Stevenson – another reincarnation proponent who is known to ask leading questions of young children.) Bowman 'encourages' James in his fantasies, also with leading questions. Unsurprisingly, the child cooperates in this fantasy building. After all, they're telling him he was a real pilot.

On what does Rockley base his massive assumption that a young child taken to an air museum is automatically likely to have the specific nightmare of being trapped in a burning plane? Worse still, what about his assumptions concerning Bowman's influence? Apart from the throwaway slur against both her professionalism and that of Ian Stevenson – of whom more in a moment – there is no suggestion in any of the reports that Bowman traveled halfway across America from her Pennsylvania home to visit James and ask supposedly 'leading questions'. Instead it appears that she and Andrea merely talked on the phone at this point.

Rockley then suggests that the signing of drawings with 'James 3' could simply have meant 'James, three years old'. But this too is contradicted by James' own explanation in the full report when quizzed about it by Bruce: 'Because I'm the third. I'm James 3.' Finally we come to Rockley's pièce de résistance:

> 'Natoma' is the name of a ship he could no doubt have seen in one of his father's books. But 'Natoma' is not quite 'Natoma *Bay*' – and did he say 'Natoma' or just something similar? We'll never know. Only 'John Larson' [sic] can't be explained easily. But even with this we really don't know a) if James really said these words, b) if he was prompted, c) if he said it after his father had read the name to him, and the father's timeline is confused, d) if he said something close that the father mis-remembered later when he read the name John Larson [sic], e) how many other things the kid said over the course of four plus years that did not match up but that the parents have forgotten.

A brief response to these equally ill-founded objections will suffice. According to the full report, it was James' mention of the word *Natoma* that *led* Bruce to look it up on the internet and find the Natoma *Bay*, which he established was involved in the battle of Iwo Jima, which is *why* he bought the *single* initial book from his book club about the battle, *in which* James then identified the more obscure island of Chichi Jima on a map. Surely for Bruce to be *that* confused about the order and causation of events he would have to be either a halfwit or a complete charlatan, and not even Rockley has dared to suggest either. Then, in seeming desperation about something he admits cannot be explained so easily, Rockley suggests that James might not even have said the name of his former colleague – unfortunately Rockley's failure to even get this name right is symptomatic of the superficiality of his analysis – and that his father might have read it in a book instead. Yet Bruce could not even find Jack Larsen in detailed military records, let alone in a recently published book.

James' recall of the little-known names of his former aircraft carrier and former colleague, his insistence he had previously flown a Corsair when all the initial evidence suggested otherwise, and various other obscure memories, are surely impressive enough. But arguably superior even to all this is one key aspect of the case that Rockley does not mention because it only appears in the full report. How could little James have known about Huston's fellow pilots Leon Conner, Walter Devlin and Billie Peeler? Although as Bruce found there are a number of reports about the *Natoma Bay* on the internet, their names do not appear at all except in more recent write-ups *resulting from* this case. There can surely be no doubt that the only way Bruce could be 'mistaken' about this would be if he were a complete charlatan making it up, and coaching James to lie into the bargain. Is this the most rational and likely explanation, given the facts and context of the case? Or is it simpler just to accept that James Leininger really is the reincarnation of James Huston Jr? [5]

Charlie and James Kellow

A similar but rather earlier American case comes from Frederick Lenz, whose research in the late 1970s will be discussed further at the end of this chapter. One of his correspondents was a real estate broker from Tampa, Florida called Mary, and she reported that one day her four-year-old son Charlie suddenly started talking about his death in a previous life.[6] In fact he seemed to be in a sufficiently distressed state – indeed he seemed to be reliving the events – that she encouraged him to reveal whatever he wanted.

He said it was the 'big war of 1942' and he had been killed when he was 'hit in the leg... and it hurt; it hurt bad'. Further questioning revealed he had lived as an only child with his parents in San Francisco, and his name had been James Kellow. James had volunteered as a naval officer – Charlie was quite indignant at the suggestion he might merely have been enlisted – and it seems his ship was bombed because he described a hellish scene of screaming and explosions. But he must have survived the initial attack even though badly wounded, because Charlie continued: 'I was in a raft, and there were some fellas with me. One of them fell off, and the other one died on the raft.' He managed to land the raft on a beach but died himself shortly afterwards. He was apparently single and in his twenties. Finally Mary asked Charlie the name of the ship and she thought he said *Alabama*, although he had difficulty pronouncing the word.

Mary was sufficiently intrigued to check this story out, and she established that the USS *Alabama* was now a museum ship docked not too far away in the port of Mobile, in its namesake state. She took Charlie to visit the ship and he seemed to instinctively know his way around, swinging through the hatches like an experienced sailor. But unfortunately the list of officers had no James Kellow, and the ship had never taken a direct hit such as the one Charlie described. Yet when she spoke to the commander he revealed that its sister ship the *Arizona*, with which it was often confused, *had* taken just such a hit.

Mary was able to obtain a copy of this ship's crew list some months later, and there he was: James Kellow, from San Francisco. Obviously Charlie had been saying 'Arizona' not 'Alabama', but she had not heard him correctly. She did consider contacting James' parents, but decided it would be better to hold off until her son was somewhat older. Nevertheless, this case gains most strength from the checking that Lenz himself did. Not only did he confirm that James Kellow was an officer on the ship at the time of its destruction, but a more detailed search of Navy records showed that he and at least one other member of the crew had indeed escaped on a raft, and their bodies were found on a nearby island.

To wrap this case up we can add that a quick search on the internet reveals the *Arizona* was destroyed during the attack on Pearl Harbor.[7] An aerial bomb ignited its munitions store, blowing the forward part of the ship to smithereens and setting of fierce fires that burned for two days. Nearly twelve hundred lives were lost, representing more than half of the entire Pearl Harbor casualties. Moreover she was moored next to Ford Island. The only inaccuracy in Charlie's statements was that the attack took place in December 1941, not in 1942.

Common Characteristics

In the last two centuries there have been a number of reports of cases of children who, like James and Charlie, spontaneously remember past lives. These have been collated and investigated by paranormal researchers from Europe and the US, including for example George Brownell, Gabriel

Delanne and Karl Muller.[8] In particular the latter's 1970 study *Reincarnation: Based on Facts* provides an extremely thorough review of a variety of reincarnation cases.

However the foremost pioneer in this field is indisputably the aforementioned Ian Stevenson.[9] Born in Montreal in 1918 he originally qualified as a medical doctor, but transferred to psychiatry and in 1957 became the head of department at the University of Virginia. Over time he had developed an interest in researching survival after death, perhaps in part because his mother was a keen theosophist, but at least as much, apparently, as a result of Aldous Huxley's influence and his personal experimentation with LSD. In 1960 he published the first paper to reflect his growing interest in child reincarnation cases, and this caught the eye of Chester Carlson, the inventor of the Xerox machine, who funded field trips to India and Sri Lanka the following year. On his death two years later Carlson went much further and bequeathed a million dollars to endow a chair for research into the paranormal, which resulted in Stevenson setting up the separate Division of Personality Studies. Further field trips to Burma, Thailand, Lebanon, Syria, Turkey, West Africa and Alaska followed, and now the department has nearly three thousand child cases on record – a huge body of painstakingly collected evidence.

Stevenson published some three hundred books and academic papers before his retirement in 2002, the best introductory overview being his *Children Who Remember Previous Lives*, first published in 1987 and revised in 2001, which contains brief summaries of twelve cases. However his earlier works always contained fully detailed case reports. The best known are *Twenty Cases Suggestive of Reincarnation*, first published in 1966 and revised in 1974, and the three volumes of *Cases of the Reincarnation Type*, published between 1975 and 1983.

Just as others have with near-death experiences, Stevenson identifies a number of common characteristics of typical children's past-life cases.[10] First, most subjects start to talk about their previous life at some time between the ages of two and four. This is hardly surprising given that this is more or less when we would expect a child to start talking with any degree of lucidity, and it suggests that the memories are with them more or less from birth. It also seems that they work like any other memories in that they fade over time, because the vast majority of subjects stop talking about their previous life between the ages of five and eight. However here there is more variety based on the extent to which they are encouraged or discouraged by their families, and on the degree of forcefulness with which their memories impinge on them. In any event Stevenson concludes that ideally cases need to be investigated early in the child's life if they are to have real merit.

Second, subjects' memories almost always relate to the later years of the previous personality's life, while the length of the apparent interval between the current and former lives is in most cases relatively short at less than three years, with an average of fifteen months.[11] Again this suggests an element of normal memory operation. In particular they also remember their mode of death, and given that most cases involve either a violent or at least a sudden and unexpected departure, it seems that unfinished business and strong unresolved emotions may again be playing a part.[12]

Third, subjects often express an intense desire to visit the location and family of their previous life, which if identifiable is usually not that far away. In the more forceful cases they often use the present tense when mentioning it, as in 'my name is...' or 'I live in...', or they may refer to their previous parents as their 'real parents'. They also adopt attitudes to others that are completely inappropriate for a young child and their current life, but entirely appropriate for the previous personality – for example showing friendship or animosity to former family and friends in exactly the measure that would have been expected of the deceased, or acting as a parent or older sibling to former relatives.

Fourth, subjects often display behavioral traits that are completely out of character for their present life, but entirely in keeping with the previous one. These can include phobias, such as of guns, knives or water, which are usually related to the manner of their previous death and can emerge even before they start to speak about it. Or they may display a fondness for unusual types of food, or for tobacco or alcohol, or interests in and aptitudes for a particular profession to which they have had no exposure in their current life. In a small number of cases they even reject their current gender on the basis that they still identify with the opposite gender of their previous life. Finally, in rarer cases still they display 'subliminal cognitive' skills, such as speaking a foreign language to which, again, they have had no obvious exposure.

Two More Strong Cases

Swarnlata Mishra and Biya Pathak

One of Stevenson's most impressive cases is that of Swarnlata Mishra.[13] Born in 1948 in Madhya Pradesh, a huge, central state in India, she was only three years old when she began to reveal amazing details of another life. On this occasion her father – an inspector of schools – had decided to take her on a trip from their home city of Panna in the north of the state to the central city of Jabalpur, some 170 miles to the south. On their return they were less than a third of the way home when, on the outskirts of the city of Katni, Swarnlata asked the driver to turn down a road towards 'my house'. Shortly afterwards, when they had stopped for a meal in Katni, she again insisted that they would obtain much better food in *her* house nearby. Of course this puzzled her father, but it was not until some time later that he discovered she was continuing to talk about her previous life in Katni to her brothers and sisters. She said her name had been Biya Pathak.

A number of years passed, during which time Swarnlata and her family moved some forty miles west to the district of Chhatarpur so that her father could take up a new post. Every now and then she would refer to her past life, but it was not until she was ten years old that he started to take her more seriously. The breakthrough came when a local professor, having heard a vague rumor about Swarnlata's claims, invited her and her father to dinner. During the meal Swarnlata learned that the professor's wife originally came from Katni, and asked to meet her. Swarnlata's recognition of an old friend of Biya's was instant, while the lady herself was stunned when Swarnlata reminded her of how, in her former life, they had had difficulty in finding a toilet at a wedding in the village of Tilora.

For the first time her father now documented the key statements she had made to date, including that Biya had had two sons, and that her family had owned a motor car – a rarity in this part of India even by the 1950s. She especially recalled a number of details about Biya's home. Apparently it was white on the outside, with black front doors fitted with iron bars for security. Inside there were four decoratively plastered rooms, while others were less well finished, and the front of the house had stone floor slabs. Behind it lay a girls' school, while a railway line and lime furnaces were also nearby. Katni is well known as one of the largest railway junctions in India, and also for its lime deposits, so the last two statements might be regarded as easy guesses if Swarnlata were making it all up. But what about the other less obvious details?

Not long after the incident at the professor's house the leading Indian paranormal researcher, Hemendra Banerjee, learned of the case and spent two days with Swarnlata and her family in their home in Chhatarpur. He was so impressed that he made up his mind to go to Katni to try to locate Biya's family. But he knew that Pathak was an extremely common name in the region, so he would only have her statements about Biya's home to guide him. Nonetheless in time he was able to find a house that matched the external description, in the right location near to a school, railway and lime furnaces. The family who owned the house was well known in the Katni-Jabalpur area for their extensive business interests, and were indeed called Pathak. So far so good. But in his wildest dreams Banerjee could not have expected to find that they did indeed have a deceased daughter called Biya. After her marriage she had moved to Maihar, a town some forty miles to the north, where she and her husband had raised two sons. But unfortunately she had died in 1939 from heart disease.

In that same summer of 1959 several members of Biya's family decided to visit Chhatarpur to test Swarnlata out. First her eldest brother arrived unannounced at the Mishra family home, but Swarnlata quickly recognized him and called him by the nickname Biya had used, 'Babu'. Then, in conjunction with Swarnlata's father, Biya's widowed husband and one of her sons arranged a meeting in which they were anonymously present amongst nine other local men. Not only did Swarnlata identify them both, but she did so despite Biya's son trying to throw her off the scent for a full twenty-four hours. He insisted that he was someone else, and that a friend he had brought along was Biya's other son. But on both counts Swarnlata stuck to her guns, quite correctly.

Not long afterwards Swarnlata traveled to Katni to visit Biya's home for the first time. Here she correctly identified a number of people without any leading, and even, again, with a certain amount of deliberate *mis*leading. These included Biya's other three brothers and various other relations; a Pathak family servant; the family cowherd – refusing to be put off by claims that she was wrong because he was dead; and one of Biya's family friends and his wife – commenting on his spectacles, which he had not worn when Biya was alive. She also asked about a neem tree in the compound and a parapet at the back of the house, both of which had been there in Biya's time but were now missing.

Further visits to Katni and Maihar followed in which more people were recognized and statements verified, up to a total of nearly fifty in all. But perhaps the most compelling piece of evidence came from Swarnlata confiding to Biya's husband that he had taken 1200 rupees from her money box. This was something of an embarrassment that, he confirmed, had been known only to himself and his former wife.

Faced with such overwhelming evidence, it was not long before all parties fully accepted the reality that Swarnlata was Biya reincarnate.

Indeed she continued to visit her former family regularly, and their close bonds were reestablished. What amazed onlookers was the way that, in the company of her former brothers, she would adopt the attitude of an older sister, while they in turn seemed to accept this as perfectly reasonable – despite the fact that in this life she was their junior by some forty years.

Gopal Gupta and Shaktipal Sharma

'I *won't* pick it up!' shouted the two-year-old. His parents had merely asked him to remove their guest's empty glass from the dinner table, and all three were completely taken aback by this temper tantrum. 'I am a Sharma!' he exclaimed as he dashed several further glasses to the floor. Once he had calmed down his father demanded an explanation, and without hesitation the young boy announced that he came from Mathura, a city in Uttar Pradesh that lay some one hundred miles to the south of their home in Delhi. He added that he had another father and two brothers, that he owned a number of large houses, and that he had multiple servants to clear tables for him. Most chilling, he suggested that his youngest brother had shot him in the chest.

Thus began another of Stevenson's more impressive cases, that of Gopal Gupta.[14] It appears that his parents reacted to this initial episode with indifference at best, but over the next few years he seems to have provided further snippets of information about his former life. He said that he had had a car, that he had traveled to college in it, and that he had obtained a degree there. In particular he also said that he had owned a company that made and sold medicines, and had a large showroom in Mathura. Gopal's father worked at a petrol station, and at some point he mentioned all this in passing to his boss, who vaguely remembered that some years before there had been a murder of a businessman connected with a company called Sukh Shancharak in Mathura that fitted the description.

But nothing further of note happened for some time until 1964 when, with Gopal now around eight years old, his father traveled to Mathura to attend a religious festival – although neither he nor his wife had ever been there before. While there he decided on a whim to locate the Sukh Shancharak Company's premises, where he met with the sales manager. When this man heard what Gopal had been saying he confirmed that the company *had* been run by three brothers, and that the middle one, Shaktipal Sharma, had indeed been shot in the chest by his younger sibling in the showroom. This had occurred back in 1948, when he was thirty-five years old, and he died several days later in hospital.

The sales manager was sufficiently impressed that he asked Gopal's father for his address, and passed the details on to Shaktipal's widow Subhadra. She in turn asked a friend in Delhi to investigate, and the details were confirmed by letter after a meeting with Gopal's mother. This was sufficient to persuade Subhadra and one of her late husband's sisters to visit Gopal's family at their home in the Krishna Nagar area of east Delhi. When they arrived unannounced he correctly identified Shaktipal's sister, but seemed reluctant to acknowledge the presence of Subhadra, or even say 'hello' or 'goodbye' to her. Shortly afterwards, when his father pressed him on why he had been so rude, he admitted that she had been his wife but he was not happy with her. Further questioning then revealed that as Shaktipal he had attempted to borrow money from Subhadra to give to his younger brother, who drank and caroused and always had money problems. But she had refused him, and this had escalated tensions between the brothers until the fateful day when the shooting took place. It was clear that in some sense at least Gopal blamed Subhadra for Shaktipal's death.

Over the next few months Gopal received two more visits in Delhi, both unannounced. Shaktipal's elder brother and his wife arrived one day in their car and told Gopal's parents only that they were from Mathura, yet when he came outside he correctly identified them too. However when Shaktipal's other sister arrived at his house he seems to have become confused between her and an aunt. Undaunted, this sister invited the Guptas to the forthcoming wedding of her son. Perhaps this was not such a good idea, because she had also invited her younger brother, the one who had shot Shaktipal, who had been released from prison early. It seems that Gopal did spot Shaktipal's nemesis while there, and became somewhat agitated. Afterwards he told his father that he had looked like a 'guilty thief', which seems to tie in with the fact that Shaktipal and his elder brother had suspected their younger sibling of stealing funds from the company. He also noted that he had grown a beard, which he had not had when Shaktipal was alive.

On a few occasions Gopal had asked to go to Mathura, and at the wedding Subhadra repeated an invitation for the Guptas to visit her. So in the spring of 1965, when Gopal was nearly nine, he and his parents finally made the journey south. They took along two friends for support, and also to act as independent witnesses. They first made their way to a central temple, and Gopal's father asked him to find the way to the showroom of Shaktipal's company. He knew the way himself because of his previous visit, but he and the others were careful to stay behind the boy and not influence him. His father even attempted to put him off, but for the entire journey of about a mile Gopal walked confidently ahead. 'Don't consider me a child,' he said. 'I *know* the way.' Of course once they got close the showroom had a sign on it proclaiming the 'Sukh Shancharak Company', which Gopal would have been able to read by that time, but he still led them straight there. His father then asked him to find Shaktipal's main house, which *none* of the small number of people present had ever visited. Apparently this was nearby, and he went down one lane but came back and reported that there should have been a betel shop at the end. He then found the correct lane, walked down it confidently and stopped outside a large house. 'Here it is!' he proclaimed proudly, and indeed when they knocked at the door he was proved absolutely correct.

It was here that Gopal provided considerable further confirmation of his apparent former personality. He identified Shaktipal in several photographs, even though only his body could be seen in one and his back in another, and asked if he could take one of them home. He recognized one of Shaktipal's close friends in another photograph, and his father in two more. He also pinpointed his bedroom, and the piano he had played keenly. The eldest of Shaktipal's brothers was particularly impressed to learn of Gopal's recollection that in his supposed former life he had kept all his accounts in a diary, because he was able to confirm that this unusual assertion was entirely accurate. It was either at this meeting or the previous ones in Delhi that certain of Gopal's unusual behavioral traits were also discussed. We already know about his refusal to do housework, which continued right throughout his childhood. But also like Shaktipal he displayed a marked fondness for oranges, while he was unusually generous to those less well off than himself – whereas members of Gopal's caste would normally be frugal to say the least.

However the two most impressive aspects of this case were still to come. First of all, it appears that Gopal's coolness towards his supposed former wife Subhadra continued at this meeting in Shaktipal's house. Nevertheless it was here that she learned for the first time that he remembered asking her for money for his younger brother in his former life and, with echoes of the Swarnlata case, it seems that he may even have stated the exact amount: five thousand rupees. Apparently when she heard this, she fainted. Admittedly Shaktipal's death had received significant news coverage in Mathura at the time, because not only was he a prominent businessman but he was also Chairman of the Municipal Board. It would almost certainly have been reported in Delhi as well, but only to a far lesser extent. On top of this, it had happened some seventeen years previously. So when Subhadra revived she initially told Gopal's mother that her shock was because his information was so accurate, even though it had never been made public at any time. In fact this information was *so* sensitive for the Sharma family, and for Subhadra in particular, that she apparently then retracted her confirmation of it – although only for a limited period of time before subsequently reconfirming it.

The second impressively obscure piece of recall came after this meeting at the house, when the assembled party moved back to the showroom and Gopal was asked to identify exactly where Shaktipal and his younger brother had been positioned at the time of the shooting. The exact details were known to those closely involved, of course, but they were actually trying to put him off. Nevertheless he stuck to his guns and correctly pointed out exactly where both the victim and his assailant had been standing.

Gopal never returned to Mathura after this. It seems the latter part of his life there held too many painful memories. Indeed after this his contact with Shaktipal's family was relatively sparse. He did make a few trips to Delhi to see the sister he had easily recognized when she visited him – and this accorded well with the fact that Shaktipal was closer to her, and also to her husband, who had stayed with him in hospital after the shooting and had been holding his hand when he died. In addition some time in the early 1970s the elder of Shaktipal's brothers visited him. But it seems that by this time, now in his mid-teens, Gopal had somewhat switched off from his former life.

Skeptical Critiques

Unsurprisingly Stevenson's work has attracted a great deal of interest and admiration from those who regard it as the most impressive evidence for a reincarnatory worldview so far produced. However, much of this tends to be relatively uncritical. So is his research as thorough and scientific as is usually suggested?

Probably the most quoted of Stevenson's critics is the aforementioned Paul Edwards, whose *Reincarnation* contains a comprehensive compilation of the various critiques we will consider in due course. For this we should be grateful, although his opening is not particularly impressive when he lays out his 'initial presumptions against reincarnation'.[15] As with his arguments against the astral body he relies on the strictly materialist argument that as yet we have no 'scientific' explanation of the mechanism by which some form of consciousness not only survives death but transfers back into another physical body. As a result he describes the assumptions that would have to be made to accept reincarnation as 'fantastic if not pure nonsense', requiring us to 'crucify our intellect'. Then, echoing the brain-mind debate that we discussed in the last chapter, he asks how a 'nonphysical body' can 'retain memories of life on earth although deprived of a brain'. How lucky we are that the many of the gifted scientists who continue to push the barriers of consciousness research are not similarly preoccupied with flushing themselves down a logical plughole.

In any event the first widespread criticism of Stevenson's research is that the vast majority of his cases are, again, purely anecdotal – that is, only in a very few was he able to investigate and obtain independent corroboration when the child was still young, and before there had been any contact with the previous family. Edwards is rather more constructive here, quoting correspondence with Champe Ransom who, after graduating from law school and developing an interest in parapsychology, joined Stevenson's team as a research assistant between 1970 and 1973.[16] He makes a number of criticisms of their methods, some of which we will discuss in due course – although others seem highly questionable given the way Stevenson presents his material so meticulously in *Twenty Cases*, the first edition of which had already been published at the time, and *Cases of the Reincarnation Type*. Perhaps more damning, however, is Ransom's conclusion:

> Stevenson's cases then do not amount to even half-way decent evidence. In only 11 of the approximately 1,111 rebirth cases had there been no contact between the two families before an investigation was begun. Of those 11, seven were seriously flawed in some respect. What this means is that in the great majority of cases, the two families had met years before a scientific investigation began, and that the likelihood of independent testimony was quite small. The rebirth cases are anecdotal evidence of the weakest sort.

We cannot avoid the fact that Stevenson's cases often rely on the memory and objectiveness of family and friends of both parties, which can clearly be questioned from a general perspective. Sometimes they also rely on the memory and notes of prior researchers, whose investigative standards probably vary in quality. Added to this most of the researchers in or associated with the Virginia team are clearly supporters of the reincarnation hypothesis, which can only reduce their objectivity. But then skeptics are hardly objective either. All of us are encumbered by greater or lesser degrees of preconception and bias. Nor could Stevenson have done anything about his relatively late investigation of many cases. He could only become involved after he was made aware of them, while the geographical logistics meant that he often clocked up as many as fifty-five thousand miles a year. But he was very much aware of the problem, and always hoped that one day he would be able to afford more staff on the ground in several countries, ready to investigate as soon as a case came to light.[17]

In any case Jim Tucker, one of Stevenson's successors whose own book *Life Before Life* was published in 2005, reports that the team now have of the order of thirty cases in which written records were made before there was any contact between the two families.[18] He also provides what is surely a reasonable assessment of the problem:

> Though it would obviously be ideal for us to solve every case ourselves, others have usually done so before we arrive on the scene. I don't think that means we should discount all these cases. That would be analogous to saying that we should only prosecute crimes that police officers personally witness. Memory is certainly imperfect, but that doesn't mean it's worthless.

Apart from the anecdotal issue, as already suggested various skeptics have also criticized Stevenson's methodology.[19] Often quoted is a 1994 article in the *Skeptical Inquirer* by another philosopher, Leonard Angel from Douglas College in British Columbia.[20] It is an analysis of the case of Imad Elawar from the Lebanon, described as apparently one of Stevenson's most impressive because it is one of the few where he managed to arrive relatively early and control much of the investigation. But in fact it is indubitably one of his weakest cases in terms of the quality of information obtained from the child, and in view of the doubts surrounding which deceased member of the Bouhamzy family the boy was actually identifying as his former personality. It is therefore extremely easy for Angel to accuse Stevenson of failing to 'skillfully record, present, or analyze his own data' by concentrating on this one case in respect of which he may have a point. But had he tried to extrapolate his criticisms to, for example, Swarnlata's case – which is also reported in *Twenty Cases* – he would have faced a far harder problem. It is also relevant to look at Gopal's case here, because there is some confusion on a minority of the forty-six statements tabulated by Stevenson. However he goes to great lengths to explain exactly what the uncertainties are, even down to admitting in one place that 'my notes are not quite clear on this point'. But Angel, of course, did not choose to widen the scope of his study, instead falling back on the general assumption that 'the other cases, in which data was first gathered by untrained observers' must be 'even less reliable than this one'. Selectivity and reductionism again.

Rockley has also criticized Stevenson's research, although in rather less detail than the Leininger case. The main point of his review of *Children Who Remember Previous Lives* for the internet-based *Skeptic Report* is that he would 'expect the book to consist of the more convincing cases'.[21] To some extent this is a fair criticism, and he can certainly be forgiven for making the assumption that 'the cases and comments in this book are representative of his work'. This was Stevenson's first foray into more populist writing, intended to belatedly introduce his research to a far wider audience than his more academic previous books. However one of his admitted intentions was to show that it covered far more than just Eastern cultures already imbued with a belief in reincarnation.[22] So he selected four cases from the United States, despite the fact that they significantly weakened the book. This was also in part because, with commendable professionalism and impartiality which Rockley is either unaware of or reluctant to acknowledge, he deliberately included weaker cases in all his publications to demonstrate both the 'strengths *and* weaknesses' of his research.[23] Nevertheless it is hard to see the twelve cases chosen here as fully representative, and their strength is not enhanced by being presented in summary rather than in full detail as elsewhere. So Rockley does not find it difficult to selectively pick a number of the weaker cases and briefly pick holes in them.

American philosophy teacher Robert Carroll adds a few criticisms we have not yet considered in his internet-based *Skeptic's Dictionary* article on Stevenson.[24] In fact the first was raised originally by the Indian philosopher C T K Chari from Madras Christian College in his 1967 critique of *Twenty Cases*.[25] It is that his use of translators in most of the countries he visited meant he could not fully control the objectivity of the questions put to subjects and witnesses, especially if the translators had their own cultural biases towards reincarnation. Of course this may have had an impact on a few occasions. But one of Stevenson's associates in India, the psychologist Satwant Pasricha, conducted an independent study without translators and reported similar findings in her 1990 book *Claims of Reincarnation*. Stevenson also provides important details about how he worked with translators in the introduction to *Cases of the Reincarnation Type*.[26] The second criticism raised by Carroll is that of 'confirmation bias', which means that researchers selectively look for information and answers that support their prior hypothesis and disregard those that do not – as if such accusations of selectivity can be leveled at Stevenson alone, and not his detractors. In any case, later in this chapter we will consider some fascinating testimony from Stevenson himself that rather mitigates against this suggestion.

Normal Explanations

Let us now turn to the possible normal explanations for Stevenson's cases, most of which he discusses with far greater thoroughness than the skeptics themselves.[27]

Pure Imagination

The first and most simplistic is that they derive from pure imagination alone. The finest exposition of this argument, at least for its entertainment value, comes from Richard Wiseman. A former professional magician turned psychologist from the University of Hertfordshire, he is one of the UK's most prominent members of the CSI, consistently appearing in the media to debunk supposedly paranormal phenomena. He decided to investigate whether such cases could derive purely from the imagination of young children, and so set up an experiment in which he asked a small sample to simply make up an imaginary friend and to describe the things that happened to them. There are no published results for this, even on his extensive website that lists over seventy journal articles and conference papers.[28] But one example of a three-year-old girl called Molly was used in a documentary entitled 'Past Lives: Stories of Reincarnation' that aired on both the Learning and Discovery Channels in 2003. She came up with a description of another child called Katy, who was also three. Molly said Katy had red hair, blue eyes, and was wearing a pink dress with flowers on it when she ran away. The experiment then continued as follows:

> *When Katy ran away, Molly, did good or bad things happen? [Pause while Molly is unresponsive to Wiseman] Was there anything bad that happened to Katy?*
> Bad.
> *Bad? What's bad that's happened?*
> The monsters got Katy.
> *What were the monsters like?*
> Ugly.
> *They were ugly monsters? What happened?*

Don't know.
[Molly's mother interjects] What happened to Katy when the monsters got her?
The monsters bit her.
[Molly's mother again] They bit her? So what happened to Katy?
Died.

Wiseman then tried to see if he could find a match for this story by looking through newspaper archives for children that had been abducted and killed, and managed to find one in which he says thirteen of the seventeen statements made by Molly were verified – although how he managed to get anywhere near this number from the sparse details mentioned in the documentary is not clear. Triumphantly, he proclaims he has proved that all such cases are based merely on imagination and pure chance: 'If Molly were claiming to have lived before, this would be the reincarnation case of the decade.'

Apart from Wiseman's massive exaggeration, which displays a rather shameful ignorance of the far greater depth of real cases, was this a valid experiment? First, and most obvious, we can see that he deliberately led her down a negative or 'bad' route by the emphasis in his question – which is hardly objective evidence that children spontaneously evoke bad memories more than good, as he claims in the program. So where are the rigorous scientific controls that skeptics – and, at least to a far greater extent than this, Stevenson himself – insist upon? Even more damning is that Molly's responses to questioning are brief, and have an obviously childish tone. So where is Wiseman's explanation for the much more detailed and obscure memories of people, places, nicknames, private facts and so on that are provided by the children in Stevenson's better cases, and even more by James Leininger? Can these really be so easily dismissed as the products of mere imagination? Worse still, Molly may have made up an imaginary friend, but in no way did she identify with her as a past life of her own. Yet again, just as with near-death experiences, we have a supposed expert using reductionism to a quite ridiculous degree without even attempting to examine the full range of the phenomenon in question.

Cryptomnesia and Self-Deception

To turn to more serious explanations, first there is the possibility already mentioned of a child picking up information from perfectly normal sources that have been entirely overlooked or forgotten by those close to it – the technical term for which is 'cryptomnesia'. Most obviously the information might have come from someone who knew the deceased, because another weakness in Stevenson's cases is that in the majority there was some degree of prior acquaintance between the two families, or at least they lived close to each other. Alternatively skeptics suggest that the high incidence of violent deaths arises in these cases because they are more likely to be reported in the media and discussed in cafés, bars, shops and the like, and are thus more likely to travel around and be overheard by a child. This too is undoubtedly true, although Stevenson counters that violent deaths would make them more memorable anyway, which is relevant if past-life memories operate in a similar way to normal ones.[29]

In any case he also worked hard to analyze and account for these various possibilities, and his detailed reports always contain a section headed 'Relevant Facts of Geography and Possible Normal Means of Communication Between the Two Families'. Moreover he often admits that in terms of information alone a child in a particular case might have come up with nothing that they might not have overheard perfectly normally, but nevertheless emphasizes that this does not account for their unusual behavioral traits, for example. In addition, skeptics offer no convincing explanation as to why so many children might turn merely overheard information into a strong identification with a past life of *their own*.[30] We can perhaps conceive of this happening if the child lives in a culture that believes in reincarnation, as most do, and if the deceased had the sort of heroic and fascinating death that skeptics like to assume. But in many cases the former personality had a downright unpleasant death and even life, recollection of which was painful to the child, while in many others their former lives were quite ordinary and unheroic, even if their deaths involved a degree of violence.

Stevenson also acknowledges that significant parental exaggeration of sparse early comments made by a child, similar to the idea of false memories that a person may firmly believe to be true, can lead to a case appearing to be far stronger than it really is. So the possibility of such self-deception must be taken into account as well.

To turn to specific analyses by skeptics, in his 1976 review of *Cases of the Reincarnation Type I* in the *Parapsychology Review*, the US-based parapsychologist John Fraser Nicol analyzed two Indian cases and concluded that they could be explained by normal means.[31] Meanwhile in his 1981 book *The Philosophical Possibilities Beyond Death* yet another philosopher, Brooke Noel Moore from the California State University, did likewise with a Sri Lankan subject from *Cases of the Reincarnation Type*

II.[32] However again it seems both were cherry-picking easy targets. A potentially more serious indictment came from an anthropologist called David Barker, who was hired by Stevenson to work alongside Pasricha in India. In an unusual article in the *European Journal of Parapsychology* in 1981 they each presented a different interpretation of the case of Rakesh Gaur, which they had thoroughly and jointly investigated.[33] But while Pasricha insisted it had a paranormal component, Barker's interpretation was that the case could be explained by normal means – this time because there had apparently been significant leading of the child when he was attempting to recognize people from his supposed former family. Nevertheless several years later Pasricha published new information that she felt favored a paranormal explanation.[34]

Whoever is right about this latter case, it is appropriate to remind ourselves that none of the other skeptics who make such strong pronouncements about Stevenson's work ever accompanied him on any of his field trips. The only person who did was the award-winning journalist and editor of the *Washington Post*, Tom Shroder. Previously a hardened skeptic, he took years to persuade Stevenson to allow him to observe his work first-hand. But when they did finally travel together, first to the Lebanon and India, then to South America, Shroder found himself completely convinced – and his 1999 book *Old Souls* did much to raise awareness of Stevenson's research.

But even if skeptics are right that many of Stevenson's cases are weakened by cryptomnesia or self-deception, despite his attempts to uncover and eliminate these possibilities, would it follow that we could safely write them *all* off? What about cases like those of Swarnlata and Gopal? In both the respective families' testimony that there was no prior acquaintance seems reasonable given that they lived more than one hundred miles apart. Biya's death due to ill-health would not exactly have been a big story and, while Shaktipal Sharma's murder probably would have made the news even some way away in Delhi, it would have been forgotten well before Gopal was born eight years later. Both children are reported to have made some impressive recognitions of people or places without prompting, sometimes without the accompanying adults having any knowledge of the place or person recognized, or even when being actively *mis*directed. Both recalled private nicknames of acquaintances of the former personality, or private events in their lives known only to themselves and one or two others. And both exhibited strong and unusual behavioral traits. All this seems to eliminate the possibility of normal acquisition or significant self-deception. Remember too that, even if he came to these cases relatively late, Stevenson interviewed significant numbers of people from both sides – in Swarnlata's case thirteen, and in Gopal's nineteen. Even if there were some minor discrepancies in the detailed testimony, especially in the latter case, in neither did any of these witnesses or any other bystanders – of which there would have been many at various times – express any serious doubts about their authenticity.

Fraud

The only other normal explanation for such cases, therefore, has to be deliberate fraud. Stevenson reports that in a very few cases it has been proved, and accepts that in just a few more it may have occurred but not been unearthed. But in his 1981 book *Mind Out of Time*, and the 1987 follow-up *The After Death Experience*, the British historian turned paranormal investigator Ian Wilson pinpoints several Indian cases in which he suggests fraud *should* have been concluded from the very facts that Stevenson himself uncovered and reported.[35] The first is that of Veer Singh, who did specifically ask for a share of the property of his significantly wealthier supposed former family, and then lost interest when they suffered a reversal in fortunes.[36] This case is pretty much unique in having an openly expressed financial motive, but there is nothing in the detail to explain *how* any fraud might have been committed. In particular it is difficult to see how the boy was 'coached' to make a number of relatively obscure statements that were verified by his former father when there was no prior acquaintance at all – especially because of the differences in caste – nor any notoriety in the death of the former personality, which had taken place more than ten years previously.

The same difficulties afflict the simplistic suggestion of fraud in the case of Dolon Mitra, except here there was not even an open request for financial reward on her part, merely a suspicion in the former family that was perfectly understandable given their great wealth.[37] Meanwhile in the case of Puti Patra, although there were some allegations of coaching, we find her openly accusing her former husband of murder when it had been commonly assumed that she had hanged herself.[38] Even the most ardent skeptic must surely admit that this would not be the most sensible approach to trying to swindle money out of someone – unless you were trying to blackmail them entirely in private, an idea that is clearly not supported by the other details and context. Not only that but Puti never expressed any desire to visit her former home because of the bad memories it held for her, and she stopped talking about her former life at the early age of four – at least in part, it seems, because she was discouraged by her own parents. So again the idea of fraud motivated by financial gain simply does not hold up.

Can we see a pattern emerging here? Despite the apparently greater effort put in by Wilson to investigate Stevenson's detailed reports, yet again he is selectively picking on specific aspects of a few of them and taking them entirely out of context. Moreover, remember, these are all details that Stevenson himself provides and comments on in great detail. In fact Wilson's misrepresentation is much clearer in the next case, that of Sunil Dutt Saxena: 'Despite being told directly by a doctor that Sunil had been coached... Stevenson preferred to dismiss the doctor as unreliable, concluding, against all the odds, the case was genuine.' What he fails to mention is that Stevenson goes into great detail about the reasons for his rejection of this person's testimony, which included obvious lies, and nor was he the conventional, reliable, medical doctor implied by Wilson, but an Ayurvedic physician.[39] Meanwhile the huge amount of testimony from nearly twenty other witnesses who did not support this claim hardly backs up his contention that Stevenson's conclusion went 'against all the odds'.

The last of Wilson's specific cases, that of Ravi Shankar, involves a somewhat different motivation.[40] Here we find a few neighbors on each side suggesting that early on the boy had been taken by his father to visit the father of his supposed former personality, which contradicted the testimony of the prime witnesses. This case is again unique in that it certainly could be interpreted as involving fraud, but here motivated by the *former* father who was keen to see his son's killers brought to justice. So he would have had to bribe Ravi's family. Not an impossible scenario by any means and one that, this time, is not necessarily weakened by the broader context of the case. Nevertheless it is certainly not typical and cannot be used to explain others.

On a more general note Wilson also provides a tabulation of the thirty cases from India and Sri Lanka discussed by Stevenson in *Twenty Cases* and *Cases of the Reincarnation Type I* and *II*, which shows that in twenty of them, or two-thirds, the previous personality's family was wealthier than the current one.[41] But the twenty include all the cases mentioned above whose broader context does not support the contention of fraud, and it seems reasonable to suppose that the same might be true of many of the others. In any case he follows these efforts up by admitting that 'there are considerable numbers of cases where such an interpretation cannot be justified', and then fails to provide any useful alternative explanation for these. Similarly Angel is forced to admit in his *Skeptical Inquirer* article that 'most reviewers of these materials hold that outright deliberate deception, on the part of enough of the participants to warrant dismissing the data [in its entirety], is highly unlikely'.

Nevertheless, given that they are both on Wilson's list of twenty, we ought briefly to check whether the fraud hypothesis can be applied to our two lead cases. Although Swarnlata's former family were reasonably wealthy while her father was a civil servant whose financial position remains entirely unclear, there is nothing else in the more detailed facts of this case to suggest there was ever any attempt to gain financial reward, and nor did any of the numerous informants ever suggest such a motive. As for Gopal, it was many years before any contact between the two sides was initiated, and even then it was relatively short lived and broken off primarily from his side. Yet again there is absolutely nothing in the huge mass of detail concerning this case that supports Wilson's general contention.

The other fraud motivation mentioned only in passing by Wilson could be publicity and fame, and Stevenson himself reports that he did come across this on a few occasions, but not regularly.[42] In fact Gopal's father was one such who apparently enjoyed the publicity of his son's case.[43] Wilson of course seizes on this, but what he makes less clear is that this only occurred late in the investigation, *after* the visit to Mathura. By this time Gopal was nine years old, so if his father was perpetrating a fraud he came to the idea very late on. Not only that but the broad context of the case in terms of the distance involved, the obscurity of much of the information and so on, suggests that fraud is unlikely and would have been extremely difficult to enact.

On top of all this, in many cases there are strong mitigating reasons why either family would prefer *not* to be involved. As Stevenson so eloquently points out:[44]

> I cannot emphasize too strongly that these cases impinge unexpectedly and often in an undesirable way on the lives of the persons concerned. The nagging demands of a four-year-old boy that he be taken immediately to another remote village, his revelations of sordid murders or other crimes, his claim that he has in the 'other' home electricity, good food, automobiles, and maybe a wife, cannot possibly increase the pleasure of a poor farmer who must listen to such talk in the morning before he leaves to till the soil and again at night when he returns weary from doing so.

Moreover the families of these children often face unwanted rivalry for their affections from the previous personality's family, and the fear that they might run away or even be 'claimed' and taken away. Meanwhile, of course a wealthy previous family will sometimes suspect the motives of the child's family, which is almost certainly why Swarnlata was given such a hard time with them repeatedly trying to trick her. The previous family may also be fearful of skeletons in the closet that they would prefer remained private, Puti Patra's aforementioned allegations of murder being a perfect case in point.

But what if there was a genuine motive for fraud in any given case? A daunting number of people might have to be coached and even paid off to make it watertight; and what about the strong emotions and unusual attitudes, behavioral traits and phobias displayed by a great many child subjects? These too would have to be painstakingly coached and acted.

It is also worth pointing out that in many of Stevenson's cases we find subjects achieving some seriously obscure spontaneous recognitions, and then failing to recognize certain other people who should have been obvious. This was certainly true in Gopal's case because, despite the impressive 'hits' described previously, he failed to recognize two of his previous personality's brothers-in-law, one of his sons and one of his employees. Skeptics blithely suggest this makes such cases weaker, but is this actually the most considered and rational interpretation? Certainly if fraud is the potential motive we might expect the research and coaching to be rather better than this, and to at least take care of all the obvious people. So arguably this augments rather than lessens the authenticity of such cases.

Cultural Conditioning

So much for the normal explanations of cryptomnesia, self-deception and fraud. The last major possibility is that Stevenson's cases can be explained by a mixture of these and cultural conditioning. The prime example of this is that they primarily occur in countries where a belief in reincarnation is already strongly ingrained. But Stevenson argues that in decades past, when such belief remained rare in Western cultures, any child mentioning something even hinting at a past life would have been at best ignored and at worst silenced – either through lack of understanding, or fear of ridicule or even ostracization if such information became public. Edwards counters that if such suppression had been widespread teachers and child psychologists would still have noticed and reported the phenomenon.[45] But how many children who had already obtained a negative reaction from their parents would have gone on to confide in a teacher, especially in decades past when schooling remained relatively strict? Indeed how many run-of-the-mill psychologists would take past lives seriously even now, let alone in earlier times?

In addition we have seen that near-death subjects were reluctant to come forward until the phenomenon became more commonly discussed and accepted, and the same has been true of past-life recall. Stevenson found that he was increasingly contacted by people from the US and Europe saying their child had talked about another life many years before, but they had discouraged them because they thought it was all nonsense. That is why in 2003 he was able to publish *European Cases of the Reincarnation Type*, which included thirty-two cases investigated by his own team, and why around the same time the Leininger case was able to command so much media attention in the US. It is also why the researchers who continue in this line – like Tucker and the rest of the team in Virginia, and Bowman – are now collating far more data from Western countries.

Of course skeptics will suggest this is a circular argument that only proves their original point. But the Leininger case is a perfect example of parents who did not even *consider* the idea of reincarnation until James' unusual behavior was well underway, while Bruce in particular did not fully *accept* it until long afterwards. But it was *introduced* to them by Andrea's mother because it is now more widespread and acceptable. By contrast in times gone by this would probably never have happened, and they would likely have become so frustrated by their son's behavior that they would have attempted to silence him. How many Western cases might we have already lost in this way? More importantly, what might the future hold?

In general, therefore, it seems reasonable to suppose that there *has* to be a certain degree of acceptance of reincarnation in a culture for cases to be taken seriously and reported, but it does not then follow that it is this belief that creates them. Nevertheless the other aspect of cultural conditioning that purports to show that reincarnation is not the best explanation is the apparently marked difference in certain characteristics of Stevenson's cases depending on where they arise. In other words, as Chari first suggested in his 1967 paper, the *type* of reincarnatory belief influences them. So let us examine the three key characteristics that are supposedly culturally conditioned.

The first is the length of the interval between lives. Wilson discusses these in some depth, even going as far as to produce another detailed tabulation, but he completely misses the point.[46] He seems to think they should all show either no interval or a consistent one, whereas there is no logical or philosophical reason why this should be the case; as Stevenson found there are generally no hard-and-fast rules on this, with variations from as much as twenty years to zero, although the lower end of this scale is far more common.[47] Instead the more productive argument for skeptics is to suggest that any variations can be shown to be culturally influenced, and their favored example is that of the Lebanese Druses who, along with certain other cultures, are quite specific in their belief that reincarnation is instantaneous. So is this what we find in Lebanese cases? Stevenson reports on only two in his two main books, but for Imad Elawar it was some nine years and for Suleyman Andary twelve.[48] But in fact if there is an interval of any length the Druses simply assume there must have been an intermediate life in which nothing of note occurred, which is why it was not remembered. So this, surely, is the real cultural artifact; and it has no impact on the underlying nature of the cases.

The second characteristic is the relative locations of the two lives, for which once more there are usually no definitive rules. But Wilson provides a representative tabulation showing that in the majority of Stevenson's cases the child returns to not only the same country but also the same region, and sometimes even the same town or village.[49] Nevertheless he again misses the key point, which is to look for cultures that show a marked peculiarity conforming to preexisting beliefs. This time we find that a majority of cases in Burma and Thailand, and amongst the Igbo of Nigeria and the Tlingit of Alaska, do conform to the local belief that the deceased reincarnate into the same broad family.[50]

The third characteristic is gender change, and again most cultures have no definitive rules about this. However in all the cases from the Lebanon, Turkey and the tribes of Alaska and British Columbia there were no changes in gender from one life to the next, and this again conforms to local beliefs.[51]

These findings concerning location and gender certainly cannot be dismissed lightly, because they affect a significant number of cases. But they fall well short of a majority, so it would surely be reductionist to suppose that we can dismiss the entire body of Stevenson's research as a result. Not only that but he has a ready paranormal explanation for them, albeit one that skeptics will dismiss as nonsense.[52] We have already seen that thoughts and intentions are of supreme importance in the nonphysical realms. So, if someone dies believing strongly that they will come back in the same family or gender, perhaps they fulfill that expectation psycho-spiritually, especially if they return in something of a hurry. We can also conjecture that some groups of souls might choose to stick to one location for their incarnations together, at least for a period of time.

Genetic Memory

The final normal explanation that has been offered is that these children's memories do not relate to a past life but are genetic, and have somehow been passed on through the offspring of the deceased. But this is easy to counter. In most cases it is absolutely clear that there is no possibility whatsoever of even a distant blood relationship, if for no other reason than that the interval between the two lives is so short.

Paranormal Alternatives

If we accept that the normal alternatives cannot provide full and complete explanations for the entirety of Stevenson's research, then like him we must consider the paranormal alternatives before we can take any definitive view about the extent of its support for the idea of reincarnation.[53]

The first of these is extrasensory perception, the alternative championed by Chari in his 1967 paper. Under this hypothesis the memories are assumed to come from telepathic communication either with living acquaintances of the deceased person, or with their discarnate soul. A variant of this alternative is that the memories arise from tapping into some sort of 'universal memory' or consciousness. But Stevenson's child subjects are hardly ever reported to have any particular paranormal gifts. Nor does this alternative seem to offer a sensible explanation for the depth of emotions and unusual behavioral traits so often encountered or, again, for why the children identify so strongly with the memories as being from a past life of their own.

The second is possession of the subject by the soul of the deceased, and Stevenson certainly accepts that this is the best explanation for those few cases in which the other person did not die until *after* the subject was born. As for the main body of cases, on the face of it possession might better account for the strong emotions, behavioral traits and identification. Stevenson himself offers four objections to this idea, but arguably none of them are particularly strong. The first is that the memories of the other life almost always fade at a relatively consistent, early age; but we know from other paranormal research that children are more likely to attract not only poltergeist activity but also certain types of possessing spirits. The second is that subjects are often ignorant of changes that have taken place in and around their former home and so on since the time of the previous personality's death; but Stevenson at least partially accepts that a possessing spirit's self-imposed imprisonment in the intermediate plane might 'freeze' them in time as well. The third is that subjects' memories can be stimulated by visits to their former home and relatives; but, on a purely practical level, this is usually where they would *need* to be to make spontaneous recognitions of former acquaintances, possessions and so on. The fourth relates to cases involving birthmarks and defects; we will discuss these shortly, but they may be rather less secure than the main body of evidence.

However there is another argument for reincarnation rather than possession that Stevenson does not use, presumably only by oversight, which is that a number of child subjects seem to remember brief details of what happened to them *between* lives.[54] Some remember staying in a discarnate state somewhere near the site of the previous life, and may occasionally make statements about events after their death – descriptions of funerals and so on – that have been at least partially verified. Others describe meeting a sage or guide. In either situation they find themselves drawn or directed to the parents of their new life. They key point is that these memories display a clear continuity between the previous and current lives. This suggests that reincarnation is a better explanation than possession in at least some cases, and it is then a matter of opinion whether this is likely to be true in the majority of cases. But it is germane to point out now that in later chapters we will come across extensive, broader evidence from adult regression subjects about what happens in the period between lives, or 'interlife'; and this, by definition, supports the notion of individual soul reincarnation.

It is worth casting our minds back to the allegation of 'confirmation bias' made by Carroll. But instead of relying on the armchair musings of yet another philosopher, let us leave the final word on alternative explanations – whether normal or paranormal – to a highly trained university professor with a passion for psychology and psychiatry and an obsession, while regularly out in the field, for examining all possibilities in as much depth as possible. This is, of course, Stevenson himself:[55]

> I have some interest in fraud and much curiosity about cryptomnesia and also about the subtle ways in which extrasensory perception works. I have found that my interest never flags when we encounter features of the cases

that suggest these interpretations instead of supporting that of reincarnation. Without claiming that I always like what I hear, I do believe that I am willing to listen to anything that anyone cares to tell me about a case, and I have often gone out of my way (sometimes to the exasperation of my associates) in order to trace out some remote informant who might throw light on the possibilities of normal communication between the two families concerned in a case or who was reputed to speak unfavorably about it.

Birthmark and Defect Cases

There is a subset of Stevenson's cases that, if fully authenticated, would provide quite astonishing evidence of reincarnation, which is why he devoted a considerable amount of time to their investigation and documentation. They involve children who have birthmarks or other physical birth defects that appear to correspond to the fatal wounds of the deceased person whose life they remember. He collated over two hundred such cases and they are all reported in detail in his lengthy medical monograph *Reincarnation and Biology*, the two volumes of which deal with birthmarks and defects respectively, while over one hundred of them are summarized in the shorter *Where Reincarnation and Biology Intersect*. All of these books were published relatively late in Stevenson's career, in 1997.

Most skeptics do not pay much attention to these cases because they have already concluded that the conventional ones are deficient. But in his 1967 paper Chari expressed doubt about the validity of the small number of early birthmark cases. Meanwhile in *Reincarnation* Edwards critiques one of the early cases, that of Corliss Chotkin.[56] This is an easy target because both child and deceased came from the same family, as is usual with the Tlingit, although his selection was limited because Stevenson's specialist books on this topic had not been published at the time. In any case Edwards' main objection is the 'modus operandi problem' – that we do not know the scientific mechanism by which such birthmarks and defects could be transferred from one body to the next.[57] Of course this is just as narrowly materialist as his aforementioned objection that we do not know the exact mechanism by which a soul might reincarnate in the first place.

However he does present one other argument, which was speculative at the time given that he had only studied one case, but which arguably turns out to be pretty accurate when the full set of cases is examined:[58]

> What happens is that when a child is born with some birthmarks, the parents or other interested parties try to remember or look for somebody who died

fairly recently and of whom it was known that he had wounds whose location corresponded to the location of the birthmarks of the child.

Edwards is assuming here that such cases always come from cultures with an existing belief in reincarnation, and this does seem to be true because there are very few if any from Western countries.[59] To make matters worse Stevenson admits, without apparently seeing it as a major problem, that certain cultures do exactly what Edwards suggests:[60]

> Much depends on the care with which they examine the baby. This, in turn, varies with the importance they give to identifying the baby as a particular person reborn. Some cultures, such as those of the Tlingit of Alaska and the Igbo of Nigeria, attach great importance to such identification. In those cultures, if you had been, for example, a famous warrior or even a successful trader, you can pick up some of your previous prestige as you are reborn – provided, that is, that your parents recognize you for who you were.

Elsewhere we find that the Burmese too regard birth defects as stemming from a previous life:[61]

> Burmese people call birth defects and wounds… *ta-gyun-nar*, which means an affliction from a previous life. One treatment consists in applying to the wounds a paste made from a human bone, or perhaps bamboo or other wood, from the cemetery.

Stevenson also discusses cases that involve what he calls 'experimental' birthmarks:[62]

> These involve the marking of a dying or recently dead person with some substance, such as charcoal. The mark is put in a particular location, and later-born children (of the extended family or area) are examined to see whether they have a birthmark at the site of the marking.

Not only this, but we have already seen that the general cases from Burma, Thailand, Nigeria and Alaska always involve the same broad family, and the birthmark and defect ones follow the same rule. Meanwhile in most of the rest of these cases from other countries or cultures the two families are still from the same village or area. Indeed in virtually all of them there is some degree of prior acquaintance, unlike in the more conventional cases in which at least a substantial minority – including those of Swarnlata and Gopal, for example – do not suffer from this drawback. What all this means is that there does appear to be a far greater likelihood of widespread self-deception, and even on occasion of fraud, with birthmark and defect cases.

Birthmark Cases

To be sure that this is not an unduly harsh judgment we should examine a few of what might be thought of as the stronger cases in each category. If we start by considering those involving birthmarks we should first appreciate that, although almost all of us have them, they usually only take the form of small areas of increased skin pigmentation or moles. By contrast Stevenson insists that most of his cases involve 'hairless areas of puckered, scarlike tissue, often raised above the surrounding tissues or depressed below them', and also usually more than one mark.[63] There is therefore some validity to his claim that they are unusual *as birthmarks*, but the problem is that they also tend to resemble the sort of scars that arise from common injuries. So Stevenson is almost always relying on uncorroborated family testimony that the marks were there at birth. That is not to suggest that fraud is widespread in these cases, merely that there can easily be confusion between marks existing at birth and those arising from typical childhood knocks. However in the worst-case scenario, as distasteful as it may be, it is not impossible that in certain cultures a family with a strong motive for making an identification with someone who was powerful or wealthy might have deliberately manufactured appropriate scars on their child.

Our first example of this type of case is that of Chanai Choomalaiwong.[64] He was born in central Thailand in 1967, apparently with one small, round mark on the crown of his head and another larger and more irregular one above the hairline on the left. These did roughly correspond to the mode of death of the previous personality he claimed to have been, a schoolteacher and minor gangster called Bua Kai who was shot in the back of the head – although there was no postmortem report to establish the exact location of his wounds. Moreover Chanai apparently made a number of correct statements and recognitions, in addition to adopting a fatherly attitude to Bua Kai's children. On the other hand, although the two relevant villages were some fifteen miles apart, the grandmother who brought Chanai up was at least 'casually acquainted' with Bua Kai. There is certainly nothing in this case to overtly suggest fraud but, given the element of prior acquaintance, self-deception is surely a possibility. Much hinges on the statistical likelihood of such birthmarks, if that is what they are, and it is not easy to form an objective judgment about this.

By contrast there is every reason to suppose our next case involved self-deception at the very least, because it was apparently preceded by an 'announcing dream'. This is a reasonably common occurrence among several of the cultures that Stevenson investigated, and particularly in birthmark and defect cases. In this example he reports that the night before Cemil Fahrici was born in Antakya, Turkey, in 1935, his father dreamed that a distant relative, Cemil Hayik, would be reborn as his son.[65] Hayik was a local hero, a bandit who had only recently killed himself by firing his shotgun from under his chin when his hideout had been surrounded by the occupying French police. Apparently the baby Cemil was found to have a prominent scarlike birthmark under the right side of his chin, about two centimeters long and one wide, and then from the age of two he made a number of accurate statements about Hayik's life. But Stevenson himself admits that nothing the boy said was not already well known after recent and prominent reporting, on top of which the two parties were distantly related. The boy supposedly had nightmarish dreams about the police, and identified with Hayik so much that he insisted on being called Cemil even though he had been christened Dahham. But, unlike the often somewhat obscure behaviors encountered in more conventional cases, these are obvious reactions if from an early age he had been encouraged to believe he was the heroic Cemil Hayik reborn.

On the face of it this case is strengthened when we find Stevenson reporting on something that transpired some years into his investigation. When he found that the decisive bullet had exited through the top of Hayik's skull, he was also able to establish that the younger Cemil – albeit that he was by now thirty-five years old – had a linear hairless area about two centimeters long and two millimeters wide at the top of his head. But on further reflection something does not sit quite right here. Apparently the younger man immediately pointed to it when asked, so he himself knew it was there; and so, surely, must his parents and others. So why had it never been mentioned previously? Doubts about this second mark are not improved when we find from Stevenson's more detailed report that witness testimony about whether or not it had been there at birth was extremely varied and unreliable. Given the popularity of the supposed former personality, and the very late stage at which Stevenson became involved, it is not impossible to conceive of fraud playing a part in this case.

A worse problem arises when we find in this same more detailed report that there was at least one other child in the vicinity, born several years later, who apparently had a birthmark on top of his head and was identifying himself as Cemil Hayik reborn. Stevenson did not learn about this until some time after his own visits, and the details of this other case were sparse. But what we might justifiably consider his far greater impartiality when dealing with more conventional cases seems to go out of the window with this one. He ruminates about the high likelihood that both of these cases might have been manufactured given Hayik's popularity but then, with no additional justification, comes to the following conclusion:

> My own opinion is that Cemil Fahrici had memories of the life of Cemil Hayik and that if anyone should be regarded as the reincarnation of Cemil Hayik it is he. If this is correct, then the case of Sabri Aynaci [the other claimant] belongs in the category... of cases developed by self-deceiving parents.

Birth Defect Cases

If we turn now to birth defects, it seems that they originally caught Stevenson's attention during his medical training and played a significant role in his future career development. He wondered how they could be fully accounted for by purely physical phenomena when, for example, genetic and hereditary factors alone cannot explain why only one twin in an identical pair sometimes suffers from a defect. It was undoubtedly this conundrum that caused him to devote so much time and energy to these cases. In addition, by their very nature it is virtually inconceivable that those involving birth defects would involve deliberate fraud. So do these fare any better when put under the spotlight?

From a physical correspondence perspective one of the more impressive cases appears to be that of Semih Tutusmus.[66] His birth in Sarkonak, Turkey, in 1958 was supposedly preceded by his mother dreaming that a man called Selim Fesli would be 'coming to stay' with her and her husband. In the dream his face was covered in blood, and he said he had been shot in the ear. This was accurate in that only shortly before this same man, a local farmer well known to Semih's father, had been shot in the side of the head while dozing in a field and had succumbed to his injuries in hospital several days later. A neighbor had been accused of his murder, but he pleaded that it had been a hunting accident and only received a two-year jail sentence.

Again the identification of the newborn Semih with the deceased was strengthened when he was found to have only a linear stump where his right ear should have been, and the right side of his face was markedly underdeveloped. We are then told that from an early age he made a number of accurate statements and recognitions relating to Selim's life and death – but again none that he could not have obtained by normal means, while there were virtually no independent witnesses who could testify to their authenticity. From a behavioral point of view he apparently showed intense hostility towards the man accused of his murder, which continued up until his late teens, but this would be a rather obvious reaction if he had always been identified with the deceased.

Although there is nothing to suggest a strong motive for self-deception in this case – apart from Semih seeming to enjoy the attention of Selim's family during regular visits to their home – once more if we ignore his defects it is not a strong one. But do they force us to rethink? Stevenson reports that studies show the incidence of microtia with hemifacial hypoplasia as something like one in every three-to-five thousand, which is not especially rare. Far worse, however, is that again we find two rather damning pieces of additional information in his more detailed report. Not only were Semih's parents cousins, although they did not seem to know to what degree, but his mother had taken some form of abortifacient during her pregnancy. As Stevenson himself admits in the small print, both of these factors significantly increase the chance that Semih's birth defect had an entirely natural explanation.

Another interesting birth defect case is that of Ma Htwe Win, who was born in Upper Burma in 1973.[67] During pregnancy her mother supposedly dreamed that a man walking on his knees, or perhaps on stumps, was following her and she could not shake him off. Then at birth she was found to have, among other things, partial constriction rings just above both ankles and a severe one around the middle of her left thigh. Stevenson reports that her parents did not understand any of this until Ma Htwe Win started to talk, when she said she had had a previous life as a man called Nga Than, who had been attacked by three other men and then dumped, still partly alive, in a well. She also said he had been placed in a sack and his lower legs tied up behind his thighs to reduce space. This story did correspond rather well with the life of a man called Nga Than whose wife had encouraged his murder to continue a long-standing affair with one of his assailants. Then some time later they quarreled and a neighbor overheard them discussing the murder and the location of the body. The police duly found it in the well.

This sounds rather impressive, but it is aided by the order in which Stevenson presents the events. It is only towards the end of his summary account that we establish, somewhat in passing, that in fact Ma Htwe Win's mother had walked past the well just as the police were bringing up the body. Stevenson says that she 'glanced at the body and ropes and went on her way', but we then find that this made enough of an impression on her that the aforementioned dream occurred that night. Meanwhile, of course, the murder would have been reported in the papers and thoroughly discussed, and then Ma Htwe Win was born some six months later with defects that appeared to correspond well with those of the murder victim – into a culture that, remember, deliberately looks for past-life explanations for such defects.

Like Semih she apparently retained a strong determination to take revenge on the murderers, but this is again an obvious reaction. The only information she provided that was not already well known were some uncorroborated details of the murder itself, such as being stabbed in the chest and having her hands or fingers – the reports varied – cut off. This vaguely corresponded with an extremely faint, small birthmark on her chest and some defects in her left hand. But the key fact not even mentioned by Stevenson is that he seems to have made no attempt to relate this to any sort of postmortem on the recovered body. So her own or her family's imagination could easily have developed this aspect of the story *from* these defects, rather than them acting as corroboration for her supposed past-life. This leaves us with her main defects of the legs, and their statistical likelihood is not easy to establish. But there must again be a clear possibility that all this was just coincidence and that self-deception, motivated by a parental desire to explain some rather debilitating defects, played the major role.

A Question of Balance

Any skeptic reading this chapter might easily suggest that this heavy criticism of Stevenson's birthmark and defect cases, contrasted with ongoing support for the bulk of his more conventional ones, is indicative of double standards. But it is easy to adopt a position in advance and then make selective facts fit that position, even when apparently examining the evidence thoroughly, which is what the vast majority of Stevenson's supporters and critics do in equal measure. Whereas this evidence is so detailed and complex that to handle it reductively is a nonsense. So the arrival at a less than black-and-white conclusion may be perceived, by some at least, as a strength and an indication of reasonable objectivity.

What can we conclude, then, about where the balance really lies? It seems there are fundamental weaknesses in *all* of the birthmark and defect cases. It also seems that Stevenson's objectivity was unquestionably reduced in this area of his research, and we have already seen that there were strong motivations for this – on the one hand because of his medical training, and on the other because such cases, if proven, would constitute incredibly strong evidence of reincarnation. They would also provide unparalleled support for the argument that we are dealing with the reincarnation of the individual soul, and not with subjects tapping into a universal memory or being possessed, which is particularly crucial to the general thread of this book. However our conclusion must surely be that the birthmark and defect cases so far collated really do not stand up well enough to provide such proof. That is not to suggest that our normal explanations of the specific cases discussed above are definitely correct, merely that they are at least as likely as paranormal ones, if not more so. Nor can we discount the possibility that far stronger cases may emerge in the future. But so far the evidence in this area can only be regarded as inconclusive at best.

What about the more conventional cases? Again there can be no escaping from two general weaknesses. First, that in most of them there was contact between the two families before professionals were able to investigate. Second, that many of them involve either the same family, or two families who vaguely knew or lived reasonably close to each other, or a previous personality whose death was well known in the locale. Moreover we have seen that skeptics have been able to show significant weaknesses in some of the handful of cases they have chosen to analyze.

However we have also seen that they chose these cases somewhat selectively. Far more important, though, is that their blanket rejection of *all* Stevenson's cases as being explainable by cryptomnesia, self-deception, fraud or cultural conditioning does not appear to stand up well when we examine the full details and context of certain stronger cases – such as those of Swarnlata and Gopal from his collection, and the more recent Leininger case. Indeed it is probably fair to go further and suggest that these normal explanations do not easily explain anywhere near as many cases as skeptics would have us believe. It is because of this that it is arguably justifiable to grant a reasonable degree of credence to the conventional cases while simultaneously rejecting those involving birthmarks and defects, where no equivalently strong cases appear to exist and normal explanations seem far more widely applicable.

Let us also remember that Stevenson himself was a trained psychiatrist, that he was well enough respected that originally he was made head of department at Virginia, and that he traveled the world for more than three decades investigating and collating these cases. However much skeptics might suggest a general lack of objectivity, the man was no idiot, and his work was sufficiently impressive that the originally skeptical Shroder – one of the few people to accompany Stevenson on a field trip, and who set out to refute his research – found himself persuaded of its authenticity. Again we must ask, how well does the testimony of these two and of others in the field compare to that of armchair philosophers, who make blanket assumptions about the motives or integrity of the subjects and their families without ever meeting them – assumptions that usually turn out to be completely unsupported by the context and details of specific cases?

As Stevenson rightly observes when discussing Nicol's criticism of one case:[68] 'I am aware that personal impressions about the honesty and reliability of informants count for little in the minds of some critics; but an informant's good reputation should have due weight in appraising a case.' Of course sometimes his subjective judgments of the people involved will have let him down, and led to a case getting through that should otherwise have been rejected, as he readily admits. But we all make mistakes; and across the board the final position arrived at by allowing such subjective considerations to play a part – as they do, for example, in any court of law – will surely be far more balanced than a blanket rejection in complete ignorance of the details.

Of course a hardened skeptic will remain unmoved by any of this. But others may agree that there remains a case to answer – especially when spontaneous childhood memories are placed in the broader context of other areas of research.

A Strong Adult Case

One of these areas of research involves the spontaneous memories of adults. Although modern commentators seem to place less emphasis on these, older sources such as Brownell, Delanne and Muller document many cases with impressively obscure and subsequently verified details.[69] The triggers for these memories can be internal – for example dreams, illness or emotional stress similar to that experienced in the apparent past life; or they can be prompted by something external – for example an object, location or person somehow related to it.

Some of the finest research into spontaneous memory in adults was conducted by Frederick Lenz, who we mentioned briefly at the beginning of the chapter. As a university professor lecturing in Eastern philosophy he had some interest in reincarnation, and after various radio and television appearances in 1975 he was contacted by one hundred and twenty-seven people who reported spontaneous recollections of a past life. He spent the next three years interviewing them, documenting the results in his 1979 book *Lifetimes*. Intriguingly, one hundred and nineteen of his respondents said they had no interest in reincarnation before their experience.[70]

One of the fascinating features of Lenz's research is the common features he identifies. Paralleling near-death experiences, the majority of his subjects reported that at the onset of their recall they heard a ringing sound, often accompanied by a sense of everything vibrating and a certain lightness; and they felt a profound sense of wellbeing mixed with a heightened state of awareness. After this the scenes from the past life were initially watched as if they were movie clips, but gradually the subjects identified with one character until they actually entered the movie as that person, feeling all their emotions and so on. In about a quarter of cases the subject felt some sort of 'guide' was taking them through the whole process.[71]

Yet perhaps Lenz's greatest contribution, for our purposes at least, is the veridical cases he provides. We have already discussed Charlie's child case, but that of a writer from Venice, California called Phillip is arguably even more impressive.[72] The events leading up to his recall began when he was away from home and asked a girl in a car for directions. Her name was Anne and they both sensed a strong connection. They met the following weekend and talked a little, but they were very different types of people, and he did not hear from her again until she phoned him late at night some five months later. Although they only chatted generally, this was the trigger, and when he put the phone down his recollections began.

In the opening scene he saw a woman walking towards him and realized it was Anne in another life. Her name came to him as Martha Williams, and he realized he was a minister called Walter Morris. They were friends and lived in Colorado. In the next scene he found himself preaching to a congregation of several thousand, fully feeling the power of his oratory. Then it shifted again, and he was telling his wife he was going to have to leave her for Martha. Various further scenes unfolded, centered on him and Martha performing missionary work in China for many years. In the final scenes they were attempting to take some orphaned children back to the US after the Japanese invasion during World War II, but they were boarded by a Japanese ship. The women were raped in front of the men, then they and the children were killed. The men were tied up below, seemingly bound for a life of forced labor, but they managed to escape. In a corridor Walter came across the soldier who raped Martha and took a certain pleasure in strangling him. But when be emerged on deck to fierce fighting he was shot in the shoulder, and then flung overboard by an explosion. He clung to a box and drifted throughout the night, before being rescued the next day by a Chinese boat. He recovered and returned to the US via Australia and England. He began preaching again but, weakened by his ordeals, died within a year.

Phillip was sufficiently intrigued by all this that he decided to do some digging. He found out that a revivalist preacher called Walter Morris had become reasonably well known in Colorado in the 1930s, and had then become a missionary in China. He contacted family members who confirmed that Walter had escaped from the Japanese, and had indeed returned to the US via Australia and England. So far so good. But no one knew anything about Martha, and it seemed that a hugely significant element of his recall was inaccurate. He began to doubt the authenticity of his memories.

And then he received a call from a Mrs Crowley, who had been told about his investigations by other family members. It turned out she was Walter's daughter – which on the face of it made matters worse, because he had had no recollection of even having a child. Nevertheless he flew to South Carolina to meet her, and once there he relayed his whole story while she sat impassively, betraying no emotion. When he had finished he expected her to ask him to leave. But instead she took his hand and told him that every word was true, including the role of Martha. As to Walter's ignorance of having a daughter, unbeknown even to his wife she had been pregnant when he left, and she never spoke to him again. Nevertheless he continued to write to her regularly over the years, to send money and to tell her about his adventures. Mrs Crowley herself had, of course, grown up feeling abandoned by her father.

In a fitting finale she asked if Phillip would like to see the letters, which she still retained in a chest. He was more than eager, and in them he found confirmation of all the details of the life he had recalled, in particular the descriptions of Martha and how hard she worked. Poignantly the letters were falling apart because his former wife had read them so often, even though she never replied.

Subsequently Lenz himself was able to meet with Mrs Crowley and to read the letters, all of which confirmed Phillip's account of his former life.

Another area of research into adult past-life recall is, of course, regression. It is interesting to note that Stevenson himself remained a resolute critic of this technique, arguing that the memories arising are far too subjectively influenced. But are there nevertheless past-life regression cases involving details so obscure, yet still verifiable, that they should be accorded the same status as the stronger cases of spontaneous recall?

3

PAST-LIFE REGRESSION

Normal Explanations

Although there are other techniques, the most common approach to past-life regression is to use hypnosis to take a subject back into what may at least appear to be a previous life, and the potential normal explanations for such recall are similar to those for children's spontaneous recall. So first we might again ask whether past-life memories retrieved under regression are somehow passed down physically through the genes of the subject's ancestors. Even more here we can see that this cannot be so because for many individuals recalling multiple lives there is such rich variety in the geographical setting and racial type – at times, remember, when the world's population was relatively immobile. Moreover, unlike with children's recall, in this line of research we can usually dispense with fraud because even most skeptics accept that in the majority of cases on record the therapist is genuine, if somewhat deluded. As for the subjects themselves, anyone who is properly hypnotized finds it almost impossible to lie deliberately, while any professional hypnotherapist ought to be able to detect if they are not really in trance but just pretending.

But related to this is the whole issue of suggestibility. Many skeptics and, for example, Ian Stevenson insist that the majority of past-life memories are bound to be false because the subject is simply trying to please the therapist.[1] Yet hypnosis is commonly misunderstood, because many people's only exposure to it is via stage performers. They do undertake brief, initial tests on their audiences in order to find subjects who will be extremely malleable, but such people tend to be in the minority. Moreover this kind of hypnosis is very different from a typical, modern, past-life exploration where relatively light levels of trance, typified by the alpha brainwave state, are used. Under these circumstances subjects retain their critical faculties because their normal consciousness is still operating in the background. This is how one therapist, Helen Wambach, describes her subjects' behavior in trance:[2]

> Certainly, their responses are the result of the hypnotist's suggestions and they do respond immediately when you tell them to see something. But when I have misunderstood what my subjects have said, or my questioning is not clear, they will not change the image to suit my interpretation of what it is they are doing... Subjects have a strong desire to tell the truth under hypnosis. They become very concerned about the truthfulness of their answers, and will cling stubbornly and literally to whatever it is they are experiencing.

To balance this, however, we should remember what is possible when a therapist has a particular agenda. When certain of them in Europe and the US decided to focus on apparent child abuse they inflicted terrible and unnecessary suffering on many families, resulting in many legal battles and the coining of the term 'false memory syndrome'. So the nature of the approach adopted by the therapist, and the degree of openness of their direction and questioning, has a significant bearing on this issue. As an example Ian Wilson knew that British hypnotherapist Joe Keeton, of whom more later, insisted that there is no interval between lives; and when he tabulated the seven apparent past lives of one of Keeton's subjects, this is more or less what he found.[3] So in this case Keeton was clearly and explicitly influencing the timing of the subject's lives.

However there is a crucial and often overlooked point to be made here. In the context of past-life cases that might result in *verifiable* evidence of reincarnation, and in the absence of fraud, any potential leading by the therapist tends to be irrelevant. It is true that Keeton in particular sometimes had reference books on hand to check historical information as he went along, and others might at least be tempted to check up on easily sourced information between sessions. Any of this could result in a degree of leading if the therapist was not careful. But here we will set rather more stringent rules, whereby a case is only fully admissible as evidence of the paranormal when the subject provides factual information *so* obscure that the therapist and most other people *could* not be aware of it without months or even years of research.

Modern studies suggest that somewhere between seventy-five to ninety percent of people can enter a trance state sufficient to remember at least one apparent past life, and sometimes many more. Usually these produce few factual details, but some subjects seem to be able to come up with copious information including dates, names, places and so on – and these are obviously the types of case for which verification can be attempted. But we should recognize that past-life regression research again differs significantly from spontaneous childhood recall in that it often takes the subject back into lives that occurred centuries ago, and in other countries, so attempting to check the details by identifying the specific deceased personality is often impossible. Verification is further hampered in that, contrary to popular opinion, past lives revealed during regression are almost always those of unremarkable rather than famous people. However in the cases we will study here some sort of verification was possible.

Nevertheless skeptics argue that even cases that appear to contain plenty of authentic detail can be explained by subjects with a more vivid imagination combining this with normally acquired but long-forgotten information to construct what may seem at first sight to be a thoroughly impressive and detailed past-life narrative. So cryptomnesia is, of course, the main normal explanation on which they focus. What is more this time, unlike with children's spontaneous memories, adult subjects have had far more time to acquire historical information and then to consciously forget not only the information itself but also its source. So we should be quite clear at the outset that not all apparent past lives revealed under regression are genuine. As to what proportion may have at least some degree of authenticity, we will return to this topic in the next chapter.

Our previously established skeptical sources, that is Wilson and Paul Edwards, have written about cryptomnesia at some length. But this time they are joined by Melvin Harris, a British journalist, broadcaster and indefatigable debunker of past lives whose 1986 book *Sorry, You've Been Duped* – which was republished in 2003 under the less confrontational title *Investigating the Unexplained* – is a prime source. The same is true of American psychologist Robert Baker's 1992 book *Hidden Memories*.

The cases we will study can usefully be divided into three groups. In the 'weak' ones cryptomnesia seems to have been proved beyond doubt; in the 'inconclusive' ones it has been offered as an appropriate explanation but some puzzling aspects remain; and in the 'unexplained' ones it is hard to credit any sort of normal explanation.

Two Weak Cases

When an acquaintance first suggested to BBC producer Jeffrey Iverson that he should visit the renowned hypnotherapist Arnall Bloxham in their shared home town of Cardiff, he had little expectation of it coming to much.[4] Bloxham was by then nearly eighty years of age, but for the past twenty years he had been regressing subjects into previous lives, and had tapes from sessions with more than four hundred subjects to prove it. Despite his initial skepticism, Iverson made a number of visits and spent many hours listening to the tapes, becoming increasingly intrigued. Like most people he had accepted the misconception that people always remember only famous and exciting lives, yet here he encountered regression after regression that was ordinary, humble and often somewhat boring. Not only that but many subjects used entirely different voices and words from their normal, conscious personality. But he also knew that the only way to satisfy his mounting curiosity would be to concentrate on cases containing detailed and obscure historical facts that might be verifiable. This he did, even bringing in the famous journalist and broadcaster Magnus Magnusson to assist in the investigation. The results were aired in 1976 in a BBC documentary entitled 'The Bloxham Tapes', accompanied by Iverson's book *More Lives Than One*. Between them they caused quite a stir.

Graham Huxtable and The Aggie

Iverson was fascinated by one of Bloxham's subjects, a mild-mannered Swansea man called Graham Huxtable who, when regressed, transformed into a coarse, illiterate gunner's mate in the English Navy of the late eighteenth century.[5] Using what appeared to be contemporary naval slang he described how he was on board a ship called the *Aggie*, which was part of a fleet of ships involved in blockading the French just off Calais. Indeed this case had come to the attention of two high-ranking naval officers, in the shape of no lesser personages than Lord Mountbatten and Prince Phillip, who had been sufficiently impressed that they helped to investigate it. Some partial names were given but, coupled with incomplete naval records for the time, the details were insufficient to prove exactly what ship Graham had described. What is more, the trauma he suffered when he apparently relived his leg being shot off in battle convinced both him and Bloxham not to attempt to elicit more details.

Needless to say skeptics like Harris are not at all convinced by cases such as this. We all know that most researchers attempt to trace the *factual* historical records for past-life cases in their attempts at verification, but he reminds us that it is easy to forget that historical *fiction* is an even more likely source. In this instance he suggests that Graham provided no information that could not have been easily digested from the scores of historical novels and boy's adventure stories about life in the Royal Navy at that time.[6] He also insists that naval records for the period are not incomplete and that, although there was one similarly named ship at the time called the *Agamemnon*, it had a massive sixty-four guns – double the number on the *Aggie* reported by Graham.

Jane Evans and Livonia

For Iverson the case that seemed to hold out most promise was that of a local housewife, who he dubbed 'Jane Evans' to protect her identity. She originally visited Bloxham in the late 1960s after seeing a roadside poster about his health treatments, but she also proved to be an excellent regression subject. Over a number of sessions she explored what appeared to be six different previous lives, the earliest in Roman Britain in the late third century, the most recent as a nun in Maryland who died around 1920. Iverson asked to meet her, and established that by coincidence they had attended the same secondary school in Newport, although a few years apart. From this he was able to independently check that she had never studied history at an advanced level, and none of the relevant periods in any detail, and that neither of her parents had read much or showed any great interest in history when she was younger.

Some of Jane's regressions provided little in the way of verifiable detail, but others appeared to be more promising. The earliest involved a woman called Livonia who lived in Roman Britain towards the end of the third century.[7] She was married to Titus, a tutor to the boy Constantine who would go on to become known as 'the Great', and whose father Constantius eventually became Caesar. Jane provided many details that were reasonably obscure yet known to be historically accurate, but in fact Constantius' whereabouts in the earliest years discussed in the regression, that is around the year 286, are unknown. She reported that he was in York, and already acting as the Roman governor of Britain – a country to which history does not link him until a decade later, when he invaded to crush the independence movement of Allectus. So was she really a first-hand witness who could fill in the missing blanks of history, as Iverson suggests?

Unfortunately it appears not, because Harris remembered a book by best-selling novelist Louis de Wohl that covers exactly this 'missing' period.[8] In *The Living Wood*, first published in 1947, de Wohl effectively lays out a fictional narrative interspersed with known historical facts to tell a story that is in parts identical to Jane's recall of the life of Livonia, except that he has Constantius serving merely as a legate in Britain during the missing period. As Harris points out, the only major discrepancies in the fictional elements are that Livonia and Titus are extremely minor characters in the novel, but Jane's imagination appears to elevate them somewhat. In fact Livonia is merely a lady-in-waiting in the book, but she has 'pouting lips and smoldering eyes' and in Jane's story becomes much more identifiable with the lead character – Constantius' first wife Helena, who would go on to be canonized for supposedly discovering the 'true cross'. Meanwhile Titus appears to be based not so much on his namesake, a briefly mentioned Roman soldier, but on the romantic lead, another fictional character called Hilary; because what happens to him – he is converted to Christianity by a woodcarver called Albanus, ordained by the Spanish Bishop Ossius and then killed shortly afterwards as part of the persecution of Christians at the time – is exactly what happens to Titus in Jane's version.

Not only that but in other places the correspondences in terms of names and actions are even more exact, and again what is most damning is that they relate to fictional rather than historical characters. For example both stories have a 'military tutor' to Constantine called 'Marcus Favonius Facilis', de Wohl's inspiration for whom came from the tomb of a Roman soldier at Colchester Castle that is known to date to the *first* century. Moreover both contain Roman deputies to the governor of Britain called 'Curio' and 'Valerius', but these were again made up by de Wohl. Meanwhile Wilson adds that in both stories everyone refers to Helena as 'domina', and the Roman name for the modern town of St Albans is shortened from Verulamium to 'Verulam'.[9] Rechecking *The Living Wood* proves that all this is correct.

Research into Cryptomnesia

Despite the apparently foolproof explanation for this case of Jane's, in fact we will find in due course that her other notorious regressions may not be as easily explained as Harris and Wilson suggest. But in the meantime we can see from this example that cryptomnesia should not be underrated. It seems to be possible that someone can be exposed to a normal source of information sufficiently briefly that they completely forget it, while their subconscious memory of it remains virtually photographic in its detail and accuracy; and that source could be anything from a book, a magazine, a newspaper article, television, radio, cinema or even an overheard conversation. It also seems that the use of different voices and accents, and displays of intense emotion, may still emerge even if only cryptomnesia is in operation.

The research that underlies these conclusions has in fact been available for many decades.[10] The general fact that our underlying memory is photographic, even though we cannot consciously access most of it, was proved by the poorly recognized research of Wilder Penfield at the Neurological Institute in Montreal in the late 1930s.[11] He worked mainly with epileptics, but as a by-product he found that something incredible happened when he applied a small electric current to the cortex of the temporal lobe of the brain while his subjects were only locally anesthetized and therefore fully conscious – apparently there was no suffering or distress involved. This stimulation triggered *complete* memories of what were, usually, entirely insignificant events from earlier in their lives.

However the pioneering research into cryptomnesia in a past-life context was performed by Edwin Zolik of Marquette University in Wisconsin.[12] In 1956 he began a program of regressing subjects into apparent previous lives and then, in subsequent sessions, regressing them again and enquiring about the source of their information. This was followed up in the 1960s by psychiatrist Reima Kampman of the University of Oulu in Finland, and his experience with one girl in particular will serve as an example.[13] She regressed into the seeming life of an innkeeper's daughter in England in the thirteenth century, and at one point sang what she called 'the summer song' using certain medieval words and phrases. She had no conscious knowledge whatsoever of having heard it before, but when Kampman regressed her again to ask about its source she reported that she was thirteen and taking a book from the shelves of a library. Apparently she selected it at random and merely flicked through it, and yet under hypnosis she not only recalled its title and authors but also where inside it the song could be found. On further investigation Kampman found a copy of the book and there was the song written out in modernized Middle English, exactly as she had sung it. This seems to show beyond reasonable doubt that it is possible for someone to have only the briefest exposure to something to which they do not even pay much attention, but which information is then stored for subsequent retrieval if the right method is used.

We will find in the next chapter that most past-life therapists are interested only in the therapeutic benefits of their treatment, and not in whether the apparent past lives that emerge are real. But those few that have been interested in verification research have been slow to pick up on the work of Zolik and Kampman, and in none of the cases that follow have the subjects been re-regressed and asked about their sources. It is very much to be hoped that in future this shortcoming will be rectified in any new, strong cases that emerge, to see what happens. In the meantime we should be careful not to write off *all* cases just because of this research. What we will need to bear in mind, however, is that a case will have to contain *seriously* obscure information – which may not have been recorded *anywhere* before, or perhaps just in one or two extremely inaccessible places – if we are going to use it as strong evidence of a possibly paranormal source.

Five Inconclusive Cases

Virginia Tighe and Bridey Murphy

One of the best known, most interesting and most misunderstood cases came to light with the publication in January 1956 of *The Search for Bridey Murphy*, a book that took the world by storm and sold nearly 170,000 copies within two months.[14] Its author Morey Bernstein was an amateur hypnotist who, some three years earlier, had conducted a series of six regression sessions with a housewife from Colorado, who he referred to as Ruth Simmons in an attempt to protect her identity. In the first experiment she proved to be a good subject and, talking with a soft Irish brogue, identified herself as Bridey Murphy who lived in Cork.

Over time more details emerged. She was born in 1798 with the full name Bridget Kathleen Murphy, her father Duncan was a barrister married to Kathleen, and they were Protestants living in an area outside the town called 'the Meadows'. At twenty she married Sean Brian MacCarthy, the Catholic son of another Cork barrister, first in a Protestant service in their home town and then in a second, Catholic one in Belfast presided over by a priest called Father John Joseph Gorman of St Theresa's Church. They settled in Belfast, living in a cottage in Dooley Road while Brian taught law at Queen's University. She died some time in 1864, aged sixty-six. Not only did Ruth use a number of contemporary Irish words and phrases but, when she mentioned the 'Morning Jig' during one session and Bernstein gave the post-hypnotic suggestion that she should dance it on emerging from trance, she gave a passable performance – despite apparently being a poor dancer under normal circumstances.

Bernstein was under an embargo from his publishers not to travel to Ireland to attempt to validate the case. But a reporter from the *Denver Post*, whose three-part article had originally brought it to publisher Doubleday's attention, had managed to confirm in correspondence that two grocery shops in Belfast mentioned in the sessions, Farr's and Carrigan's, were listed in a directory for 1865. Then, after the book's publication, this same reporter traveled to Ireland and located an 1801 map of Cork on which an area called 'Mardike Meadows' was shown on the outskirts. He also found out on his return that the 'tuppence' mentioned in the sessions had only been in use in Ireland in the first half of the nineteenth century. So much for the positives. On the negative side, none of the birth or marriage details could be verified because regular, official records only began in Ireland in the year of Bridey's death – although this clearly did not invalidate the case. Worse, perhaps, was the fact that there was no record of a Dooley Road or a St Theresa's Church in Belfast at that time.

In the meantime the Randolph Hearst-controlled *Chicago American*, which had been outbid for local syndication rights by its rival the *Chicago Daily News*, had decided to gain its revenge by rubbishing the story in any way possible. Their task was made far easier when reporters managed to establish that the real identity of Ruth Simmons was a woman called Virginia Tighe who had been brought up in Chicago. By May of 1956 the Hearst newspaper empire had the evidence it wanted, and went into overdrive across the US with its revelations of the normal sources of Virginia's information. The main allegations were, first, that she had a now-deceased Irish aunt who had regaled her with stories during her childhood. Second, that her former schoolteacher had heard her reciting Irish songs including 'Mr Dooley on Archey Road'. Third, and perhaps most damning, that she was well acquainted with a neighbor called Brid*ie* Murphy Corkell who had originally come from County Mayo.

This supposed exposé gained so much publicity across the Western world, including from all the outlets that had originally supported the case, that it has been widely dismissed ever since. But was the exposé itself flawed? Such was the power of the Hearst empire's onslaught that few people took any notice when, in mid-June, the *Denver Post* published a rebuttal showing beyond doubt just how exaggerated and in some respects fabricated the *Chicago American's* exposé had been. For a start, although Virginia's aunt had been of Scots-Irish descent, she had been born in New York and had lived mainly in Chicago; what is more, Virginia insisted she had only got to know her aunt in her late teens and that she had never 'regaled her with stories' of Ireland. Second, when Virginia's schoolteacher was traced she insisted she hardly remembered her, and certainly had no recollection of her performing Irish songs. Third, and perhaps most revealing, not only did Virginia not know Mrs Corkell or that her name was Bridie, but the lady in question would not talk to the *Denver Post* reporter; and the reason soon became clear, because her son was in fact the editor of the *Chicago American* in which the exposé had first appeared. Worse still there was no record whatsoever of her having the middle name 'Murphy', while other complete fabrications included a supposed stillborn baby brother.

The Bridey Murphy case remains, therefore, a complete enigma. Hardened skeptics like Edwards write it off by concentrating on the few aspects of Virginia's recall that were almost certainly factually incorrect.[15] But we know that memories of even our current lives are fallible, so surely we can conjecture that the same may be true of past lives.[16] Meanwhile other commentators like Wilson are rather more open in their conclusions, if still largely skeptical.[17] But probably the most dispassionate assessment comes from a detailed 1960 paper written by Curt Ducasse, a professor of philosophy at Brown University on Rhode Island.[18] He showed that there were rather more details in Virginia's recall than are normally reported, and that while some aspects could not be checked, others that were quite obscure were verified. In particular he showed that some elements originally thought to be anachronisms for the period in question – such as Bridey having an iron bed and eating muffins, and the idea that her Catholic husband could teach at Queen's – subsequently proved reasonable.

Above all, no one has been able to prove conclusively what the normal source of the entirety of Virginia's memories might have been. It seems to be generally accepted that she and her husband virtually never read books, and as yet not even a possible fictional source has been identified. Admittedly Harris was able to establish that in 1893 the World's Columbian Exposition in Chicago included a complete Irish village, with natives of that country shipped over to perform songs and jigs and so on.[19] Apparently in excess of three million people attended this exhibit over six months, so he is right to assert that, even though Virginia was born some thirty years later, someone could have talked to her about it in her childhood. But this is far from conclusive.

Jan and Joan Waterhouse

In *Mind Out of Time* Wilson investigates a number of past-life regression cases in considerable detail, many of them coming from the casebook of the aforementioned Keeton. Another amateur, he discovered at an early age that he had a gift for hypnotizing people, and by the time he had become well known for his lecturing and television appearances in the late 1970s he had apparently performed more than eight thousand regressions. Seven of these were described in his 1979 book *Encounters With the Past*, co-authored with Peter Moss, and his integrity was proven by the fact that he consistently refused to charge for his services, relying instead on the income from his main job as a catering manager.

One of his most fascinating cases concerned a young woman called Jan who responded to a television appeal for subjects made by Keeton in 1977.[20] She regressed to the apparent life of a young girl called Joan, the 'daughter of Mother Waterhouse', who lived in 'Hadfald'. However, from the start of the session there is an air of terrible anxiety in her speech and breathing, the cause soon revealed as her being at the 'assizes'. Asked why she is there she blames her mother and spits venomously into the crowd of onlookers, before revealing in a seething whisper that they are both accused of 'witchery'. Keeton then manages to establish that it is 1556 and that the assizes are at Chelmsford, presided over by Judge Southcote. At this point he vaguely remembers hearing about the Chelmsford witches and pulls an encyclopedia on witchcraft from his shelves, quickly finding the relevant section; and there is the name Joan Waterhouse, an eighteen-year-old girl who was tried with her mother Agnes by John Southcote, and who came from what is now called *Hatfield* Peverell. Armed with this historical account Keeton continues to obtain confirmations, such as that they were being tried with Elizabeth Francis, that the prosecutor was 'Master Gerard, Queen's attorney', and that their accuser was a young girl called Agnes Brown – to whom, not surprisingly, she showed special enmity.

So far this seems like a reasonably impressive case. Jan did not consciously recall ever having read details of these trials, and again we have the archaic language and intensity of emotions. However, late on in the regression she was asked the name of the reigning king or queen and she replied Elizabeth. But Keeton's wife knew that she did not come to the throne until 1558, two years *after* the date previously given by Jan. So she interjected and pressed Jan as to why it was not her predecessor Mary, to which she replied with some anger: 'You *too* say I lie!' Such confusion piqued Wilson's interest. The first thing he needed to do was establish the genuine date of the trial, which he did by examining the original 'chap-book' published only months afterwards – of which only one copy remains, in the library at Lambeth Palace. He found it was 1566, indeed during Elizabeth's reign, and not 1556 as reported by Jan. This date was confirmed by other contemporary records of the Chelmsford Assizes. Far more interesting, however, was Wilson's discovery that some relatively commonplace records of this trial *do* put the date, wrongly, at 1556. He even traced the apparent source of this error back to a nineteenth-century reproduction of the original chapbook whose cover page carried a clear transcription error of 1556 instead of 1566.

As a result Wilson felt he had done more than enough to show that, in getting the date wrong but the monarch and other details right, Jan must have at some point read one of the modern accounts in which this date was also wrong. Moreover when he interviewed her in late 1978, although she continued to insist that she had never read or heard a word about the trial and was truly awful at history, she revealed that anything involving witchcraft had terrified her for as long as she could remember. Wilson puts all this down to a mild form of multiple personality disorder with its roots lying in whatever normal source must have terrified her when young, which she would then have consciously repressed until it was awakened by hypnosis. Meanwhile, although he does not mention it, his argument is strengthened by the fact that this trial is infamous because Agnes Waterhouse was the first woman to be hanged for witchcraft in Britain. So information about it is not in short supply – indeed, we know that after she testified against her mother Joan was let off.

All this looks fairly conclusive. Admittedly there are certain aspects of Jan's recall that seemed quite obscure at first sight, even to Wilson himself, and that are not found in the more obvious references to this trial.[21] However they were traceable, without too much difficulty, to a popular-style book from 1973 called *Essex Witches*.[22] For example, she revealed to Wilson that she had subsequent flashbacks involving visions of her mother seeming to look too old, but her age is given in the book as sixty-four – meaning she had Joan at the relatively old age for the time of forty-six. In addition in these flashbacks her mother's face was covered with disgusting spots, but again the book includes the original trial report that these were uncovered when the jailer removed the 'kerchief' from her face. She also recalled while in trance that 'Master Foscue' – in reality Sir John Fortescue – had assisted the Reverend Thomas Cole in presiding over the first day of the trial, but again these details are in the book.

Despite all this, though, the relatively detailed account in *Essex Witches* does *not* include the following even more obscure but verified facts that emerged during the regression. First, Jan remembered the heat and oppression in the courtroom, which was recorded in the original report and is consistent with the case being heard in late July. Second, Keeton knew about Cole presiding over the first day and so during the regression asked Jan about him; and Wilson was able to establish that her response that 'he spake too much' was entirely in keeping with contemporary reports that he was noted for his eloquence. Third, she kept holding out her hands with the fingers curled up as if in intense pain, and her response when asked why was 'they're burnt... 'tis a rod of iron'; this kind of trial by burning is known to have taken place as a method of torture that she might well have suffered beforehand. Fourth, we also know that suspected witches were stripped, shaved and examined thoroughly for the extra nipple by which they were supposed to suckle demons; but does this fully account for Jan exclaiming, 'No imp sucked from me!' when asked if they found one?

In no sense is this case as strong as others that are to come. Nor, as we have seen, is anything in it intrinsically unexplainable by cryptomnesia alone. But there is no question that these latter aspects of her recall are relatively obscure. Nor, as it turns out, do *any* of seven more recent sources picked more or less at random contain the 'wrong' date.[23] Indeed most of the authors are well aware that the relevant legislation was passed only three years before in 1563, and that it was in this trial that it was used for the first time. So it seems quite possible that the incorrect date was, in fact, just a coincidence. In any event, just as with the Bridey Murphy case, it is clear that no one has so far come up with the definitive source containing not only the wrong date but also all the obscure details. So perhaps this case should not be fully written off just yet.

Jane Evans and Rebecca

The Jane Evans regression that is most commonly referred to by supporters of reincarnation is that of a persecuted Jewess called Rebecca, again in York but this time in the late twelfth century.[24] In outline she reported that she was married to a wealthy moneylender called Joseph, and they lived with their son and daughter in a large stone house in the north of the city. But Iverson had to approach Barrie Dobson, the professor of medieval history at York University, to help with the analysis of the more specific details of Jane's recall.

First, she reported that her fellow Jews were made to wear yellow circles over their hearts. History records that this identification was only enforced by papal decree in 1215, but Dobson suggested it would have been quite conceivable for this to have been a practice in York or even the whole of England several decades earlier. Second, she said that the Jews lent money to the king, Henry Plantagenet, to finance the war in Ireland, and that as a result he was well disposed towards their attempts to recover money in the courts – although they had to pay him a levy of 'ten parts' of any such sums; and this was certainly historically accurate. Third, she described how a priest came to York to recruit men for what would now be called the Third Crusade, and that both Jews and Muslims alike were regarded as 'infidels', this hatred being stirred up by the Pope himself. Moreover she said the Jews of York were so worried by uprisings against their kinsmen in other cities that her husband had shifted much of his money to their uncle in Lincoln for safekeeping. Again, all this is perfectly feasible, because Dobson himself had documented the emerging ties between the Jews of York and Lincoln at the time. Fourth, she recalled that a young man called 'Mabelise' had borrowed money from her husband, and that they had to take him to 'the assizes' to recover it. This is pretty close to the name of a local noble recorded by chroniclers of the time, Richard Malebisse, who did indeed owe money to the Jews of York and led the subsequent uprising against them, in part to avoid paying his debts.

Fifth, she recounted how after Henry had died and his successor Richard had immediately left for the Crusades, her community felt they had lost their last protection and were getting ready to flee the city. She also gave the date as 1189, and said that Henry had protected them for thirty years, both of which are exactly correct. Sixth, she recounted how an elderly Jew called Isaac had been killed in the lead-up to the riots in 'Coney Street', and this too is recorded although without the name. She further recalled that at about the same time their neighbor Benjamin's father had been murdered while on a visit to London. Apparently some months passed before the rioters then broke into his house, and because it was next door she heard the screams and smelled the smoke as they set fire to it. Again these obscure details are confirmed when we find that a wealthy resident of York called Benedict was one of thirty Jews killed in riots in London at the time of Richard's coronation, and Dobson himself records that it was the subsequent attack on this man's house, and the killing of his wife and children, that sparked the uprising.

Jane reported in trance that as a denouement to all this Rebecca and her family fled their own house and headed for the castle where they took refuge with all the other Jews. History confirms that this siege lasted for several days before those inside, realizing their position was hopeless, took each other's lives. But, according to Jane, on that first night they were only allowed 'just inside the gates', and they could hear the mob screaming at them to come out and be killed – and asking if they had 'crucified any little boys', a known accusation of the time. Then they started to ram the gates, and the terrified Jews resorted to killing their children to save them from their persecutors' clutches – another poignant and distressing fact confirmed by contemporary chroniclers. It seems that Rebecca's husband managed to bribe someone to get his family out, and they fled to a Christian church 'just outside the big copper gate' where they tied up the priest and his clerk and then hid 'down below in the cellars'.

According to Jane's report it seems they must have stayed in this cellar for several days, terrified for their lives and growing increasingly cold, tired and hungry. In desperation Rebecca's husband and son went off to find food, but while they were gone she heard rioters on horseback preparing to enter the church. In the final, highly charged scenes of the regression she prays in vain for her menfolk to return as she hears the rioters entering the church and approaching their hiding place. Then she sees her daughter being dragged away, at which point she herself becomes, simply, 'dark'.

We can see that much of the information Jane came up with was relatively obscure and yet still factually correct. Dobson was apparently impressed by the accuracy of much of her recall, and felt some of it would only have been known to professional historians. He did question one point, which was why she had referred to the modern name of 'Coney Street' when in the Middle Ages it was marked on maps as Cuninga or King Street. But Iverson suggests that the more modern name, derived from the sale of rabbits, may have been in everyday use for some time before the change was noted on maps. Moreover Dobson himself refuted another potential problem, which is Jane's reference to the 'big copper gate'. Although there was no gate actually made of copper, there was a street called Coppergate at the time and it would have had a large gate at the end leading into the precincts of the castle. In addition it would probably be a moot point whether she said it as two words or just one.

Dobson also apparently identified St Mary's, Castlegate, as the prime suspect for the church in which Rebecca and her family hid. It was close to Coppergate and in sight of the castle. But the problem was that, in common with all the churches of the area, it had no crypt or cellar. Then in late 1975 he wrote to Iverson with the news that is still, in many quarters, trumpeted as the pièce de resistance of this and indeed all reincarnation cases:

> In September, during the renovation of the church, a workman certainly found something that seems to have been a crypt – very rare in York except for the Minster – under the chancel of that church. It was blocked up

immediately and before the York archaeologists could investigate it properly. But the workman who looked inside said he had seen round stone arches and vaults. Not much to go on, but if he was right this would point to a Norman or Romanesque period of building, i.e. before 1190 rather than after it.

There is a rarely reported problem with this, however, which is that over the next decade more was established about this supposed crypt. Harris corresponded with Dobson in 1986, and this time he revealed that 'it now seems overwhelmingly most likely that the chamber... was not an early medieval crypt at all but a post-medieval charnel vault.[25] This seems to have been based on the findings of a Royal Commission Survey in 1981 that it was 'probably a later insertion'.[26] In fact to Harris' delight Dobson seems to have been put off the case completely by this revelation: 'The evidence available is now revealed as so weak in this instance that it fails to support any thesis which suggests that Rebecca's regression contains within it genuine and direct memories of late twelfth-century York.' But let us step back for one second. What about all the other elements of Jane's recall that had so impressed Dobson ten years previously, which had not changed at all? One cannot help but wonder whether an ambition to progress to the higher echelons of the academic world might not have had some influence on this apparent change of heart; after all, within another two years Dobson would take over the chair of medieval history at Cambridge.

But what of Rebecca hiding out in a crypt? Harris himself reports that originally Dobson identified *three* potential churches close to Coppergate, and St Mary's was simply the most convenient for filming the documentary. So perhaps one of these others contains a crypt that has yet to be discovered? Or perhaps one of them had a rather different configuration in 1190, or there was even an entirely different building on one of the three sites, or at another nearby site that has now been lost to time? One of these is surely not impossible.

Harris has only two other possible criticisms of this case. First of all he repeats the obvious criticism of Jane's assertion that the Jews of York had to wear badges several decades before the formal papal decree, and he argues that the yellow circle was only used in Germany and France. But we have already seen that Dobson originally accepted this as a possibility, and that he was *the* expert even if he decided to make a general about-face later on. The other apparent problem is that Jane repeatedly referred to living in a 'ghetto', a word only invented several centuries later. But we know that regression subjects can use a mixture of modern and archaic language, and nor does her use of the word necessarily infer, as Harris suggests, that this was the only area the Jews lived in. He makes great play of the fact that these passages were left out of the book and documentary, but in fact there may be nothing in this at all. Above all it seems fair to say that he has done nothing but snipe around the edges, without tackling the wealth of accurate and obscure facts that emerged during this regression.

Harris must have accepted that Jane was unlikely to have read any of the relatively obscure, non-fictional sources that might have played a part in her recall, but nor does he come up with any possible fictional sources. However Wilson does, reporting that three of his correspondents recalled having heard a radio play on the subject of the York massacre some time in the 1950s.[27] Nevertheless none could remember the name, and he was unable to trace it. All in all, therefore, these rebuttals are nothing like as convincing as those of Jane's Livonia regression, which is why it seems fair to regard this case as inconclusive.

Bruce Kelly and James Johnston

Our next such case is described by Californian hypnotherapist Rick Brown in his 1989 book *The Reincarnation of James, The Submarine Man*.[28] It involves a furnishings salesman called Bruce Kelly, who consulted Brown in 1987 because he suffered from several extreme phobias – of flying, due to the claustrophobia brought on when the cabin door was fastened, and also of water, which he could not stand as soon as it was deep enough to cover his knees. He also complained of an intermittent stabbing pain that had troubled him for most of his adult life, which started in his stomach and traveled up to his left breast, and which doctors had diagnosed as merely psychosomatic.

In his first regression session, when asked to go to the source of the problem, Bruce reported 'I'm in a submarine... I'm dying'. From a therapeutic perspective Brown instructed him to relive the separation of his former personality's spirit from the body, and to accept it. But he also had some interest in collating factual data that might be verified, so in that same session he asked Bruce for details. He recalled without effort that he was a crewman called James Johnston serving on board the submarine USS *Shark*, code number SS-174, which was part of the Asiatic Fleet stationed in Manila. He also gave the date and time of his death as 11.30am on February 11, 1942 – some eleven years before Bruce's birth.

Although both men were delighted that the therapy was an apparent success they were also intrigued by the details that had emerged, so Bruce agreed to further sessions to explore James' life. Meanwhile Brown began checking out the details, consulting the US Navy Operational Archives and the Military Reference section of the National Archives, both in Washington DC, before writing letters to and eventually visiting James' family and acquaintances in Alabama. He was able to confirm that James Edward Johnston had served aboard exactly that submarine, and that it had been sunk by depth-charges from a Japanese destroyer – as Bruce had also described – on exactly the date he gave. There were no survivors.

Bruce was also able to provide the following details. First, he said his closest colleague was Robert Miller, and they are both listed in military records as Firemen Second Class on the *Shark*. Second, he gave the name of a man with him when he died in the hallway of the submarine as Walter Pilgram, who he said was 'a mechanic or engineer... older... maybe in his mid-thirties'; and records again showed Pilgram was a Chief Electricians Mate aged thirty-one. Third, he correctly named two of the accompanying submarines in the fleet, the USS *Porpoise* and the USS *Spearfish*. Fourth, he said that he had been confined to his bunk at the time of the fatal assault because he had already suffered rib injuries in a depth-charge attack three days previously. Were these the source of his chest pain in his current life?

It must be said that all this information is now easily found on the internet, on multiple sites that mention not only the *Shark* and its counterparts but also its crew members. However that does not mean to say it was easily accessible in the pre-internet days when this case first developed. On top of this, nobody can be absolutely certain how and when the *Shark* met its end. One site indicates that at least three antisubmarine attacks in that area around that time are mentioned in a Japanese report, any of which could have been on the *Shark*.[29] One was east of Menado on northern Celebes on February 11, the second north of Kendari on the southeast coast of Celebes on February 17, and the third east of Kendari on February 21. Most reports seem to agree that the first of these is the most likely candidate because the submarine had been ordered to northern Celebes several days before. They also agree that it was probably lost through depth-charge attack.

All of this suggests that Bruce was actually confirming something about which history is uncertain. But another more detailed report on the internet seems to indicate not only that he was wrong about the timing of the final attack, but also that he and all the other sources are wrong about its nature:[30] 'At 01:37 on 11 February, the Japanese destroyer *Yamakaze* opened fire with her five-inch guns and sank a surfaced submarine. Voices were heard in the water, but no attempt was made to rescue possible survivors.' By contrast, of course, a depth-charge can only attack a submerged target – which is what Bruce said the *Shark* was at the time of his death.

This case is too recent to have been considered by Harris or Wilson, for example. But at this point it is difficult to know what to make of it. Of course the last-mentioned account could be wrong, because websites do mention that Japanese reports were notoriously inaccurate and incomplete. Or there could have been more than one attack in that area that morning. Or Bruce's recall might just have been confused about this one aspect, without it invalidating the remainder. Nevertheless, the information that he came up with cannot be regarded as *especially* obscure given the ease with which it has now been published on the internet. So it is not entirely inconceivable that he might have come across some sort of dramatized account of the sinking of the *Shark* when he was younger, which was at least partially based on fact and contained real names.

If that were correct, however, the question then arises as to the source of Bruce's phobias and chest pain – and this is much harder to answer. It is again not beyond possibility that the normal source of his memories, whatever it was but perhaps in childhood, shocked him so profoundly that he developed the phobias *as a result*. As for his chest pains, they would have to have been completely unrelated but might have caused him to *invent* the one piece of recall that could not be verified – that he already had broken ribs before he died. But in truth this explanation smacks of the kind of desperation often employed by skeptics themselves. So, while we are just about persuaded to categorize this case as inconclusive, it may well be that it is in fact paranormally derived.

Bob Snow and Carroll Beckwith

Our final inconclusive case is that of Bob Snow, who was the commander of the homicide branch of the Indianapolis Police at the time his book *Looking for Carroll Beckwith* was published in 1999. It deals with his recall of the life of this little-known American painter who lived at the turn of the twentieth century, which first emerged when, to fulfill a dare, he visited a local regression therapist called Mariellen Griffith. Needless to say, as a hard-nosed police officer he was entirely skeptical of anything to do with past lives from the outset; and his description of how he internally resisted the induction of trance for some time before he suddenly began seeing incredibly vivid scenes from three different lives is well worth the read for anyone interested to know what past-life regression feels like.[31] But it was to the life of an as yet unidentified painter that he kept returning.[32]

We will come to the other details in due course, but in particular Bob vividly recalled a scene in which he was in his studio painting a portrait of a woman with a hunchback. Indeed even after he emerged from trance and for many months afterwards the painting was still vivid in his memory, and the experience left him shocked and bewildered. But, despite a nagging intuition, he refused to accept that it had anything other than a normal explanation; and, aware of the concept of cryptomnesia from his police dealings with hypnosis, he set about 'solving the case'.[33]

Bob's first approach was to go to the Central Library in Indianapolis and look for the painting in the art history books there, of which there were several hundred. But over the course of several months this exhaustive research revealed nothing similar.

Another few months were spent visiting every art gallery in the city, again without result – apart from the advice that without the name of the painter or painting he was wasting his time. Then another few months were taken up with trawling through the art history sections of all the bookshops. He even attempted regression again, both with Griffith and using self-hypnosis, in the hope of obtaining more details and perhaps some names; but this time he kept going to older lives, so little new information surfaced. It looked as if he had drawn a blank so he tried to forget the case, although with little success.

Two months later Bob made a startling breakthrough that seemed to be no coincidence.[34] He and his wife had taken a short holiday in New Orleans, and on the last day were wandering into art galleries in the French Quarter when in the corner of one, on an easel, he saw the portrait of the hunchbacked woman. His shock at the coincidence and inner knowledge that this was undoubtedly the painting he had seen so vividly in trance left him bewildered. The curator told him the artist was Carroll Beckwith and then, clutching at straws in his efforts to maintain his materialist view of the world, Bob asked if the painting had ever been exhibited. But it had been in a private collection for many years.

On his return to Indianapolis he again visited the Central Library, this time, of course, armed with a name.[35] His aim at this point was still to disprove the case, perhaps by showing that at least some of his trance recall about Beckwith's life had been incorrect. But the large art history books contained only a few sentences, while the smaller ones did not mention him at all. Bob followed this up in the library of the Museum of Art, where more obscure reference works gave a few more details, as did a number of more obscure art history books he found on returning to various bookshops. But they only tended to support the idea that his recall had been largely accurate. Moreover his excitement on finding that Beckwith's work had indeed been exhibited in Indianapolis was short-lived – this had happened back in 1911.

But he also found out that the painter had kept a detailed diary from age nineteen until his death aged sixty-five, and had penned an unpublished autobiography not long before, although it was unfinished and it only covered the early years of his life. Both of these were held in the archives of the National Academy of Design in New York, where Beckwith had lived for much of his adult life, but they were also on microfilm and available on loan via the Smithsonian Institute. Bob spent many more months trawling through them, before also visiting the library of the New York Historical Society that retained six large and two small scrapbooks kept by Beckwith.

Gradually, as Bob's recall was increasingly validated, his desire to disprove the case was replaced by a reluctant acceptance that it could not be explained by normal means. So now he wanted to validate every statement as far as possible if he was going to take the huge risk of publishing his research. This he was persuaded to do, despite his wife's initial reluctance, when subtle canvassing of a number of his police colleagues revealed that many had had paranormal experiences – such as traveling out-of-body at moments of extreme stress, and attending a disturbance apparently caused by a poltergeist.[36]

So what were the main elements of Bob's recall, and how accurate were they? He tabulates twenty-eight facts, but some must be regarded as easily guessed: for example, that as a painter Beckwith was constantly short of money, at least in his early career; that he argued about this with his wife; that his studio was full of unsold paintings; that he was feted at some sort of awards ceremony; that he spent some time in France; that he had a happy marriage; and that one of the studios he worked in had many windows and skylights.[37]

What follows are the more obscure facts, although Griffith did not push him hard for follow-up details during his regression, preferring to flit swiftly from one scene to the next:

Bob's Recall	Verification
Beckwith had been a young man in the late 19th century	Published references show he was born in 1852
He painted portraits because he needed the money, but he hated doing them	Confirmed in several obscure reference works, and repeatedly in his diaries; they also show that he was obsessed with money and his perceived lack of it
He painted the portrait of a hunchbacked woman	No published source either written or pictorial, but verified in New Orleans gallery; also mentioned several times in his diaries as painted in the winter of 1912
He had had a fierce argument with someone about the poor lighting on one of his paintings	Such conflicts with exhibitors are mentioned nine times in his diaries; one incident at the Catholic Club in New York in 1913 stands out in his scrapbooks, with eight different newspaper articles about it
He drank wine, which was unusual for men at that time	No published source, but confirmed several times in his diaries, his unusual taste having been acquired in France
His wife played the piano	No published source, but confirmed repeatedly in his diaries
He would have liked children but his wife could not have them	No published source, but his diaries confirm that his wife had had a bad miscarriage in 1888, after which there are several mentions of his envy of couples with children
A woman very close to him died from a blood clot	No published source, but his diaries indicate that in 1886 his mother died exactly this way
He felt he had to persevere for a long time before he became a decent artist	No published source, but his diaries confirm that he had a poor opinion of his own work right up until his last few years
Under self-hypnosis Bob had a flash of the importance of the date 1917	Published references show Beckwith died in this year

In fact Bob's only real failures came with names. Under regression he called himself Jack, whereas Beckwith's first name was actually James. However it was well known that he did not like and eventually dropped it, while in the intervening period he used the first initial 'J' alone. Moreover one obscure source said that when he was young he had invented and used other first names, and of course Jack would have fitted the initial.[38] Bob also gave the name of Beckwith's wife as Amanda, when in fact it was Bertha. However he insists that at the time he said this during the regression he felt it was wrong. As for the painting of the hunchbacked woman, when he returned to New Orleans hoping to buy it the gallery had closed down. He traced the stock to another gallery, but the dealer said it had been sold and that privacy rules dictated he could not give out the address of the buyer, merely pass Bob's on to them. Unfortunately he never heard from them, even though he only wanted to take a photo.

Again this case is too recent to have been considered by, for example, Harris or Wilson. But it clearly does involve some extremely obscure yet verified facts, so why should it be classified as inconclusive? Admittedly this may be harsh, but there are two factors that count against it. The first is that it was entirely investigated by Bob himself, with nothing in the way of independent corroboration. This could of course be overcome if, for example, Griffith was to confirm the details of the regression sessions. The second and probably worse problem, which unfortunately Bob does not consider, is the perfectly conceivable possibility that all of his information could again have come from some sort of semi-fictional, dramatized account of Beckwith's life, for example in film or book form, which was properly researched by a writer who accessed the autobiography, diaries and scrapbooks just as Bob did. The requisite sources here are narrowly defined and reasonably easily traced. Moreover the portrait of the hunchback is mentioned in the diaries, even if our putative author would be unlikely to have seen it unless they had known the private owner.

Does this properly account for the highly emotional rollercoaster that Bob's investigation turned out to be; or for the coincidence of him finding the painting in New Orleans; or for his apparently vivid images of the painting and instant recognition of it? Perhaps, perhaps not. In conclusion, we have not traced such a fictional source, and nor are we suggesting that one definitely exists. Yet on the evidence available – as with some other cases in this section, but *unlike* the ones we will consider next – the possibility of such a source cannot be ruled out.

Five Unexplained Cases

Whatever we might make of the cases discussed so far, there are some involving details *so* obscure that cryptomnesia would appear an impossible explanation.

Jane Evans and Alison

Jane Evans' previous regressions as Livonia and Rebecca appear to be normally explainable and inconclusive respectively. Moreover Harris and Wilson separately managed to track her down, and both insist that she refused to speak to them, although this may be perfectly understandable and not the indictment they suggest.[39]

In any case another of her regressions is in a different category entirely. In this she found herself in mid-fifteenth-century France, acting as a servant to an important contemporary figure called Jacques Coeur.[40] We should state at the outset that Iverson established that Jane had never studied the period in question in any detail, and certainly not French history of the time; and she had only been to France once, to Paris for two days, whereas the town of Bourges on which this regression centers lies some 150 miles to the south.

Before we examine Jane's recall we should acquaint ourselves with a few known historical facts.[41] Coeur was born around 1395, in the middle of the 'hundred years war' with England. The son of a rich Bourges merchant, he began building up his own trading empire in his early thirties, and in time his massive fleet of ships would become preeminent in the import of all manner of goods from the eastern ports of the Mediterranean. As his wealth grew, so did his estates, his portfolio of debtors and his influence in royal circles. In 1436 Charles VII summoned him to the recently reacquired Paris to become master of the mint, two years later he was made steward of the royal expenditure, and within another ten he had started lending the king himself money to finance his new thrust to oust the English from his northern territories. It was not least because of this that Coeur formed part of the royal procession that triumphantly entered the recaptured city of Rouen in 1449.

His service to his country was ill rewarded, however. Many merchants whose profits had been squeezed by Coeur's monopolies were keen to see his downfall, as were those who owed him money – the king and many of his senior courtiers included. Meanwhile the king's mistress Agnes Sorel, whose huge influence and inordinate beauty caused much jealousy in royal circles, died suddenly in 1450 at the tender age of only twenty-eight. Unsurprisingly rumor soon spread that she had been poisoned, with the king's son Louis the chief suspect – he had been agitating against his father since his forced marriage to Margaret, daughter of James I of Scotland, in his early teens. However events took a rather different turn when, more than a year after Agnes' death, a courtier who owed Coeur money formally accused him of her murder. It seems everyone knew this was a ridiculous accusation, but the king showed his gratitude by having him arrested for this and other charges, financial and otherwise. His estates and stocks were seized and distributed to various royal favorites, including the men chosen to preside at his trial, while the king reserved a substantial portion of Coeur's money to finance further war efforts. After nearly two years of imprisonment he was finally convicted, but he escaped from prison in 1455, only to die a year later on the Greek island of Chios.

So what of Jane's recall? The broad thrust is that her name was Alison, and she was found by Coeur in Alexandria. As a young servant girl she had been ill and effectively unwanted, but he took pity on her and brought her back to France, where she remained in his employ until he was taken into custody. Apparently he gave her a draft of poison at this point, and it seems reasonable that if she was of infidel Arab descent then, robbed of his protection in such a staunchly Christian country, death might have been the kindest option. This suggests she may have grown quite close to him by this time and, as we will see, he certainly seems to have taken her into his confidence on many things about court life.

There are many more details of her recall that we will come to shortly, but first there is one unusual aspect picked up on by Harris.[42] When she was asked whether Coeur had ever been married her response was 'not that I know of'. Yet history clearly shows that in his early twenties he married Macé de Lodepart, the daughter of a wealthy Bourges family, and that they had a number of children together. Harris reports that again he found an appropriate fictional source, this time *The Moneyman* by the renowned historical novelist Thomas Costain, first published in 1947 and republished in 1961. Moreover he admits in his introduction that he deliberately omitted Coeur's family from his novel 'because they played no real part in the events which brought his career to its climax'.[43] So at first sight Harris appears absolutely right to suggest that this cannot be mere coincidence, and Wilson again praises his sleuthing without adding to or questioning it.[44] But, unlike with Livonia and *The Living Wood*, Harris says little more about Costain's novel except that 'it is based on Coeur's life and provides almost all of the flourishes and authentic-sounding touches included in her past-life memory'.

To anyone who takes the trouble to read the full five hundred pages of *The Moneyman*, this is something of a generalization at best and a downright misrepresentation at worst. It is a romantic tale in which many of the key characters apart from Coeur are entirely fictional, along with much of the narrative, and its main thrust involves Coeur supposedly attempting to find a successor for the 'ageing' Agnes Sorel as the king's mistress. One of his associates chances upon a fictional teenage girl called Valerie, who had been fostered and then orphaned, and is also Agnes' double – in fact she eventually turns out to be her illegitimate niece. Valerie is tutored for the part of royal mistress and easily wins the king's affections, but then she runs away with a fictional friend of Coeur's and marries him. This tale of a blonde-haired, porcelain-skinned girl attempting to become the king's mistress bears no resemblance to Alison's life as a humble servant of Eastern extraction, who remains in Coeur's mansion at Bourges. Indeed the latter location is hardly mentioned in Costain's novel, and there is no character on which Alison could be based.

More important even than this, Jane came up with a significant number of historically accurate facts of varying degrees of obscurity, the majority of which are not mentioned in *The Moneyman* at all. Nor did she repeat *any* of its many fictional 'mistakes'. All of which leaves Harris' proclamation of the 'overwhelmingly strong evidence' that this was her source looking rather misplaced. His only other comments relate to her recollections of Agnes' tomb and of Coeur's house in Bourges, pictures and descriptions of which are reasonably widespread – especially of the latter, whose unusual mixture of architecture remains a significant tourist attraction. But we do not even need to discuss these, given the wealth of other accurate information Jane provided. So the explanations proffered by Harris in this instance are entirely unsatisfactory.

But before we carry on with the rest of the case, we must attempt to provide an explanation for Jane's apparent ignorance of Coeur's family. It is certainly true that historians pay them scant regard, even though one of his daughters married the son of the Viscount of Bourges, and a son became archbishop of the city. So it is entirely conceivable that he only married at an early age as an aid to social mobility, and that his wife played little role in his later life before she died around the time of his arrest. As for his children, it is equally conceivable that a man with his widespread business interests and political responsibilities would have had little time for them. Alternatively there are some subtle hints that Alison was very much in love with her master, although she flatly denied being his mistress, so Iverson's suggestion that perhaps she could not even bring herself to acknowledge his marriage may also have some merit. If these explanations sound at all forced, they will be put into perspective by what follows.

So let us commence our detailed examination of this case by summarizing various aspects of Jane's recall:

Jane's Recall	The Moneyman	Known Facts
Her name was Alison	No one of that name	Common name of period
She was found in Alexandria	City never mentioned specifically	One of the ports with which Coeur traded
The king was Charles 'de Valois'	Surname never mentioned	This is the king's proper surname
Agnes was known as the 'Maid of Fromenteau'	Never mentioned	Birth place is correct
The currency was 'écus d'or'	'Écus' are mentioned once, as separately is 'a royal d'or'[45]	The combination of the two words to make 'gold crown' is correct
The king borrowed 2000 écus from Coeur for an early war effort but spent the money on one of his castles	The only sum mentioned is 200,000 'écus' for the main thrust into the north [46]	Coeur lent the king money at various times; a smaller, earlier sum could have been misused by Charles, although Jane may have got the scale of the loan wrong
The king's mother was 'Duchess Yolande'	Mentioned once as 'Yolande' only [47]	Yolande was referred to as Duchess; although the king's mother-in-law she had been his protectress from an early age
The king handed the 'maid of Orleans' over to the English	Mentions that the king did not attempt to rescue or bargain for her [48]	The king could have paid a ransom to Joan of Arc's Burgundian captors, but he let them sell her to the English instead
Coeur was 'argentier' to the king	Term mentioned once in author's intro; in main story he is referred to as 'comptroller' [49]	This was the correct, specially created title for his stewardship of the royal expenditure
Louis was banished from court for threatening Agnes before her death, and Coeur suspected he would attempt revenge	Louis gains one brief and irrelevant mention [50]	His banishment is commonly recognized, but Coeur's private concerns are reasonable given Louis' subsequent status as prime murder suspect

These facts are certainly reasonably obscure, and for the most part cannot be traced to *The Moneyman*. But they do not relate purely to Coeur but to French history of the time more generally, so a skeptic might still argue that there are probably plenty of sources, fictional or otherwise, that contain said details. Nevertheless Jane did come up with some rather more obscure information about the period that to his credit, and by some painstaking research in France, Iverson was able to confirm as correct. None of this appears on the internet even now, so it is not likely to have been included in other easily accessible sources that Jane might have consulted, whether fictional or otherwise. Nor is any of what follows found in *The Moneyman*.

First, Jane reported that the king's nickname was 'heron legs', which Iverson confirmed in discussions with French historians. Second, she specifically commented on how his son Louis was 'very wicked, very cruel and yet pious sometimes', which exactly matches the description by another French historian that his character consisted of 'piety combined with ruthlessness'. Third, she reported that Coeur suspected Louis had poisoned his wife Margaret, who was only twenty when she died, and again historians confirmed this was a popular rumor at the time. Fourth, she said that Coeur had been to Paris after its recapture from the English and had watched the king enter the city with both his queen and mistress in tow. He said Agnes was spat upon by the crowd because even her two beloved pet dogs were clothed in 'coats of white fur with jeweled collars', after which the queen appeared with her on a balcony in a show of support. Jane talked about this happening some time after Louis' banishment but before Agnes' death, which places it somewhere between 1446 and 1450. Iverson was able to confirm that in her letters Agnes often mentioned her two pampered pet greyhounds. More than this, though, he found a contemporary although anonymous account describing just such a visit to Paris, in April 1448, in which the queen and Agnes regularly appeared together much to the dismay of the people.

Jane also came up with rather more obscure information relating specifically to Coeur himself, and Iverson was again particularly thorough in his attempts to research at least the non-fictional sources for his life. What he found was that, despite his huge importance, only two detailed reference works about him existed in English at the time of Jane's sessions, and both were obscure books written in 1847 and 1927 that did not mention the facts that follow. Of course skeptics might still point out that Jane learned some French at school, and therefore must have read about Coeur's life in books from his homeland. But in fact even French history books provide few details of this enigmatic character. So again Iverson had to spend considerable time with French scholars and historians, in Bourges and elsewhere, attempting to verify these seriously obscure aspects of Jane's recall.

First she indicated that Coeur, who was very close to Agnes, gave her the first polished diamond in France on a chain with a sapphire clasp. Iverson was able to establish that he probably was the first person to have diamonds shaped and cut, and that Agnes probably was the first person in France to model them for him. Second, Coeur's father is referred to in general modern sources merely as a 'rich merchant', but French historians told Iverson there are two more detailed versions of his story, one that he was a furrier and the other that he was a goldsmith; and while the former view is mentioned once in *The Moneyman*,[51] Jane clearly stated the latter. Third, she discussed this in the context of rumors that Coeur was Jewish, and again historians were able to confirm that these were current during his life. Fourth, when describing how the king's men were coming to arrest her master, she showed extreme indignance at the ingratitude of it all that would have been entirely appropriate after everything Coeur had done for him. Fifth, she reported that he was an avid collector of art, and that in his main gallery hung paintings by 'Fouquet', 'van Eyck', 'Giotto' and 'John of Bruges'. Iverson established that Jean Fouquet was the court painter to the king, and that receipts show Coeur lent him money; that Jan van Eyck was the court painter to the nearby Duke of Burgundy; and that Giotto was an Italian master who had lived in the previous century. John of Bruges, also known as 'John Bondolf', was harder to trace; but a specialist art-history book revealed him to have been a Flemish court painter for the king's grandfather, Charles V. Jane also mentioned a painting depicting Agnes with one of her babies, and said that Coeur badly wanted to acquire it. She was wrong that this was by van Eyck, but it is a reasonably renowned painting by Fouquet known as 'Madonna and Child'. Sixth, Jane indicated that Coeur had a 'body servant' called Abdul, who was 'dressed differently from the others'; and Iverson was able to establish from his trial records that he did indeed have an Egyptian body slave.

Yet we still have not come to the most impressive aspect of this case, which is Jane's recall of a 'beautiful golden apple with jewels in it' that Coeur said had been given to him by the Sultan of Turkey. All of Iverson's initial attempts to verify the existence of such a piece drew a blank, until his last night in Bourges when he returned to his hotel to find a message from a local historian, Pierre Bailly. The latter reported that he had been searching through contemporary archives when he found 'an obscure list of items confiscated by the Treasury from Jacques Coeur'; and in that list was a 'grenade' of gold – a pomegranate. As Iverson points out, this is so like an apple in shape and size that the English word contains the French root *pomme*.

However photographic memory might be it is almost impossible to conceive of any obvious way in which such obscure information could find its way into any normal source, whether fictional or otherwise, that an ordinary person like Jane, with no special interest in Jacques Coeur, might have encountered. Moreover in general her case is a fascinating and instructive one, which is why we have explored it in some depth. Given Harris' foolproof evidence against Jane's Livonia regression, it is easy to see why others might assume that his superficially similar proof against this case would be equally watertight. As a result both his and Wilson's less impressive explanations for the Rebecca regression tend also to be accepted, by skeptics at least, without further comment. Yet as soon as we find that in fact the Alison regression is almost impossible to explain by normal means – and Harris himself must have at least partly realized this unless he never actually read the full text of *The Moneyman* – perhaps we become more favorably disposed towards a paranormal explanation for the Rebecca regression as well.

Nevertheless, we are still left wondering how a single subject could show all the signs of cryptomnesia in one regression and of a paranormal source in another. Of course we all tend to hanker for simple, reductionist explanations that come down definitively on one side or the other, and at first sight this case might seem illogical and baffling. But in fact, if we take a step back, there is no practical reason why such a 'mixed' case might not occur. We might even suggest that it has a certain poignancy for a book such as this that attempts to show both sides of the argument, and to follow the evidence where it leads with at least some degree of attempted objectivity.

Laurel Dilmun and Antonia

Our next unexplained case comes from American psychologist Linda Tarazi, and features the incredibly detailed and obscure recall of a subject called Laurel Dilmun. This is described in Tarazi's 1997 book *Under the Inquisition*, and in two earlier articles.[52] The background is as follows.[53] The case first emerged in 1977 within the context of a group that met regularly to engage in past-life regression. Laurel was initially hypnotized by a Dutch member of the group, and over the course of eight sessions over some eight months many details emerged about the apparent life of a

Spanish girl called Antonia, who lived in the late sixteenth century. Laurel then drifted away from the group for several years before contacting Tarazi to ask for personal therapy. She said she had had dreams and flashbacks about Antonia's life, and had developed something of an obsession with certain highly charged romantic elements.

Over the course of a further thirty-six sessions an enormous quantity of further information about Antonia's life was revealed, although much of this new material was of a more emotional nature. Indeed most of the verifiable facts of this case emerged in the initial eight sessions. But, as well as providing therapy, between 1981 and 1984 Tarazi devoted considerable time and effort to investigating the case in various libraries in the US, also making several visits to Spain to consult historians and the municipal and diocesan archives in the central city of Cuenca around which much of Antonia's life had centered. Indeed it is worth pointing out that Tarazi's initial reaction was one of skepticism, and she was perfectly aware of and comfortable with the concept of cryptomnesia.[54] At first she was able to locate many of the historical figures Laurel mentioned in the earliest sessions, although only with some difficulty. But as the information became more and more obscure she became more intrigued; and when she was able to verify these aspects too, although only with great difficulty and on occasion many years later, her skepticism was finally replaced with a firm belief that Laurel's memories could not have derived from normal sources. Needless to say investigations also revealed that she had no affinity with or interest in Spain, had no ancestors from the country, had never visited it and did not speak the language.

Antonia's life is described in the main chapters of *Under the Inquisition*, which runs to well over six hundred pages. Unfortunately for the research importance of this case, Tarazi decided to write these in the form of a historical novel, rather than present the huge volume of transcript information in what she felt would inevitably be a dry, chronological format. To make matters worse, much of this reads like a rather salacious Mills and Boon novel, with romance interspersed with repeated scenes of sex, flogging and torture, some of which are seriously depraved and unsettling. It is impossible to tell the extent to which this reflects the original transcripts, but one would normally regard this much-repeated detail on the same topics as the product of a fevered and somewhat obsessive imagination, rather than of genuine past-life recall. On the basis of this alone the case would easily be dismissed, were it not for the extremely obscure information Laurel came up with and the scrupulousness with which Tarazi attempted to verify it. Her description of these key elements is contained within the Introduction and Notes sections of the book, the professionalism of which are in stark contrast to the novel sandwiched between them.

But first an outline of Laurel's recall of Antonia's life. She was born in 1555 on the island of Hispaniola where her father, Antonio Ruiz de Prado, owned a plantation. For most of her life he was away on military campaigns in various parts of the Spanish empire. When she was fourteen she and her mother moved to live with her scholarly and recently widowed uncle Karl in Germany, but her mother died shortly after their arrival. For the next three years he tutored her in German, Latin and Spanish, and a smattering of science and philosophy. Her education continued when they moved to Prague, and then in Leipzig she began dressing as a man to sneak into university libraries and even lectures. She also learned to excel with the rapier. When they moved back to Germany she changed her name to Antonio and enrolled at university full time. Not long afterwards her uncle was called to teach at Oxford, where she again led a double life as a male student during the day and an occasional Spanish barmaid in the evening. But her devout Catholicism had to be carefully hidden in the England of the time, and she longed to move to her beloved Spain to be with her father. This dream became more realistic when he retired from the army and bought an inn called El Toro de Oro in the beautiful surroundings of the Sierra de Cuenca; and when her uncle died not long afterwards there was no further obstacle. She was now in her late twenties.

Unfortunately her arrival in Spain brought the news that her father had died while she was en route. She was forced to take over a business that was badly in debt to a ruthless creditor, but soon turned it around. She then found out that she had a protector in Francisco de Arganda, one of the inquisitors at Cuenca who had been a close friend of her father. Despite appearing before him in his official capacity, despite suffering flogging and torture at various times, and despite the initial repulsion she felt for the machinations of his office, she fell under his spell. Their affair was tempestuous and he was totally controlling, but also highly persuasive. After some years they sailed for South America, where a dispute had arisen between Francisco's nephew and the commissioner of Popayan in New Granada, with inquisitor Ulloa of Lima aligned against him as well. Also involved was inquisitor Juan Ruiz de Prado, the uncle Antonia had never met, but when she arrived in Lima he confided that he was actually her father. The nephew was pardoned, but on the return journey their ship was attacked by English pirates and Antonia drowned trying to escape.

To turn now to the obscure facts Laurel recalled, excluding the obvious references to reigning monarchs and so on, in the Notes section of Tarazi's book these number in excess of one hundred and thirty.[55] She tabulated sixty and sent them to all the professors of Spanish history in the six universities in the Chicago area, asking them to rate the ease with which the information could be found and to identify the relevant sources. Many of these turned out to be obscure volumes, and for twelve facts only sources in Spanish could be traced. Some other facts Tarazi only located by fortune after the professors had drawn a blank, while a few even contradicted archival sources that were subsequently found to be incorrect. She tabulates the results for twenty-four of these obscure facts in her Notes, and comments on a number of the most obscure and hard to verify in her Introduction. So what are they?

First, in Laurel's early sessions with the Dutch hypnotist he quizzed Antonia on various aspects of the sixteenth-century history of his homeland, because the Low Countries were at that time Spanish colonies. She gave a detailed account of the assassination of William of Orange in 1584, which she had overheard being discussed in the inn, and expressed relief that the Spanish governor Alesandro Farnesio would find it easier to control William's seventeen-year-old son Maurice. When asked why she did not refer to the governor as the Duke of Palma, as most history books do, she replied that he was not a Duke even if he was the son of Margaret of Palma. Importantly this was true from the perspective of the exact point in time that Laurel was reliving, because he did not go on to become the Duke until two years later. Second, she referred to the previous governor as Fernando de Toledo, and the hypnotist responded that surely she meant the Duke of Alva, which again is the name given by most history books. She replied curtly: 'Of course. That is his *title*. I gave his *name*.'

Second, for a long time no one could trace the names she gave for the two inquisitors in Lima, that is Ulloa and de Prado, or any information about an auto da-fé she attended while there. But finally Tarazi found it all in an obscure book published in Spanish in 1887 – although the outer margins of the pages of the copy that she consulted in the library at Northwestern University had never been cut, indicating it had never even been opened. Similarly, the names she gave for people involved in the Inquisition in Cuenca could only be traced to contemporary municipal and diocesan archives, again of course in Spanish. These included Bishop Zapata; the Corregidor, Jeronimo de la Batista; the two inquisitors,

Francisco de Arganda and Ximenes de Reynoso, and a range of biographical data about them that matched her statements; and various people arrested by them, including Andres and Maria de Burgos who she knew were tried for sorcery, and the Jesuit priest Fray Fernando Mendoza. Indeed, the experts originally indicated that there would always have been three inquisitors at any tribunal, but Laurel's insistence that there had only been two while Antonia was in Cuenca was again proved right by the Episcopal archives.

Third, Laurel recalled that there had been a college in Cuenca when Antonia was there, because the students would come to drink in her inn. But local historians were unaware of such a college existing at that time, until one American expert suggested she might try a multi-volume work in Spanish published between 1912 and 1925 – and there she found confirmation that one had indeed been set up in the mid-sixteenth century. Fourth, when Laurel traveled to Spain with Tarazi and saw the address originally given by the authorities in Cuenca for the 'Casa Sancta' where the Inquisition was based, she insisted it was not the right place. Instead she said it had been moved to the castle not long before Antonia arrived in May 1584. Again she was later proved right when Tarazi found an obscure book about Cuenca's history, again in Spanish and published in 1944, in the appendix of which she found confirmation that the Inquisition's move to the castle had taken place in December 1583.

This is just a small proportion of the highly obscure yet subsequently verified information that Laurel recalled about Antonia's life. What is more it would appear that, of the facts that could be checked out, none was found to be incorrect.

Three of the finest veridical past-life cases on record come from the diligent research of Australian psychologist Peter Ramster. From the early 1970s he used hypnosis in his therapeutic practice to regress patients into their childhoods – a reasonably conventional process referred to as 'age regression' – but he was initially skeptical when some appeared to be regressing into past lives without any prompting. Yet, as with so many of his colleagues in other parts of the world who we will meet in the next chapter, when he experimented further the therapeutic results he consistently achieved changed his mind. He documented a number of these cases in his 1980 book *The Truth about Reincarnation*.[56]

Ramster then developed an admirable determination to see past-life regression taken seriously as a key tool by the rest of his normally skeptical profession. So he conducted an experiment in which he chose four subjects from his home town of Sydney who had particularly vivid recall of what appeared to be previous lives in various countries in Europe, and arranged for them to visit the locations they described on the other side of the world to see whether the facts could be verified. With one of these – Jenny Green, who had relived the life of a young Jewess taken to the gas chambers in Nazi Germany – his efforts were not particularly successful. But the other three produced incredible results, especially when we remember that none of them had ever been to the countries in question, which were France, England and Scotland. In each location they were accompanied by independent witnesses and a film crew, the results appearing first in a stunning television documentary entitled *The Reincarnation Experiments* that Ramster produced in 1983, then seven years later in his second book *The Search for Lives Past.*[57]

Cynthia Henderson and Amelie de Cheville

The first of these three cases involves a young woman called Cynthia Henderson.[58] The most detailed of a number of apparent past lives that she described over the course of a number of sessions was that of Amelie de Cheville, which she described as follows. As the daughter of a wealthy French merchant who owned a chateau to the northwest of the market town of Flers in Normandy, she grew up alongside her brother Philippe, their every whim attended to by servants, watching with amazement and envy as the beautifully dressed guests arrived for an endless procession of lavish balls. Often these were held by the lake in the grounds of the estate, and minstrels played on as the guests danced long into the night. But the carefree days of youth could not last forever. Before long she found herself marrying an army officer called Jean-Pierre Victoir St Claire, and leaving the family home to move to a house on the Rue St George in Paris. She was still comfortably off, with servants of her own, but life was not quite as lavish as it had been with her father. She had two children, Edouarde and Marianne.

As time went on, life became increasingly difficult. The pressure for revolution was building as the gulf between rich and poor widened. Amelie decided to send her children, by now in their mid-teens, to the chateau for their safety. She rarely left the security of her home to venture into the streets of Paris, and when she did she found the streets filthy and overwhelmed by rats. Then came the fateful day when she was dragged from her house by the mob and thrown into a small, dark cell. Nor was it long before she found herself being forced into a cart. Her hair had been cut short at the back, and she knew what was to come, but first she had to face the crowd on the journey to the square and their hatred left her numb with fear. She watched as the victims ahead of her met their fate. So great was the bloodlust of the crowd that as soon as one head had fallen they were ready for the next. Every available vantage point was taken, every window and balcony, like some great sporting occasion. The heads were trophies to be stuck on spikes, while the bodies were flung over a wall and left to rot. The streets were literally rivers of blood.

Finally Amelie's turn came. She stumbled up the steps to the guillotine – confused, petrified, jostled and pulled from all sides. Her hands were tied behind her back, and as she was pushed down into position her throat struck the block so hard she nearly choked. Then, staring into the basket, with everything covered in a thick blanket of glistening blood, she heard the final 'swoosh'.

All this was enough to convince Ramster to take Cynthia to France to see if they could find her former home, but it was a big risk because none of the team had even been there before, at least not in *this* life. However they would be aided by a young French Catholic with little interest in reincarnation called Antoine le Breton, who would act as the independent witness. What follows is described in *The Search for Lives Past* and confirmed in the documentary.

Starting from the bustling marketplace in Flers they followed the route she had described in trance: 'You go past the church for a while, and then you come to a road, a big road that goes between Rouen and St Michel. Go right there for about an hour [by coach], and then it starts to go up after you leave Flers, the road goes over the top of a hill. You can look down mainly on the left side, you can see woods, trees and fields... Then you turn left down to the chateau.' Coming out of the town past the church and finding the main road north was no great problem, and before long they came to a long incline. At the top there was a spectacular view over a wooded valley on the left, and at the bottom a turning to the left, all just as Cynthia had described. The smaller road wound around for a while, but then they found a new estate had been built and the roads had changed completely. They could not go in the direction she wanted, so was this to be the end? Fortunately after asking for directions they were able to pick up the original road on the other side of the estate, and soon she was sure that the long wall running alongside it belonged to the chateau, and that the entrance lay just ahead. As they drove into what was now a public park and slowly made their way up the tree-lined driveway, Cynthia's tension mounted: 'Oh God! I can't look... Oh God, there it is... It's a *tower*!' Previously it had been a tantalizing dream, but now it was a reality, and the emotion was too much. Cynthia began to sob deeply. She at least felt she had come home.

The chateau was a derelict ruin now after suffering bomb damage during the war, but it was not difficult to imagine its former splendor. Two stories high and crafted from cut sandstone blocks; the large porch with huge doors and long windows on each side; the imposing tower at the rear that she and her brother had been forbidden to climb; the lake nearby. All was exactly as she had described it in trance. Once she had had time to get over the initial shock, they walked around and she soon found everything flooding back to her: 'I feel fantastic here. I feel as if I belong. It's incredible. I recognize everywhere... I have all these images of the coaches and the clothes and the people, the servants and the parties and everything, the whole bit... It's only just now that the impact has hit me, how real those people were, and this was my life! It's all so real to me. It's sort of like a big tunnel being opened up and my whole memory being brought back.'

The team then took her to Paris to see if they could locate her house there. This time she could not lead them from the outskirts because the environment had changed beyond recognition, but when they arrived at the Rue St George she knew where to look. Unfortunately the building at the site of her former home was completely different; and given her unpleasant memories of this latter part of this life, which were in such stark contrast to those of the chateau, the team agreed not to linger.

Nevertheless they had rather more success in tracing a regular holiday destination she had described as being within a few miles of the picturesque Mont St Michel, on the coast some fifty miles to the west of Flers. This was a large country house that she said had been owned by a friend of Amelie's father. As the team left the car park at Mont St Michel they were once again relying on the clarity of Cynthia's recall. This time she had said little about the journey in trance, so they were instead relying on her recognizing the route consciously as they went along. But they need not have worried, because the country roads had not changed too much and she retraced her steps as if it had been only yesterday. She directed them to take a number of turns, without making a single mistake. Then she told them they were approaching a stream, and that their goal was coming up on the right just around a bend – which it was. Again emotion got the better of her and she burst into tears.

Cynthia had described the house itself back in Australia, and the details were borne out when they pulled into the courtyard of a u-shaped mansion, with a central archway through which coaches would once have passed. The only difference was that a well lay in the centre of the courtyard rather than the fountain she had described, but even this could have been the one feature to change significantly in the intervening centuries. As the team walked around Cynthia again felt her surroundings coming to life. She was particularly captivated by the chapel in the grounds of the house, which she had also described previously. Apart from many other details that could perhaps be put down to intelligent guesswork, she had reported that it had a hexagonal stone font on the left, dark wooden pews and, even more obscure, diamond-shaped blue-grey tiles on the floor. When the team obtained permission to enter the chapel, yet again all these details proved to be accurate.

This was the initially skeptical le Breton's reaction in the documentary:

> It is difficult to work it out. It is a fascinating and intriguing experiment. It has reached the limit of credibility. It's absolutely different, I can't understand it. There is something spiritual at the heart of it.

Gwen McDonald and Rose Duncan

The second of Ramster's key cases is that of Gwen McDonald.[59] When she first arrived in Ramster's office she had only come to provide moral support for a friend, who wanted to see if she could experience a past life under hypnosis. Gwen herself was a down-to-earth, middle-aged woman who had no belief in reincarnation at this time, and no desire to be regressed, so when Ramster said that he could just as easily work with both of them to see how well they reacted she was initially reluctant. Nevertheless after some persuasion she agreed, and how grateful we should be that she did because she turned out to be one of his finest subjects. She regressed easily and, albeit with some further reluctance that Ramster had to overcome, agreed to return to help with his ongoing research. Initially he uncovered what appeared to be ten different past lives with her, which took place in various parts of the world, with the earliest as far back as prehistoric times. But for research purposes he decided that the most promising regression occurred in eighteenth-century England, a country that again Gwen had never visited in this life – indeed she had never even held a passport.

In trance she initially revealed that her name in this life was Rose Duncan, and that she lived with her father Adam and stepmother Bessie in a small dwelling called 'Rose Cottage', which was part of a larger estate.

Although she did not say where this was, it is obvious to anyone just reading Ramster's written transcripts that when she became Rose she talked with a broad Somerset brogue. The full details of this life then emerged over the course of a number of subsequent sessions. She was born in 1765, and had a happy and relatively uneventful childhood – although she later found out that at birth she had been taken away from her real mother, whose maiden name was Lethbridge and who was married to a Lord Somerville, and with whom her father had had an affair. He went away for long periods so she was mainly left with Bessie, of whom she was very fond, and Dobbs, Bessie's grandfather, who kept her entertained with many local tales and legends.

The highlight of her week was when she crossed fields and a stream to visit the nearest village to buy provisions, where she could look in the shops and meet local people. She knew that the master of 'the big 'ouse' was called James Mackenzie, and that he owned various ships that traded around the globe. But he had taken the estate over from a Lord Panmure of Forth, a friend of her father's who was very kind to her when she was young. So she was less fond of Mackenzie, and even less of his annoying son Nicholas. Apparently he chased her for amusement when she was a girl, and for entirely different reasons as she developed into a young woman. But her greatest pleasure was reserved for when she could walk right through the woods and fields and on to the ruins of the abbey at Glastonbury, which she reckoned to be some six miles away. Sadly, it also proved to be her ultimate undoing.

As she approached the age of eighteen her father began to cast about for a suitable husband. Mackenzie, Lord Panmure and her father were all expatriate Scotsmen – indeed it seems the latter had come to Somerset to hide away in the aftermath of the failed Jacobite rebellion of 1745. In any case, when he returned one day he announced that he had found a suitable candidate from the clan McCrae, and that after their marriage she would go to live in Scotland for good. Rose was thrown into confusion. The poor girl did not want to leave the home and people she loved, and was not at all sure she was ready to be married, especially not to a complete stranger. Worse still, the McRaes were relatives of the Mackenzies – who by this time Rose had come to hate with a passion.

Desperately confused and scared she ran for miles until she reached the abbey, her favorite place when she needed time to think, but as night started to close in it was too late to try to make her way home. Gradually the temperature dropped and the cold became more intense, so she took refuge in one of the ruined buildings and huddled up in a corner to fight off the cold as best she could. Her parents had no idea where to look until they asked Dobbs, who knew of Rose's love for the abbey, but by the time they found her it was morning and she was already very ill. They took her home on their cart, and Bessie nursed her in bed. But after several weeks she succumbed to pneumonia and died.

Gwen's regression as Rose became Ramster's 'lead' case because it was so rich in detail. But before he could commit to taking her and others halfway around the world, he needed to do some preliminary checking of the accuracy or otherwise of Rose's story. He and a colleague devoted hours to poring over old records in the New South Wales Library, and it proved well worth the effort. He had specifically asked Rose to name the villages in the surrounding area, and the majority of these checked out on modern maps as clustered together in southeast Somerset. Langport, Somerton, Alford, East and West Pennard, West Bradley, and Croscombe – which she correctly pronounced 'Crocom' – were all there within about a twelve-mile radius of each other. Better still she mentioned the villages of Hornbl*aw*ton – again her pronunciation was quite precise – and Stone Chapel, both of which were correct for her time, although the former is now called Hornblotton while the latter no longer exists.[60] Ramster also managed to unearth a manuscript from this period that recorded all the landed gentry in Somerset, and he was delighted to find the Lethbridges, James Stuart Mackenzie and Hugh Somerville all listed. Meanwhile Rose had also described how Mackenzie had hired the architect James Wyatt to renovate the stairs and banisters in the main house, and how a curse had been placed on the Mackenzies by Coinneach Odhar, the 'Brahan Seer'. Both these aspects of her story checked out too.

These signs were encouraging. Ramster was also satisfied there was no way Gwen was attempting to perpetrate some sort of elaborate fraud by having accessed similarly obscure manuscripts. So he was now ready to depart for England to conduct his own further research before Gwen and the others joined him. In the library at Taunton he enquired about the word *tallet*, which Rose had used in connection with the roof of their cottage, and found that it meant a loft.[61] More impressive again was a discovery he made by pure luck. Rose had mentioned that a group of Quakers used to pass through her neighborhood to get to Alford, where they had a small 'meeting house'. When he looked into this further he discovered that, although in more recent times there have been meeting houses in virtually every town and in many villages, at that point they were rarer. But Alford was not listed in the main Quaker records from that time, and nor did anyone in Alford itself know of such meetings having taken place. However, during his local research he and some assistants chanced upon a hoard of magazines from the period, and they happily flicked through them out of general interest and to get a feel for life in Somerset at that time. They did not expect to find a brief but clear reference to a meeting of Quakers in Alford. This was starting to be the sort of obscure information that even the most determined hoaxer was unlikely to have uncovered.

As if all this were not enough already, Gwen and the film crew then flew out to meet Ramster in London. After a little rest and acclimatization, Ramster again regressed Gwen to her life as Rose, and afterwards discussed the details consciously in the hope that her memories would now be closer to the surface as they tried to verify them. This seemed to work because they then traveled to Somerset to meet Basil Cottle, an expert in local history from the University of Bristol who was to act as an independent witness throughout. She was given an unmarked map of Glastonbury and asked to point out any landmarks she recognized, and immediately identified Wearyall Hill, which lies to the southwest and which she had referred to back in Sydney. She also identified Tor Hill to the east, on which stands the famous ruined tower of St Michael's Church. She then pointed out the ruins of the abbey on the map, and for the first time described how two low pyramids had sat in the middle of the ruins, acting as a doorway. A local historian subsequently confirmed that this observation was correct according to medieval records.

As described in *The Search for Lives Past* and confirmed in the documentary Gwen's next stop was to be taken to the abbey itself, although blindfolded so as not to prejudice later attempts at navigation. When she first saw the ruins again she was clearly moved. The major difference, apart from the absence of the two pyramids, was apparently the way in which the site had been cleared of rubble and generally cleaned up for tourists – which in fact she found rather sterile and depressing. But as she walked around the memories seemed to come flooding back. She lovingly caressed the carved feathers on the pillars of an arched doorway, exactly as she had described Rose doing all those years before. At this point she became quite understandably overwhelmed because, despite the detailed nature of her hypnotic recall, she had never been consciously certain of its validity. Until now when, just like Cynthia, she realized she really had stood in exactly this spot nearly two hundred years previously: 'The memory of this place brings the same old feelings and the feelings of peace. You wouldn't believe the feelings I get inside from seeing this place, you really wouldn't.'

The next task was for Gwen to attempt to find her former home, which the team felt sure had been in Hornblotton. She was blindfolded and taken to the outskirts of Ansford several miles to the east, which they also felt sure was the local village she had walked to once a week. Standing in a field she spotted a line of trees to the west that she thought were familiar, and the search was on. She took them along a road for a short distance, but then stopped at a bend in the small village of Clanville. She said that in Rose's day there had been five houses at this point, one of which sold cider. Now there were only two new houses and two old ones, one a mere ruin. But in the other the owner confirmed that his house had been built in 1742 and that a number of its contemporaries had only recently been knocked down. Not only that, but his family had a tradition that one of them had been a cider house – a point subsequently confirmed on an old map.

Gwen now left the road to the north and began to traverse the fields. It was not long before they came to the stream she had said would be there, but it was getting late so they decided to stop for the day. The next morning they returned and she led them along the stream, still heading west. In trance she had described how they would come to a fork, near which was a small waterfall, all of which they encountered after about a mile. In addition, although she had described some stepping stones near the fork that were no longer there, a local man was able to subsequently confirm they had been removed some forty years previously. At the fork Gwen sensed she was close and sped off across a field, with the rest of the team struggling to keep up. After about half a mile her mood changed to one of trepidation as she stopped and stared at a building that could just be made out through the trees. When they reached it there were tiles on the roof rather than thatch, and it seemed to be just an old barn attached to a more modern home. But she insisted this was her old house.

Cottle asked Gwen to sketch the back of the house on the spot, and she came up with a rough drawing of a back window and door, and of a lean-to that she referred to as the drying room. When they walked around there was a lean-to, but only one window that looked as if it might have once been a door. Cottle was skeptical, yet Gwen was convinced this was her former home and, facing it again after an interval of two centuries, she broke down in tears for the first time. Their differences were soon resolved. The team obtained permission to look inside, and the outline of an older window that was now bricked up lay exactly where she had said it would. Meanwhile there, in the roof, was a loft room or tallet.

This, surely, must be the end of Gwen's incredible story? No. There is one final, and even more amazing, twist. While in Sydney she had described how Rose had been at the abbey one day when she had cut her foot quite badly, and a local farmer called Brown had taken her to his cottage nearby to bandage it up. He was kind, but the forthright Rose was upset that he had been stealing flagstones from the abbey ruins to cover the floor of his home, because on this particular journey she was sharing the cart with one that had unusual markings on it. Ramster asked her to draw these while still in trance and she roughly very sketched a variety of curved lines and spirals.

Of course they had already had incredible success with Gwen, far more than they could possibly have hoped. But Ramster knew that the crowning glory would be if they could locate the farmer's cottage and the flagstone, even though the chances were probably slim at best. So, on their final day together, they assembled at the abbey and Gwen headed off. On the way they passed the George and Pilgrim Inn, which she had described and accurately drawn for Ramster back in Sydney – with a long bow window on one side, an arch in the middle for coaches, and two triangular, pointed structures on the roof. The only difference was that she had called it 'The Pilgrim's Inn', which was correct for Rose's time.

They pressed on, heading west out of Glastonbury towards Meare. At one point they had to skirt an embankment where a new ring road was being constructed, and of course the majority of the buildings had changed too. Nevertheless she persevered, and they eventually came to a bridge over a stream. Now they needed to locate what Rose had described as the second in a row of five thatched cottages that lay nearby. Gwen left the road and walked along the stream for a short while before pointing to a dilapidated building on the other side that on closer inspection turned out to be a chicken shed. The farmer, Dennis Simmonds, confirmed that it had been a row of five thatched cottages, which had deteriorated so much that the end ones had been pulled down. What was left had a corrugated iron roof, while the windows were open holes, but it looked as though the basis of the original, second cottage was still there.

The next problem was that for decades the floor had been covered in droppings. Simmonds kindly agreed to clean it overnight, and was himself amazed to find dark blue flagstones that clearly matched others still remaining at the abbey.[62] But what of the one with the markings? Gwen pointed to one that seemed to have faint patterns on it, and anticipation mounted as they washed it off and brushed it with talcum powder so that the markings stood out. Although faint, there were some definite similarities with the ones Gwen had drawn. And even if one were to take the view that this was purely a coincidence given their relatively random nature, the mere fact that she knew there were flagstones from the abbey buried underneath all the detritus is surely impressive enough.[63]

In the documentary Cottle summarizes his views on the case, and admits that after initial skepticism he was impressed:

> When we arrived at Rose Cottage Gwen showed signs of distinct emotion, which might be convincing but need not be. What convinces me much more is that she did give beforehand a quite reasonable plan of what it was going to look like – she showed us a pent roof and windows in approximately the right places for a building that was nearly two hundred years old – and that is fairly convincing. One of the things that impressed me most was her pronunciation of Hornblotton as Blawton, because I happen to know that that is the former pronunciation and I happen to believe that Gwen probably didn't have access to this fact... And there is one word she has used that could be a crucial proof that she is really repeating something heard in a previous existence, and that is the obsolete West Country word *tallet* for a loft.

Helen Pickering and James Burns

Our third key case from Ramster's experiment involves another young woman by the name of Helen Pickering. This case is not described in *The Search for Lives Past*, so the lesser quantity of information that follows is all taken from the documentary. In trance she described the life of a Scottish doctor called James Archibald Burns, who lived in the middle of the nineteenth century and whose practice was in the town of Blairgowrie, about sixty miles to the north of Edinburgh. When she was taken there she was blindfolded and asked to orient herself from a local landmark, which she did, taking the team across a bridge to a grassy square around which James' local pub and practice offices had been situated. She was able to locate both but the buildings had completely changed, so nothing further could be accomplished. Nevertheless they were able to establish from the local county archives that a doctor and local dignitary called James Burns had indeed lived in the town at the time.

However Helen had also described while in trance how James had studied medicine in Aberdeen in the 1830s, so now they traveled north where they were joined by two independent witnesses – Ann Gordon from the history department of the university, and local reporter Joanna Buchan, who would go on to become a well-known BBC radio presenter. Again blindfolded Helen was taken to the docklands area, from where she led them towards the centre of the city. On the way she pointed out a building that she insisted had once housed the Seaman's Mission, which proved to be correct when contemporary maps were subsequently checked. They carried on and she led them past what to her were modern buildings fronting the street near the college, not recognizing them but feeling that their target was close by.

Then she spotted the entrance into the courtyard of Marshall College, which was now one of many Aberdeen university buildings. Just as with Cynthia and Gwen, when she entered the memories seemed to come flooding back – even though it had changed considerably, with the grass quadrangle now covered in tarmac and a new tower in the centre of the building. They went inside, and at the top of the main stairs she pointed to the library on the left. It was now a museum, but in James' day it had indeed been a library. Gaining in confidence, she led them all around the interior of this huge old building, pointing out the location of passages and hallways long ago blocked up or demolished. Then when they emerged at the back, there was the long protrusion or 't-shape' that she had described back in Sydney; and she indicated the new portion and top floor that had been added on, both of which were confirmed by one of the witnesses, and neither of which were so recent that they were obvious to the casual observer. Indeed, one of the witnesses confirmed that Helen's knowledge of the building was far superior to her own, even though she had recently spent five years there as a student.

Back in Sydney Helen had used her talents as an artist to draw a detailed picture of the courtyard, on which she pointed out where the library and lecture theatre were. Some aspects compared favorably to an old drawing they were able to locate in local archives, but not all. Yet even this drawing was more recent than when James was supposed to have attended, so were there inaccuracies in her recall or had the building changed even between the times of the two drawings? The only man who would know was David Gordon, an oil sciences expert who had also researched the history of the building in great detail, collecting every plan and drawing available, to write an unpublished postgraduate paper on it.

Initially somewhat skeptical, he asked her what she remembered of the building at the time James was there. She reported that the right-hand side of the quadrangle as you faced the main entrance had been a chapel; that the main building had been only three stories high, with the then top floor housing the dormitories; and that there was another stone staircase in the interior that must have been demolished. At this point he was sufficiently impressed at her accuracy that he pulled out his file of historic plans and architects' drawings and showed her confirmation of all these facts. She then pointed out first where it had been possible to look down from the main landing onto the main assembly hall, and second the location of the main lecture theatre, both of which facts had now changed but were true of James' time. Finally, in a fine display of his own detailed knowledge from the old plans, Gordon asked her how she would have found her way to the nearest toilet if she had been working in the library. She said you would go along a small corridor off the main staircase and it was on the right, which was again confirmed.

Gordon summed up his feelings as follows:

> It would seem more than coincidental. It may be inexplicable in my terms, what she has discussed with me before she saw these plans or even knew they existed... The only place there would be a copy of my work is in the Open University archives, and I don't think that Helen has been anywhere near those, especially never having been out of Australia.

Summary

To summarize, unfortunately in none of these cases was the subject hypnotized and asked about the source of their memories. But, whereas in some of our inconclusive cases cryptomnesia might be thought of as possible even if unlikely, these unexplained cases contain certain features that suggest it is close to impossible. To recap:

- Jane's recall of the 'golden apple' given to Coeur could only be verified in one place, the local archive records in Bourges that even local historians knew little about.

- Laurel had information about the college in Cuenca and about the change in location of its Inquisition headquarters of which even local historians and archivists were unaware.

- In Gwen's case, nobody else can have known about the flagstones that had been hidden under the detritus on the floor of the chicken shed for decades.

- Helen had information about the college in Aberdeen that was only partially contained in one archived and never published paper.

- In general the chance of any of these obscure facts having been unearthed and then included in some sort of fictional account seems entirely remote.

- In the three Ramster cases the subjects were able to find and recognize places while not in trance at the original locations, which almost certainly discounts merely reading or hearing about them.

- All of these cases involve *seriously* obscure information that had to be verified using *multiple* sources. This contrasts with the inconclusive cases, in which the information tended either to be only reasonably obscure, or to be traceable to a single, prime source.

- Although we have already recognized that the accuracy of past-life memories may vary, these unexplained cases contain few if any facts that are demonstrably incorrect. Again this contrasts with the inconclusive cases.

All of these unexplained cases except Jane's are again too recent to have been considered by Harris or Wilson, and nor do there appear to have been any attempts by other skeptics to comment on or analyze them, even on the internet. To be charitable this may be simply because they have not yet heard of them, in which case time will tell. In any event, we should play devil's advocate for ourselves. If we are right that cryptomnesia is not just unlikely but can be completely eliminated in these cases, the only other normal explanation that could account for them would be deliberate fraud. So, despite skeptics' general acceptance that normally this can be discounted when we are dealing with past-life regression, is fraud likely or even possible in these particular cases that some might regard as 'too good to be true'?

To commence with Jane, her case originated with Bloxham and was then investigated independently by the initially skeptical Iverson. All three also appeared in a television documentary together, so that not even Harris and Wilson suggest fraud is a possibility here. As for Tarazi, the sheer depth and detailed referencing of the obscure factual data in her book does not suggest complete fabrication, and as her publisher Frank DeMarco pointed out in his preface: 'If this is fantasy, the author is a genius, and a pretty industrious one at that.' Indeed, despite his general reservations about past-life regression, it was Stevenson who introduced the two of them, so impressed was he by the details of the case.[64] Finally, what about Ramster? Again his cases were shown in a documentary not just in Australia but also in the UK, and he used independent witnesses in each.

As for the minute possibility that even these were actors, Basil Cottle, for example, was a well-known lecturer at Bristol University at the time.

Group Regressions

We mentioned Helen Wambach briefly at the beginning of this chapter. She qualified as a psychologist in New Jersey in the mid-1950s, and because the Bridey Murphy case had been treated with disdain by her college professors she continued to be skeptical of past lives in her practice for more than a decade. Then in 1966 a vivid *déjà vu* experience piqued her interest, followed by several encounters with children who appeared to have spontaneous past-life recall.[65] She became determined to research past lives in general, initially investigating individual subjects' recall and examining the extent to which it could be verified from a historical perspective. But she gradually decided that a better direction would be to regress *groups* of volunteers in order to gain statistical data that might or might not suggest reincarnation as the best explanation for their past-life memories.

So between 1974 and 1978 Wambach undertook a series of group regressions with more than three hundred volunteers, not just from her base in California but from across the mid-west of America. Once she had refined her methods she found that of the order of ninety-five percent of her group subjects would experience some sort of recall – this slightly higher than normal rate presumably being explainable by the fact that they were interested volunteers.[66] With each group the session was split into three segments, in each of which they were given several options as to the time period they might regress to, the earliest being four thousand years ago. After each regression they were asked to write down what they had experienced, which produced nearly eleven hundred individual data sheets. The findings from such a large and controlled survey, as reported in Wambach's 1978 book *Reliving Past Lives*, were at the very least interesting.[67]

Over the four millennia, almost half of her subjects' past lives were lived as a male and half as a female, exactly as we would expect – and this despite her sample of volunteers being considerably biased towards females. Between sixty and eighty percent of past lives involved the lowest social class of the time, suggesting that imagination and ego were not significant factors. Her subjects' descriptions of their race, geographical location, clothing, footwear, food and eating utensils in the different eras all conformed to historical patterns that certainly make logical sense, even if they were difficult for Wambach to verify with any great accuracy. As for their deaths in previous lives, consistently across the different eras more or less eighty percent died naturally or accidentally, with the remaining twenty percent of violent deaths only rising to thirty percent for the start of the twentieth century – coincident with World War I.

Xenoglossy

The term xenoglossy was coined by the French physiologist Charles Richet around the turn of the twentieth century. Of course the phenomenon had been known long before that, because 'speaking in tongues' had been regarded as a sure sign of demonic possession for centuries. But in the modern context of speaking previously unlearned languages while in hypnotic trance, *responsive* xenoglossy is defined as a subject being able to hold a two-way conversation in the language. With *recitative* xenoglossy, on the other hand, they simply recite a word or phrase they may have previously memorized, or repeat those used by the questioner, without really understanding what is being asked. In this context, while the former might suggest that some form of paranormal process was at work, the latter would not.

To begin with the less than impressive cases, Wilson reports on one from the north of England in the 1930s involving an amateur hypnotist called Frederic Wood and a subject to whom he gave the pseudonym Rosemary.[68] She apparently recalled the life of a Babylonian princess called Nona who was part of the harem of the eighteenth-dynasty Egyptian pharaoh Amenhotep III. But most important was her apparent ability to speak the language of the time, something that has fascinated but eluded scholars for centuries. After he published a brief report Wood was contacted by a supposedly professional Egyptologist with the impressive-sounding name of Alfred J Howard Hulme. Over the next five years transcripts containing some nine hundred phrases were produced, and in 1937 they published their joint findings in *Ancient Egypt Speaks* – proudly proclaiming that they had 'completely restored its language'. The problem with any such claim is that Egyptian hieroglyphs incorporate consonants only, while any vowel sounds can only be guessed at best. As Wilson points out, translating it is therefore like having only the 'b', 'n' and 'd' of the English word *bend*, from which one could, for example, derive band, bend, bind, bond and boned. Not only that, but Wilson was able to establish that Hulme was not really a professional Egyptologist at all, with there being no record of his having gained his 'honors certificate in Egyptology' from Oxford University as he claimed. So it should come as no surprise that a genuine, contemporary Oxford Egyptologist called Battiscombe Gunn was easily able to show the flaws in Hulme's interpretations.[69] Moreover, to double check Wilson asked the Cambridge Egyptologist John Ray for his opinion, and he was appalled at Hulme's poor understanding of Egyptian grammar and the way he confused Middle and Late Egyptian. It seems likely, therefore, that Rosemary's subconscious was simply making the language up while she was in trance.

A rather stronger case appears in George Brownell's 1946 book *Reincarnation*, and it involves an apparently famous compatriot who he does not name out of respect for her privacy.[70] Apparently she had an unhappy childhood, not least because she refused to speak in anything other than a strange language that her parents did not recognize, although they did attempt to record many of her utterances phonetically in a notebook. She grew out of the habit after seeing a psychiatrist. But much later in life she and her husband found themselves in Egypt as the guests of a man of high standing, and one of his servants spoke an ancient Arabian dialect that only his mother could understand. They were astonished when their guest indicated that she too understood every word, and when she subsequently arranged for them to inspect the notebook from her childhood the words were all verified. But this case is, unfortunately, entirely anecdotal.

Ramster regularly directed his subjects to speak the language of their previous incarnations, and he reports that a number of them were successful in speaking, for example, Greek, Italian and French even though they had had no exposure to them in this life. The most linguistically prolific of his subjects was reported to be Jenny Green, who apparently recalled a rich variety of past lives in different times and places.[71] The one covered in his documentary, in which she was a young Jewish girl, was briefly mentioned above as being less than a complete success when it came to verification. But what is relevant for our current purposes is that she is shown in trance being interviewed by a German speaker. However quite why is a mystery because, as they are forced to admit, her responses are complete nonsense made to sound a bit like German – and like Rosemary it seems absolutely clear that they are merely the result of her imagination working overtime. However, in *The Truth about Reincarnation* Ramster describes how Jenny too recalled the life of an ancient Egyptian priestess, this time in a temple dedicated to the goddess Isis. Moreover she too attempted to speak the language of the time when directed, and he was apparently impressed by the fluency of her utterances. But the aforementioned problems that face anyone attempting to prove the authenticity of supposed, spoken, Ancient Egyptian, coupled with her false German, suggest that this case should probably not be regarded as a strong one – apart from a brief rider that we will come to shortly.

The other case of Ramster's that is relevant here is that of Cynthia Henderson.[72] We have seen that her recall of the *facts* of the life of Amelie de Cheville was impressive, but what about her apparent ability to speak French when in trance? Ramster had established that at the age of twelve she had received some basic French tuition for two months at the most, while on their first morning in the marketplace in Flers it was clear that she retained little or no conscious ability to speak the language. So they retired to a nearby chateau to see what would happen when she was placed in trance and le Breton, the independent witness, spoke to her in his native tongue. Although Ramster provides no detailed transcripts of this session in his book, he suggests that the results were astonishing:

> To the surprise of everyone in the room, she fully understood what Antoine had said to her and answered him in fluent French. There ensued a long conversation in French. Sometimes Cynthia answered his questions in French and sometimes in English. Sometimes Antoine spoke in English and she answered him in French. It was apparent at all times that she was aware of what was being said and was able to answer. Antoine had gone off on a tangent asking her all sorts of questions and she correctly answered him. Her knowledge of French seemed to far exceed anything she might have been able to learn from a short period in classes at school.
>
> Antoine was astonished. He said she spoke French well, as a Frenchwoman spoke it, devoid of any English accent. Furthermore, he said she spoke in a manner more in keeping with the eighteenth century, as some of her words were old-fashioned. Sometimes she hesitated, however, as if the words came easily one minute and only with difficulty the next. Yet, Cynthia displayed that she had enough of a command of the French language to understand all that was said to her. The startling fact was that her French accent was perfect, her English accent disappeared, and even the English she spoke while in trance had a French accent.

Unfortunately these results are not exactly confirmed by Ramster's documentary. Generally speaking when in trance her pronunciation of French names and words carries a reasonable accent, although on a couple of occasions it seems somewhat poor – for example, when she pronounces the name of the city of Rouen as more like Roo-enne, and her own name as de Che*au*ville with an 'o' sound rather than as de Che*v*ille. Nevertheless her accent remains reasonable in the brief extract from the session with le Breton shown in the documentary in which she replies in French. But what about what she actually says?

The Spoken French	Accurate Translation	Subtitles in Documentary
A: [Inaudible] plus le jour de votre marriage?	...still the day of your marriage?	Do you remember your wedding day?
C: Oui. Marriage. Famille. Au chateau.	Yes. Marriage. Family. At the chateau.	Accurate.
A: Est-ce que vouz avez connu quelqu'un à St Michelle?	Did you know someone at St Michelle?	How well do you know St Michelle? [Seems to have been adapted to better fit her answer.]
C: Un petit maison. L'Abbaye St Michel. La mer.	A small house. The Abbey of St Michel. The sea.	Accurate.
A: Est-ce que l'on a déjà fait un portrait de vous?	Has anyone ever made a portrait of you?	Have you ever had your picture painted? [Close enough]
C: D'accord, un peu [untranslatable] de Versailles. Je fait rien.	Agreed, a little... of Versailles. I'm doing nothing.	Yes, certainly. On a visit to Versailles. [There is no word for 'visit' similar to the sound she makes] I don't think much of it. [This seems to pretend she says 'ca ne fait rien']

From the transcript of this extract we can see that there are minor problems with specifics, such as that she seems to use the wrong gender for the word *maison*, and omits the 'ne' from the last sentence. But the arguably far bigger problem is that her responses are, for the most part, far less than fluent. Indeed at this point at least she is suffering from all the typical weaknesses of responsive xenoglossy: fragmentary words and phrases, most of which are either repeated from the question, close to the English equivalent or could easily have been picked up from films and so on. It is true that le Breton speaks so swiftly that reference had to be made to a French acquaintance to reveal exactly what he was saying in several places, while Cynthia did not ask him to repeat anything. But whereas Ramster insists that she understood everything that was said to her, in this extract at least that seems to be debatable – especially when the proper words are recorded and accurate translations made instead of relying on the less than accurate subtitles used in the documentary. Ramster maintains that this particular extract is not actually representative of the whole session.[73] But based on the evidence placed in the public domain so far this case must surely be regarded as far weaker from the xenoglossy perspective than it is in terms of its normal historical verification.

Stevenson too has documented three xenoglossy cases in his usual great depth and, despite his skepticism about regression in general, in two of these the foreign language only emerged under hypnosis. The first involves the wife of an American doctor who was also an amateur hypnotist, although their names were never published to protect their identities. When in trance she seemed to be recalling the life of a Swedish peasant farmer called Jensen. This case developed in the late 1950s, but Stevenson did not become involved until much later, publishing his report in his 1974 book *Xenoglossy*. However even he is forced to admit that the woman, who was also supposedly a medium, was less than reliable.[74] Twice she was caught channeling messages about biological research, the first time using information she had previously written down on a notepad, and the second from a passage in a book she had borrowed from the library. Stevenson seems to accept her explanation that these things must have happened when she was in an amnesic trance – or at least he did not allow this to deter him from taking her apparent xenoglossy seriously. But Wilson tracked the couple down, and without going into detail he maintains the case was completely fraudulent.[75]

Stevenson's other two cases are reported in his 1984 book *Unlearned Language*. The first involves an Indian girl called Uttara Huddar, who lived in Nagpur and whose family spoke Marathi.[76] From 1974, when at thirty-three she was far older than Stevenson's typical child cases, she began to have periods when she would spontaneously become a completely different personality who called herself Sharada. Sometimes this personality would take over for weeks at a time. But most important for our purposes is that Sharada spoke fluent Bengali, even though Uttara had supposedly had no significant exposure to this language as a child or adult. This case is also unusual in that Sharada did not seem to feel, or know, she was dead. From the statements she made when she was the dominant personality it seems she merely recalled being bitten by a snake, falling unconscious, then waking up again in Uttara's body. Nor did Sharada say when she had lived. But in fact she gave enough information about her former life in the vicinity of Burdwan in West Bengal, which lies some six hundred miles to the east, that a number of the contemporary members of her family whose names she gave could be accurately traced to a genealogy of the Chattopadhaya family from that area. But she is again different from Stevenson's typical cases because they had lived much, much earlier, in the early part of the nineteenth century.

Whether or not this case is a strong one in terms of its historical verification, what about the xenoglossy aspect? The most cited critique of Stevenson's language cases is a 1987 paper by Sarah Thomason in the *Skeptical Inquirer.*[77] She argues that Bengali and Marathi are closely related languages, and adds that there was a distinct possibility that Uttara gained her knowledge via perfectly normal means, although her only non-speculative information about this is actually provided by Stevenson himself. For example, he reports that one critic insisted they had seen Uttara taking a test in Bengali, and although Stevenson suggests they may have mixed her up with her sister, it appears that at the very least both this sister and her younger brother had some knowledge of Bengali.[78] This case was also independently investigated by V V Akolkar, who wrote a report on it in 1992.[79] From a critical point of view he adds that a friend of Uttara's claimed they had studied Bengali together during their final year in high school, and that her older brother confirmed this. Nevertheless for various reasons both Stevenson and Akolkar remain convinced that these normal sources are not capable of explaining her fully responsive xenoglossy. But even if they are right, although we will not discuss the paranormal alternatives to reincarnation properly until the end of the chapter, in this case more than most possession must be regarded as a distinct possibility.

The last of Stevenson's xenoglossy cases is that of Dolores Jay.[80] Her husband Carroll was again an amateur hypnotist who began experimenting with past-life regression in the late 1960s, and found his wife was an excellent subject. But he was merely hypnotizing her to relieve some back pain one day when she unexpectedly answered '*nein*', the German for 'no', to one of his questions. Over the course of several sessions, and with the help of a German dictionary, Carroll managed to establish that Dolores was regressing to an apparent life as a young girl called Gretchen Gottlieb from Eberswalde. But it was only a year later that he invited a friend who spoke German to attend a session with her in which she was questioned in German for the first time, and responded. This was the only session in which an outsider was present before Stevenson became involved in 1971, and he attended a number of subsequent sessions with Dolores, accompanied by a variety of other German-speaking witnesses. She spoke only German in these, although she was happy to be questioned in German or English. After extensive investigations into her childhood Stevenson established to his own satisfaction that Dolores had had no significant exposure to the German language in her current life, and had certainly not been taught to speak it.

This case has drawn the usual criticism that it merely displays repetitive rather than responsive xenoglossy. Thomason discusses it in her aforementioned paper and argues that Dolores used only fragmented words or phrases rather than full sentences; that her use of grammar was wrong or even nonexistent; that she repeated words used by the questioner, or used words that are very close to their English equivalent; that she repeated stock phrases about being frightened and her situation being dangerous; that a quarter of her responses involved merely yes or no; and that sometimes she did not understand the question put to her. Thomason also suggests that Dolores displayed a limited vocabulary, a point echoed by Wilson who indicates that in nineteen sessions held over four years she managed to speak only two hundred plus German words not previously used by one of her questioners, half of which were mere cognates of their English counterparts.[81]

Dolores' German as Transcribed	Approximate Translation
Ich beistehen der Hausfrau.	I help the housekeeper.
Gretchen nicht gut mit Zahlen.	Gretchen [is] not good with numbers.
Essen viel Sache.	[I] eat many things.
Warum er kommen wieder und wieder?	Why does he come over and over again?
Gretchen Sache sehr schlecht.	[For] Gretchen things [are] very bad.
Sehr beschwerlich.	[It is] very troublesome.
Möglicher sieben.	[I am] about seven.
Schon ich habe reden alles. Warum der Fragen wieder und wieder?	Already I have told everything. Why the questions over and over again?
Reiten das Pferd.	[I] ride the horse.
Verborgen das Wald.	[I am] hidden [in] the forest.
Ich bin nicht dieselbe.	I am not the same.
Ich versuche machen Sie verstehen.	I [will] try [to] make you understand.

Broadly speaking these criticisms are validated by a glance through the full transcripts of four sessions provided by Stevenson in an appendix to

Unlearned Language.[82] But to leave the case here, as skeptics do, would undoubtedly be selective. Her grammar may have been incorrect or incomplete, but Stevenson is surely right to argue that an uneducated young girl might well have talked with poor grammar – just think of how some poorly educated children in the modern world speak. Moreover although her pronunciation was apparently variable, sometimes it was good. Above all, however, we can see from the selections in the table that Dolores did come up with a number of words, phrases or sentences of reasonable complexity; and her range of vocabulary, as limited as it might have been, is decidedly *not* what one might be able to pick up merely from watching a few war films, for example.

This case could probably be explained if it was fraudulent and Dolores kept looking words up in a dictionary. But Stevenson arranged for her to take a lie detector test, which she passed. Nor does he think the couple had any motive for fraud, given that they received a fair degree of criticism over the case from their local community because Carroll was a Methodist minister. So even though from a historical point of view this case remains unverifiable, with respect to xenoglossy perhaps it is not as easily dismissed as skeptics suggest.

Wambach too makes a valuable contribution in a 1982 paper in which she studied the experiences of twenty-six fellow therapists who had worked with a combined total of 18,463 regression patients – of whom 17,350, or ninety-four percent, had experienced some sort of past-life recall.[83] One part of her survey revealed that only twenty-one of these displayed xenoglossy, which correlated with the findings from her own practice in which she had come across only one case out of many thousands of subjects. She put this down to them needing to be in a deeper brainwave state than is normally used for past lives. However, despite the highly anecdotal nature of the evidence, she also reported that in eleven of the twenty-one survey cases the language spoken was taped and then verified:

> In the first case, a woman was able to speak German, French, and Polynesian in three separate regression sessions to three different past lives. These sessions were recorded and the therapist was able to recognize both German and French phrases and sentences. The Polynesian dialect was never verified. Another case involved a subject who recalled being a German aircraft designer during World War II. His use of German was recorded and verified by the therapist... Another undocumented case also included a subject regressed to Nazi Germany who spoke some German phrases, this time as a concentration camp inmate. One therapist reported

the case of a young woman subject who, while recalling a life spent in eighteenth-century France, spoke fluent French, although totally ignorant of that language ordinarily. Two other subjects spontaneously answered questions in Italian while remembering lifetimes spent in that country. Finally, a twenty-three-year-old woman began speaking ancient Hawaiian during her past-life regression to those islands. The session was recorded and later verified as authentic by a Hawaiian Kahuna or native healer-priest. When translated the woman's words implied a message on ancient Kahuna healing techniques virtually unknown to outsiders.

Let us finally turn to xenography – that is, the ability to *write* an unknown foreign language. Another of Ramster's subjects called Alexander Cochrane recalled the early twentieth-century life of a Welshman called George Evans.[84] Alexander was born in England of Anglo-Scottish parents and had lived in various parts of the world – but never Wales, and he had had no exposure to the Welsh language. Yet using it he wrote down a number of words and a short sentence, all of which were subsequently verified in a Welsh dictionary. With strong echoes of the nature of that life they included 'sorrow', 'fear', 'coward', 'weak', 'church', 'was killed' and 'battle'. In addition, despite the doubts previously expressed about the authenticity of Jenny Green's spoken Ancient Egyptian, she also wrote down a number of hieroglyphs while in trance.[85] Ramster reports that he sent these to an unnamed 'eminent professor of Egyptology' for his appraisal and his verdict was apparently that, while some of the writing was difficult to make out because it had been scribbled down too quickly, many of the words could easily be distinguished as genuine.

Meanwhile another intriguing case conducted by the Canadian psychiatrist Joel Whitton, who we will meet properly in the next chapter, is documented in his 1986 book *Life Between Life*.[86] His subject Harold Jaworski regressed to one life as a Viking sailor called Thor, and at Whitton's request wrote down twenty-two words and phrases that, when examined by a specialist, were revealed to be primarily nautical terms in Old Norse – the precursor of modern Icelandic – with a smattering of words of Russian, Serbian and Slavic derivation. Perhaps even more impressive was Harold's regression to the life of a Zoroastrian priest in seventh-century Mesopotamia called Xando, under which guise Whitton asked him to write down his version of a number of common words such as 'brother', 'house', 'clothing' and 'village'. Whitton was convinced that the resulting spidery lettering might have some validity, although his initial attempts to validate it against ancient scripts in library books failed. Then he approached Ibrahim Pourhadi, an expert on ancient Persian and Iranian languages in Washington's Library of Congress; and he confirmed that what Harold had written was an authentic reproduction of the long-extinct language Sassanid Pahlavi, which was used in the area at that time and bears no relation to modern Iranian. Unfortunately Whitton provides no further details of what, if corroborated, might have proved a crucial piece of evidence in support of a paranormal interpretation.

Paranormal Alternatives

We might take the view that the group regression and apparent xenoglossy and xenography evidence reviewed above is not entirely compelling. Nevertheless, the unexplained veridical cases discussed earlier seem to leave us little option but to accept that they at least involve paranormal processes. So we should now consider other possible paranormal explanations, which are exactly the same as those we considered for spontaneous childhood recall.

First, although Laurel did seem to have some psychological problems when she visited Tarazi for therapy, these were not apparent in her earlier sessions with the Dutchman. More importantly Jane, Cynthia, Gwen and Helen had no such problems when they visited Bloxham and Ramster respectively. So possession seems unlikely to be the best explanation for these cases at least – although it may be for some, such as that of Uttara-Sharada. As for extrasensory perception, again tapping into the memories of discarnate personalities or into a more universal memory would not, at least on the face of it, explain the depth of emotions displayed by the subjects in our stronger cases. Above all, however, once more neither of these alternatives fit into the broader context of the interlife regression evidence that we will consider in later chapters.

There is of course one other logical argument that supports the concept of reincarnation, and that is that it explains the inequalities faced by different people from birth better than any other theory. How can we justify one child being born into a life of financial and emotional deprivation, while another has all the advantages that money and a loving family can provide, without appreciating the context that each of these souls will experience all varieties of circumstances in turn? The alternatives are either sheer luck and blind chance on the one hand, or the vagaries of a capricious deity on the other – and neither option is remotely as satisfying from a philosophical perspective.

4

PAST-LIFE THERAPY

Background

When we turn now to the use of past-life regression for therapeutic purposes, a common misconception is that all practitioners are poorly qualified amateurs who already believe in reincarnation. This may have some truth in respect of what is now a significantly expanded community, although a number of professional bodies on both sides of the Atlantic are making considerable attempts to introduce professional standards of both training and practice.[1] But when we look at the background of the pioneers who first dabbled with this therapy we find that nothing could be further from the truth.

Those who published the results of their work in book form shared a number of common traits. Nearly all had qualified as professional psychologists or psychiatrists, so their scientific training had given them an atheist or at least agnostic outlook. Nearly all came to use past-life therapy more or less by accident, or at least reluctantly. And, like Peter Ramster, nearly all were profoundly skeptical of the results initially, but over time could not escape the fact that it was sometimes able to produce dramatic, rapid and permanent improvements in patients – some of whom had spent years in conventional therapy with no significant remission. Nevertheless they all recognized that it should form just one element of a professional therapists' overall toolkit, to be used only when appropriate and not as a complete replacement for more conventional treatments.

The history of past-life regression goes as far back as the late nineteenth century, when a Parisian military colonel by the name of Albert de Rochas dabbled with a form of hypnosis based on the 'animal magnetism' techniques first developed by Austrian physician Franz Anton Mesmer in the late eighteenth century.[2] In regressing his subjects back before birth de

Rochas found that many recalled details of their previous life. Needless to say he was roundly criticized by a Western world to which reincarnation was largely anathema at the time, apart from in theosophical circles, and his work was dismissed as entirely explainable by his suggestive control of his subjects. But we can now see that his research with nineteen subjects, recorded in 1911 in *Les Vies Successives*, shows remarkable consistency with modern findings. He in turn inspired his compatriot, the physician Charles Lancelin, to perform similar research that was written up in his 1922 study *La Vie Posthume*.

Then in the mid-twentieth century the leading Swedish psychiatrist John Björkhem used hypnotic regression on many hundreds of patients over several decades, but his work is not well known because it was not translated.[3] At around the same time the British psychiatrist Alexander Cannon regressed more than a thousand patients over a lengthy period, and consistently found that symptoms that could not be cured by conventional treatment were significantly reduced. In his 1950 book *The Power Within* he emphasized his change of stance over time:[4]

> For years the theory of reincarnation was a nightmare to me and I did my best to disprove it and even argued with my trance subjects to the effect that they were talking nonsense, and yet as the years went by one subject after another told me the same story in spite of different and varied conscious beliefs, in effect until now, well over a thousand cases have been so investigated and I have to admit that there is such a thing as reincarnation. It is therefore only right and proper that I should include this study as a branch of psychology, as my text bears witness to the great benefit many have received psychologically from discovering hidden complexes and fears which undoubtedly have been brought over by the astral body from past lives.

We will assess whether he is right to suggest that the success of past-life therapy provides further proof of reincarnation throughout this chapter. But in the meantime we can see he also stresses, as do many of the other pioneers, that his patients' existing religious beliefs – or indeed lack of them – had little or no impact on their ability to experience past lives or their therapeutic benefits.

Another British pioneer was Denys Kelsey, a medical doctor turned psychiatrist who began using hypnosis for conventional age regression in the late 1940s. But he had no interest in the idea of past-life regression until 1958 when he teamed up with the psychic Joan Grant, who had published a number of autobiographies of previous lives in ancient Egypt and elsewhere. Their way of working was unique in that Grant would sit in on therapy sessions and pass Kelsey notes to confirm whether or not she too was 'seeing' what the patient was remembering about a past life. In this way they could direct the therapy even more accurately, as the following example from their 1967 collaboration *Many Lifetimes* indicates. A patient had repeatedly undergone age regression with Kelsey to alleviate feelings of guilt and inferiority about his identification with being a woman, but had found his symptoms only partially alleviated. After an intermission of several years he contacted Kelsey again complaining of a severe recurrence of his problems, and with Grant now involved past-life regression had become an option:[5]

> Within a few minutes he began to describe scenes in which an elegant young woman appeared, always with a handsome escort. But the scenes changed abruptly: swathed in white ermine she was alighting from a Daimler at the entrance to the Savoy, and then, without any thread of continuity, she was on the deck of a large yacht and then in the paddock at Ascot.
>
> Joan handed me a note. 'This is a genuine recall. But he is not seeing the girl he really was: these are the girl's daydreams of the woman she longed to be. Tell him to see the girl herself.'

Intriguingly these images had come through in previous sessions, but because Kelsey had no awareness of past lives at that time he had been unable to make therapeutic use of them. This time, however, the patient went on to describe how his previous personality had fallen pregnant, had been rejected by her high-society lover leaving her dreams in tatters, and had died when a back-street abortion went wrong. He was apparently cured in this single session, reporting no recurrence of his problems for many years after. It was repeated therapeutic success of this nature that convinced the scientifically trained Kelsey of the reality of reincarnation.

Despite the successes of these early pioneers, it was only really in the 1970s that past-life therapy took off. It was then that Ramster began his pioneering work in Australia, while in Europe psychologist Hans TenDam was leading the way – his seminal work *Exploring Reincarnation* was first published in 1983 in Dutch. Meanwhile in the US Morris Netherton was one of the main pacesetters. Raised as a Methodist with no belief or interest in reincarnation, he trained as a psychologist but in the late 1960s decided to experiment with past-life regression after some interesting experiences with self-analysis. Over the next ten years he regressed many thousands of patients, although rather than using hypnosis he adapted Gestalt therapy –

which relies on picking up on trigger phrases patients use repeatedly when describing their current problems. Although some lingering skepticism about reincarnation remained with him for some time, it had been completely dispelled by 1978 when his book *Past Lives Therapy* was published. Based on the success of his therapy at effecting lasting cures for his patients, he had this to say:[6]

> Patients recreate scenes in past lives for the purpose of understanding certain problems they have in the present; it would be pointless to question the veracity of the material they are reporting. Past-lives therapy does not depend on the 'truth' of reincarnation, but on putting aside the question of 'truth' in order to work toward curing the patient's behavioral problem.

This of course suggests that the success of past-life therapy does not necessarily provide further support for the idea of reincarnation. But Netherton continues:

> Having made this point, I must state my own belief at once, which is that reincarnation does in fact take place. I have been influenced in this belief by neither occultism nor Eastern religion, however. The belief has evolved by following my own observations to their logical conclusions. On the basis of the cases I have handled personally, and the independent research I have done, I feel that the theory of reincarnation most logically explains the phenomena I have witnessed... As far as my patients are concerned, the success of their therapy is unaffected whether they embrace a belief in reincarnation or remain skeptical throughout.

Edith Fiore was brought up attending various branches of the Protestant church, but became an agnostic while gaining her doctorate in psychology because it was more in keeping with her scientific bent. In her 1978 book *You Have Been Here Before* she describes how she had been in psychiatric practice for many years before she moved to California and started to use hypnotherapy in 1974, and it was another two years before she stumbled upon past-life regression. But when she did she quickly began to question her agnosticism:[7]

> Until two years ago I was totally uninterested in the idea of reincarnation. Then one afternoon, while using hypnosis with a male patient, I witnessed something that radically affected both my professional life and my personal beliefs. He had come to me because of crippling sexual inhibitions. When I asked him, while he was under hypnosis, to go back to the origin of his problems, he said, 'Two or three lifetimes ago I was a Catholic priest.' We traced through this seventeenth-century lifetime, looking at his sexual attitudes as an Italian priest, and found the source of his sexual difficulties. I

was aware that the patient believed in reincarnation. Therefore, I felt his vivid description of his past life, colored by a great deal of emotionality, was a fantasy. However, the next time I saw him, he told me he was not only free of his sexual problems, but felt better about himself in general.

As with so many of her colleagues Fiore then decided she would use past-life regression whenever a patient's own subconscious indicated that the origin of a problem was to be found in a previous life. After conducting many thousands of regression sessions she too came to believe in reincarnation, but like Netherton she stresses that for therapy purposes it does not matter whether the experience has any underlying 'veracity':[8]

> Actually, whether the former lifetimes that are 'relived' are fantasies or actual experiences lived in a bygone era does not matter to me as a therapist – getting results is important. I have found past-life regression consistently helpful, often resulting in immediate remission of chronic symptoms that do not return, even after months and years.

Joel Whitton, who we met briefly in the last chapter, initially qualified as a medical doctor at the University of Toronto before moving on to become the chief psychiatrist for the city's school system. He is something of an exception among the pioneers in that he had dabbled with hypnosis from an early age, and openly admits that reincarnation had always been part of his worldview – although he allied himself to no particular religious sect or creed. So it was natural that he would use past-life regression in his practice, which he did from the early 1970s. This is how his co-author Joe Fisher describes his work in their 1986 book *Life Between Life*:[9]

> As Dr Whitton gained a more intimate understanding of the unconscious mind, he instructed his patients, while in trance, to bring traumatic past-life memories into their conscious awareness. This resulted in rapid and dramatic healing which he himself cannot fully explain... Occasionally, people contacted Dr Whitton after having traipsed in vain from one clinic to another. They would tell how the ministrations of innumerable physicians had made no appreciable improvement in conditions ranging from disabling phobias to terminal disease. Because past-life regression sometimes worked where conventional medicine had failed, Dr Whitton was dubbed the 'Lost Cause Doctor'.

British-born Jungian therapist Roger Woolger had studied comparative religion as a postgraduate, but was no believer in reincarnation when he set up his practice in Vermont in 1976. So he was somewhat skeptical when, three years later, a colleague suggested he should experiment with a technique for self-regression into a past life – but he was professionally curious enough to try it. What he did not expect was to recall vividly and in detail the life of a mercenary involved in the brutal repression of the Cathars in southern France in the thirteenth century, who then changed sides and ended up being burned at the stake. Indeed there was a supreme irony to this, in that eight years earlier he had reviewed a book called *The Cathars and Reincarnation* in which the British psychiatrist Arthur Guirdham described how a patient had recalled obscure details of the life of a repressed Cathar – which eventually led to Guirdham believing he too was involved as her lover. When Ian Wilson tried to investigate this case personally with Guirdham he found there were some serious question marks hanging over it.[10] So at the time Woolger may have been justified in dismissing it as mere 'transference' between patient and therapist. But he now realized that his own experience could not be so easily dismissed, especially because he had always had a fear of fire, a total distaste for orthodox religion and especially Christianity, strong pacifistic tendencies based on the deliberate repression of a violent streak, and regular dreams about torture and killing. Despite his vocation, he had never been able to properly explain any of these facets of his personality.

From that point on he began to experiment with past-life regression, although like Netherton using Gestalt and other therapies rather than hypnosis, and by the time he wrote his 1988 book *Other Lives, Other Selves* he had reached the following conclusion:[11]

> From nearly a decade of taking clients and colleagues through past-life experiences and continuing my own personal explorations, I have come to regard this technique as one of the most concentrated and powerful tools available to psychotherapy short of psychedelic drugs.

We cannot close this section without mentioning one of the best-known, modern exponents of past-life therapy, Brian Weiss. In his 1988 book *Many Lives, Many Masters* he describes his initial skepticism as the Head of Psychiatry at a university-affiliated hospital in Miami:

> Years of disciplined study had trained me to think as a scientist and physician, molding me along the narrow paths of conservatism in my profession. I distrusted anything that could not be proved by traditional scientific methods. I was aware of some of the studies in parapsychology that were being conducted at major universities across the country, but they did not hold my attention. It all seemed too farfetched to me.

But he goes on to describe what happened when, in 1980, he started to treat a new patient called Catherine. Although an outwardly attractive woman of twenty-seven, she suffered from a mass of phobias – of water, of choking, of the dark and of death. She was an insomniac who often spent the night in a cupboard to feel safe, and when she did sleep fitfully she had terrible nightmares. She was deeply depressed, and suffering increasingly from acute anxiety and panic attacks.

Throughout eighteen months of weekly appointments Weiss tried everything he knew, but could make no real progress with Catherine. Finally he persuaded her to overcome her fear of hypnosis, and regressed her into her childhood. At the age of five she recalled having been pushed into a swimming pool and having nearly drowned, while at the age of three she remembered having been abused late at night by her drunken father. Weiss was confident he had finally cracked her case, but she returned a week later with her symptoms stubbornly intact. He wondered if he could have missed something from even earlier in her childhood, and took her back again. When nothing emerged at age two, somewhat in desperation he told her to go back to the time from which her symptoms arose. His scientific mind was not prepared for her to suddenly start describing a big white building with pillars and steps, and to tell him that she was living nearly four thousand years ago. As a girl in her mid-twenties called Aronda she had apparently drowned, clutching her baby daughter, when a natural catastrophe engulfed her village in a tidal wave. Although still skeptical, when Catherine returned a week later looking far more radiant, announcing that she now had no fear of drowning and that her nightmares had lessened, he knew he had to take her experience seriously.

Over the next few months Catherine regressed into a number of other past lives out of which various traumas emerged, each one seeming to work its magic on her current personality so that her phobias and anxieties were mere shadows of what they had been. But the real shock was still waiting for Weiss. It was not long before Catherine began to regularly enter the interlife *after* her various deaths in previous incarnations; and when she did, some startling messages started to emerge – not least a personal one for Weiss that left him reeling:[12]

> Your father is here, and your son, who is a small child. Your father says you will know him because his name is Avrom, and your daughter is named after him. Also, his death was due to his heart. Your son's heart was also important, for it was backward, like a chicken's.

Weiss had always been careful to maintain a professional distance from his patients, and Catherine was no exception. He felt it was almost inconceivable that she could have known his young son Adam had died nine years earlier, when only twenty-three days old, because he had a one-in-ten-million defect whereby the pulmonary veins entered his heart on the wrong side. Nor did he think it likely she had learned from any normal source that his daughter Amy had been given the same Hebrew name as his father. This was his reaction:[13]

> My life would never be the same again. A hand had reached down and irreversibly altered the course of my life. All of my reading, which had been done with careful scrutiny and skeptical detachment, fell into place. Catherine's memories and messages were true. My intuitions about the accuracy of her experiences had been correct. I had the facts. I had the proof.

Unfortunately, for all his professional training, Weiss became considerably influenced by and personally involved in this case after these initial disclosures. Catherine went on to reveal in subsequent sessions that he had been a great teacher in a number of their previous incarnations together, and many of her trance messages related to him and the writing of his book. So, just as with Guirdham, some aspects of Weiss' work do lay themselves open to the possibility of transference. We might also note that Weiss has more recently turned his attention to *progressing* patients forward into their potential future lives, a technique that should perhaps be regarded with rather more suspicion.[14]

Research Studies

In addition to the anecdotal evidence of the pioneers, the success of past-life therapy has been reinforced by a number of studies conducted by other professional psychologists and psychiatrists. They were all published in the *Journal of Regression Therapy*.[15]

In 1986 Johannes Cladder reported on his work with a group of thirty Dutch patients with serious phobias, for whom conventional therapies had done little.[16] Five of these dropped out during the program, and another five completed it without significant improvement – although these ten were noticeably more compulsive, depressed or psychotic at the outset. The remaining twenty made rapid improvements using regression therapy when directed to go to the source of their problems, and of these fourteen, or seventy percent, found their subconscious taking them to a previous rather than the current life.

In 1987 Hazel Denning, one of the earliest past-life pioneers, analyzed the outcomes from the work of eight past-life therapists working with nearly a thousand patients, for whom again conventional treatments had achieved little. Of the four hundred and fifty who could still be traced five years after their therapy, twenty-four percent reported that their symptoms had completely disappeared, while twenty-three percent reported a considerable or dramatic improvement, and a further seventeen percent a noticeable improvement.[17]

Back in Holland, Ronald van der Maesen of the Department of Clinical Psychology at the University of Amsterdam conducted two studies on which he reported in 1998 and 1999 respectively. First he used past-life regression with ten patients who suffered from Tourette's syndrome, for which there is little in the way of a conventional cure.[18] He contacted them again one year after therapy to check on their progress, which can best be understood using a tabular summary:

Patient	% Reduction in Motor Tics	% Reduction in Vocal Tics	Medication Originally	Medication Afterwards
1	95	99	N	N
2	0	0	Y	More
3	0	0	N	N
4	80	80	Y	N
5	20	40	N	Y
6	65	65	Y	N
7	0	0	Y	Y
8	95	90	Y	N
9	25	80	N	N
10	80	25	Y	N

We can see that seven out of the ten patients experienced reductions in both their motor and vocal tics, often of over eighty percent, while only three experienced no improvement at all. In addition, while three patients were not on medication originally and remained so, four found that they no longer needed medication. Meanwhile one needed the same amount, and only two – numbers two and five in the table – found they needed more.

In his second study van der Maesen used past-life therapy with fifty-four volunteer patients who heard hallucinated voices, the majority of whom had been receiving conventional psychiatric treatment for schizophrenia.[19] Only twenty-seven of these completed the treatment for a variety of reasons but, when they were independently reexamined after six months, fourteen – more or less fifty percent – showed significant improvements, with four reporting that they were completely cured. A further eleven were sufficiently improved that they were no longer classified as psychiatric patients.

These are only brief summaries of the studies, and certainly it could be argued that none of them is sufficiently replete with control groups and so on to be considered properly scientific. Nevertheless even that most hardened of skeptics, Paul Edwards, is forced to admit that past-life therapy can produce impressive results.[20]

But does this success necessarily provide further proof of the reincarnation hypothesis? In fact, unlike many of the pioneers, most modern, professional hypnotherapists tend to shy away from making too direct a link. For example in her 1995 book *Past Life Therapy: the State of the Art* Rabia Clark, a therapist from Texas, published the results of a survey of more than a hundred colleagues who responded to her questionnaire about their work. Although the majority were not interested in authenticating any personal belief – preferring instead to concentrate on helping their patients with their problems – as with the pioneers ninety-eight percent had come to believe in reincarnation. The difference is that, despite this, a full seventy-five percent took the view that the apparent memories arising during regression are a mixture of real past lives and metaphors or fantasies.

Linda Tarazi, who we met in the last chapter, adopts an even harsher stance:[21]

> For some years I have practiced hypnotic regression in the hope of relieving the suffering of neurotic or phobic persons for whom no other treatment seemed beneficial. If material from their childhood was not pertinent, and they desired to attempt a past-life regression, this was performed. In my own experience, nearly all of the 'previous personalities' evoked during these sessions are unverifiable and almost certainly derive from fantasies on the part of the subject. That many of the patients benefit from this procedure in no way confirms the authenticity of the 'previous personalities' whose lives the patients claim to remember. Still, in a small number of cases, information turns up in one or more of these sessions that cannot be readily accounted for.

So can the success of past-life therapy instead be explained merely by known therapeutic principles such as emotional catharsis, desensitization, cognitive restructuring or post-hypnotic suggestion? A complete skeptic would suggest this must be the case. But we have seen in the last chapter that at least *some* past lives recalled under regression appear to be veridical. Moreover, even Edwards is confused as to why some patients automatically regress to past lives as the source of a problem, even when not directed to so do. So it may be that even if the full details of most past lives are not entirely accurate, those elements in many of them that relate specifically to a current-life problem probably have some grounding in fact.

Admittedly there is some evidence to suggest that occasionally past-life memories can be 'projected' by spirit guides and similar to provide some sort of understanding and catharsis for the subject.[22] But this is by no means a complete explanation for the memories retrieved during past-life therapy. On top of this the suggestion that they tend to have some basis in fact is surely strengthened by those cases reported by therapists in which a patient regresses into multiple past lives that have clear connections and threads running through them – of which more shortly – and even more when accompanying interlife regression reveals more details about these threads.

Nevertheless, unless we are to be accused of a circular argument, it appears we have little option but to conclude that past-life therapy does *not* provide additional, objective proof of reincarnation.

Emotional Dynamics

Even if we accept that past-life therapy works at least in part because the key memories that emerge under regression have some basis in fact, this does not really tell us *how* it works. What are the underlying dynamics that allow healing to take place? Of course it is at this point that most people invoke the concept of karma – about which, unfortunately, there seems to be a great deal of muddled thinking.

Many spiritual commentators who write about karma still tend to refer to it as a 'law' of 'action and reaction', thus maintaining the traditional view handed down from its Hindu origins that it determines our fate or even punishment from one life to the next. This view is also adopted to a greater or lesser extent by at least some regression therapists. But how accurately does this terminology convey what is really going on? An obvious place to start is with case studies involving subjects who find themselves in related traumatic situations in multiple lives. Although some of the cases that follow may seem a little sensational, we should remember not only that in times past life tended to be more brutal, but also that we are no longer concerned with the potential historical accuracy or otherwise of these cases, merely their therapeutic aspects.

A fine example is provided by one of Woolger's patients, who he refers to simply as Chris.[23] Abused as a child in the harsh, drunken environment of a farm, he repeatedly attempted to run away, and had been in and out of prison in a dismal spiral of depression, alcohol and suicide attempts. Even his efforts to start a family had been thwarted by the cot death of his infant son. His opening statement said it all: 'I'm all alone. I'm a piece of shit. I want to die.' When regressed to his birth he discovered that his mother had not wanted him and had attempted her own abortion by falling down the stairs – as a result of which he was born three months premature and placed in an incubator for an equivalent period. Alone and isolated, he already knew he was not welcome and just wanted to die.

A number of Chris' past lives revealed a depressingly similar pattern. As a prisoner in a dungeon in Scotland he had been beaten and was sick with dysentery when he was left alone in chains to die a slow and lonely death, full of hatred for his callous English captors. He had been a sickly adolescent in a besieged native tribe in the American Northwest where, unable to fight and with the medicine man proclaiming his sickness as a sign of evil, his father left him to die – again without food and alone – in the tribal burial grounds. This time his dying thoughts were that he was no good, and deserved to die. In a much earlier tribal life he recalled having been an old man abandoned to die alone in a cave, where he was eaten by a bear while still half-alive.

But further investigation of Chris' case revealed at least two lives that might be thought to justify so much suffering. In one in China his intense anger at his prostitute mother – for whom he acted as lookout, and whose only affection lay in attempts to seduce him – boiled over into a life of violent crime and a hatred of all women. Tragically one woman whose house he was robbing bore the full brunt of his frustrations when he stabbed and mutilated her pregnant body, although at least he felt intense remorse afterwards. But in another life as an uncontrollably psychopathic Eskimo he indulged his hatred of women in general by forcing himself sexually upon as many female members of the tribe as he could, and of his shrewish wife in particular by murdering her. The tribe staked him out in the cold to die. This time a polar bear provided the finishing touches, and he apparently remained unrepentant.

We do not know in exactly what order Chris' lives took place, or what other lives he may have had, but that there was clear alternation between lives as primarily perpetrator and victim is not in doubt. Both Woolger and

Netherton, for example, describe a number of similar cases, and on the face of it these seem to be reasonably understandable within a classical karmic framework of supposed 'action and reaction', or more particularly of 'paying off debts'. But even then one is bound, logically, to ask how subjects are supposed to bring such terrible cycles to an end; and even more how all this works out when apparently unconnected people are, for example, murdered – what are they supposed to do in their next life, murder their previous killer in a never-ending cycle of violence?

That the concept of direct 'action and reaction' is seriously flawed is demonstrated clearly by those cases in which the subjects are consistently the victims, and where regression uncovers no traces of perpetrator lives that might account for their apparent punishment. For example, one of Netherton's patients came to him suffering from impotence and abdominal pains that signaled a potential ulcer brought on by the stress of running his business.[24] Under hypnosis he revealed that he had had an early tribal life in which his lover's husband caught them together, cut his penis off and ran him through the stomach with his spear. A later life was that of an aristocrat in which this former guilt resurfaced when he was about to have sex with a mistress. It was sufficient to cause a perforated stomach from which he eventually died, even though such behavior was generally regarded as perfectly acceptable at the time. In a later life still he was a businessman whose wife conspired with her brother to obtain his money by setting him up to be caught with a prostitute. This time his recurring guilt unhinged him mentally so that he was committed to an asylum, in which he died from the plague. On the face of it this man had repeatedly been the victim, and had done nothing of real note to deserve his succession of unpleasant lives.

Perhaps the most heart-rending case reported by any of the pioneers involves one of Whitton's patients called Jenny Saunders.[25] Identifying that she was masking some strong repressed emotions, over a prolonged and difficult period of conventional regression he managed to establish that she had been cruelly abused by her mother as a child. She therefore avoided sex because any feelings of pleasure brought on by sexual stimulation were immediately replaced by emotional pain and intense anger. This realization might at least have started the healing process, but Jenny's symptoms persisted. Whitton had also discovered that she was terrified of having a child of her own, and not long before becoming his patient had had an abortion after a rare sexual encounter. Apart from the obvious fact that she might not want to repeat the mistakes of her own mother, he could find nothing else in her current life to explain this fear. So he decided to extend the regression back beyond her childhood, at which point the following two lives unfolded.

As Lucy Bowden she had been the poverty-stricken single mother of a mentally retarded child in London in the late seventeenth century. In those days everyone regarded such children as a mere burden to be disposed of, but Lucy cherished and protected her child with all her might. She rarely left her rented attic room because of her fear that someone, whether well meaning or not, might try to rid her of her 'burden'. But one day she went to fetch some provisions, and stopped to have a drink with some friends at an inn. Not used to alcohol, time slipped by quickly until she realized she had been gone for some hours, and rushed home. But when she turned the corner into her street her blazing house was surrounded by curious onlookers. Pushing through the crowd, she realized there was nothing she could do to save her child – and her unbearable inner torment was to set up a recurring pattern.

In another life in the mid-nineteenth century Jenny was Angela, a young girl abandoned by her parents and brought up in a Chicago orphanage. At sixteen she left the harsh institution behind to seek a new life in the mid-west, ending up as a barmaid and part-time prostitute in a small town in Colorado. The local doctor fell in love with her and she became pregnant by him. But, unbeknown to her, the local parson began berating the doctor that his child would be born out of wedlock to a woman of ill repute. Eventually he blackmailed the doctor into agreeing that it should be committed to an institution to preserve its moral sanctity. So as soon as the child was born the parson, the doctor and two assistants came to collect the baby, wrestling it from the convalescing Angela's startled grasp. Instinctively she reached for a shotgun she always kept under her bed for protection, but in the ensuing struggle the weapon discharged right at the baby and the assistant carrying it, killing both instantly. Again Angela's shock and remorse was unbearable, but worse was to come. Their curiosity piqued by the sound of a gunshot, and with the parson egging them on to punish the 'murderer', six cowboys entered the room and dragged her off to a cattle shed, from which she never emerged.

After reliving these horrors Jenny wept uncontrollably in Whitton's office – maybe for the first time in her life. But, for the purposes of the current discussion, again we can see that she was repeatedly the innocent victim. Some therapists would nevertheless maintain that, like Netherton's impotency sufferer, she must have done something awful in other lives that she did not recall under regression in order to deserve such 'punishments'.

Yet this suggestion is entirely undermined when we find that, when Whitton regressed Jenny into her most recent interlife, the primary issue that confronted her was her failure to *forgive herself* for letting her children down in her former lives. But with this insight she did relent and happily, when she left his office for the last time, she was determined to have a child in this life too. Some might suggest that this was Jenny 'paying off debts *to herself*', but surely this hardly helps our understanding.

So if it is rather less than useful to view the dynamics of past-life therapy from the perspective of traditional karmic notions such as 'action and reaction' and 'paying off debts', on what do they depend? Additional clues can be obtained from the relatively simple cases that all therapists report, in which a major trauma from a past life is found to lie at the heart of a patient's current problem. Kelsey's patient who identified with being a woman earlier in the chapter is a good example, and Fiore derives the following list of typical linkages.[26] Patients who are chronically overweight, or by complete contrast have anorexic tendencies, have often been close to starvation in a past life. Fear of the dark and insomnia often relate to previous lives in which the patient was either molested or killed while asleep. Assorted phobias of fire, water, guns, knives, snakes, flying, crowds, enclosed spaces, heights and so on can often be traced to corresponding past-life traumas, usually related to the mode of death. And chronic pains in various parts of the body often stem from injuries, again usually fatal, received in previous lives.

Whatever conflicting signals they might send out when they talk about karma, nearly all therapists do appear to understand the underlying dynamic of such cases. It is that intense emotions – for example of loss, guilt, failure, shame, remorse, sorrow, humiliation, jealousy, anger, hatred or revenge – are always attached to the past-life experiences; and it is our failure to deal with them at the time that leaves them unresolved or unassimilated. In some cases this can lead to a traumatized soul remaining trapped in the intermediate plane, as we saw in chapter 1, but in most cases the emotion is carried forward into a new life. In fact as we will see in later chapters most souls make deliberate choices to work with particular emotions, often over several lives; and this work will be facilitated not only by the deliberate planning of life circumstances, especially in the formative years, but also by certain 'triggers' that act as reminders. These might take the form of phobias or compulsions, and the more severe they are the more intense the unresolved emotion is likely to have been. The exact dynamics will depend a great deal on the level of experience of the soul, and especially on the extent to which they are able to use the interlife to heal emotional trauma.

In any case, the key to healing in a therapeutic context is that the therapist should help the patient to 'reframe' their current problem, either by recognizing it as part of a longer-term destructive pattern that they now want to break free from, or by gaining appropriate insights from the interlife – as, for example, Jenny did. But the dynamics are usually complex, which is why the best modern therapists tend to avoid making simplistic pronouncements about the healing process, and especially about 'action and reaction', 'paying off debts' and so on. They also realize that the patient's higher self is the best judge of what they most need to re-experience, which is why they tend to use 'non-directive' techniques as much as possible.

We will return to the concept of karma, and even more to the whole issue of *why* we reincarnate, in the final chapters.

5

INTERLIFE REGRESSION

Opening the Gateway

The earliest reports of regression not just into a past life but into the time *between* lives actually come from Charles Lancelin in the early twentieth century, but for reasons that will be made clear in chapter 7 this work cannot be regarded as entirely objective. So the first research to deserve that honor is probably that of Alexander Cannon, who in *The Power Within* briefly mentions one subject's experience of being in a 'garden of waiting' before she incarnated into her current body – although it seems he was not inclined to follow this up.[1] By contrast Morey Bernstein deliberately attempted to elicit some information on the topic from Virginia Tighe by asking her what she experienced after Bridey Murphy's death, but her sparse responses provide little of real interest.[2]

Rather more productive, however, was a partnership prompted by this case. Robert Huffman was a staunch Colorado Christian who would not even countenance reincarnation, unlike his wife who risked his wrath by showing him local newspaper reports.[3] But he had had some training in hypnosis and in fact had met Bernstein, so he was persuaded to invite several like-minded people to his home to see if any of them would be good subjects for a similar experiment that would attempt to prove the matter one way or the other. Irene Specht, a housewife in her mid-thirties, entered deep trance easily and was repeatedly able to furnish details of the life of a poor farmer's wife in mid-nineteenth century France. More pertinent here, however, is that in their 1957 collaboration *Many Wonderful Things* we find that she was also able to provide a reasonable amount of information about what happened after this woman's death.

In the following decade the New York parapsychologist Hans Holzer decided to turn his attention to past lives, although at the outset it seems he

146

had no fixed view one way or the other. Again he had had some training as a hypnotist, so when people who had read his books wrote to him about spontaneous visions of the past and so on he was able to regress them to obtain further details that might be investigated. He documents a number of fascinating cases in his 1970 book *Born Again*, although for various reasons none of them are quite strong enough to merit inclusion in chapter 3. But he did ask several of his subjects about the interlife and one in particular, Ruth Macguire, was able to provide interesting details.[4]

It is clear from his transcripts that Holzer, like Huffman before him, was deliberately asking questions about the time between lives. By contrast many of the more professionally trained pioneers who now began to enter the fray seem to have stumbled upon the interlife experience entirely by accident. For example, in 1973 the Toronto Society for Psychical Research agreed to Joel Whitton's proposal to conduct a controlled, long-term study of past-life regression, and after interviewing over fifty candidates he chose Paula Considine. She was a temperamentally stable and unexceptional forty-two-year-old housewife, who was deeply hypnotizable and had no particular feelings about reincarnation one way or the other. In *Life Between Life* his co-author reports how, in their weekly sessions, she regressed into a number of different lives in different eras – when events took a most unexpected turn:[5]

> Paula's inventory of lives had been traced back to an existence of a slave girl in ancient Egypt when, unpredictably, her hypnotic traveling suddenly changed course. One Tuesday evening in April 1974, as she was talking in a deep trance about Martha Paine's life on the farm [an incarnation in the early nineteenth century], Dr Whitton remembered there were further details he wished to learn about the last days of Margaret Campbell [the previous incarnation in the early eighteenth century]. First he interrupted his garrulous subject. Then he told her:
> 'Go to the life before you were Martha.'
> Expecting Martha's childlike voice to be exchanged for that of the elderly Canadian housekeeper, Dr Whitton waited several minutes for the familiar French-accented enunciation. But no sound, save the occasional sigh, came from Paula's mouth. Her lips moved only with a constantly shifting facial expression which indicated she was watching events unfold. But what events were these? Not knowing where she was in time, Dr Whitton was wondering where he had erred when Paula interrupted his bewilderment with a rapid flickering of her eyelids. Her lips, too, puckered repeatedly as if she were searching for words and not finding them. Then, slowly and with great difficulty, she announced in a dreamy monotone:

'I'm in the sky. I can see a farmhouse and a barn. It's early morning. The sun is low and making long shadows across the burnt fields, stubby fields.'

Dr Whitton could barely believe what he was hearing. Paula wasn't supposed to be 'in the sky'. So he must have made a technical error; but which one? Hypnotic subjects have much in common with computer programs in that their wondrous responses rest upon the most literal commands. They must be told exactly what to do. Make one mistake and the show won't go on – at least not the show anticipated by the hypnotist. Dr Whitton had told Paula, 'Go to the life before you were Martha.' Normally, he would have commanded, 'Go to the incarnation before you were Martha.' Clearly there was a difference between the two.

'What are you doing up in the air?' asked the puzzled hypnotist.

'I'm waiting to be born. I'm watching, watching what my mother does.'

'Where is your mother?'

'She's out at the pump and she's having great difficulty, difficulty filling the bucket.'

'Why is she having great difficulty?'

'Because my body is weighing her down. I want to tell her to take care. For her sake and for mine.'

'What is your name?'

'I have no name.'

This is typical of the way in which several other pioneering therapists' imprecise commands led to their discovery of the interlife, as we will shortly see. As was his professional duty Whitton restricted the remainder of his study with Paula to her past lives alone, and objectively concluded in his report: 'There is no reason as yet to suspect that hypnosis will successfully carry the burden of proof of reincarnation.' However, once this was completed his curiosity had been sufficiently aroused that he decided to devote a specific proportion of his practice to interlife research, and over the next decade he conducted multiple between-life sessions with more than thirty subjects.

Of the other pioneers that we have already mentioned, Edith Fiore tantalizes us with the following statement: 'A description of the interim between lifetimes, taken from my patients' fascinating accounts, will have to wait for a future publication. It is a book in itself!' Unfortunately this separate work has never appeared.[6] Nevertheless she found that, of over one thousand patients she took through the death experience in a previous life, many were able to achieve some sort of interlife recall, about which she provides some information in *You Have Been Here Before* and the 1988 follow-up *The Unquiet Dead*, in which she concentrates more on possession. Helen Wambach, spurred on by her initial past-life research results, decided to concentrate specifically on pre-birth questions with seven hundred and fifty volunteers, publishing the results in 1979 in her second book *Life Before Life*.[7] In the late 1970s Peter Ramster too made some interesting discoveries about what happens after death, reporting on them in both *The Truth About Reincarnation* and *The Search for Lives Past*. Meanwhile in *Many Lives, Many Masters* Brian Weiss provided brief reports of the interlife from working with his patient Catherine in the early 1980s.

There are three more pioneers not mentioned in the previous chapter because their books were published somewhat later and they tend to specialize in the interlife. Although she is one of the few not to have a professional background in psychology or psychiatry, Dolores Cannon qualified as a hypnotherapist and set up a practice in Arkansas in 1979. Like Whitton she already had an interest and belief in reincarnation and, rather than work as a therapist, she was specifically motivated to undertake general research into her subjects' past lives. As she relates in her 1993 book *Between Death and Life*, she too appears to have come across the interlife by accident:[8]

> I can still remember the first time I stumbled through the door and spoke to the 'dead'. It was during a past-life regression and when the subject 'died' on me – it happened so quickly and spontaneously that I was taken off guard. I was not fully aware of what had happened. I don't know what I expected would occur if someone were to go through a death experience. But as I said, it happened so quickly there was no time to stop it. The person was looking down at their body and saying they looked just like any other corpse...
>
> When I overcame my shock and wonder of being able to speak with someone after they had died, my curiosity took over and I was filled with questions I had always wondered about. From that time forward, each time I found a subject who could go into the deeper states of hypnosis required for this type of research, I made a practice of asking some of the same questions. Religious beliefs seem to have no influence on what they reported. Their answers were basically identical each time. Although worded differently, they were all saying the same thing – a phenomenon in itself.
>
> Since I began my work in 1979 I have had hundreds and hundreds of people go through the death experience.

We can see from this that Cannon was deliberately asking her more receptive subjects some highly philosophical questions, and as a result some of her session transcripts, like Weiss', read rather like channeled material. But clearly they are still regressions. She also provides little summarized commentary of her own, so in her case in particular we are forced to take extracts from the reports of individual subjects.

When Shakuntala Modi set up her psychiatric practice in West Virginia, she quickly realized that hypnotherapy paid great dividends where other treatments failed. So for many years she conducted conventional age regression, but knew nothing about past lives. Like so many others before her she was completely taken aback when, one day in 1986, she instructed a patient suffering from claustrophobia and crippling panic attacks to go back to the time when these problems arose – and she found she was a young girl who had been buried alive.[9] Modi was even more stunned when the patient was almost immediately cured – a speed of remission that she had never before come close to achieving but, as we have seen, is not unusual with past-life regression. In fact she would go on to concentrate heavily on spirit possession as a potential source of the ailments of many of her patients, like Fiore before her, and her 1997 book *Remarkable Healings* contains a great deal of somewhat dubious material about demonic possession in particular – which seems to be at least partly fuelled by a strong Christian bias. However she also makes it clear that in the intervening decade she had taken hundreds of her patients through the death experience and into the interlife.[10]

Last but by no means least we come to the best-known interlife pioneer of them all, Michael Newton. He qualified as a psychologist and set up in practice in Los Angeles in 1956.[11] As he explains in his 1994 book *Journey of Souls*, although he regularly regressed patients into their childhoods, for some time he resisted the use of past-life therapy – regarding it as 'unorthodox and non-clinical' – until he came across one particular client in the mid-1960s :[12]

My interest in reincarnation and metaphysics was only intellectual curiosity until I worked with a young man on pain management. This client complained of a lifetime of chronic pain on his right side. One of the tools of hypnotherapy to manage pain is directing the subject to make the pain worse so he or she can also learn to lessen the aching and thus acquire control. In one of our sessions involving pain intensification, this man used the imagery of being stabbed to recreate his torment. Searching for the origins of this image, I eventually uncovered his former life as a World War I soldier who was killed by a bayonet in France, and we were able to

150

eliminate the pain altogether.

With encouragement from my clients, I began to experiment with moving some of them further back in time before their last birth on earth... I came to appreciate just how therapeutically important the link is between the bodies and events of our former lives and who we are today.

Following on from this, in 1968 Newton too chanced upon the interlife:[13]

Then I stumbled onto a discovery of enormous proportions. I found it was possible to see into the spirit world through the mind's eye of a hypnotized subject who could report back to me of life *between* lives on earth.

The case that opened the door to the spirit world for me was a middle-aged woman who was an especially receptive hypnosis subject. She had been talking to me about her feelings of loneliness and isolation in that delicate stage when a subject has finished recalling their most recent past life. This unusual individual slipped into the highest state of altered consciousness almost by herself. Without realizing I had initiated an overly short command for this action, I suggested she go to the source of her loss of companionship. At the same moment I inadvertently used one of the trigger words to spiritual recall. I also asked if she had a specific *group* of friends whom she missed.

Suddenly, my client started to cry. When I directed her to tell me what was wrong, she blurted out, 'I miss some friends in my group and that's why I get so lonely on earth.' I was confused and questioned her further about where this group of friends was actually located. 'Here, in my permanent home,' she answered simply, 'and I'm looking at all of them right now!'

From this point on he realized he wanted to find out as much as he could about the interlife, apparently working with subjects numbering in the 'thousands' for over two decades to elicit some of the finest material we have available. He used twenty-nine of these as the case studies for *Journey of Souls*, and sixty-seven for the follow-up *Destiny of Souls*, published in 2000.[14]

The Consistency of the Reports

So much for the attitude of the pioneers to their discoveries. But ultimately all interlife research relies on material arising from regression sessions, which we know can be less than reliable. Moreover, unlike with past-life regression, with the interlife there is no independently verifiable data. So why should we take this research at all seriously?

The key factor is the consistency of the reports that the pioneers' subjects have provided. Although we must be careful to recognize that the experience is far more fluid for each individual subject than some researchers would suggest, there can be no question that it has certain broad elements that consistently emerge. Typically we can identify the following five, which form the basis for the detailed descriptions in the next chapter:[15]

- Transition and Healing
- Past-Life Review
- Soul Group Interaction
- Next-Life Planning
- Returning

Crucial to this argument, however, is whether this consistency merely derives from either the pioneers themselves, or their subjects, being preconditioned as to what to expect. So let us now examine these possibilities.

The Independence and Objectivity of the Pioneers

Virtually none of the interlife pioneers explicitly mention any prior knowledge of the others' work, with two main exceptions. First, Weiss admits that in the early stages of Catherine's treatment he avidly read up on other general past-life research, and specifically mentions the work of Fiore and Wambach, although his subsequent exposure to the interlife still appears to have come as a complete surprise.[16] Second, Modi specifically mentions consulting the work of Wambach and Whitton, among others, after she had stumbled across past lives in general – and, because she provides no details of how she came across the interlife, it is possible that her material is less objective.[17] Apart from this, Weiss and Modi are joined by Holzer and Ramster in mentioning Stevenson's non-interlife-related work.[18] Moreover Weiss, Wambach and Whitton discuss Raymond Moody's contemporary and highly publicized work on near-death experiences, but this is only the tip of the iceberg in terms of the interlife, so it does little to compromise their research.[19]

We should also remember that the bulk of this early work was performed before widespread use of the internet revolutionized the communication in any line of research. What is more Hans TenDam, who knew most of the pioneers at the time, confirms that their work was indeed conducted independently of each other.[20] Meanwhile Newton, whose pioneering research spanned several decades, insists that he 'stayed out of metaphysical bookstores because I wanted absolute freedom from outside bias'.[21]

What about subjective leading of their subjects by the pioneers? There is far more potential for this in interlife than in past-life regression, precisely because of the apparent consistency of the experience. Moreover anyone who has studied a wide variety of transcripts from different therapists can see that some of them tend to push their subjects to answer specific questions and stay within a given framework, while others tend to adopt the more open style of 'so what happens next?' This is why various more detailed aspects of some pioneers' reports will be omitted from the next chapter. But the possibility of subjective leading cannot be used to write off the entire body of interlife research – precisely because, as we have seen, the experience was only independently discovered by many of the pioneers *as a result* of their early subjects leading *them* somewhere they were not expecting to go, and about which they maintain they knew nothing.

The Objectivity of the Subjects

Many of the past-life pioneers stress that their patients came from highly varied backgrounds, both religious and nonreligious, and that many had an initial attitude of total skepticism towards reincarnation. This continues to hold true for those who did some interlife work without concentrating on it exclusively – in particular Fiore, Ramster and Modi – and whose research therefore remained based on a wide cross-section of patients. The same is also likely to be true of Cannon and Newton, despite their rather greater interlife specialization, because they both maintained a large body of subjects. As Newton stresses:[22] 'The clients in my cases represent some men and women who were very religious, while others had no particular spiritual beliefs at all. Most fall somewhere in between, with a mixed bag of personal philosophies about life.' By contrast the fact that Wambach's group subjects volunteered probably suggests that many of them had at least a passing interest in reincarnation, while Whitton says nothing about the backgrounds of his relatively small number of interlife subjects. And Holzer, Huffman and Weiss' information is only provided by one subject each.

In any case, it is highly improbable that anything more than a tiny handful of all the pioneers' original subjects had any significant prior knowledge that could have conditioned their experiences, precisely because of the minimal public exposure this early research received. If we start with the most recent publications and work backwards, certainly Cannon's and Newton's books have sold extremely well, with Modi's perhaps somewhat behind, but none of them is exactly a household name. Not only that but, even if their books have had some reasonably widespread cultural influence since their more or less simultaneous publication in the mid-1990s, this does not discount the experiences of their own subjects that obviously arose beforehand. Prior to that the research of Whitton and Wambach, published in the mid-1980s and late 1970s respectively, did not gain widespread public exposure. On top of that we have seen that Fiore published few details of her interlife research in any of her books, while Ramster's work has always remained little known outside of Australia. As for those researchers who had only one main subject, Weiss' book sold well when it was published in the late 1980s but this is far too late to have influenced the main pioneering research, while Catherine's case is not exactly fully representative of the interlife experience anyway. The same is true of Holzer's subject Ruth, even though he himself would go on to become well known for his investigation of the 'Amityville Horror' among other things. And Huffman's work did not receive widespread attention in the 1950s when it was first published, or thereafter.

As for other potential sources, we will see in chapter 7 that a number of mainly channeled books published previously did discuss the time between lives in some detail and in highly similar terms. However it is probably fair to suggest that they too were insufficiently well known and far reaching to be likely to have exerted a significant influence on the broad span of the population represented by most of the pioneers' subjects.

Of course we should be clear that since the turn of the century Newton's books in particular have become widely read in spiritual circles, even if he is still not a general household name. That is why more recent research, such as that conducted by good friend and colleague Andy Tomlinson – who is now one of Europe's leading interlife regression specialists, having trained under Newton himself – must be treated with rather more caution. His 2007 book *Exploring the Eternal Soul* is the first to properly follow a number of clearly identified subjects right through the whole interlife experience. But when we were working together to select the subjects we were forced to recognize the extent to which he had tended to attract people who had varying degrees of prior knowledge of the interlife. Nevertheless we knew that at least some of them had never read or heard anything about the topic, and yet still managed to come up with consistent reports. Accordingly some of this testimony will be incorporated in the next chapter where it adds to the pioneering research. We also worked very closely together to produce *The Wisdom of the Soul*, and certain elements of that research will be included where relevant.

The underlying consistency of interlife testimony from thousands of disparate subjects working with a variety of independently operating pioneers would seem to give it a great deal of credibility. Indeed it is arguably one of the most profound sources of spiritual wisdom that has ever been available to humanity. Its strength lies in its very derivation from countless ordinary men and women, with no fixed preconceptions, no pretensions as spiritual gurus, and no axe to grind.

6

THE INTERLIFE
EXPERIENCE

Fluidity and Individuality

We have seen that mere past-life regressions can be conducted using the relatively light level of trance characterized by the alpha brainwave state. By contrast, despite the pioneers often stumbling upon the interlife, therapists generally seem to agree that regressing subjects into their time between lives requires the deeper levels of the theta state.[1] However there is no significant tendency for people to be able to enter the alpha but not the theta state, so anyone who responds to hypnosis should be able to regress not only to a past life but also to the interlife.

As to the experience itself, it is impossible to overemphasize the extent to which it should be seen as fluid and individual. We have seen that Michael Newton is by some margin the best known and most widely read of all the pioneers, and his dedicated efforts to investigate and report on the interlife have rightly earned him widespread praise. However, if we are to remain objective and professional, Newton's work in particular must come with a health warning. On first acquaintance with the regression transcripts in his books, the untrained observer tends to be overawed by the quality and detail of the information that emerges. This feeling is reinforced by the regularity with which they laugh at, scold or contradict him when he appears to be ignorant of any particular issue, suggesting that they are in no mood to be led to experience something that is not validly happening in their trance at the time.

However, at least off the record some professional hypnotherapists make rather more critical assessments of his work, even when they are not necessarily skeptical about the broad concept of the interlife.[2] They suggest that, in his determination to investigate and especially to classify the experience, Newton has ended up leading his subjects rather too much to stay within the specific framework he has devised. Particular areas of concern include his classifications of levels of soul 'advancement', symbolized by the colors of their energy fields; of the various types of 'soul groups'; of the specific makeup of various 'councils', and of the symbols worn around the necks of the wise 'elders' that make them up; of the specific terminology used for various 'places'; and of certain types of more advanced activity and specialist training. Most of these are found in both of his main books, although there is far more detail in the second, and they are arguably aspects of his research where subjective influence may have played a part. Of course the same problem afflicts certain aspects of the other pioneers' research as well, but in most cases to a significantly lesser extent, not least because they were not investigating the experience as thoroughly as Newton. We will not be examining any of these more suspect areas in the sections that follow.

What we will be doing is seeing just how consistent a thread is woven by all the pioneers' subjects around the five broad elements of the experience described in the previous chapter. But even then we should appreciate that they are not all experienced by every subject during every interlife regression. For example, sometimes the emphasis may be more on review than on planning, or vice versa. This does not necessarily mean that each of the elements is not experienced by most souls during the interlife *proper*, at least to some degree; but it does mean that, when we are *recalling* the experience in human form, some aspects may be more important than others. We should also recognize that, broadly speaking, each interlife experience between each pair of earthly lives is unique and different for each of us. However, subjects also report that existence in the light realms represents an 'eternal now', in which not only elapsed but even sequential time becomes largely unimportant. So our recall of our time between lives under regression can only approximate to the true, timeless experience – and it will be deliberately framed in terms that our somewhat restricted human perceptions can understand.

Before we start to look at the details, there are two further riders that should be placed on this material. Just as we saw in chapter 1 with near-death and out-of-body experiences, the interlife pioneers confirm that souls tend to project quasi-physical qualities onto their surroundings and the other souls they encounter in the light realms – rather than perceiving them in more purely energetic terms – to make them feel at home. In seems this tendency may be more prevalent when they are reorienting themselves after death, or if they are less experienced. But we will also find that most subjects continue to describe all aspects of the light realms in quasi-physical terms – indeed there seem to be certain archetypes, for example of 'libraries' containing 'life books', and of 'elders and councils', that arise repeatedly. This could be because this is what they *actually* perceive in the real experience, or it could be merely because these provide the easiest way of *explaining* various aspects of the interlife in human terms when recalling it while still incarnate. In general, however, it remains likely that this tendency to project will reduce with experience.

Related to this, we have also seen that research into near-death and out-of-body experiences suggests the realms we encounter after death are in large part created by our own thoughts, feelings and emotions. So surely our perception of these must also be influenced by our cultural conditioning and expectations. On that basis, we should recognize that virtually all of our pioneers' subjects have come from the Westernized world in their current life. Admittedly some interlife regressions are preceded by a life in another part of the world, but the fact that these do not seem to make a great deal of difference to their experience could simply reflect the overriding influence their current culture has on their *recall*. In any case, as yet there have been no published studies of the interlife from, for example, Asia, Africa or South America – and it would be fascinating to establish whether the five broad elements, and the main archetypes, would be corroborated without any subjective leading by the therapist.

Transition and Healing

There are various aspects of our transition to the light realms. In chapter 1 we discussed the typical near-death features of the tunnel and light, and of some sort of welcoming party, and broadly speaking these are corroborated by interlife research. But it also provides descriptions of various aspects of healing and reintegration that only occur during death proper, as well as a view of what happens to more traumatized souls.

Leaving the Body

Joel Whitton's co-author provides a typical summary of the dying process:[3]

> The much publicized 'tunnel' experience – an archetype of transition – is a common feature of the withdrawal from earthbound existence. Time and

time again, Dr Whitton's subjects have told of 'seeing' their bodies lying beneath them before being pulled rapidly through a high, cylindrical passageway. They then discover they have left their physical bodies and cannot comfort and reassure relatives and friends who have been left behind. In most cases, however, the onset of strange and wonderful experiences soon dissipates all earthbound attachment. The tube or tunnel appears to serve as the channel of conveyance to the afterworld.

This idea that departing souls cannot comfort their loved ones is confirmed by Peter Ramster, who also emphasizes the consistency of his subjects' reports:[4]

> The same sorts of statements are made over and over again by many different people. A statement one might feel to be a bit fanciful is sometimes actually confirmed by someone else, without that person having been asked to confirm it. Many people describe how, after death, they felt themselves being pulled along a tunnel. They speak of a bright light towards which they move after emerging from the tunnel. Many of them also describe how, after death, they remained watching their relatives, sometimes still trying to talk to them, but to no avail.

But elsewhere we find that the tunnel experience is by no means universal amongst Ramster's subjects:

> After this the world seemed to become blurred, and they found themselves being pulled along, slowly at first, then faster. Some people said that they were pulled along at what seemed to be a very high speed. Some described this as a wind or a force; others didn't seem to know how or where they were traveling; and still others described themselves as moving through a tunnel, or something resembling a tunnel or a tube. It was after this stage that most people saw a light... described as being very bright... seeming to come from everywhere.

Newton too confirms the difficulty in talking to loved ones, and agrees that the tunnel is by no means there for all subjects:[5]

> They find themselves floating around their bodies in a strange way... They say they are frustrated in their attempts to talk to living people who don't respond. They state they feel a pulling sensation away from the place where they died and experience relaxation and curiosity rather than fear. All these people seem to report a euphoric sense of freedom and brightness around them. Some of my subjects see brilliant whiteness totally surrounding them at the moment of death, while others observe the brightness is further away from an area of darker space through which they are being pulled. This is often referred to as the tunnel effect.

Meanwhile Edith Fiore provides the following summary of the initial transition:[6]

> Almost all people experiencing dying under hypnosis use the word 'floating' to describe the immediate bodily sensations after death. They feel themselves rising into the air and viewing the scene below. They report hearing loud noises – ringing, buzzing, celestial music. A few have experienced going through a tunnel with a light at the other end.

We can again see from this that the tunnel is not always reported, and this theme continues. Hans Holzer's subject Ruth describes 'moving on a floating ribbon of light towards the light'.[7] Similarly Shakuntala Modi does not mention the tunnel at all:[8] 'My patients describe being lifted up and drawn toward the bright white Light. They describe feeling loved and free of the concerns they felt before and just after the death of their body.' Nor does Dolores Cannon mention it, although one of her subjects does provide a wonderful and rather unique description of what it is like to die:[9]

> Have you ever dived into a deep pool, to where it's dark and murky at the bottom? As you come back up towards the surface of the water it gets lighter and lighter. Then when you break through the surface of the water there's sunlight all around. Death was like that... Dying is pleasant. If people are worried about it, tell them to go to a place in the river that has a deep pool. Tell them to dive down to the bottom of the pool. And then, at the bottom push up vigorously with their feet and come plunging up to the surface.

This same subject goes on to discuss the fact that souls can release themselves from the body even *before* death in order to escape undue trauma from any physical pain and shock, unless this is a lesson they particularly need. And another of Cannon's subjects discusses the fact that – unlike with near-death and out-of-body experiences, where there is a need to return – during death proper the ubiquitous 'silver cord' is severed.

Welcoming Parties

Holzer's subject Ruth describes meeting her then mother after her previous life;[10] and more generally Whitton's subjects report being met by 'a deceased relative or friend, a conductor, or a guide who has been watching over their charge during the last life'.[11] Newton confirms that his subjects are usually met by soul mates or by a guide – the latter especially if they are somewhat traumatized.[12] He adds that 'souls often use their capacity to project former life forms when communicating with each other', and that 'they will show you what *they* want you to see... and what they think *you* want to see'.

One of Cannon's subjects supports this idea of flexible projection of earthly identity:[13]

> There is a period of orientation or *reorientation*, which can be confusing to some as they figure out where they should go from here. But they needn't worry because help is sent immediately. Usually a handful of souls will come that you have had close karmic connections with in former lifetimes... So you'll recognize those souls. First, initially in the relationship you knew them in the life you just left. Then you'll start remembering other relationships where you've known them.

Modi reports along similar lines:[14] 'Patients often describe being greeted by Light beings, who can be angels, a religious figure, a guide, or anyone they believe in. At times they see their departed loved ones in the Light.' She too indicates that these departed souls from that past life tend to project their best image: 'They look younger and in perfect health... Patients usually describe them as beings of Light with loving eyes, wearing white robes and totally surrounded by the white Light.' She adds that her patients are able to recognize how these people from their previous lives relate to those in their current life.

Several of Ramster's subjects also emphasize the wisdom and love emanating from those who come to meet them:[15]

> One woman described the person who met her in the following terms: 'He wasn't very old, but he had a beautiful face, and I felt I knew him before, but I didn't. All around him was wisdom.' In another description, from another subject, I was told that 'He was neither young nor old, he was a beautiful person, very kind, and he had a sort of peacefulness about him. He seemed very wise.'

And Fiore confirms this impression:[16]

> After the sensation of floating, often within a few seconds, the presence of spiritual guides or a 'guardian angel' is felt. Many experience them as a bright light – but a light with a benign, loving essence – there to help. Sometimes, the transition is aided by more definitive entities. The person is often greeted by deceased relatives or friends.

Initial Perceptions of the Light Realms

Newton reports that his subjects often hear celestial music, and that they see familiar and comforting images to ease their transition that include 'fields of wildflowers, castle towers rising in the distance, or rainbows under an open sky'.[17] Whitton's subjects similarly describe 'splendid palaces... beautiful gardens... landscapes with waves lapping on the shore... and churches and schools and libraries and playgrounds'.[18] Ramster's too report seeing 'animals and birds, houses and cottages, rivers and streams, grass, flowers, music, big buildings'.[19]

We have already introduced the idea that the returning soul's expectations will largely create the environment they encounter, a point one of Cannon's subjects emphasizes:[20]

> That which you expect to find or that reality you create, you do indeed find... Anything is possible if they believe in it... If they expect to meet guides or friends along the way to help them toward the light, this is what they will see. If they were steeped in the belief of damnation and hellfire and if they believe that they deserve this, this is what they shall also perceive. Most of this is based upon the preparation of the individual soul prior to death.

We will return to the possibility of hellfire shortly. In the meantime Modi makes a distinction between the 'outer' and 'inner' sections of 'heaven'.[21] The outer section is used for rest and recuperation, and it is here that quasi-physical form is still recognized: 'Different patients have a different representation of this place in heaven. The more common representation is of a beautiful garden, an open field with a meadow with trees and flowers, or a house with a bed.' Then, when they enter the inner sanctum, they shed all vestiges of physicality and everything is now in energy form. This is consistent with other reports, except that it is probably a misinterpretation to suggest these are two separate 'places', rather than the different perceptions of souls who have different levels of experience, or who are at different stages of reorientation.

Perhaps one of the most sophisticated discussions of how we form our impressions of the light realms is provided by Kenneth Ring.[22] He bases his arguments on the work of holographic theorist Karl Pribram, to whose ideas we will return in the final chapter. But for now, according to Ring, when we step away from this physical world – either during a near-death experience or after actual death – we need some time to become reacquainted with the way this quite different holographic domain operates.

Healing and Delayering

Ramster emphasizes: 'One of the most common experiences... is the feeling of tiredness. Almost without exception my subjects remembered sleeping or resting after they had died.'[23] Brian Weiss' patient Catherine confirms the idea of at least initial rest and recuperation by referring to souls going to the 'plane of renewal', while Robert Huffman's subject Irene similarly makes repeated references to a 'resting place'.[24] Newton too discusses the idea of general rest, especially for less experienced souls or those who have had a difficult life.[25] But one of his subjects also provides an interesting description of a 'shower of healing':[26]

> I'm propelled in and I see a bright warm beam. It reaches out to me as a stream of liquid energy. There is a vapor-like steam swirling around me at first, then gently touching my soul as if it were alive. Then it is absorbed into me as fire and I am bathed and cleansed from my hurts... I am suspended in the light, it permeates through my soul, washing out most of the negative viruses. It allows me to let go of the bonds of my last life, bringing about my transformation so I can become whole again.

A similar experience seems to be hinted at by Whitton's subjects who 'find themselves enveloped in a brilliant vault of light that radiates sensations of blissfulness and peace'.[27] One of Cannon's subjects briefly mentions a 'place of healing', while another goes into rather more detail about a 'temple of healing' that projects 'waves of color and energy all around me, taking out all my pain and soreness' and 'negative energy'.[28] Meanwhile yet another provides what is perhaps a rather more perceptive description:[29]

> When you die it's a lifting of weight. It's relaxing. People carry all those problems around. And it's like they are carrying around a weight because they are heavy and laden with all these other things. When you die it's like tossing them out the window and it feels good.

But perhaps Modi sums up this healing best:[30]

According to my patients, everybody goes through the stage of cleansing before they enter the main part of heaven. Patients describe different representations or symbolism for this stage. Some mention the similarity to taking a shower, where a burst of Light cleanses them; a sauna; a process of dry cleaning; bathing in the river; or walking through a river of Light. Some report standing under a waterfall and being cleansed from all impurities. Others describe a mechanical spinning process where the negative stuff is thrown off, or a vacuum cleaner sucking out all the impurities. Negative emotions and attitudes are removed, but not the memories of them.

She carries on to report how, as a therapist and as part of this healing process, she actively helps her patients to retrieve all the fragments of energy that split off from them during particular emotional or physical traumas in incarnate life. And it may be that after death most souls go through some sort of similar process as part of their proper transition and healing.[31]

To return to the topic of the tunnel for a moment, we saw earlier that it is by no means universally reported by interlife subjects. Perhaps one of the most interesting explanations for this comes from another holographic theorist and consciousness researcher, Itzhak Bentov. According to Ring, Bentov suggests that the tunnel actually represents our limited human perception of the shift in consciousness that takes place as we free ourselves from the physical body and its limitations – although he adds that for more experienced astral travelers this perception is no longer required.[32]

Perhaps now we can go even further and suggest that the whole idea of the tunnel and of the shift in consciousness is combined with our shedding of the heavier and denser emotions and energies associated with the physical plane, so that our energy becomes lighter and less dense. We might refer to this composite process as 'delayering', because several of Andy Tomlinson's subjects specifically describe 'moving through or shedding layers'.[33] One in particular has this to say:

> I feel that these layers are somehow preparing me, helping me to shed the different aspects of life that I can't take with me. I feel like they're preparing any residue of physicality that I bring with me, any links to my body. It's part of a healing process, but I seem to be just visiting each layer and moving on very quickly.

It seems that this represents *the* essential process by which we raise our vibration level sufficiently to return to our true home in the light realms – because without it we simply would not be able to operate at these higher frequencies. It also seems that while more experienced souls learn to do all this for themselves, other might receive some assistance. One of Tomlinson's more experienced souls provides a fascinating description of how he goes about providing such help:

> I can see the energies of the whole person, and just after they die it's like a tangled knot. It's just like a knotted ball of string inside them, and together we draw it out and I help them untangle it. There's something very intimate about it. It needs a lot of mutual trust and sensitivity. You cannot just grab hold of it and tug it, you have to understand what the strands are, each one is a feeling or thought. All the fears, anger and pain.

Meanwhile, although Fiore says little about healing per se, one of her patients does provide what seems to be a similar description of how her guide and various other souls help her during a difficult transition:[34] 'I'm leaving my pain. They are making me feel happy. They are giving me strength, eliminating my confusion, guiding me.'

Reintegrating Soul Energy

Newton alone explores the idea that souls make a deliberate decision about how much of their energy to take into incarnation, dependent upon their level of experience and the challenges of the life they are about to face.[35] As to that element that remains in the light realms, it would almost certainly be appropriate to suggest that this is exactly our higher or 'soul' self. So an additional aspect of the transition is that at some point the returning soul will reunite with the energy it left behind. Newton provides reports from several subjects on this dramatic infusion of soul energy and awareness:

> Once contact is made, the rest of my energy comes into me as a magnet. I feel so expanded by it.

> She [the subject's guide] moves close to me, stimulating my natural vibrational frequency to accept more easily what I left behind. As my core center is filled with my own essence, the outer shell of my physical body imprint is melted off.

However this last subject carries on that 'it is as if I were a dog shaking off water droplets from my fur after getting wet... the unwanted earthly particles are jarred loose'. The similarity of this with the previous descriptions of healing seems to suggest that this reintegration may, at least sometimes, be just another part of the delayering process.

Modi seems to corroborate this idea when she reports on what happens as part of the initial 'resting phase':[36] 'Here patients report that they let go of the past life personality. They do not destroy it, but incorporate it into themselves, making themselves much greater than the individual personality they just lived... They get their real spiritual self on the surface.' For her, this integration is tied into the entry into the inner sanctum where the astral body is shed completely – which seems to support the suggestion that all these aspects are very much interlinked, if not all part of one composite transition and healing process.

Dealing with Trauma

We have already seen in chapter 1 that those who have suffered a sudden and perhaps traumatic death can remain so focused on unfinished business, or so aggrieved by what they perceive as a great injustice, that they remain trapped in the intermediate plane. Whitton reports that 'the shock of violent death often causes the disembodied soul to linger on the earthbound plane, perhaps out of bafflement, fury, self-pity or the desire for vengeance'.[37] Meanwhile one of Cannon's subjects confirms a number of general perceptions.[38] Some spirits may not even realize or at least accept they are dead, while others know they have passed on but are expecting to return to a physical body straight away. They continue to hang around the intermediate plane, tending to remain attracted to the geographical location of their home or death and, because of their confusion and frustration, they can make a nuisance of themselves to incarnate humans – perhaps attempting to attach to or even possess them.[39] It seems that such spirits are simply unable to see the light or any welcoming party because their own energy vibrations remain so dense. However Newton reports that sooner or later such souls *will* perceive and enter the light, with help from either human mediums or spirit guides.[40]

So what happens when more traumatized souls enter the light realms, whether after a period trapped in the intermediate plane or not? Modi reports as follows:[41] 'If the life just lived was extremely traumatic and they are still feeling confused, angry or guilty, then they are taken to a room where there are some Light beings waiting for them. Here the patients are allowed to ventilate their feelings about what happened.' One of Cannon's subjects talks in similar terms:[42] 'There is a special place for damaged souls to go to rest and restore themselves before they can enter the company of other souls or enter the plane of incarnation again... Some people, if it is a traumatic death, go into a period of deep, deep resting until they can handle the experience of knowing that their body has ceased to exist.' Ramster reports that there are 'hospitals' for 'spirits who are in a state of confusion, such as those of people who will not or cannot accept their death, or who still try to exist on the earth plane even though they can't be heard or seen'.[43] And Newton follows a similar line by suggesting that seriously damaged souls are taken to a secluded part of the light realms where they undergo a process of isolation and rehabilitation.[44]

A good example of this seems to be provided by Holzer's subject Ruth, who had just relived a traumatic previous life as a colonial wife in mid-nineteenth century India.[45] She was raped by a local man during an uprising, after which her husband regarded her as unclean, so when on board ship on their return to England she decided to end her life by drowning. Although somewhat confused after her death, she does seem to confirm our ideas about delayering when she describes herself 'growing or breathing, or something of that sort, and it just happened to you, and then I continued onwards towards the light'. She was then given instructions by a 'wise man' or 'elder of some sort':

I remember being told to be good and to be compliant and I would learn why the terrible things had happened to me, and that I must learn that no matter how cruelly I had been treated, or how senselessly, savagely, I must treat it all with love, love, love. No resentment, no sharp edges, just kind of a soft, lovely, relaxed receptiveness... They said if I did that I would grow. I was very frightened when I went over, and I hated my husband for being so stubborn and stupid, and I hated the man who had assaulted me.

Her companion then reemphasized that she must 'lose all the resentment that she was still holding', after which she went into a 'kind of sleep' during which she 'seemed to be learning things'.

Hellish Realms

In chapter 1 we also conjectured that near-death and out-of-body visits to the intermediate plane, in which tormented earthbound spirits remain trapped, are the most likely source for historical reports of hellish realms. It is important to emphasize that most interlife subjects do not report anything of this nature, probably because after death proper most of us raise our vibrations sufficiently that we automatically pass through this plane. However Ramster does briefly mention that some of his subjects experience 'places of trouble and unrest' before they move onto 'places of great beauty and tranquility'.[46] So we must surely allow for the fact that *some* souls might find themselves having to traverse or negotiate the intermediate plane in some fashion – especially if they were carrying particularly heavy energies and emotions – and we will return to this topic later.

More than this, though, is there any interlife evidence for a more permanent hell that might act as a counterpoint to 'heaven' – as proposed, for example, not only in Christianity, Judaism and Islam, but also to some extent in Hinduism?[47] Or, instead, are there merely experiences of self-imposed and temporary exile that do not involve separate realms at all?

Fiore explicitly reports that she has never encountered anything approximating to the popular concept of hell.[48] Newton too is adamant there is no such thing, but he accepts that disturbed souls can project their own mental torments onto their surroundings while in seclusion.[49]

Meanwhile, although Roger Woolger does not discuss the interlife in much detail for reasons we will discuss later, his patients do sometimes provide corroboration of the main pioneering research. In the current context he reports on one called Madeleine who, in a past life as a pirate, had taken great pleasure in the torture and execution of her captives.[50] After death in that life he entered a hellish interlife exile, clearly of his own making, in which he saw all the people he had made to suffer:

> I'm punishing myself. In this dimension a part of me knows that this is what I have to do to atone for what I have done to others, and in order to be human again I have to feel what my victims must have felt before they died, desolate, alone and without hope.

Nevertheless as we might expect this self-imposed torment did not last forever:

> There's a light ahead of me; it's starting to get warm. I'm stepping onto the grass. There are people and voices ahead of me and I hear an authoritative voice which says: 'Enough, enough. You have done enough.' I know now that my punishment is over.

One of Cannon's subjects confirms in some detail the extent to which any interlife exile is self-imposed and temporary, and to which traditional religions have relied on misinterpretations of near-death experiences:[51]

> The nearest thing I can see that would possibly equate with purgatory would be the place of resting for the damaged souls. But it is not a place of punishment, not like the Catholics imply with their term of purgatory. There's really no such specific place as purgatory or hell... The condition of hell is all a matter of what state your mind is in during the period of transition. The idea of heaven or hell has become somewhat of a fable or a legend from your perspective. Those who choose to believe this create their own reality to such an extent that when they do pass over they find that elemental reality that they themselves helped to create, and therefore it is indeed real. The descriptions of heaven and hell in your holy writings are a result of people who have had near-death experiences. They come back and describe what they saw. And what they saw was how they perceived the spiritual energies around them during the period of transition. But they did not cross over far enough to be able to realize what was actually going on. If they reported something that was good and very pleasant, that was reported as being heaven. Those who reported something that was very horrible and terrible, that was reported as being hell... Religion was corrupted into a political or power play, such that what was spiritual became a tool for the sublimation of the masses in order to control their behavior. There are in

their embellishments some aspects which would perhaps be true in a very elementary sense. However, the overall picture is grossly misunderstood at this time by most on the physical plane.

This is how another of Cannon's subjects reinforces the point about power:

> There's no such punishment as saying this person is going to be thrown into the pit of fire for everlasting. There's no such thing, unless that person is punishing themselves in that manner. 'They' don't do it... For centuries that was the control they had over the people, the masses. By saying, if you don't do what we say, then you will burn in – as they called it – hell.

Past-Life Review

In the Christianized world we are familiar with the idea of St Peter judging us at the gates of heaven, and most religions down the ages have incorporated some form of life review after death. So it comes as no great surprise that interlife subjects report that, either as part of their initial healing or not long afterwards, they participate in some kind of review of the life just passed. They tend to do this either with a spirit guide, or with some sort of council of elders.

Guide Reviews and the Library of Life Books

Newton alone talks about reviews with spirit guides forming part of the initial healing and orientation.[52] Most of the other pioneers' subjects tend to place non-elder reviews in the archetypal 'library' setting. This aspect of the light realms bears all the hallmarks of the universal memory that we have discussed previously – or the 'akashic records' as it is commonly known in esoteric circles, the Sanskrit word *akasha* meaning 'ether' or 'boundless space'. Subjects describe conducting reviews in this library either with their spirit guide or with the assistance of one or more 'librarians', who locate the correct 'life book' from the subject's collection. These books then take on a three-dimensional screen quality that allows the subject to 'replay' scenes from a past life in total detail. Or they can also be used to 'role-play' alternative courses of action, which can be played out so the subject can observe how their life would have evolved if they had made different decisions at key points.

As an example, one of Newton's subjects committed suicide as a pregnant farm girl in Victorian England.[53] Her young lover had just died, and she was unable to face telling her parents that she was about to be an unmarried mother, or the horrors of running away to London to a life of almost certain prostitution. She was shown a number of alternatives, one of which was indeed a pretty wretched life in London as a prostitute who died young – but also others in which her parents, although angry, helped her to have as normal a life as possible with her child. The life books can even be used by souls to place themselves in the shoes of others, to see exactly what effect their actions had on them. For example, another of Newton's subjects was shown scenes from his early childhood in a past life when he had been a bully at school and, as well as reliving these events as himself, he switched and became another young child who was on the receiving end. Nothing could have better shown him the pain he caused others at this time.

Ramster reports that his subjects consistently refer to conducting reviews in a library setting.[54] In particular Gwen McDonald, who we met in chapter 3, describes visiting a 'Hall of Records' after her life as Rose Duncan:[55]

> We walked to the Hall of Records and that was where I met the Egyptian. He was so kind, he showed me all I had done, things I should have done but didn't do. The place was like a library and it's full of records. It was a big place, a very big place. It had a long corridor with a sort of gold light everywhere inside. He showed me my life, but I could see it in my mind, not on paper, all the things I'd done, things I needed to do and didn't do. The thing I needed to do was to be more conscious of other people. I was selfish, I only thought about myself and where I lived, my home and not the poor people in the village and the poor children. I should have helped, but I didn't. His voice is almost music, and there is a light that shines around him. When he looks at you his eyes seem to read what you are thinking, he seems to know. I was told that in the Hall of Records there is a file on every living soul that ever incarnated and each time we have to see what fools we've been, what mistakes we've made. We have two paths to choose. If you take the wrong path it's all against you, if you take the right path it's all for you, and it's balanced out in the Hall of Records, and it's all there, every page, almost every thought and every deed is there, every book, every spoken word you can find. It's gold inside, lit up with a gold light, pure light. Everything in there is knowledge, and the keeper, the Egyptian in this plane, looks after and controls the records.

Bearing in mind that neither Gwen herself nor Rose showed any inclination towards ancient mysticism, it seems that the Egyptian setting and symbolism – which is often encountered in interlife reports – may represent a particularly popular version of the library archetype. In addition her description of a 'right and wrong path' has echoes of the idea of 'right action' that we will discuss in the final chapter.

Meanwhile Weiss briefly indicates that, according to his patient Catherine, life reviews occur on the 'plane of recollection' in which 'you are allowed to collect your thoughts... and see your life that has just passed'.[56] And Fiore merely reports that many of her patients confirm the general idea of learning from life reviews, although we will see shortly that she discusses the idea of life films separately in the context of the elder review.[57] We will also encounter the library setting again, with other pioneers, when we come to the ongoing learning element of the experience.

Reviews with the Elders

Whitton's co-author provides a typical and detailed description of elder review meetings:[58]

> Nearly all who ventured into metaconsciousness have found themselves appearing before a group of wise, elderly beings – usually three in number, occasionally four, and in rare instances as many as seven – perceived in a variety of guises. They can be of indeterminate identity or they may take on the appearance of mythological gods or religious masters...
>
> The members of this etheric tribunal are highly advanced spiritually and may even have completed their cycle of earthly incarnations. Knowing intuitively everything there is to be known about the person who stands before them, their role is to assist that individual in evaluating the life that has just passed and, eventually, to make recommendations concerning the next incarnation.
>
> If there is a private hell in the life between life, it is the moment when the soul presents itself for review. This is when remorse, guilt, and self-recrimination for failings in the last incarnation are vented with a visceral intensity that produces anguish and bitter tears on a scale that can be quite unsettling to witness. While incarnate, one's negative actions can be rationalized and repressed; there are always plenty of excuses available. In the interlife the emotions generated by these actions emerge raw and irreconcilable. Any emotional suffering that was inflicted on others is felt as keenly as if it were inflicted on oneself...
>
> The judges radiate a restorative, healing energy that abolishes any handicaps and assuages all guilt... Rather than confirm the self-loathing and dissatisfaction of the contrite soul, the board of judgment expresses encouragement, pointing out where the life has been positive and progressive. It's as if they are saying, 'Come on now, your life wasn't *that* bad'...
>
> For the purposes of self-assessment, the soul is confronted with an instantaneous panoramic flashback which contains every single detail of the

last incarnation... Said one subject: 'It's like climbing inside a movie of your life. Every moment from every year of your life is played back in complete sensory detail. Total, total recall. And it all happens in an instant.'

The review tells the soul more about the last life than the individual alone could ever hope to realize, even with full restoration of memory. An entire world of which the individual was not aware is given expression. The larger picture is etched in vivid detail so that the soul realizes for the first time when happiness was thrown away or when thoughtlessness caused pain in another or when life-threatening danger was just around the corner.

The soul absorbs every jot of meaning from this personalized videotape and this precipitates a rigorous exercise in self-analysis. This is the soul's moment of truth and, as it proceeds, the judges tend to remain in the background. They do not, according to Dr Whitton's subjects, act in the authoritarian manner suggested by cultural tradition. Rather, they behave more like loving teachers whose aim is to encourage their student to learn and benefit from past mistakes. The board of judgment frequently initiates discussion of critical episodes in the last life, offers retrospective counsel, and instills reassurance that each experience, no matter how unsavory, promotes personal development.

The individual's hopes, friendships, ideals, esthetic inclinations, and mental processes all form part of the review. Emotionalism is kept to a minimum as the judges gently assist the soul in an objective understanding of its actions within the larger context of many lives. Only by observing karmic trends and patterns – always difficult to discern within a single lifetime – can the soul gain some measure of its progress on the long, long journey of spiritual evolution.

We can see clearly from this the supreme difference between the testimony of interlife subjects and traditional religious views: it is that during the life review the only judgment comes, if at all, from the recently arrived souls *themselves*. Any more experienced souls in attendance merely seem to act as benevolent counselors. In fact, far from making harsh judgments, when souls are being too hard on themselves they encourage them to look at the positives. The soul's own judgment arises because its newly rediscovered 'soul perspective' is totally unlike human perception, and cannot include self-deception or excuses. All actions and – even more important – intentions are laid bare. This extract also confirms the idea of feeling the pain we have caused others, and of gaining the broader perspective of other potential outcomes if we had acted differently.

Modi's description of elder reviews confirms these common themes of self-judgment and the ability to replay past events from different perspectives:[59]

Patients describe going to another room after cleansing, where there are one to five or even more beings waiting for them... These beings serve as counselors who help in reviewing the life. They usually have a broader perspective and clear understanding of the nature of the Light and the universe.

Patients describe reviewing their whole life with the help of these counselors. Together they review their purpose for that life and the lessons they learned or failed to learn. They also evaluate their spiritual achievements.

According to patients, the function of the Light beings who help them review their life is not to judge or condemn them. Their function is to help them get the information out in such a way that the patients can see and understand it clearly. Patients usually say this is the most difficult stage, because it is they who judge themselves. There is no judgment or punishment by God or the Light beings who are helping them. Patients are their own harshest judge and jury.

Patients often describe this as a process of self-analysis and evaluation of the life they just lived. They alone interpret their success or failure in meeting the goals they set in the Light for that life. Their feelings of disappointment and bitterness over lost opportunities and wrong actions cannot be adequately described. Their feelings of success and triumph about goals they achieved and good acts are just as remarkable and hard to convey. This is the stage in which patients come to grips with the harm they did to themselves and others by suicide, murder, and other negative actions.

During the review, patients not only assess every good and bad thing they did, but also experience other people's feelings. In heaven, patients describe themselves as nonphysical spirits. There are no barriers of time and space. Patients can return to any moment in the lifetime they just departed and observe the events from different points of view.

As we might expect Newton discusses the idea of the elder review in some detail, and his thrust is broadly similar.[60] Perhaps most useful is the way one of his subjects emphasizes that, to the elders, it is the little things in life that matter:[61]

'We are not here to judge you, punish you, or to override your thoughts. We want you to look at yourself through our eyes, if you can. That means to forgive yourself. This is the most challenging aspect of your time with us because it is our desire that you accept yourself for who you are with the same unconditional love we have for you. We are here to support you in your work on earth. Toward that end, we would remind you of the bus stop incident... You do not remember this incident? The woman who you helped one day while she was sitting at the bus stop?'... They wait for my memories to kick in and someone sends a picture into my mind. I'm beginning to see – there was a woman once – I was walking toward my office with my briefcase. I was in a hurry. Then I heard this woman crying softly to my left. She was sitting at a bus stop next to the sidewalk. It was during the Depression, people were desperate. I stopped. Then on an impulse, I sat down next to her and put my arm around her, trying to comfort her. This was a very unnatural thing for me to do. My god, is this what they are interested in? I was with this woman for only a few minutes before the bus came. I never saw her again... It's so crazy! An entire lifetime of giving money to charity and they are interested in this! I gave this woman no money, we only talked.

As for the other pioneers, Cannon merely describes how one type of council is involved with reviewing former lives, in conjunction with the soul's spirit guide and with the assistance of 'holographic projection'.[62] As previously mentioned Fiore combines the idea of the review council with that of life films:[63]

If the regression continued, they reported experiences of a rich, full existence in another world. At one point, with wise counselors, they reviewed the life they had left and saw it all as though watching a film... It was clear to them that the purpose of this review was to enable them to see where they passed key challenges and failed others.

Meanwhile Huffman's subject Irene does not mention any sort of life review, but she does repeatedly talk about learning, especially from 'every side', and emphasizes that 'God is wonderful, beautiful, loving... we punish ourselves'.[64]

Near-Death Reviews

We all know that people who think they are going to die describe their entire life flashing before them. Raymond Moody provides an excellent description of the panoramic and film-like life reviews that occur not infrequently in conjunction with near-death experiences:[65]

This review can only be described in terms of memory, since that is the closest familiar phenomenon to it, but it has characteristics which set it apart from any normal type of remembering. First of all, it is extraordinarily rapid. The memories, when they are described in temporal terms, are said to follow one another swiftly, in chronological order. Others recall no awareness of temporal order at all. The remembrance was instantaneous; everything appeared at once, and they could take it all in with one mental glance. However it is expressed, all seem in agreement that the experience was over in an instant of earthly time. Yet, despite its rapidity, my informants agree that the review, almost always described as a display of visual imagery, is incredibly vivid and real. In some cases, the images are reported to be in vibrant color, three-dimensional, and even moving. And even if they are flickering rapidly by, each image is perceived and recognized. Even the emotions and feelings associated with the images may be re-experienced as one is viewing them. Some of those I interviewed claim that, while they cannot adequately explain it, everything they had ever done was there in this review – from the most insignificant to the most meaningful. Others explain that what they saw were mainly the highlights of their lives. Some have stated to me that even for a period of time following their experience of the review they could recall the events of their lives in incredible detail.

Many of Moody's subjects also place their review in the context of being educated by a 'being of light', in particular about love, as the following case shows:

All through this, he kept stressing the importance of love. The places where he showed it best involved my sister; I have always been very close to her. He showed me some instances where I had been selfish to my sister, but then just as many times where I had really shown love to her and had shared with her. He pointed out to me that I should try to do things for other people, to try my best. There wasn't any accusation in any of this, though. When he came across times when I had been selfish, his attitude was only that I had been learning from them, too.

Ring reports similar review experiences associated with the near-death phenomenon:[66]

A person may experience the whole or selected aspects of his life in the form of vivid and nearly instantaneous visual images. These images usually appear in no definite sequence (though they sometimes do), but rather as a simultaneous matrix of impressions, like a hologram.

He too confirms that when any light being is present there is no judgment involved. He also makes the fascinating suggestion that this being may in fact be the subject's own higher self – except that they are so unused to its wisdom and soul perspective that they see it as all-wise and maybe as some sort of angel, or even as Jesus or God. However we might expect interlife as opposed to near-death subjects to be aware of being met by themselves in this way if it was a regular occurrence.

Meanwhile Peter Fenwick specifically confirms not only the lack of judgment but also the re-experiencing of our actions from the perspective of those we have wronged:[67]

> In the 'classical' life review the person is shown his or her whole life in a panoramic fashion. Although actions which have been carried out are often seen as shabby and self-interested, the person does not feel judged; guilt is made more tolerable by the supportive quality of the surrounding light of love. Often the person experiences himself the emotional or physical pain that he has caused to others. Usually he is left with a feeling that he has learned from this and a determination to change and do better.

He also reports on a case in which the subject emphasized it was not just his actions but also his innermost thoughts and intentions under review:

> After the life review I spent some time resting and considering the implications of what had happened. I did not feel that I had been judged except by myself. There was no denying the facts because they were all there, including my innermost thoughts, emotions and motives. I knew that my life was over [wrongly as it turns out] and whatever came next would be a direct consequence of not only what I had done in my life, but what I had thought and what had been my true feeling at the time.

Fenwick indicates that in most studies only about a quarter to a third of near-death subjects experience life reviews, although in some the figure is far less, while Ring emphasizes that they tend to be more prevalent in cases involving accidents – such as falls, drowning or vehicle crashes – when the brush with death is sudden and unforeseen. Skeptics argue that the phenomenon is triggered because the brain is searching through its memory banks for some way to cope with the trauma, but as usual this seems to be a highly simplistic explanation for the variety and depth of the review experiences on record – and especially for the *new* insights that are derived from them. Moreover there are sufficient similarities between the life reviews that occur during near-death and interlife experiences – such as their ultimately detailed and even holographic nature, the lack of judgment except from the subject, and the re-experiencing of events from the perspective of others – that they must surely be regarded as related paranormal phenomena.

It is also worth returning briefly to Frederick Lenz's research with adults who spontaneously remember past lives. We have already seen in chapter 2 that these recollections are very much like reviews in which the subject can enter the movie to feel what was going on, and that they are sometimes accompanied by some sort of telepathic commentary. But he too emphasizes the guides' impartiality and lack of judgment, and that it is only the subjects themselves who consistently feel sad at the extent to which they have wasted their opportunities.[68] What is more some subjects were shown whole 'chains of lifetimes' in one go, which can only add further support to our contention that these are *individual* soul memories.

Hallucinogenic Reviews

At this point it will be useful to consider that there is another, independent source of confirmation of the concept of the life review, and it comes from reports of ingesting a specific type of hallucinogen called ibogaine. This is an alkaloid derived from the roots of the iboga shrub that grows abundantly in West Central Africa, which have long been used by local tribes of the Bwiti religion to enter altered states of consciousness and induce visions that assist spiritual development. But pioneering Western researchers like Howard Lotsof and Eric Taub argue that it is the most effective psychotherapeutic tool they have ever come across because of its profound impact on the subject. Not only can it help to cure alcohol and drug addictions overnight, but in more general terms it acts as an incredible tool for self-analysis and learning.

Although this process is again fluid and individual, Taub points out that it regularly involves some form of life review:[69]

> The person ingesting the ibogaine may seem to journey backward in time and to re-experience significant life events. Some people undergo a 'life review' similar to that described in *The Tibetan Book of the Dead*, and in modern accounts of near-death experiences. If the person is an addict, he or she is sometimes brought to the place where the core issue that helped facilitate the addiction began. The emotional content of that experience is relived, along with the visual, pictorial gestalt of the experience itself. In most cases, the experience is complete with 3-D effects and the sensation of actually 'being there'... It is this understanding that seems to allow the former addict to begin again, making new, healthy choices.

It seems that ibogaine-induced reviews can replicate other more specific aspects of near-death and interlife reviews too. In one episode of the documentary series *Tribe* first aired in early 2005 on BBC2, the anthropologist Bruce Parry ingested iboga while living for a month with the Babongo people of Gabon. Afterwards he explained that he had been transported back in time to specific situations in which he had caused hurt or offence to others, swapping places so that he became acutely aware of the effects of his actions on them. One example he gave was of the pain of a former partner he had jilted – and although he reported that he had some

177

feelings of guilt, he was equally imbued with a deep-seated understanding and awareness, and with a desire to let that particular person know that he now had a far better idea of what he had put them through.

Another hallucinogen, the DMT-based ayahuasca, is a brew created by natives of the Amazonian rainforest by mashing and boiling the forest vine and adding chacruna leaves. Some people suggest this has a similar capacity for psychospiritual therapy, in terms of removing blockages and allowing a closer union with the higher self. However specific reports of life reviews appear less common with this substance.

Soul Group Interaction

The idea that we have a group of soul mates with whom we work closely in varied relationships over many lives is pretty well established, and it explains the immediate chemistry all of us sometimes experience on meeting someone new for the first time.

Helen Wambach does not mention the transition or past-life review elements of the interlife at all, because the 'pre-birth' questions she put to her group subjects did not cover these areas. But she did ask them to visualize whether in their past lives they had been associated with anyone they knew in their current life:[70]

> Eighty-seven percent of all my subjects reported being aware of how they had known important people in their current life from past lives. These relationships were quite varied [with friends, spouses and family members being mixed up again and again]... My subjects all tell the same story. We come back with the same souls, but in different relationships. We live again not only with those we love, but with those we hate and fear. Only when we feel only compassion and affection are we freed from the need to live over and over with the same spirits, who are also forced to live with us!

Ramster reports in similar fashion:[71] 'Although the roles may change and the gender of the individual may change, in some cases people report reincarnating in groups so that people remain related in some way from lifetime to lifetime... Matters that remain unresolved within the span of one lifetime become resolved over the course of another lifetime.'

But do any of our pioneers provide more detail about how we interact with our soul mates between incarnations?

The Learning Environment

Fiore and Modi both make brief references to the idea that we work closely with other soul group members during the interlife, attempting to learn various lessons with them.[72] Holzer's subject Ruth is rather more forthcoming when she describes learning amongst certain 'friends':[73]

I stayed with these people for a while... There were so many things I had to get over. I had felt I was quite a nice lady, you know, the English gentlewoman, making little visits to the poor. That was silly. That isn't being good, you know... You have to start from scratch... and it mostly involves *attitudes*. That is what I learned. Not just the outer words. And then, I used to be very good with the Bible. I read it every day and I prayed a lot, and I was what you would call a pious person. But when I looked back from over there, I had to laugh at my little vanities. I didn't know anything. I just went through the motions. It isn't until you get your moves all straightened out that you really know and you've really learned of things.

Unsurprisingly Newton goes into even more detail, indicating that his subjects set aside considerable time to discuss former lives with other members of their soul group that were involved – including the lessons learned, the good and bad choices made, and the aspects not yet properly mastered.[74] He reports that to this end they can again make use of the library environment for both replaying and role-playing, to build on the lessons learned as part of the review process, and to see how each of them could have reacted differently to various circumstances. Of course such discussions are also teeing them up for the lessons they would like to learn, and the sort of experiences they will need, in the next life – of which more shortly.

Whitton's co-author briefly corroborates the general idea of learning alongside other soul group members, and then moves on to that of ongoing learning in a library environment:[75] 'Most of Dr Whitton's subjects have found themselves hard at work in vast halls of learning equipped with libraries and seminar rooms.' And one of Cannon's subjects confirms the idea of interacting repeatedly with the same souls to learn with them.[76] He also describes the educational classes he attends on an ongoing basis with the other members of his soul group:

It is the school of knowledge. I see the hall. It has tall pillars and it's all in white... It has classrooms off of it. This is a kind of main walkway, I guess. You can see anything that you want to see here. Just by visualizing it, it occurs. You can make it as nice or as bad as you wish. If you're dealing with a guilty conscience and want to make yourself suffer, you can make yourself do that also... There are about fifty people just in my class. There are others here, but we don't have much to do with them. They are working

out other problems. They have different lessons that they have to learn...
I'm studying life experiences and effects. I study long and hard in order to
learn and to know. I put the pieces of my experiences together and compile
them to make sense of my existence... I try to understand why I acted and
reacted in such a way so as not to repeat previous errors. We amass great
knowledge here of lessons to be learned.

Meanwhile another of Cannon's subjects describes a 'tapestry room'
that apparently has a similar function but can only be used by more
experienced souls:

The guardian is explaining that every life that has ever been lived is
represented as a thread in this tapestry. This is where all the threads of
human life, the souls that incarnate are connected. It illustrates perfectly
how each life is interwoven, crossing and touching all these other lives until
eventually all of humanity is affected. The absolute oneness of humanity is
represented by the tapestry. It is one but composed of all these many parts.
Each cannot exist without the other and they all intertwine and influence
each other... It's like looking at the most beautiful creation of art... These
are the akashic records that advanced souls understand. He says some of the
records are kept in book form, but those are for souls who are not as highly
advanced.

Different Aspects of the Light Realms

Weiss' patient Catherine refers to 'seven planes, each one consisting of
many levels'.[77] Similarly Ramster describes the different planes and levels
in the light realms:[78]

It seems from all the accounts of past-life recall, that the number of places
one may go after death are many, as if the world on the other side of death
is composed of various levels. The level to which one belongs is determined
by one's advancement. It seems that each person goes to a plane of
existence where they find people similar to themselves. The people on each
plane will be such that each has a great affinity with the other people on that
same plane. Sometimes they will meet dead relatives or friends after they
die, however, this seems to depend upon the level to which those relatives
and friends belong.

Note that this suggests not all of our friends and family will be close
soul mates, and this idea is expressed by Newton and others. More than
this, though, the broad idea is that of souls and soul groups at similar stages
of spiritual development, and Huffman, Cannon and Newton generally
corroborate it.[79] However, to the extent that the idea of *levels* and of soul

advancement generally sounds somewhat hierarchical and even elitist, it is perhaps subtly better to refer to soul *experience* and to the different vibrational *aspects* of the light realms. It is of course vital to remember that soul evolution is not a race, that some of us assimilate certain experiences more swiftly than others and vice versa, and above all that all souls will evolve completely and exactly as they should in the fullness of time.

Next-Life Planning

Unlike the life review, the whole idea that we might be actively engaged in planning our own incarnations, including the trials and tribulations we all encounter to varying degrees, has little provenance in mainstream metaphysical thought ancient or modern – although in the next chapter we will find that it is present to varying degrees in certain more obscure sources from the last two centuries. It is undoubtedly one of the most important aspects of this book, not least because of the profundity of its revelation that we, as individual souls, are entirely in control of our own destiny. This is reinforced by the idea that we create our own reality as we go along in incarnate life, albeit often unconsciously, which we will discuss fully in the final chapter. The implications of these twin concepts are *so* far-reaching that some people struggle with them, especially initially, so we will examine them far more in the final chapters – aiming to show that, taken together, they are the most individually empowering concepts ever presented to humanity. Of course skeptics might argue that the idea of a life plan merely panders to our egotistic belief that our life must have some sort of 'purpose and meaning', perhaps even an important destiny to be fulfilled. But when we find that we deliberately choose unpleasant as well as pleasant aspects of our lives this becomes a far less self-aggrandizing concept.

In any case, for now let us examine the pioneers' evidence that we do indeed plan our lives, and look at some examples of the mechanics of the process. Interlife subjects indicate that at the very least their planning involves an awareness of who their parents will be, where they will live, what their family's circumstances will be and what sex they will be. But some subjects describe rather fuller, film-like previews that seem to have similar qualities to past-life reviews, and they may even be presented with several different lives from which to choose the one they think will be most beneficial to their growth. As usual, spirit guides and elders are on hand to provide advice, while some subjects also report that they discuss their plans with other members of their soul group who will be involved.

Destiny versus Free Will

Before we start looking at the detail we should clarify one crucial issue: any life previews glimpsed in the interlife represent major *probabilities* and lesser *possibilities* only. The idea of life planning does *not* mean that our lives are predetermined.

Newton discusses these important issues at some length.[80] The other pioneers are less explicit, but they all describe life reviews in one form or another – the purpose of which is to see where we went right and where we went wrong. Of course, implicit in this process is the idea that we have free will in the actions we take when incarnate, and their subjects are unanimous that this concept of complete, unfettered free will reigns supreme.

Simple Planning of Parents, Location and Circumstances

Two of the primary considerations for any soul will be where to reincarnate, and into what family. Newton's subjects report that affiliations to particular countries or races are rare and, if they do exist, relatively short-lived – after all, the underlying point of repeated reincarnation is variety of experience.[81] Nevertheless he does allow that the soul of a child who has died young might return to the same parents as a subsequent child, the dynamics behind which we will discuss in the next chapter. We also saw in chapter 2 that many of Ian Stevenson's child subjects do come back in more or less the same location and even the same family, perhaps because they are in a hurry to return – of which more later. We also saw that in those native cultures around the world where these ideas form part of the religious belief souls may choose to operate in this way, at least for part of their development. So this is an area where different 'soul cultures' might well come into play.

Whitton affirms that 'the choice of one's parents, in establishing the setting and direction of the lifetime to come, is immensely important'.[82] And Cannon's subjects confirm this, with one describing a similar experience of studying her mother before incarnating to that of Whitton's subject Paula in the previous chapter:[83]

> I watch the woman who is to be my mother. In this manner I will know what to expect... I am very unsure. They are very demanding. They have definite ideas of what they wish to do. The final decision hasn't been made... I have a choice. I have to decide whether the lessons I feel I need to learn can be taught in this particular existence.

Modi provides this brief description of her patients' life planning that also specifically mentions the basic choice of family, along with that of talents and skills:[84]

> All my patients describe the same cycle of life. They exist first as a spiritual being. They incarnate into a physical body, not blindly, not randomly, but with a definite plan in mind. In the Light, they describe planning their life in detail. They claim to choose their parents, spouses, children, and other key people in their lives. Patients also remember choosing their occupation, skills, and talents. They plan in detail all the important events.

Meanwhile Weiss' patient Catherine does not discuss any specifics, but does briefly confirm the basic idea of life planning:[85] 'We decide when we want to return, where, and for what reasons.' And later she reaffirms this: 'You are responsible for the life you have. You choose it.' Similarly Huffman's subject Irene emphasizes that 'we make our own lives... we choose the way we want to go'.[86]

Life Previews and Multiple Choices

Newton describes a 'place of life selection', which his subjects compare to a giant movie theater with screens all around.[87] Here they are able to review the various life options available to them, perhaps in a number of geographic locations, and can control the movie telepathically – fast-forwarding where necessary, and even pausing the scene to enter it. He suggests that the formative period between the ages of about eight to twenty is most regularly viewed, but major events after that may occasionally be seen. This is how one subject describes the experience:

> The ring is surrounded by banks of screens – I am looking at them... I feel a moment of quietness – it's always like this – then it's as if someone flipped a switch on the projector in a panoramic movie theater. The screen comes alive with images and there is color, action, full of light and sound... I am watching life actually going on in the streets of New York. My mind connects with the scanner to control the movement of the scenes I am watching... I'm scanning. The stops are major turning points on life's pathways involving important decisions, possibilities, events which make it necessary to consider alternate choices in time... I can move forward, backward, or stop... I suspend the scene on the screens so I can enter it... Now I have direct access to the action... I can experience what life is like with anyone in the scene, or just watch them from any vantage point.

This subject then goes on to discuss in some detail the four next-life choices available to him, in each of which he will train as a classical pianist according to his own desire, but as a boy in New York, Buenos Aires or Oslo, or as a girl in Los Angeles.

Wambach did not explicitly ask her group subjects to recall if they were offered a choice of different lives, but several provide this information anyway:[88] 'I chose this life amidst some kind of assemblage. I had a few choices but they were not unlimited.' 'I did choose to be born, and I had others helping me choose. I had the choice of several entities.' However, the extent to which her subjects might have seen full-on previews of their possible life choices is not clear.

Despite an apparent reluctance to return that we will discuss shortly, Ramster's subject Gwen McDonald concludes her interlife recall with a reference to having to make a choice between two families:[89]

> Finally, a man came, he said I must go back to earth. I didn't want to go back, but I had to. He said there were people who needed me and I must help. There were two families who needed me... I could do what I had to do with both families, but I had to choose.

Another of his subjects who is also somewhat reluctant reports on his life preview with a guide as follows:[90]

> He showed me pictures, the man showed me pictures of earth, people, places, and I said to him, am I to go back? He said it was my decision. He said I had to understand the life that I would live and then I had to decide whether I wanted it or not. He told me all the things that I'd learned through my last life and explained some of the things I could learn through another life. I asked why I couldn't learn those things where I was, and he said it was because I didn't have a physical body, and for the lessons I needed to learn I needed a physical body.

Meanwhile, although Cannon does not discuss multiple choices, one of her subjects makes a brief reference to life previews with her guide:[91] 'She sometimes shows me how certain actions will affect me in a life. She'll flash them like on a movie screen on a wall.'

Planning with the Elders

Although we should probably ignore the talk of 'karmic debts', Whitton's co-author describes the planning process as follows:[92]

> The most significant finding of Dr Whitton's research is the discovery that many people plan their forthcoming lives while discarnate. The knowledge of self gleaned from the review process equips the soul to make the vital decisions that will determine the form of its next incarnation. But the soul

does not act alone. The decision making is heavily influenced by the members of the judgment board who, mindful of the soul's karmic debts and its need for specific lessons, give wide-ranging counsel.

To add some detail, one of Newton's subjects provides the following information about a planning meeting with the elders:[93]

> They want my input to assess my motivations and the strength of my resolve towards working in my new body. I am sure they have had a hand in the body choices I was given for the life to come because I feel they are skilled strategists in life selection. The committee wants me to honor my contract. They stress the benefits of persistence and holding to my values under adversity. I often give in too easily to anger and they remind me of this while reviewing my past actions and reactions towards events and people. The elders and Magra [her guide] give me inspiration, hope and encouragement to trust myself more in bad situations and not let things get out of hand. And then, as a final act to bolster my confidence when I am about to leave, they raise their arms and send a power bolt of positive energy into my mind to take with me.

A significant number of Wambach's group subjects also report planning discussions with one or more counselors:[94] 'There was a council of twelve who helped me choose, and I did choose freely.' 'Yes, I chose to be born, but a high council seemed to be helping me to make the decision.' Others are clearly referring to assistance from a planning council without actually using that terminology: 'There was a group helping me choose. They listened to what I had planned and made some suggestions.' 'Yes, I chose to be born, and there seemed to be a board or committee – a group of authorities to help me choose.' Others still identify a single individual helping them, who is most likely their spirit guide even if only a few of them use that expression.

Meanwhile Fiore's brief report of her patients' experiences continues from her previous description of the review council as follows:[95] 'Spirit counselors pointed out what they still had to learn to make the necessary spiritual progress. The next incarnation was planned, based on this knowledge.' And Ramster indicates that certain 'superior beings' are involved in his subjects' life choices – although his view that they and not the subject might have complete responsibility for the choice is again something we will discuss shortly:[96]

> People recall being born into a family that suits the specific purpose coming and that could be one of many. If it is to learn humility, then it is unlikely one will be born into a kind and rich family, more likely into a harsh, poor

one, possibly a family of slaves or prisoners. In those cases people recall the choice being made by a superior being (or beings) as one is usually not likely to see one's own need for humility. 'The purpose of life is to learn,' people under hypnosis report. Whoever comprises the hierarchy for the decision making I don't profess to know. However, according to testimonies, they play a large part in the choice of the family one is born into and the opportunities that confront one during the course of life.

Planning with Other Souls

Of course, while we are learning our own lessons we are also playing a part in the lessons learned by others around us. So according to Newton another part of the life-planning process involves subjects coordinating their planning with other members of their soul group, and possibly with a broader group of souls who will be involved with them to a lesser extent.[97] He explains that all of these souls plan to impact on each other's lives in various ways in a complex web of probable and possible interactions, which combine to best allow for the potential fulfillment of multiple life goals for each of them. He adds that it is not necessarily the length of the potential interaction that defines the strength of the bond between the two souls, but rather the importance of its impact.

Newton's subjects report that in these planning meetings they are helped to agree 'triggers' that they should remember once they are in the next life. They add that, despite the general amnesia that progressively overtakes us when we reincarnate, of which more later, these triggers are left with us as prompts that at certain points something or someone is crucial to our life plan – usually coming through as strong intuitions. Apparently we can miss these triggers, but there will usually be contingency plans to provide us with another chance for important interactions – although if we continue to miss such signs, life goes on, but in a different direction from that originally planned as most beneficial for growth.

A huge majority of Wambach's group subjects indicate that they planned their incarnations carefully with other members of their soul group, even though they sometimes referred to them merely as 'friends'.[98] Modi too seems to confirm this idea:[99] 'Patients state that they learn, have discussions with others, and plan for the next life.' And so does Whitton:[100]

> Planning for the next life is frequently undertaken in consultation with other souls with whom bonds have been established over many lifetimes. Which is to say the choice of the time and place of birth is of paramount importance; to choose wrongly is to miss the opportunity for a productive reunion.

It also gains support from Ramster's somewhat reluctant subject who we quoted earlier in relation to life previews:[101]

> Lots of people came and we talked about it. We talked about the things I needed to learn and the things I didn't need to learn... and what best the situation would be that I be born in. It seemed to take a long time. Just before I did come back I wanted it to be quick. I felt that the sooner it was over with the better, the sooner it was started the sooner it would finish. But they said the time had to be right.

Cannon's subjects too repeatedly stress that the timing of their incarnation must be right because of the way they will need to interact with other souls. This is how one describes a planning meeting with them and their guides, although we will return to whether their repeated use of the word karma is useful in the next chapter:[102]

> I am with other spirit entities. There is a group of us gathered together. You could call it a sort of discussion and planning group. The majority of us here have been linked karmically in our past lives. There is one here who is our main guide for the group in general, and our individual guides are nearby. We are discussing and planning what karmic problems we will be working on during this next upcoming life, the one that this subject is currently living. And we are discussing and planning how our lives and our karmas will interweave and interrelate and what we hope to work out karmically.

She then carries on to discuss what such planning means as far as free will versus destiny is concerned:

> We discuss how we are going to interact with each other. We have our free will on such things from the physical viewpoint when we get there. But if we work out these things ahead of time we are more apt to be open to our spiritual guides as they try to guide us through. It is a way of not being quite so haphazard about working our karma.

This suggests that, in addition to relying on triggers, we may sometimes be actively prompted to take a certain path by our spirit guides. Nevertheless both types of assistance would come through our intuition.

The Choice to Return

Newton's subjects suggest that, not surprisingly, there can be some initial reluctance to leave the peace, tranquility and love of our true home in the light realms for the harsh environment of life on earth.[103] But they stress that souls are never coerced into returning against their will, merely reminded that their growth proceeds far quicker when facing the challenges of the earth environment. This is the same point made to Ramster's reluctant subject above, and one of Cannon's subjects confirms it, while another reaffirms that souls are never forced to do anything but sooner or later tend to see the wisdom of the advice given to them:[104]

> No one is ever made to go into a situation they absolutely abhor. It's generally done by a consensus of opinion between the person and their spiritual masters. They won't like many aspects of the life in particular, but the majority of the life will be something they can handle. And these extra things they're not too fond of are looked upon as spiritual challenges, something for them to accomplish and to work for... The people who are seemingly forced to come back know it's for their own good. After they are given time to think about it they realize that they really do need to come back or they'll be stuck in that one position for ever, and they would never progress.

Sixty-seven percent of Wambach's group subjects indicate that they were reluctant to return, with nineteen percent unaware of having any choice in the matter and some even feeling they were coerced.[105] Nevertheless a number of the latter report that they realized it was something they ought to do for their own good.

Ramster is somewhat out on a limb when he suggests that on a rather more widespread basis we may not be in full control of our choices and of our decision to reincarnate:[106]

> My research findings show that in regard to the place and time one is born into there is only a limited choice, sometimes none. People nearly always recall being told when to come back. I have seen grown men cry in trance, insisting that they don't want to come back to earth. The time of birth seems to be very important and not necessarily the choice of the person reincarnating. It seems that the ability to choose a kind mother, or an easy father, a wealthy family, or a scientific family, is not ours... It seems that one's life, therefore, may not be by chance, but instead may be predestined and not necessarily self-chosen. These are the findings as I can determine from the present stage of my research. According to the memory of those regressed, the spirit has little choice but to take part in whatever lessons are necessary to achieve advancement.

Yet we have already seen Gwen McDonald indicating that she had choices, while his other subject quoted above specifically reports that when he was reluctant to return, instead of being coerced, he was given more time to ready himself:[107]

> I told him I didn't want to go back and he said I didn't have to if I didn't

want to. He asked me why I didn't want to go back, and I said because I thought it was too hard. He said I would know when the time was right whether I wanted to go back or not. Then things just seemed to stay the same for a long time. We'd meet people and we'd talk. After a while I decided I wanted to come back.

Elsewhere Ramster takes a similar line, although he at least reflects this subject's feelings better when he concludes that there tends to be an eventual acceptance about returning:

Most people say they were told they were to go back, or that it was time they should go back. Usually they did not want to return to the earth: some people in trance even cried at this point. Most say emphatically that life is too hard on earth, and that it is much more pleasant on the other side... Another frequent comment is that after they have been told they are to reincarnate, the idea slowly grows on them and is finally accepted.

To some extent Whitton confirms these rather negative interpretations:[108] 'The judges' recommendations are made according to what the soul needs, not what it wants. So they tend to be received with mixed feelings unless the soul happens to be fanatical about pursuing its development at any cost.' However he continues by making an interesting observation concerning the extent of planning being dependent upon a soul's experience: 'Less-developed personalities seem to require the guidance of a detailed blueprint, while more evolved souls provide themselves with only a general outline, so that they must then act more creatively in challenging situations.'

Overall, therefore, it does seem that less experienced souls might be less actively involved in the details of their plans, and may also be given fewer choices and less freedom for maneuver. So they might effectively be presented with a plan into which they had little input – which would explain any initial reluctance to face a difficult life, and the human perception that they were coerced. But ultimately it seems likely that free will continues to reign supreme, in that any soul can reject any life if they think it is too hard. Not only that, in the end most souls seem to appreciate that their elders and guides have their own best interests at heart, and are offering them a life that is do-able but at the same time affords them the best opportunity for growth.

Impetuous Souls

By way of contrast with this apparent reluctance to return, Whitton's co-author makes the following observation:[109] 'Less-developed personalities...

may wish to exchange their bodily vehicles as quickly as possible for a new "suit", and rapid reentry into physical existence.' He then confirms that some rebellious or impatient souls may occasionally decide to reject all advice and return into incarnation with no real plan:

> To be reborn without a plan is also a matter of choice. The trouble is, with no script to follow, the soul becomes a reed shaken by the wind – a victim of fate rather than a participant in destiny... Occasionally a trance subject has learned that he or she made no plan in the between-life state – knowledge that is invariably communicated to Dr Whitton in fear... Nothing could be worse, or so it seems, than to have an open future.

This idea receives some backing from Newton, and also from one of Cannon's subjects who confirms that some impatient souls are in such a hurry to reincarnate that they make no real plans in the interlife – and then inevitably find their lives 'messed up and confused'.[110] Meanwhile some of the most revealing of Wambach's group responses involve the small minority of subjects – less than three percent – who did not listen to the planning advice of their counselors or guides before their return:[111]

> When you asked about the prospect of living the coming lifetime, I became aware that I should have been more selective and waited a few years.

> When you asked about the prospect of being born, someone kept saying, 'Wait till a better time. A smaller family would have more time for you.' But I felt, 'No, it has to be now.'

> Yes I chose to be born, but I was in a hurry, and I wasn't sure of my choice. When you asked if anyone helped me choose, I became aware that someone, I'm not sure who, gave me a warning, but I felt that I had to get something done and solve something.

> Yes, very clearly, I chose to be born. Some entities were trying to advise me, but I didn't listen. I was impatient to finish something I had started.

> Yes, I chose to be born, but it was in panic. It was not a decision made at leisure. When you asked if anyone helped me choose, I was aware of guides that seemed to be large light beams, guiding me not to be born now – but I was determined.

Our more recent research confirms the view that impetuous souls can indeed reincarnate rather more swiftly than is ideal, and without the healing and life planning that would have been more appropriate.[112]

Returning

Relayering with Specific Emotions and Strengths

We have already seen that souls leave a certain amount of their soul energy behind in the light realms when they reincarnate, and Newton reports that the decision about how much can be quite important.[113] He suggests that, although souls may want to leave as much behind as possible in order to carry on with various aspects of learning and growth in the light, if they return to the physical with too little – especially if they face a difficult life – then they reduce their ability to see their plan through. On the other hand, apparently, if they were to bring too much they would retain far too many memories of the light realms – we will see why amnesia is regarded as important shortly – and might even risk 'blowing the circuits of the human brain'.

We also saw earlier that any strong unresolved emotions must receive some healing on transition in order that the soul's vibrations are raised sufficiently to enter the light realms proper, although Modi emphasized that the 'memory' of them is retained. We can interpret this as meaning that any healing does not prevent the soul from continuing to work with the core of these emotions, both in the light realms and in future incarnations. So Tomlinson has specifically built on Newton's research by investigating the extent to which souls make additional decisions in this area.[114] He suggests that these include not only the specific emotions they want to bring back to carry on working through, but also the past-life strengths they may need to help them through difficult patches. We can only assume that specific past-life abilities might come into this process too, which would account for possible xenoglossy and precocious talents in young children. Some of Tomlinson's subjects indicate that all this is achieved by what we now refer to as a 'relayering' process, in which they take on these heavier emotions, strengths and so on as if putting on various layers of 'clothing'. This is effectively the opposite of the delayering process that formed part of the transition.

Of course this idea is implicit in the broader concept that souls reincarnate to learn and grow, in particular by working with the full range of emotions over many lifetimes, which is supported by all the pioneers. However only Weiss' patient Catherine explicitly hints at it when she discusses the 'plane of transition':[115] 'In that plane is determined what you will take back with you into the next life. We will all have a dominant trait.'

Merging with the Body

Newton suggests that the process by which the soul merges its energy with the impressionable and developing brain of the unborn child takes some time and must be carefully handled.[116] He adds that some immature souls go at it 'like a bull in a china shop' and cause significant disorientation, while those who are more experienced take great care to gradually match their unique energy vibrations to the unique circuitry and wave patterns of their host's brain.

As to the timing of incarnation, Newton's subjects report that they enter the fetus any time during pregnancy, with the onus on the soul itself to choose;[117] Whitton's from several months before birth to as late as just after it;[118] and Cannon's right from conception until some days after birth.[119] As for Wambach's group subjects, eleven percent entered in the first six months of pregnancy, fifty-six percent between six and nine months, while thirty-three percent delayed until just before or even during birth.[120] Perhaps the most balanced view is provided by Modi's patients, who describe entering properly at any time between conception and birth, but also suggest that they place at least a portion of their soul energy into the fetus at conception.[121]

Eighty-six percent of Wambach's subjects indicate an awareness of their mother's emotions while in the womb, as do most of Cannon's and Modi's.[122] In particular, the knowledge of whether they are loved and wanted can have a profound impact on their subsequent development. Cannon also indicates that the soul finds its reemergence into the physical world at birth somewhat traumatic.[123] And this idea is given fuller expression by Wambach's subjects:[124]

> Most impressive in the reports was the degree of sadness experienced about emerging into the world. Even though for many of my subjects the actual birth was not physically traumatic, a sense of sorrow pervaded the experience... Many subjects reported that the onrush of physical sensations on emerging from the birth canal was disturbing and very unpleasant. Apparently the soul exists in a quite different environment in the between-life state. The physical senses bring so much vivid input that the soul feels almost 'drowned' in light, cold air, sounds. Surprising to me was the frequent report that the soul in the new-born infant feels cut-off, diminished, alone compared to the between-life state. To be alive in a body is to be alone and unconnected. Perhaps we are alive to learn to break through the screen of the senses, to experience while in a body the transcendent self we truly are.

Apparently this deep sense of isolation was made worse if there was any delay in the newborn child being held and comforted by their mother, and these views echo the findings of numerous other researchers.

Most of Wambach's subjects mention their ability to 'absent' themselves from the fetus even after they have initially entered it.[125] But Newton's subjects report that they do this not only while still in the womb but for some years after birth, usually up until the time when the child goes to school and becomes more constantly active.[126] Apparently they stay in earth's intermediate plane to be nearby in case of emergency, but one even describes these early years as a time when they can 'goof off' and just have fun with other souls without too much responsibility. Cannon too describes how her subjects can regularly absent themselves for short periods not only before birth but also for several years after, and more occasionally up until about age five.[127] This is perhaps at least one reason why babies sleep so much, and it must ease the trauma of the transition back into the physical. Such absenteeism is surely also related to the idea that, even as adults, when we sleep, meditate or enter other altered states, or are unconscious or in coma, our incarnate soul energy can leave the physical body via the astral body.

The Veil of Amnesia

The pioneers are pretty much unanimous that when we return to the physical plane we must pass through the 'veil of amnesia' that eradicates our memories of past lives and the light realms. According to Newton's subjects this ensures that we do not allow preconceptions from memories of past lives, and of our current life plan, to limit our potential for learning and freedom of choice.[128] Whitton confirms this, likening it to ensuring we do not have all the answers before we take an exam, but he also emphasizes that it is important for us to forget our spiritual home otherwise we would constantly pine for it.[129] Meanwhile Modi adds that to keep so many often-traumatic memories of past lives in ready recall would overwhelm us and stop us functioning on an everyday basis so that, just as with memories of the current life, some repression is necessary; and Cannon agrees with this view.[130]

Some pioneers somewhat simplistically regard the onset of this amnesia as instantaneous when we leave the light realms. But Cannon echoes the more common view that it is progressive, so that babies and young children have far greater ability to tap into etheric memories than adults, but then increasingly lose it over time.[131] This ties in well with Stevenson's research;[132] and with George Rodonaia's ability to communicate with the baby during his near-death experience that we discussed in chapter 1. Of course, although most of us cannot consciously remember events before the age of about three, we know that they can be recalled with great lucidity under hypnosis. Coupled with the only-gradual onset of amnesia, it is surely right that more and more people are recognizing the very young for the experienced soul travelers most of them undoubtedly are.[133]

Blank Experiences

We cannot leave this subject without briefly discussing the issue of whether all souls have some sort of interlife experience between every pair of lives. We have seen that most people are capable of achieving the requisite level of trance, so this should not affect the question. We have also seen that some impetuous souls reincarnate relatively swiftly, without any real planning, while others might spend plenty of time just resting. But do subjects ever go into trance and then remember absolutely nothing of the interlife? And, if they do, does this mean that nothing actually happened?

There remain two past-life pioneers whose somewhat restricted investigations of the interlife are relevant here. The first is Woolger, who we have only mentioned briefly above. This is because he talks about eighty percent of his patients feeling peaceful after death and then finding themselves straight back in another past life or in this one.[134] However he then admits that he refuses to actively explore any possible interlife because 'such experiences are graces that are freely bestowed by the wisdom of the Greater Self only when and if a person is ready'. As for the other twenty percent who did experience it, his brief report follows a now familiar pattern:

> There are those who spontaneously (as opposed to being directed by me) see non-embodied or spirit figures... These will frequently be the departed companions or family from the life just remembered... Many of the smaller proportion will meet old teachers or gurus from the life just lived or known from another one... A quite common experience of this nature is one where, after death, the discarnate personality meets some robed figure in white who radiates love and wisdom. Frequently several of these figures come in small groups, a kind of 'karmic committee', as I have come to call them affectionately. This group helps review and advise the departed personality about the lessons of the life lived. One woman reported being taken by such a luminous being to a celestial temple, where she was shown a huge book in which the life she had just remembered and many more were clearly

written. Another woman was similarly guided by a spirit figure and shown part of a huge tapestry that represented her many interwoven lives. Celestial gardens, mountains and islands are sometimes glimpsed.

The second of the more unusual pioneers is Morris Netherton:[135]

My experience with this 'space' has been far too shallow to make any definitive statements. Patients describe a life outside the body as easily as they describe their births and deaths. I rarely let patients linger in this area, however, although it is very tempting, with its mysteries and promises of sudden revelation. In fact, in my experience, life outside the body reveals very little. It does not seem to be a state of exalted wisdom or extraordinary perception at all. The problems that plague a particular life are carried into the space between lives. Our inability to deal with these problems influences our choice of the next body we enter.

Not only does Netherton indirectly confirm the idea of life planning and learning, but he clearly admits that even more than Woolger he actively shied away from investigating the interlife. We have also seen that they both used methods other than hypnosis to regress their patients, who as a result may not have been entering the deeper brainwave states required for interlife recall. So neither of them has provided any convincing evidence to detract from the suggestion that all souls have some sort of genuine, etheric experience between lives, however brief. But what about the minority of subjects encountered by the main pioneers who actually do report little or nothing happening in the interlife? Our recent research confirms Newton's view that almost certainly this would result from spirit guides blocking the experience because it would not be helpful for those particular individuals to recall it – due to their level of soul development, or particular challenges in this life, and so on – rather than because nothing had actually happened.[136]

Anonymous Pioneers

There is another source that is worth discussing, albeit that it may be regarded as less dependable because the author refuses to name her sources, apparently to protect their anonymity. However if it is at all reliable it represents some of the earliest written material about interlife regression in the modern era. In the 1960s the former journalist turned psychic Ruth Montgomery began automatically writing on behalf of an entity signing herself as 'Lily'. As she describes in her second book *Here and Hereafter*, published in 1968, although she had previously shied away from the idea of reincarnation, before long she found herself writing about how souls come back repeatedly to gain experience; about how those leading apparently difficult lives might be growing rather faster; and about how some return rather more quickly than they should.[137]

This prompted her to investigate the subject more thoroughly, and she began attending regular regression sessions at the Los Angeles home of an apparently eminent scientist she refers to using the pseudonym 'Jane Winthrop'. These sessions had seemingly been going on for some years with a British psychologist, Major Arthur Knight, at the helm.[138] However it seems that at some point Winthrop herself also trained in hypnotherapy, and in one session in early 1968 Montgomery witnessed one of her subjects responding to a question about the time between lives as follows:[139] 'You have to evaluate, to weigh the past life and formulate what it is that you'll need, and what you'll seek, in the next one.' Meanwhile another subject from about the same time, who was adamant that reincarnation was 'for the birds' prior to her session, provided the following details:

> I have certain obstacles that I have to overcome in order to learn, and the parents I choose also have something to learn by having me, so it's a double attraction. Sometimes you make a mistake in your selection, but you don't need to waste that particular lifetime as a consequence. Even though you may not be able to work on the particular lessons that you intended to return for, you can be learning other things… Our greater period of development is on earth, rather than here, because there we pit ourselves against obstacles, and as we surmount them we grow in understanding. Between earthly lives we have an expanding knowingness, and after assessing the errors of our past life, we decide the kind of obstacles which will best help us to advance in the next incarnation.

Montgomery also cites a 'prominent psychiatrist' who had apparently regressed 'more than a hundred patients' in the previous ten years, and claimed that his 'good subjects could talk just as easily about the period between lives as about former earthly incarnations'.[140] They stressed their 'freedom and aliveness' after physical death, and described the purpose of incarnation as being to learn how to be more 'selfless, kind and loving'. They added that 'we return together time and again, as friends, relatives and enemies' and that 'we can earn the right to choose our own parents'. This latter echoes the aforementioned idea that less experienced souls may have rather less choice about their lives.

Spontaneous Memories

Before we leave this chapter we should note that there is another corroboratory source of interlife material, and that is again spontaneous past-life memories. We have already discussed the way in which they resemble life reviews in themselves. But on top of this Lenz notes that fifteen of his subjects remembered their time in various nonphysical realms between lives.[141]

His findings as largely corroboratory of regression evidence, once we have seen through his insistence on matching his subjects' experiences with the various worlds of the *Tibetan Book of the Dead* – to which we will return in the next chapter. So, for example, his 'psychic world' filled with 'the pleasing scents and fragrances of flowers', 'beautiful lights and music' and 'luminous beings of all types', where his subjects are greeted by deceased friends and relatives, can be correlated with our transition experience. And his subjects' reports of there being 'millions of levels' in the 'soul's world' that they journey onto, which 'correspond to the soul's stage of development' and in which they 'assimilate' the life just passed, entirely corroborate our pioneers' findings. Some also experience what he refers to as 'mental' and 'artistic' worlds, but these can be seen as alternative experiences available during the soul's sojourn in the light realms rather than as separate worlds as such. As for life planning, Lenz refers to souls having more choice of lives the more experienced they are, while insisting that they are never forced to do anything against their will. However this latter information seems to come less from his subjects and more from his own reading.[142]

He also pays some attention to the horrors encountered in what he refers to as the 'vital world', which in our terms is merely the traversing of the intermediate plane as discussed above. But one further point of clarification apparently offered by several of his subjects is that their experiences in this world seemed to be related to the quality of life they had lived. For example, if they had been selfless they seemed to be little bothered by its potential torments. Arguably this can be seen as consistent with Robert Monroe's out-of-body reports, and with the law of attraction.

Summary

The major aspects of this detailed review of the interlife experience are shown in the table, indicating which ones are corroborated by each pioneer.

Circles are used rather than dots where it is reasonable to assume that the element in question is strongly implied even if not explicitly mentioned.[143]

	NEWTON	CANNON	WHITTON	RAMSTER	MODI	FIORE	WEISS	WAMBACH	MONTGOMERY	HUFFMAN	WOOLGER	HOLZER
Welcoming parties	•	•	•	•	•	•					•	•
Healing/rest/reintegration	•	•	•	•	•	o	•			o		•
Simple life review	•	•	•	•	•	•	•	o	•	o	•	o
Library of life books/films	•	•	•	•	•	o	•	o			•	
Review with elders	•	•	•	o	•	•		o			•	
Learning with group	•	•	•	o	•	•		o	o			•
Simple life planning	•	•	•	o	•	o	•	o	•	•		
Detailed life previews	•	•	o	•	o	o	o	•				
Planning with elders	•	•	•	•	o	•		•			o	
Planning with other souls	•	•	•	•	•			•				

This provides an easy visual confirmation of the consistency of the pioneers' findings. We might also remember that some of them were not concentrating on the interlife per se, only commenting on it in passing. To that extent a gap in the table may mean that the given researcher encountered the element in question but does not bother to mention it, or that they failed to ask their subjects any pertinent questions about it. Certainly in no instance can a gap be taken as a direct contradiction of the others' findings.

This has been a lengthy chapter, but there are arguably two messages that stand out. The first is that being born again into a physical body seems on balance to be rather more traumatic than the mostly pleasant experience of dying, not least because if the physical death itself involves trauma and pain the soul can choose to leave beforehand. But in passing once again into our real spiritual home we are returning to a lightness and freedom, to a heightened awareness and wisdom, and above all to a companionship and unconditional love, that are way beyond anything we can experience on earth. Yet in the Western world at least we remain obsessed with hanging on to physical life at all costs, prolonging it by any artificial means available, even when old age or severe illness has reduced its quality to near zero. Perhaps if there was more widespread appreciation of what awaits us we might be rather less scared of death, and more content to let nature take its proper course.

The other message, which is perhaps even more crucial, is the almost total unanimity of the pioneers about the extent to which we have complete personal responsibility for everything that happens to us in incarnate life. Whitton sums this up well:[144]

> In one fundamental aspect the privileged few who have visited the interlife receive the same unrelenting message. We are thoroughly responsible for who we are and the circumstances in which we find ourselves. We are the ones who do the choosing.

And one of Cannon's subjects is similarly emphatic:[145]

> You, yourself, choose that which is to be experienced, so that you may learn those lessons that you need... You are truly the master of your own fate and destiny. You, yourself, are in complete control of what you call your lifetime. You are the one who is making decisions as to when and where and how.

7

EXPERIENCE AND GROWTH

The Unhelpfulness of Karma

Even when the modern evidence for individual soul reincarnation is accepted, there are a number of very different spiritual approaches that can be adopted, whose adherents behave in very different ways. So our final objective in this work must be to attempt to answer the two crucial questions of *why are we here?* and its logical corollary of *what should we do?* Without answers to these questions we are swimming in a whirlpool – directionless, aimless, reactive, allowing the tides of our succession of lives to take us where they will.

All reincarnatory worldviews share the idea that we have many lives on earth because we are supposed to progress or evolve to the point where we no longer *have* to incarnate in the physical plane. And while this objective of 'enlightenment' or 'transcendence' is consistent, as we will see there are a number of different views as to how it can be achieved – not only from a metaphysical perspective, but also in practical, everyday terms.[1] For most people this is where the concept of karma comes to the fore, because it is supposedly the river that runs through our succession of lives and flows out into the light realms of the eternal soul. So for many their view of the workings of karma is intrinsically bound up with their view of how to achieve the progress required to depart the earth plane for good – even if souls who have achieved this enlightened state might *choose* to come back to assist with various earthly developments.

There are many different approaches to karma in the traditions of the East and West. Even the two major Eastern religions, Hinduism and Buddhism, each have many different strains – although the doctrine of *anatta* or 'no self' can tend to preclude any idea of the continuity of an individual soul that reincarnates from one life to the next in some strains of

Buddhist thought. Then there are the variants of Sikhism, Jainism, Taoism, Judaism, Gnosticism and a variety of other esoteric schools both ancient and modern. This is not intended to be a full explanation of the many intricacies of these different approaches to karma, but we can identify certain major strands of thinking.

The most simplistic, traditional approach tells us that we can be punished for so-called 'bad' karma. The harshest version of this doctrine sees the unfortunate wrongdoer devolving back down the reincarnatory chain to a lower form of animal life – or even, under some schemas, entering a terrible, hellish realm before incarnating again at the bottom of the animal chain and having to work all the way back up to human form.[2] But most modern evidence suggests that there are significant differences between the group soul energy of animal species and the fully individualized nature of human soul energy.[3] So many spiritual seekers in the West now tend to favor a more fluid approach that involves 'balancing' supposedly good and bad karma. The principle is broadly one of 'spiritual accounting' whereby we tend to accumulate karmic deficits – especially in earlier lives when we are less experienced – but over time our good karmic actions compensate for the bad ones, whether directly or indirectly. So the long-term aim is to achieve a 'balanced karmic account'. But even this is seen as too formulaic by some, so the bottom line becomes the mere recognition of myriad different forms of karma that can apply in different circumstances.[4] But does any of this karmic theory really help us to answer our two key questions?

Apparently more sophisticated approaches tend to suggest that we should live a life of non-attachment, perhaps even as a completely disinterested ascetic in solitude. In Hindu thought this frees us from generating any further karma at all, whether good or bad, thereby ending the compulsion to reincarnate. For those of a more Buddhist persuasion, by contrast, the purpose is to see through the illusion of individuality – or *maya* – and recognize our 'one-ness' with the 'universal consciousness' that pervades everything. We will return to these issues in the final chapter, but for now we might recognize that to separate oneself from the world for a prolonged period might be regarded as somewhat at odds with the idea of soul experience and growth – which we have already seen is one of the strongest themes to emerge from interlife regression. Having said that the pursuit of non-attachment does not have to be this extreme. It might be that we involve ourselves fully in the experiences of life, and yet still aim to find ourselves becoming less and less attached to particular events and their outcomes.

Rather worse, in the original Sanskrit the word *karma* means 'action', but as we saw in chapter 5 it is now widely associated with a process of action *and reaction* and of paying off debts – more commonly expressed via colloquialisms such as 'you reap what you sow' and 'what goes around comes around'. So the fundamental problem with most karmic models is the misconception that, if we are undergoing trials and tribulations in the present, they must represent our predestined fate because of wrongdoing in the past – usually thought to have taken place in a previous life. Nowhere is this flaw more blatantly demonstrated than in the idea that people who are severely disabled, either mentally or physically, are being punished – because, as we will shortly see, they may well have deliberately chosen this challenge during the interlife in order to accelerate their emotional growth. On top of this there is a seemingly irreconcilable tension between, on the one hand, this inherent suggestion of a significant element of karmic predestiny and, on the other, the total supremacy of personal responsibility and free will – which themes also emerged strongly from the interlife regression evidence in the previous chapter. Many spiritual commentators have wrestled with this problem. Most, unfortunately, have had minimal success.

With the benefit of modern regression evidence it seems that the most important distinction we can make is between the dynamics operating *across* successions of lives and those that hold sway *within* just one life. To begin with the first of these, it is clear that our accumulated experiences from past lives shape our current life plan – influencing not only our circumstances, but also the emotions we bring back to work on, and even the past-life strengths that will help us. At least this is certainly true of more experienced souls, who are closely involved in making deliberate planning choices for themselves, and in these circumstances the idea that any sort of law of action and reaction influences the process seems entirely unhelpful. As to those less experienced and more impetuous souls whose planning may be rather more directed by others, it may be that some sort of underlying law of action and reaction is applied. But if so the dynamics of this process will be so complex as to be way beyond our human understanding – and if we cannot understand something, we cannot use it to learn and grow. So expounding any number of complex theories in this area is not going to assist such a soul in deciding how to approach their life in practical terms. Worse still, who is to say whether each of us is an experienced soul who is more or less in charge of their life planning and choices, or a less experienced and perhaps more impetuous soul wielding rather less control? As we will see, outward appearances can be extremely deceptive.

So what about what happens within our current lives? If we switch the terminology slightly, it is sometimes abundantly obvious to us that the concept of 'cause and effect' holds true, especially when the effect follows hard on the heels of the cause. In fact in this context it clearly *is* appropriate to talk about a 'law' that pertains at all times – even if, again, most of the time we remain blissfully unaware of the unconscious causes that have produced the effects we consciously observe in our lives. It is because of this that, as well as having a life plan established during the interlife, we can be said to create our own reality as we go along in incarnate life – and this in turn is exactly where the supremacy of free will comes into play.

We will return to these ideas in the final chapter, but for now the clear implication is that we can break free from the 'bondage of karma' *at any time*. If we want to promote soul growth then *each and every one of us* can actively decide to start with a fresh sheet of paper and to begin 'consciously creating' our own future. This is true not only of more experienced but also of less experienced souls, because there are no obvious restrictions – except that to reinforce this process we need to become not only more spiritually aware while incarnate, but also more fully active in the time between lives, although to a large extent the one may be thought to lead to the other. Admittedly some souls may be rather more receptive to these ideas, and rather more ready to put them into practice, than others. Admittedly also, as we will see in the final chapter, real conscious creation does not just involve 'positive thinking' but also a commitment to proper self-analysis so that unconscious blockages are cleared. But, despite these riders, this undeniable fact that we use our free will to create our own destiny renders it absolutely imperative that we should shift our focus away from thinking of our present circumstances as being reactively determined by our past, and concentrate instead on how our present choices are proactively shaping our future.

We have seen that the word *karma* has many unhelpful connotations in this respect. We have also seen that there are many other ways in which it can be an unhelpful or misleading concept, at least in practical rather than purely theoretical terms and for all but the most learned spiritual seekers. So, armed with modern regression evidence, there is surely now a strong argument that we should drop it from our spiritual lexicon for good – and rely instead on a simple sentence that incorporates all three key phrases:

'*free will* gives us *personal responsibility* for our own *experience and growth*'. This is practical and, above all, difficult to misinterpret.

It seems that the Indian philosopher Sri Aurobindo recognized this imperative long ago, without the benefit of modern evidence. His master work is the lengthy, two-volume *Life Divine* and, although some new chapters were inserted when it was published in 1939, the majority of its contents stem from articles originally written for his monthly journal *Arya* from 1914 to 1919. The main thrust of this hugely erudite work is an attempt to take Indian Vedanta philosophy – one of the aspects of Hinduism – and to not only realign it with its original Vedic roots but also integrate it with modern science and metaphysics. As a result, in many crucial respects Aurobindo's arguments and conclusions form a stark contrast to those of most Eastern gurus and mystics. In the current context we are interested in his attempt to correct some of the misinterpretations of Hinduism and Buddhism with respect to karma:[5]

> The true foundation of the theory of rebirth is the evolution of the soul, or rather its efflorescence out of the veil of Matter and its gradual self-finding. Buddhism contained this truth involved in its theory of karma and emergence out of karma but failed to bring it to light; Hinduism knew it of old, but afterwards missed the right balance of its expression. Now we are again able to restate the ancient truth in a new language and this is already being done by certain schools of thought, though still the old incrustations tend to tack themselves on to the deeper wisdom... The theory of rebirth is an intellectual necessity... But what is the aim of that evolution?... The continual growth towards a divine knowledge, strength, love and purity... What of suffering and happiness, misfortune and prosperity? These are experiences of the soul in its training, helps, props, means, disciplines, tests, ordeals – and prosperity is often a worse ordeal than suffering. Indeed, adversity, suffering may often be regarded rather as a reward to virtue than as a punishment for sin, since it turns out to be the greatest help and purifier of the soul struggling to unfold itself. To regard it merely as the stern award of a Judge, the anger of an irritated Ruler or even the mechanical recoil of result of evil upon cause of evil is to take the most superficial view possible of God's dealings with the soul and the law of the world's evolution.

Elsewhere Aurobindo elaborates on the theme that most applications of any law of karma are 'ignorant', 'puerile' and 'puny'.[6] He adds that to the extent such a law exists it can and must be overruled by free will:

> If the fundamental truth of our being is spiritual and not mechanical, it must be ourself, our soul that fundamentally determines its own evolution, and

the law of karma can only be one of the processes it uses for that purpose: our spirit, our self must be greater than its karma. There is law, but there is also spiritual freedom... It is not conceivable that the spirit within is an automaton in the hands of karma, a slave in this life of its past actions; the truth must be less rigid and more plastic... Self-expression and experience are what the soul seeks by its birth into the body; whatever is necessary for the self-expression and experience of this life, whether it intervenes as an automatic outcome of past lives or as a free selection of results and a continuity or as a new development, whatever is a means of creation of the future, that will be formulated.

Repetitive, Progressive and Altruistic Behavior

If the concept of karma is unhelpful, let us now turn to the regression evidence that will help us to understand the complex growth dynamics that govern our successions of lives. We have repeatedly seen that many people's current lives will be heavily influenced by unresolved emotions carried forward from previous lives, but what do we really mean by this in practical terms? It seems likely that in the first instance all souls have to work through the full range of what we might refer to as 'emotional lessons'. That is, we all need to learn how to shift progressively away from fear-based emotions and attitudes such as impatience, guilt, shame, selfishness, humiliation, jealousy, anger, hatred and revenge towards more love-based ones such as patience, altruism, openness, understanding, forgiveness and acceptance. And in order to experience and understand them properly we need not only to feel them ourselves, but also to feel what it is like to have them directed at us by others. Such emotional learning tends to be characterized by somewhat repetitive patterns of behavior as we try to master particular emotions in a variety of life settings.

An interesting example is provided by Michael Newton, when one of his subjects reports that another soul from his group had 'hurt a girl terribly' in one incarnation, after which he reincarnated in the form of a woman who would herself be abused in similar fashion.[7] On the face of it this is directly retributive karma at its finest. But the subject emphasizes that this was entirely *his choice*, because he himself felt that this would be the best way for him to 'appreciate the damage he had done to the girl'. The clear implication is that another soul might have worked through this in an entirely different and far less directly related way.

Meanwhile Brian Weiss' patient Catherine carries on from the quote in the previous chapter about bringing back a 'dominant trait' as follows:[8]

Then you must overcome this in that lifetime... If you do not, when you return you will have to carry that trait, as well as another one, into your next life. The burdens will become greater. With each life that you go through and you do not fulfill these debts, the next one will be harder.

Although her use of the word *debts* is not particularly helpful, she is expressing a commonly held view that there is a 'self-corrective' mechanism to our spiritual growth whereby, if we fail to come to terms with a particular emotional lesson in one life, we will face it again but in rather more difficult circumstances in the next – and so on. But clearly this is not any sort of punishment, but a mechanism that automatically ensures we cannot indefinitely ignore the key issue on which we are supposed to be working – and it ties in with the idea of deliberate triggers that act as reminders. We might also note that the difficulty of the circumstances we face relating to a given issue may well increase throughout our *current* life – if, for example, it relates to an emotional problem that can easily and repeatedly be brought out by successive relationships or friendships, or even by one particular person.

However Shakuntala Modi confirms Aurobindo's view that difficult circumstances do not have to be related to repetitive patterns:[9]

Over and over, my patients tell me that not only do they plan happy, good, and productive events, but they also choose negative events, circumstances, and tragedies, to balance their negative actions from the past lives or because they need to learn something from them to grow spiritually.

Whatever else they might say about karma we have seen that nearly all the interlife pioneers discuss this more 'progressive' type of learning, in which possibly more experienced souls will deliberately take on difficult challenges to accelerate their emotional growth – and not necessarily as part of any sort of repetitive pattern; and our more recent research entirely confirms this view.[10] A prime source of case studies of such progressive choices is Robert Schwartz's 2007 book *Courageous Souls*, although he worked with mediums to gather information about his subjects' plans rather than using conventional interlife regression.

The most obvious example of this, briefly mentioned above, is the choice of sometimes-severe physical or mental disability. Joel Whitton confirms that 'bodily affliction must sometimes be accepted in the cause of higher development', and mentions one specific subject who knew there was a high probability of her developing Alzheimer's disease.[11] Several of Dolores Cannon's subjects discuss this too:[12] 'It's a humbling experience.

You are forced to really come to terms within yourself with who and what you are, and to look into yourself and not at what the people in the world think of you.' 'Much good can be gained from this. They can learn understanding. They will not be as quick to judge as others.' Similarly Ruth Montgomery states that 'some souls may have deliberately chosen to return with afflictions in order to learn some needed lesson of humility, tolerance or compassion'.[13]

Newton discusses this idea at some length too, and provides an excellent example of a subject planning a past life in the nineteenth century – in the body of a girl who she knew would have a high probability of losing the use of her legs in a carriage accident at the age of six.[14] She chose this deliberately, having had various other lives with a fully functioning and strong body, because she wanted to be fully bedridden and physically inactive to develop her intellectual capabilities. Meanwhile, for their own developmental reasons, her parents wanted to care unconditionally for a daughter that would not marry and leave them.

Different disabilities or disfigurements of course provide different opportunities, but the potential for accelerating soul growth is clearly significant. It is likely to include learning humility without being crushed by ridicule; learning to overcome discrimination; learning who we really are as a person, and not just who people think we are based on how we look; learning to be less judgmental, or how to better identify with disabled or other disadvantaged people in a future life; learning to overcome physical pain by endurance; developing other physical senses if one or more have been lost; learning trust, especially if blind; teaching others about their responses to disability, or perhaps even more to disfigurement, without letting frustration turn to anger; and showing others what can be achieved even with a severe handicap, helping them to see that anything is possible.

Another example of a demanding life choice, certainly historically, is homosexuality. One of Newton's subjects, whose previous life had been that of a wealthy and pampered Chinese empress, found himself with three options for his current life:[15]

> Of my three choices, two were women and one was a handsome young man who, I was told, 'was feminine inside'. One woman was very thin, almost frail looking, who was to live a quiet life of a devoted wife and mother. The other woman was chic, kind of flashy, and destined to be a society gadfly. She was also emotionally cold. I chose the man because I would have to cope with a life of homosexuality. I knew if I could overcome the shame of

society it would offset my life of adulation as an empress.

He could have chosen to have more fun as a society girl, but in a life so similar to that of the empress that his growth would have been little furthered. He could have chosen the quiet and devoted wife, which would probably have been a halfway-house choice in terms of adding to his experience. Instead he chose the hardest option for the swiftest possible emotional development.[16]

As souls grow in experience they also increasingly choose to take on what we might refer to as more 'altruistic lives', which tend to be primarily for other people's benefit and growth rather than their own. The most obvious example of this is when they volunteer for relatively short incarnations. Losing a loved one is one of the most severe tests we ever have to face, but it is far more severe if they are taken from us before time – whether this be by murder, accident or illness. To accept it with dignity, and without anger, bitterness and regrets, is a major challenge most of us have to face at some point. But what better service could a loved one perform than to attempt to help us learn that death is not an ending, that their soul has survived, and that we will be reunited with them in due course?[17]

Of course the most untimely deaths of all are those of young children, and although such lives can sometimes be traumatic for the infants themselves, they tend to be far more aimed at challenging parents and other close relatives to cope with the myriad emotions that surround such a tragic loss. Newton's and Cannon's subjects, Montgomery and Robert Huffman's subject Irene all confirm that in most of these cases the soul of the child will have deliberately and unselfishly chosen to have a 'filler life' that involves no learning for them at all.[18]

It would also appear that such primarily altruistic lives can sometimes be planned on a rather grander scale. Another of Newton's subjects reports that she and three other members of her soul group volunteered to incarnate as Jewish girls in Munich, knowing that they would all be taken to the same death camp at Dachau in 1941, where they would die together.[19] Although their lives may well have involved some personal lessons concerning, for example, courage or humility, it seems they may have known that they were helping humanity as a whole with a much greater lesson.[20]

Corroboration from the Past

If we turn now to the precursors to the pioneers' reports of the interlife experience, we saw in chapter 5 that while the idea of a life review after death is pretty much ubiquitous from the earliest metaphysical texts across the globe – albeit usually incorporating harsh judgments and punishments from various deities – that of next-life planning and choice is almost completely absent from those that adopt a reincarnatory worldview. However there are a few prior sources that reflect this aspect and related ideas, albeit with varying degrees of explicit detail.

The Tibetan Book of the Dead

Before we go any further we should recognize that when any commentator writes about the interlife they nearly always refer to it as the *bardo* state described in the *Tibetan Book of the Dead*. But in fact the contents of this text of unknown antiquity are almost completely divorced from the standard elements of the experience we defined previously – in particular in the extent to which it emphasizes the horrors that are encountered when traversing what we refer to as the intermediate plane. Indeed while it is not particularly long it remains somewhat difficult to put into a context that the Western mind can understand. In fact even expert Tibetan commentators struggle to give a clear interpretation, although in part this may merely reflect the general confusion that seems to abound in the different strands of Buddhism.

However from a number of quarters there comes strong support for the idea that, rather than a literal description of what happens after death, this text represents an instruction manual either for how to prepare for death or even for how to approach incarnate life – or both.[21] Even then, though, its contents arguably have only limited value in the modern world.

Plato and the Hermetica

Probably the earliest description of the interlife that is of any real interest is found in Plato's *Republic*, which dates to the fourth century BCE. In 'The Myth of Er' our hero appears to have something approaching a near-death experience, and on his return is able to describe what happens to souls in the other world.[22] He commences with a description of how 'the throng of souls arriving seemed to have come from a long journey, and turned aside gladly into the meadow and encamped there as for a festival; acquaintances exchanged greetings, and those from earth and those from heaven enquired into each other's experiences'. At some point various 'Judges' decided the fate of the newly arrived souls, who 'carried the evidence of all that they had done behind them'. They were sent 'upwards if just' or 'downwards if unjust', and although the downward path led to a hellish, punishing realm, souls did not stay there indefinitely.

More intriguingly for our current purposes the description then moves on to another location presided over by the 'three Fates, daughters of Necessity... Lachesis who sings of things past, Clotho of things present, Atropos of things to come', and who also control a complex series of spinning whorls. Here souls returning to earth were drawing numbered lots to establish the order in which they would choose from a variety of different 'patterns of life' laid out before them:

> They were of every conceivable kind, animal and human. For there were tyrannies among them, some life-long, some falling in mid-career and ending in poverty, exile and beggary; there were lives of men famed for their good looks and strength and athletic prowess, or for their distinguished birth and family connections, there were lives of men with none of these claims to fame. And there was a similar choice of lives for women. There was no choice of quality of character since of necessity each soul must assume a character appropriate to its choice; but wealth and poverty, health and disease were all mixed in varying degrees in the lives to be chosen.

The whole purpose of this elaborate ritual seems to be for Plato to show that a life of material riches does nothing to enhance soul growth, because the description continues with the drawer of the first lot 'choosing the greatest tyranny he could find... in his folly and greed... without examining it fully... ignoring the Interpreter's warning and forgetting that his misfortunes were his own fault'. Meanwhile for the soul who chooses last – in the myth cast as Odysseus – 'the memory of his former sufferings had cured him of all ambition and he looked round for a long time to find the uneventful life of an ordinary man; at last he found it lying neglected by the others, and when he saw it he chose it with joy and said that had his lot fallen first he would have made the same choice'. Having passed in front of Atropos who 'spins to make the threads of the soul's destiny irreversible', the returning souls finally enter the 'plain of Lethe' to drink from the 'Forgetful River'. If we ignore the judgment, punishment and predestiny aspects of this myth, Plato's description of the interlife is not hugely removed from our modern understanding. The question still remains, of course, as to the source of his information.

Meanwhile it is briefly worth mentioning the *Hermetica*, a body of texts of Greco-Egyptian origin dating to the second century. Here we find a discussion of how there are various 'layers' to the light realms, with souls 'inhabiting one division or another according to their worth'.[23] They are then escorted back to earth by a 'conductor of souls' and given 'a body as is suitable for them'. As with Plato's corpus, these texts are not without inaccuracies that are obvious to the modern reader, but they do hint at important concepts.

Perhaps surprisingly after these promising beginnings there is nothing else of particular relevance in the various esoteric texts of the following millennium and a half – or at least nothing that contains any great detail or clarity.

Theosophy and Anthroposophy

The theosophical movement was founded in London by Russian-born Helena Petrovna Blavatsky in 1875 and her two main treatises, *Isis Unveiled* and *The Secret Doctrine*, first published in 1877 and 1888 respectively, each run to more than fifteen hundred pages. The source of her information has always been highly contentious, with her claiming that much of it came from channeled communication with certain Eastern 'masters' who were still living. However we do know that she was not averse to faking the midair materialization of letters from them, especially in the early days. She has also been accused of plagiarism of other sources, while much of her especially historical material appears to be of somewhat dubious quality. To cap it all, her prose is so stilted as to be almost impossible to follow in places.

Despite these problems we do know that she traveled extensively in India and the Far East, while much of her writing is clearly not channeled – or, if it is, it is well referenced to other entirely physical books. As a result the rather more digestible summaries of theosophy produced by some of her followers contain at least some gems relevant to our current discussion that should not be dismissed too lightly.

Arguably the best of these is Annie Besant's *Ancient Wisdom*, first published in 1898. She makes it absolutely clear from the outset that reincarnation is one of the 'pivotal doctrines' of the Ancient Wisdom.[24] After a lengthy discussion of the evolution of souls in relation to life on planet earth, she provides an interesting postulate about the relatively reactive interlife experience of the soul of early man – although as with most theosophical writing it is interspersed with Eastern terminology:[25]

> When the man left his physical body at death he passed most of his time in kamaloka, sleeping through a brief devachanic period of unconscious assimilation of any minute mental experiences, not yet sufficiently developed for the active heavenly life that lay before him after many days.

Still, the enduring causal body was there, to be the receptacle of his qualities, and to carry them on for further development into his next life on earth.

Then we proceed to a more detailed consideration of the transition and return aspects of the interlife experience for more evolved souls.[26] These correspond well with our descriptions of delayering and relayering, although in theosophy we find much discussion of various 'bodies' – namely the physical, the astral, the mental and the causal – which can be somewhat confusing, even if they might have some real meaning and relevance for more advanced spiritual seekers. In any case, the first three of these bodies are progressively shed during the transition, leaving only the causal body to store the 'germs of the faculties and qualities resulting from the activities of the earth-life'. There is no mention of any other interlife activity at this point, merely a switch to getting ready to return again:

The experiences of the past do not exist as mental images in this new [mental] body; as mental images they perished when the old mind-body perished, and only their essence, their effects on faculty, remain; they were the food of the mind, the materials which it wove into powers; and in the new body they reappear as powers, they determine its materials, and they form its organs... The Thinker [or soul]... then proceeds... to provide himself with an astral body for his life on the astral plane. This, again, exactly represents his desire-nature, faithfully reproducing the qualities he evolved in the past, as the seed reproduces its parent tree... Meanwhile, action external to himself is being taken to provide him with a physical body suitable for the expression of his qualities. In past lives he had made ties with, contracted liabilities towards, other human beings, and some of these will partly determine his place of birth and his family. He has been a source of happiness or of unhappiness to others; this is a factor in determining the conditions of his coming life. His desire-nature is well disciplined, or unregulated and riotous; this will be taken into account in the physical heredity of the new body. He had cultivated certain mental powers... which must be considered... The man may, certainly will, have in him many incongruous characteristics, so that only some can find expression in any one body that could be provided, and a group of his powers suitable for simultaneous expression must be selected. All this is done by certain mighty spiritual intelligences, often spoken of as the Lords of Karma, because it is their function to superintend the working out of causes continually set going by thoughts, desires and actions. They hold the threads of destiny which each man has woven, and guide the reincarnating man to the environment determined by his past, unconsciously self-chosen through his past life.

This latter description of 'Lords of Karma' weaving the 'threads of destiny' is, of course, remarkably similar to that of Plato's 'three Fates'. But this time the somewhat deterministic tone seems to be ameliorated by discussion of them making adjustments to allow for free will to operate via the effects of 'causes continually set going by thoughts, desires and actions'. Finally this passage ends with a detailed description of how the astral and mental bodies merge with the brain and nervous system of the child, in a complex process that commences before birth and apparently continues for seven years afterwards. During this period the consciousness resides more in the astral than the physical, causing no few problems:

> If parents could see their children's brains, vibrating under an inextricable mingling of physical and astral impacts, which the children themselves are quite incapable of separating... they would be more patient with, more responsive to, the confused prattlings of the little ones, trying to translate into the difficult medium of unaccustomed words the elusive touches of which they are conscious, and which they try to catch and retain.

In 1912 another well-known Blavatsky follower, the Austrian esotericist Rudolf Steiner, broke away to form the Anthroposophical Society that concentrated on what he referred to as 'spiritual science' and if anything turned out to be an even more occult movement. His lectures include, for example, complex discussions of planetary influences on the different stages of the interlife, along with an insistence that spiritual understanding gained during incarnate life – especially of the 'mystery of Golgotha [the site of Christ's crucifixion]' – is crucial if the soul is not to remain largely 'asleep' between death and rebirth.[27] Meanwhile his occult investigations appear to have led him to the conclusion that, for example, Mars and other planets are *physically* inhabited, which suggests they were not entirely infallible.[28] Nor is our confidence in his occult sources enhanced when we find him tending to the view that physical incapacities represent punishments for past misdeeds.[29]

Nevertheless in some of his lectures from around this time he unsurprisingly uses similar language to that of other theosophists, and does provide confirmation of the ideas of life review and planning:[30]

> During the period in kamaloca the events of a person's last life, his good and bad deeds, his moral qualities, and so on, come before his soul, and through contemplating his own life in this way he acquires the inclination to bring about the remedy and compensation for all that is imperfect in him, and which has manifested as wrong action. He is moved to acquire those qualities which will bring him nearer to perfection in various directions. He

forms intentions and tendencies during the time up to a new birth, and goes into existence again with these intentions. Further, he himself works upon the new body which he acquires for his new life, and he builds it in conformity with the forces he has brought from previous earthly lives.

In particular Steiner also confirms the idea that during the life review we experience the pain we caused others.[31] As for our personal responsibility for our own circumstances, he has this to say:[32] 'As a result of our earlier incarnations… we resolved in the spiritual world… to occupy the very position in which we now find ourselves. Consequently it is the outcome of a prenatal, pre-earthly decision of the will that we are assigned to our particular place in life.'

If we cannot be sure about the underlying sources of both Platonic and theosophical material, the real precursors to the pioneering interlife research of the late twentieth century are, primarily, a number of undoubtedly channeled books. These discuss the time between lives in far more detail and show substantially greater synergy with modern studies. However, unlike Platonic and theosophical material, arguably none of them had a sufficiently enduring and far-reaching impact to have influenced the broad spectrum of the pioneers' subjects to any significant degree – even if each of them individually attracted significant numbers of devoted followers. The only exception to this is the work of the renowned American psychic Edgar Cayce, but as we will see this provides the least detailed corroboration, while some of the most relevant aspects of his trance 'readings' were only published in book form relatively recently. So instead it is surely reasonable to regard these channeled sources as corroboration of the messages of interlife research – indeed as laying the foundations for it. Moreover, as we might expect, these sources usually discuss the broader implications for free will, personal responsibility and so on.

Before we look at them in detail we should briefly consider the reliability of channeled material in general. Even if we take the view that most of the mediums who purport to act as channels for higher spiritual entities act with complete integrity and sincerity, how can we be sure that their ethereal source itself is reliable? The leading Qabalist Dion Fortune sums up the situation rather well in her excellent 1949 book *The Cosmic Doctrine*:[33]

> Do not think that because a piece of information is obtained in an abnormal way it is bound to be true, any more than a thing is bound to be true because it is printed in a book… A spirit communication may come from a perfectly

genuine spirit, and yet be valueless. Even if a man survives bodily death, dying is not going to cure him of being a fool; if he had no sense on the physical plane, he will not have any more on the astral.

In fact we find that in most of the channeled material we are now about to discuss the sources themselves tend to emphasize this point. They insist that we should not accept what they say merely because they are no longer incarnate, but that instead we should see whether their words appeal to our intuition or reason or, better still, both.

Spiritism

The earliest and arguably some of the finest corroboration of interlife research comes from the 'Spiritism' movement founded by a Frenchman called Léon Rivail nearly two decades before theosophy emerged – although he used the pseudonym Allan Kardec because he was also a mathematics, astronomy and science teacher and textbook writer of some repute.[34] His interest piqued by the emerging popularity of mediums and séances, he decided to conduct systematic investigations by posing spiritual and metaphysical questions to various spirits via, initially, two young female acquaintances. The resulting information was published under the title *The Spirits' Book*, which sold extremely well, and as a result many other groups began posing similar questions and sending their answers in to Kardec, who in 1857 published a completely revised edition that contains answers to more than one thousand questions.

There are perhaps some question marks over the fact that Kardec never publicly named or thanked the mediums he used, while some of the spirits who were supposedly involved are listed at the end of his prologue and include 'John the Evangelist, St Augustine, Socrates, Plato and Swedenborg'. Nevertheless, any doubts cannot fundamentally alter the superb corroboration of interlife research that Spiritism provides – nor the fact that it contains none of the dubious offerings, for example about technologically advanced ancient civilizations and so on, that are common to much channeled material.

Let us commence with its general confirmation of the central tenets of learning and growing through the experience of many incarnations, and of personal responsibility for planning our lives:[35]

When a spirit reenters his spirit life, his whole past unrolls itself before him. He sees the faults which he has committed, and which are the cause of his suffering, and he also sees what would have prevented him from committing them; he comprehends the justice of the situation which is

215

assigned to him, and he then seeks out the new existence that may serve to repair the mistakes of the one which has just passed away. He demands new trials analogous to those in which he has failed, or which he considers likely to aid his advancement; and he demands of the spirits who are his superiors to aid him in the new task he is about to undertake, for he knows that the spirit who will be appointed as his guide in that new existence will endeavor to make him cure himself of his faults by giving him a sort of intuition of those he has committed in the past.

Here we see more or less explicit confirmation of past-life reviews, and of role-playing within them; of next-life planning for growth; and of guides attempting to influence us via intuitive triggers. However there is also far more information about the various elements of the interlife. In terms of the transition, we find confirmation that the soul can leave the body before death to avoid trauma; that welcoming parties usually greet us; that our state of mind at death influences what we experience; and that the extent of our confusion and perception of quasi-physicality is dependent on our level of experience.[36] In terms of past-life reviews we have corroboration of the level of detail and immediacy:[37] 'He has the power of recalling the most minute details of every incident of his life, and even of his thoughts... All the actions which he has an interest in remembering appear to him as though they were present.' And in terms of soul groups we have confirmation that souls regularly incarnate with and recognize each other, and that there are different although un-demarcated aspects of the light realms each inhabited by souls of similar experience:[38] 'They are of different degrees according to the degree of purification to which they have attained... There is nothing like a barrier or line of demarcation between the different degrees of elevation.'

Then, in terms of next-life planning, we have a discussion of the interaction between this and incarnate free will that confirms we only plan the overall circumstances and major probabilities of our lives, while the rest is left to free will and the operation of cause and effect:[39] 'You have chosen the kind of trial to which you are subjected; the details of this trial are a consequence of the general situation which you have chosen, and are often the result of your own actions... The details of events spring from circumstances and the force of things. It is only the leading events of his new life, those which will exercise a determining effect on his destiny, that are foreseen by him.' We also have a reminder that free will reigns supreme, even in respect of interlife planning: 'He chooses for himself the kind of trials which he will undergo, and it is in this freedom of choice that his free will consists... In giving to a spirit the liberty of choice, He [God] leaves to him the entire responsibility of his acts and of their consequences. There is nothing to bar his future; the right road is open to him as freely as the wrong road.' On top of this we find confirmation that souls have a markedly different perception of difficult life choices from humans; that they have a choice of body, including the possibility of one with 'imperfections' that might 'aid advancement'; and that less experienced souls have less input and choice, and can sometimes come back with no real planning.[40]

Finally, in terms of the return, we have corroboration that all souls realize they have to do this sooner or later otherwise they will stagnate, although they retain the ability to delay until they are ready; that the union of soul and fetus begins at conception but is not complete until birth, because the link between them gradually gets stronger; that birth is a much worse experience than death; and that the death of a young baby is 'intended mainly as a trial for the parents'.[41]

As to the overall purpose of incarnation, Spiritism sums it up as follows:[42] 'In each new existence, a spirit takes a step forwards in the path of progress; when he has stripped himself of all his impurities, he has no further need of the trials of corporeal life.'

A number of European supporters of Spiritism published books containing similar ideas in the early 1920s, although most have never been translated into English. Along with paranormal researchers Gabriel Delanne, Camille Flammarion and Ernesto Bozzano, they include the aforementioned regression pioneers Albert de Rochas and Charles Lancelin. It is this prior knowledge of Spiritism that means the latter's early and fascinating research with interlife regression cannot be regarded as objective, despite his insistence in *La Vie Posthume* that his subjects themselves had no prior knowledge.[43] But however popular Spiritism may have been in earlier times, in the modern era it is not widely known or discussed – except in Brazil where it retains a huge following, and to a lesser extent in France.

Silver Birch

Silver Birch is the name of a spirit entity who, in the early part of the twentieth century, began to channel messages through a young man who was initially an outright skeptic. Although the young man's name was not originally disclosed, Silver Birch himself rose to prominence when his messages became a regular feature of weekly meetings held at the London

217

home of Helen Swaffer, which were written up for *Psychic News*. It was later revealed that the medium was in fact Maurice Barbanell, the editor of the magazine.

A compilation entitled *The Teachings of Silver Birch*, first published in 1938, begins by describing how Silver Birch and similar entities had for some time 'inspired many to let their higher selves rise in their lives' and 'helped to free many from the prison-house of creed and dogma' that had 'shamed reason with its foolish stupidities'.[44] He continues by expressing his delight at being 'a vehicle for expressing truths lost for many centuries and now restored to the world of matter, stamped with the seal of divine truth'.

Commencing with the transition, Silver Birch confirms the quasi-physical environment that can be perceived in the light realms:[45] 'We have flowers such as you have never seen, we have colors such as your eye has never beheld, we have scenes and forests, we have birds and plants, we have streams and mountains.' He continues by describing how the level of soul experience will influence what happens: 'When the soul is conscious, it sees the spirit body withdrawing gradually and it opens its eyes in the world of spirit. It is conscious of those who have come to welcome it and it is ready to start its new life. When the soul is not conscious, it is helped through the passage and is taken to whatever place is necessary – it may be a hospital or a home of rest – until it is ready to become aware of its new life.'

On the purpose of life Silver Birch has this to say:[46] 'You are on earth to build your characters. It is the way you face your problems that makes your character.' He continues on to life reviews as follows:

You do not realize that a divine thread runs throughout all your lives...
Your experiences are all part of your evolution. One day, freed from the trammels of flesh, with eyes not clouded by matter, you will look back in retrospect and view the life you have lived on earth. And out of the jigsaw of all the events, you will see how every piece fits into its allotted place, how every experience was a lesson to quicken the soul and to enable it to have greater understanding of its possibilities.

Later he adds: 'You will see everything you have done and everything you have not done which you ought to have done. You will look at those neglected opportunities, and that will cause you remorse.' He also confirms the idea of the experience-based and un-demarcated aspects of the light realms:[47] 'The world of spirit is not a world where spheres are marked off with boundaries such as you have. It is a progressive life from lower to higher stages, with no boundaries, because they all merge into one another. As the soul gradually unfolds, it expresses itself on higher planes of spirit... It cannot travel higher in the realms of spirit than the unfolding of its character has reached.'

Silver Birch does not have much to say about life planning, but he does confirm that 'the soul will choose that country and that race which is necessary for its new unfoldment'.[48] Moreover he seems to hint at the progressive soul choices that often lie behind disability:[49] 'You will find, usually, that those who start their material lives with a material defect have in their souls a compensating principle. They exhibit in their characters more kindness, toleration and gentleness to others.'

Edgar Cayce

Throughout most of the first half of the twentieth century the aforementioned Edgar Cayce, the so-called 'sleeping prophet', gave more than fourteen thousand trance readings to subjects who came from all over the world to consult him. He is probably one of *the* most quoted spiritual sources of recent times, and the books that deal with his life and work now number in the hundreds. Nevertheless, we cannot expect to obtain a balanced picture of his contribution without first being realistic about certain shortcomings.

To start with the transcripts of Cayce's readings are, unfortunately, extremely difficult to follow because he uses language that is archaic, stilted, ungrammatical and often repetitive. Another somewhat off-putting aspect of his general 'life readings' is that a significant proportion of his subjects were supposed to have had earlier lives in Atlantis. The prime source of information on this lost civilization is his son Edgar Evans Cayce's 1968 compilation *Edgar Cayce on Atlantis*, in which it is described as a highly technological civilization apparently destroyed by a massive flood around 12,500 years ago. Indeed Cayce himself was supposed to be the reincarnation of a high priest by the name of Ra-Ta who helped to organize the evacuation of survivors to Egypt. Various more detailed suggestions – such as that the Great Pyramid of Giza was built around this time, while a Hall of Records containing information from before the flood was constructed beneath the Sphinx – are also open to serious doubt. Nor was any of this helped by his prediction that these records would be unearthed in 1998, which led to unbounded but ultimately fruitless excitement in the run-up to the millennium.[50]

A similar problem is reflected in Mary Ann Woodward's 1971

compilation *Edgar Cayce's Story of Karma*, in which almost every subject has had past lives – not only in Atlantis but also in Egypt and the Near East – in which they were highly influential and powerful. Nor are extremely famous people missing from these readings. The parents of a baby boy who was less than a year old were promised great things because he had supposedly been the composer Franz Liszt in a previous life, while his brother had been the playwright Molière.[51] Meanwhile those of another boy of four had someone seriously special on their hands: not only had he been the biblical prophet Elisha, successor to Elijah, but prior to that he had been the flood survivor and savior of humanity Noah.[52] Unfortunately, follow-up revealed that this latter subject might not have been completely fulfilling his supreme potential by working as the manager of a supermarket in a small southern town. But perhaps Woodward's selection was just unfortunate, because Cayce spokesperson and chronicler Kevin Todeschi insists that less than two hundred of his readings identify famous past lives, the remainder being far more ordinary – which would better fit the pattern of usually unremarkable past lives recalled by subjects *themselves* under regression.[53]

Cayce is also regarded as one of the forefathers of the holistic healing movement, because the majority of his 'medical readings' deal with the underlying emotional causes of physical and psychological problems. This premise seems entirely sound when the problems are related to the dynamic of psychic cause and effect within the current life – and provided we also accept that some more serious problems might have been deliberately chosen in advance by experienced souls in order to accelerate their growth. However in Woodward's 1985 compilation *Scars of the Soul* it is again somewhat off-putting to find that Cayce's diagnosis for a number of the quoted cases is that current problems represent punishments for wrongdoing in previous lives – so that in 'meeting self' the subjects are reaping what they have previously sown. A similar line of argument is often found in Gina Cerminara's earlier compilation *Many Mansions*, first published in 1950. Nor is any of this helped by what now appear extremely archaic attitudes to, for example, homosexuality.[54] These must surely reflect not just the culture of the time but also Cayce's strong, traditional, Christian beliefs – which were in many respects so at odds with his reincarnation-based readings.

Nevertheless, on the positive side he repeatedly entreats his subjects to meditate regularly and to live more spiritual lives. Not only that but throughout his readings he emphasizes the idea of soul learning and growth.[55] He also echoes the suggestion that, especially in our current life, the exercising of free will reigns supreme:

> The soul comes into each experience for the express purpose of manifesting in materiality under the environs of those things builded in the past, or the hereditary influence of the entity. Whether the meeting of any experience makes for development or retardment depends upon what the entity does with the knowledge pertaining to the Creative Forces in all the activity – what the soul, the body, does about what it knows, in manifesting what the soul worships as its ideal. If that ideal is the Christ-Consciousness, well. If that ideal is selfish developments, or the aggrandizing of activities in the carnal forces, then these must bring rather the fruits of such into the experiences of the soul. As the warning has been given, there is today set before us good and evil, life and death. The growth of the soul depends upon what the will chooses.

Indeed, despite the apparent emphasis on reactive karma in many of his readings, Cayce goes further and emphasizes that at any time a person can take steps to ensure that the 'law of grace' takes over from that of karma as the dominant force in their life.[56] This is entirely in keeping with our suggestion about becoming conscious creators within the context of a more spiritual outlook on life. Moreover he explicitly confirms the view that we should take personal responsibility for how our present is shaping our future, rather than falling back on the determinism of how our past might have shaped our present.[57]

Cayce does not mention the interlife experience as such, but he does continually refer to the idea of soul groups whose members incarnate together repeatedly in different relationships.[58] As for life reviews and planning, we saw in the previous chapter that these tend to rely on the library archetype of the light realms, which is in turn synonymous with the akashic records. Most important for our current purposes is Cayce's description of using these records for his readings of the past and possible future – although as celebrated as he was this aspect of his work was not specifically publicized in any detail until 1998, when Todeschi brought together all the relevant material on how this 'supercomputer' works in his compilation *Edgar Cayce on The Akashic Records*. From a life review perspective Cayce himself compares these records to a movie that can be replayed, but with the soul's true intent understood, and with the perspectives of all participants recorded.[59] More crucially he also talks about them from a life planning perspective, and Todeschi provides an excellent description of this based on various of Cayce's life readings:[60]

Imagine that a software program had been created which could predict with astonishing accuracy the outcome of any decision or choice that you needed to make. Not only could this program foresee your personal future, but somehow it could analyze the consequence of your choices and the effect those choices would have upon the people and events around you. Imagine, as well, that this program was so finely tuned that it could also correctly anticipate how the slightest change in your thoughts, activities or decisions would impact any of the potential futures which had been envisioned. Finally, imagine that this ongoing process of calculating probabilities and evolving time lines takes place to draw together individuals and events to best provide everyone with the needed opportunities to learn the necessary lessons for personal transformation and soul growth.

In addition Cayce confirms that it is largely a question of the soul's own choice as to when and where it reincarnates, and into what family, race and sex.[61]

To sum up, despite the earlier criticisms of certain aspects of his work, we should recognize that Cayce worked tirelessly to give readings to thousands of people who requested his help – and in the process did as much as anyone in the twentieth century to bring a spiritual worldview based on reincarnation to the fore. Meanwhile the Association for Research and Enlightenment, founded by Cayce himself in Virginia Beach in 1931, continues to do a fine job of preserving and perpetuating his work.

Pathwork

'Pathwork' or 'the Path' comprises a series of over two hundred and fifty 'lectures' delivered by a spiritual entity who referred to himself only as 'the Guide'. They were channeled in New York through Eva Pierrakos – a petite, vivacious woman originally brought up in Austria – commencing in 1957 and carrying on through to her death in 1979. However the Pathwork Foundation set up to protect and foster this material has never actively sought publicity, and the first book about it – an introduction entitled *The Pathwork of Self-Transformation* – was only published in 1990. It remains little known except to devotees although the full lectures, which run into several thousands of pages, are now available on the Foundation's website.[62]

As with Spiritism this superb corpus appears to contain few if any of the dubious elements associated with most channeled material, while much of it is devoted to self-transformation – of which more later. The main interlife themes are incorporated into some of the earliest lectures, given in 1957. One in particular contains nearly all the main themes. Starting with transition it confirms the idea of initial healing and rest and talks of beautiful reception surroundings:[63]

> There are hospitals, my dear ones, where ailing souls are taken care of and healed. There are places of rest, also in different degrees, all corresponding to their development, for spirits who have left their bodies behind and also for spirits who have come to rest in the spiritual world after the completion of a great task. These beings need rest for a certain amount of time. Other spheres could be called reception spheres. They are also beautiful and often more so than your earth sphere. These spheres are for spirit entities who are perhaps not yet on a level to deserve continuous bliss. However, they have fulfilled their lives well, within the limits of their possibilities, and need and deserve a time of recovery before they can resume their path of development.

We can also see here the idea of different aspects attracting souls of different experience coming through in the 'places of rest' having 'different degrees... corresponding to their development'. Next we have some wonderful corroboration of the full re-experiencing and lack of obfuscation that characterize the past-life review, coupled with a distinction between it and a much briefer, less involving, initial review:

> There is one specific sphere where a life is viewed, sometimes even several lives. At times, the last life is connected with the one that preceded it, and only comparing the two brings about full understanding. Now the spirit who has just concluded his earthly life sees his life with such clarity that he can no longer pretend and make excuses the way humans like to do. They are prone to displace their real motives and wear a mask so that their pure currents are polluted by the unpurified qualities. But here everything is clear and open. This is not to be confused with the well-known phenomenon after dying when one sees one's life unroll in front of one's eyes in a very brief sequence. That is another thing. It always occurs, but in this case it happens very briefly, and the human spirit sees the picture of the past life almost indifferently, so to speak. It seems to concern the life of someone else. You are not affected, not emotionally moved. You see it objectively. In the sphere of purification, the process is much more extended and lasts as long as is necessary to understand what up to now you have refused to understand. This can be painful. You really come to feel that this is about you. You re-experience your life.

This extract carries on to emphasize the completely different soul perspective that operates during the review:

> It turns out that earthly life is evaluated quite differently here than on earth

where you are still in your body. As long as the body encloses the spirit and imprisons it, the suffering about each trial and blow of fate is great. To experience something difficult seems frightening to you. But as long as everything goes well on the outside, you are happy. Already in these realms of purification – which are by no means high spheres – the experience of looking at the unfolding pictures of your last life is entirely different. It is possible that a heavy fate you suffered on earth made you very sad then, but since from the spiritual point of view you have come through it well, it gives you now, as you experience it again, looking at the film, a feeling of endless peace. It gives you a sense of happiness because you passed the test and learned what there was to learn. However, a pleasant time passed in contentment may cause you great disquietude if during it the spiritual task was not completed.

This brief reference to a 'film' is backed up with more explicit confirmation of the archetypes of libraries and life films, which can be used not only for personal review and planning but also for more universal study:

One sphere in the spirit world could be called the sphere of science. Yet it is not like your human science. All the knowledge that exists, which humankind discovers only partially and gradually, is openly displayed. There is the sphere of history, if I can call it so. It does not merely deal with the history of the earth but also with the history of creation, and here everything can be observed. You only have to imagine a movie. Everything is etched in that breath of God, and you can review it again. Spirits sufficiently advanced in their development and having a specific interest may take on a particular task. They are then guided to this sphere by expert spirit beings and, with their help, study for some time to learn what is necessary and advantageous for the chosen task. They learn the plan of salvation, the history of creation, and all that pertains to it.

Moving on to next-life planning we have corroboration of the assistance of various higher beings, and of the close involvement of the soul itself:

Within an extensive sphere with different departments, there are specific places where the incarnations are prepared... Here specifically trained higher beings know exactly the laws and the past incarnations of an individual soul, have studied the load still needed to carry the merits, the abilities, what has been completed, and what still remains. They know the entire path of the individual soul's destiny so that they are capable of ascertaining and planning the most advantageous circumstances and conditions for the next life on earth, including the merits and hindrances which each entity is to bring to earth in order to make the most progress.

The being who is about to be incarnated discusses the coming life with the higher beings, speaks his wishes, and listens to advice.

This also seems to confirm that we are involved in selecting the emotions still to be worked on and the past-life strengths that will help in this – or 'hindrances and merits'. In addition the extract about the 'sphere of history' above carries on to emphasize how any plans are only outlines that have to be fleshed out by the exercising of free will once in incarnation: 'Here are also the roughly outlined plans for the future, always only as a framework giving each soul enough space to determine the time and the outcome with its free will.'

Another early lecture discusses how souls may be a little overzealous about choosing difficult lives as an aid to growth:[64]

Not every spirit will be granted such a burdened life which he, too eagerly, chooses. The high spirits of God's world who are working in this field are able to judge whether a spirit has sufficient strength to stand this or that trial. And if this seems not the case, such a spirit will be advised not to choose too heavy a burden. Sometimes it will be even rejected to choose such a lot. These high forces can exactly recognize what a spirit is capable of or not even if that spirit cannot always see it. A certain percentage of possibility must be recognizable that, if it is willed, the destiny can be fulfilled. If the margin of possibility is too narrow, it will not be granted.

Here the Guide also confirms that physical life accelerates growth:

From a spiritual viewpoint, if he lives the right human life, he can unfold spiritually in a relatively shorter period of time than it would be possible in the spirit world because of the absence of major frictions there.

Meanwhile a rather later lecture emphasizes our traditional misunderstanding of the concept of divine judgment:[65]

'The Last Judgment' or 'Judgment Day'… these terminologies mean to convey that there is a 'time' after death when all is revealed. Human beings usually react unfavorably to this concept because they think of it in terms of a punishing deity, a cruel, unmerciful ruler who imposes more unfairness on them. As you know, this was an ancient concept of God. God was confused with cruel earthly leaders and fathers. But the true meaning of the 'final judgment' is the revealing of connections that show the unutterable beauty of the faultless justice of spiritual laws.

These 'connections' again relate not only to the way successions of lives may carry the same emotional threads, but also to our often unconscious creation of our own reality within incarnate life – and lack of awareness of the original causes that create the effects we consciously observe.

Seth

Arguably the material that could have most influenced the pioneering interlife research – in terms of being contemporary, popular and covering most of the elements – was channeled by an entity calling himself Seth. He operated through the medium Jane Roberts, who lived in New York State, between 1963 and her death in 1984. His messages were first offered to the public in *The Seth Material* in 1970, while of the numerous other books that followed the 'master work' was *Seth Speaks*, published in 1972. However none of the pioneers mention any knowledge of Seth, and nor can we assume that a significant proportion of their subjects – especially Ramster's, for example, who were outside the US – would have been aware of it. Moreover, of course, some of the earliest interlife research had already been undertaken before this time.

There are some broad problems with the Seth material. When properly studied there are elements that appear to be inconsistent and conflicting; moreover it is out of step with many other sources in certain particulars, although this may be at least partly due to the complexity of some of the topics. For example, he maintains that there are multiple worlds we experience simultaneously; that time is not only linear but also circular; and, echoing Cayce, that there were a number of technological civilizations on this planet before Atlantis. There are good reasons to take issue with all of these suggestions.[66]

However as far as the interlife experience is concerned Seth's approach is entirely consistent with the pioneers' research. If we commence with the transition he confirms that the soul can choose to leave the physical body before death occurs; that welcoming parties come to meet it; that some disoriented souls may have a rest period, or require a degree of rehabilitation in what they may perceive to be 'hospitals and rest homes'; that souls create their own reality in the light realms, including hellish experiences; that more experienced souls will require less initial orientation; and that after transition there can be no hypocrisy or hiding from underlying truths.[67] As for the past-life review, he agrees that it allows the soul to 'relive' past events, to role-play different scenarios and to see how it has affected others:[68]

> You examine the fabric of the existence you have left, and you learn to understand how your experiences were the result of your own thoughts and emotions and how these affected others... The earth years will be

experienced again, but not necessarily in continuity. The events may be used in any way the individual chooses; altered, played back the way they happened for contrast... The other actors, however, are thought-forms.

In terms of soul groups, we find corroboration that souls reincarnate together repeatedly, and that the various aspects of the light realms are demarcated by 'psychological barriers' based on the soul's level of experience.[69] If we now turn to next-life planning, Seth confirms that we deliberately undergo a 'time of choosing' in which we decide on the major characteristics of our next life, including our parents and environment; that we may see 'flashes of the future existence'; that 'all counsel' is available at this time from 'guides and teachers'; that we plan our incarnations with other souls who will be involved; and that some souls are impatient to return and do not avail themselves of the advice on hand.[70] He also confirms the idea of seeing both sides of any emotional coin, and of adverse circumstances sometimes being chosen to speed up growth:[71]

If in one life, for example, you hated women, you may very well be a woman in the next life. Only in this way, you see, would you be able to relate to the experience of womanhood, and then as a woman face those attitudes that you yourself had against women in the past. If you had no sympathy for the sick, you may then be born with a serious disease, again now self-chosen, and find yourself encountering those attitudes that once were your own. Such an existence would usually also include other issues, however. No existence is chosen for one reason only, but would also serve many other psychological experiences. A chronically ill existence, for example, might also be a measure of discipline, enabling you to use deeper abilities that you ignored in a life of good health. The perfectly happy life, for example, on the surface may appear splendid, but it may also be basically shallow and do little to develop the personality. The truly happy existence, however, is a deeply satisfying one that would include spontaneous wisdom and spiritual joy. I am not saying, in other words, that suffering necessarily leads to spiritual fulfillment, nor that all illness is accepted or chosen for such a purpose, for this is not the case. Illness is often the result of ignorance and lazy mental habits. Such a discipline may be adopted however by certain personalities who must take strong measures with themselves because of other characteristics.

Perhaps most impressively Seth backs up our earlier suggestion that traditional, deterministic notions of karma are extremely unhelpful because of their conflict with the over-riding concept of free will:[72]

I have also discussed reincarnation in terms of environment because many schools of thought over-emphasize the effects of reincarnational existences, so that often they explain present-life circumstances as a result of rigid and uncompromising patterns determined in a 'past' life. You will feel relatively incompetent to handle present physical reality, to alter your environment, to affect and change your world, if you feel that you are at the mercy of conditions over which you have no control. The reasons given for such subjugations matter little in the long run, for the reasons change with the times and with your culture. You are not under a sentence placed upon you for original sin, by any childhood events, or by past-life experience. You wrote the script. Like a true absent-minded professor the conscious self forgets all this, however, so when tragedy appears in the script, difficulty or challenges, the conscious self looks for someone or something to blame.

As for the return, Seth agrees that we bring strong unresolved emotions with us to carry on working with them:[73] 'You may have brought negative influences into your life for a given reason, but the reason always has to do with understanding, and understanding removes those influences.' He also confirms that the soul can enter the fetus at any time between conception and birth; that this is a gradual merging process; that the soul can vacate the body for some years even after birth; and that identification with the light realms remains strong in these early years, but gradually dwindles.[74]

Sri Aurobindo

There is one other source that lays some firm foundations for modern interlife research, although it is clearly not channeled – which is why it has been left to the end. It is Aurobindo's *The Life Divine*, which as we saw earlier is markedly different from most other Eastern mystical works. In fact the relevant chapter was originally written for his *Arya* back in the 1910s, so it is not entirely clear where he obtained what at that time was a virtually unique view of the interlife – with the possible exception of the channeled material that Kardec had previously amassed. However it does seem that he was at pains to deduce most of his ideas from evidence and logic, and so a combination of the concepts of reincarnation, free will and soul growth may have been enough for him to develop his view. Whatever their source, Aurobindo's insights are profound and enduring.

If we start with the transition, he discusses the idea that there are different aspects of the intermediate plane as well as of the light plane, and that souls who retain strong connections to the physical or have specific expectations can create 'desire worlds' in which they may reside for some time.[75] However he adds that normally they will move on to a 'plane of pure psychic existence', or in our terms the light realms proper. He also spends some time describing what appears to be pretty close to our delayering process:

> At each stage he would exhaust and get rid of the fractions of formed personality-structure, temporary and superficial, that belonged to the past life; he would cast off his mind-sheath and life-sheath as he had already cast off his body-sheath: but the essence of the personality and its mental, vital and physical experiences would remain in latent memory or as a dynamic potency for the future.

As for the ideas of past-life review and next-life planning, Aurobindo does not discuss them in great detail, but he does make reference to them in terms that are highly consistent with modern interlife research – for example by indicating that a soul will 'assimilate the energies of its past experience and life and prepare its future'.[76] Then in a slightly fuller description he again discusses the idea of delayering in different planes of vibration, before closing with an emphasis on how, normally, souls themselves choose their next life:

> There is an assimilation, a discarding and strengthening and rearrangement of the old characters and motives, a new ordering of the developments of the past and a selection for the purposes of the future without which the new start cannot be fruitful or carry forward the evolution. For each birth is a new start; it develops indeed from the past, but is not its mechanical continuation: rebirth is not a constant reiteration but a progression, it is the machinery of an evolutionary process. Part of this rearrangement, the discarding especially of past strong vibrations of the personality, can only be effected by an exhaustion of the push of previous mental, vital, physical motives after death, and this internal liberation or lightening of impedimenta must be put through on the planes proper to the motives that are to be discarded or otherwise manipulated, those planes which are themselves of that nature; for it is only there that the soul can still continue the activities which have to be exhausted and rejected from the consciousness so it can pass on to a new formation. It is probable also that the integrating positive preparation would be carried out and the character of the new life would be decided by the soul itself in a resort to its native habitat, a plane of psychic repose, where it would draw all back into itself and await its new stage in the evolution.

In addition, 'selection for the purposes of the future' may again hint at choosing emotions and strengths to work with in the next life. Elsewhere he also confirms that impetuous souls might hurry back into incarnation, for example because of a 'strong will of earthly desire pressing for fulfillment', while other less experienced souls might effectively spend some time asleep due to their inability to attune to the higher vibrations of the light realms proper.[77]

8

THE HOLOGRAPHIC SOUL

The Unity of All Things

There is a crucial element of any spiritual approach that we have not so far discussed, and that is the whole concept of 'God'. Rather like the word *karma*, traditional religious approaches have imbued this with somewhat unhelpful connotations, but there are many alternative names both ancient and modern that attempt to convey the ineffable breadth and depth of what we might usefully refer to as an 'ultimate state of consciousness'. So whether we call this the One, the All, the Absolute, the Ultimate, the Great Spirit or whatever else, It is the Ultimate energy or force that underlies the entire universe, both seen and unseen, and the Origin or Source of everything in it.

What is most important is that we should drop any traditional occidental notion that God is something external to us. It is to be hoped that precious few people now conjure up images of a kindly old man with a long, white beard sitting on a cloud. Indeed many followers of the Christian faith, for example, now talk about inviting God *into* their hearts, and such internalization can only be a good thing. This is more in line with oriental approaches that, since time immemorial, have maintained that the divine consciousness is already inside all of us. This is why it is no exaggeration to maintain that 'we are all God'. But the corollary to this is that 'we are all One', and it is this revelation of the ultimate connectedness and unity of all things that underlies most mystical or transcendental experiences.

These can occur in a number of different contexts. If we first consider near-death experiences a prime example is provided by George Rodonaia, whose case we discussed in chapter 1 in a veridical context, although indicating that it also has a conspicuously transcendental flavor. His description of the experience of unity is typical:[1]

231

The next thing that happened was that I saw all these molecules flying around, atoms, protons, neutrons, just flying everywhere. On the one hand, it was totally chaotic, yet what brought me such great joy was that this chaos also had its own symmetry. This symmetry was beautiful and unified and whole, and it flooded me with tremendous joy. I saw the universal form of life and nature laid out before my eyes... Everything is not only connected together, everything is also one.

An American artist, Mellen-Thomas Benedict, had a similarly transcendental near-death experience after being diagnosed with terminal cancer in 1982. For our current purposes the crucial element in a lengthy description is as follows:[2] 'I became aware of a higher self matrix, a conduit to Source. We all have a higher self, or an oversoul part of our being, a conduit. All higher selves are connected as one being, all humans are connected as one being.'

In the last half-century we have also been inundated with the reports of 'psychedelic travelers' using a variety of hallucinogens to induce altered states of consciousness, and here too the experience of unity is relatively commonplace. For example the celebrated Czechoslovakian-born LSD researcher Stanislav Grof, who founded the discipline of 'transpersonal psychology', briefly discusses his subjects' reports of feeling a 'oneness with life and all creation' in his 1975 book *Realms of the Human Unconscious*.[3] This is tied into, although according to Grof not identical with, an identification with 'the consciousness of the Universal Mind' that 'encompasses the totality of existence' and is 'the supreme and ultimate principle that represents all Being'. He continues: 'This experience is boundless, unfathomable, and ineffable; it is existence itself. Verbal communication and the symbolic structure of our everyday language seem to be a ridiculously inadequate means to capture and convey its nature and quality.' He suggests that underlying even this, though, is the experience of 'the Supracosmic or Metacosmic void of the primordial emptiness, nothingness, and silence, which is the ultimate source and cradle of all existence and the uncreated and ineffable Supreme'. Whether or not these specific distinctions are useful, the general idea is clear.

In his 2001 book *The Spirit Molecule* the American psychiatrist Rick Strassman describes similar experiences in his research using DMT.[4] One subject simply reported that 'God is in everything and we are all connected', while another found themselves entering a 'white light' and experiencing a sense of 'pure being, oneness and ecstasy'.

Cosmic Consciousness & the Power of Now

Of course many spiritual seekers simply engage in meditation in their attempts to have similar transcendental experiences – although this is painstaking work, and some maintain that the use of hallucinogens can act as a catalyst to speed up the expansion of awareness. Indeed for a number of Eastern approaches, including especially Indian Vedanta and Yoga, Zen Buddhism and Chinese Taoism, achieving a state of 'cosmic consciousness' on a more permanent basis is the ultimate objective.

A number of Indian spiritual gurus exerted a significant influence on Western thinking in the twentieth century, but one of the most celebrated must surely be Paramhansa Yogananda. He studied under the Bengali guru Sri Yukteswar in his teens before heading to the US where, in 1920, he set up the Self-Realization Fellowship dedicated to the practice of Kriya Yoga. In his 1946 classic *Autobiography of a Yogi* he describes how his first experience of cosmic consciousness was brought on by his guru gently striking his chest above the heart:[5]

> My body became immovably rooted; breath was drawn out of my lungs as if by some huge magnet. Soul and mind instantly lost their physical bondage, and streamed out like fluid, piercing light from my every pore. The flesh was as though dead, yet in my intense awareness I knew that never before had I been fully alive. My sense of identity was no longer narrowly confined to a body, but embraced the circumambient atoms.

He then reveals how his vision became 'panoramic' and no longer reliant on his physical eyes so that, for example, he could see a cow approaching him from behind, then watched it with his eyes while it was in their line of vision, but was then able to see it clearly again after it passed behind a brick wall. He continues:

> All objects within my panoramic gaze trembled and vibrated like quick motion pictures. My body, Master's, the pillared courtyard, the furniture and floor, the trees and sunshine, occasionally became violently agitated, until all melted into a luminescent sea; even as sugar crystals, thrown into a glass of water, dissolve after being shaken. The unifying light alternated with materializations of form, the metamorphoses revealing the law of cause and effect in creation. An oceanic joy broke upon calm endless shores of my soul. The Spirit of God, I realized, is exhaustless bliss; his Body is countless tissues of light. A swelling glory within me began to envelop towns, continents, the earth, solar and stellar systems, tenuous nebulae, and floating universes. The entire cosmos, gently luminous, like a city seen afar

at night, glimmered within the infinitude of my being.

Yogananda carries on to describe how he could see galaxies and constellations being formed by the 'condensation of creative beams', then resolving again into 'diaphanous luster'. His experience ends with a perception that the creative centre of all this was actually 'a point of intuitive perception in my heart... irradiating splendor from my nucleus to every part of the universal structure', while he heard 'the creative voice of God resounding as *Aum*, the vibration of the Cosmic Motor'. We could not ask for a much finer description of how the Ultimate Divinity resides within us all.

He follows this up by reporting that with his master's help he developed the ability to summon this cosmic consciousness at will by 'stilling his thoughts', and to transmit it to others – but only if they had engaged in sufficient meditational practice that their mind was able to 'absorb the liberating shock of omnipresence'. He adds that in fact the sincere devotee will automatically attract the experience because their 'intense craving begins to pull at God with an irresistible force'.

Another Indian sage who has exerted a significant influence on spiritual thinking in the West is Jiddu Krishnamurti. In 1909 his father went to work as a clerk at the Theosophical Society headquarters in Madras, where the teenage Jiddu was soon 'discovered' by Charles Leadbetter, a prominent member of the movement. Leadbetter proclaimed that he was the 'world teacher' they had been searching for, and along with Annie Besant set about tutoring him for the role. However over the ensuing years Krishnamurti became increasingly disenchanted with theosophy and its leadership, until at the age of thirty-five he disbanded the 'Order of the Star' that had been set up in his honor and proclaimed that he would work alone. Not only that but from this point on he actively discouraged anyone to follow any sort of guru or leader, or any sort of formalized spiritual approach.

Several interconnected themes run throughout Krishnamurti's lectures and dialogues with other celebrated thinkers, which continued right up until his death in 1986.[6] He maintains that our lack of awareness of the unity of all things lies at the heart of all conflicts, so we should learn to 'see' properly and without separating the observer and the observed – and especially without allowing the weight of our prejudicial thought processes, which can only represent a past that is now gone, to interfere.[7] He also insists that thought hangs on to the pleasures of the past and hopes to recreate or better them in the future, which in turn leads to fear that these desires will not be fulfilled. So to do away with all these thoughts of the past and future one needs to be completely 'present in the now'.[8] And to assist in this process the seeker needs to meditate, not following any particular methodology, not forcing it as a difficult discipline, but merely by adopting the 'right way of living' so that the mind learns to become 'still'.[9]

All this is sound spiritual advice echoed by many other commentators, as we will shortly see. However we might note that Krishnamurti was not without his critics. They maintain not only that his private life was riddled with affairs and lies and therefore somewhat at odds with his spiritual teachings, but also that the teachings themselves are really rather self-evident and even vacuous – albeit dressed up to sound extremely wise and profound.[10]

The recommendation that we should strive to be more present in the now is self-help advice that anyone can attempt to follow, without devoting themselves to hours of meditation or living the life of an ascetic. Perhaps its most renowned modern exponent is Eckhart Tolle, an originally unremarkable university postgraduate whose enlightenment occurred suddenly, at the age of twenty-nine, during a particularly virulent bout of suicidal depression. His first book *The Power of Now*, published in 1999, has sold millions of copies around the world and is refreshing for its simplicity and lack of ego. His 2005 follow-up, *A New Earth*, is equally full of profound yet simple insights into the human condition.

To summarize Tolle's approach, he suggests that we are constantly preoccupied with looking both backwards and forwards – in fact anything rather than concentrate on the present, the here and now. We focus on the past because this is what gives us our sense of identity, and what has led us to the life circumstances that we currently face; and we focus on the future because this is where all our dreams, hopes and fears will play out. But we can never actually experience the past or the future. The past is gone, and in reality we only ever experienced it as a whole series of 'nows'. The same will be true of the future, when it arrives. In fact the only thing that ever has any real, underlying validity is the present. It is the only thing we truly experience, whereas we replay the past or dream about the future in our minds only.[11] Not only that but he echoes Krishnamurti's insistence that the past brings with it a whole series of conditioned responses, which keep us in chains and prevent us from seeing the now for what it really is. Meanwhile the future holds out fears or promises, depending on our outlook, which may have no validity other than that with which they are imbued by our dwelling on them. In other words we are back with the premise that we create our own future reality with our current thoughts and attitudes – and often these are only partly conscious at best, negative and based on unfounded fears.

More than this, though, Tolle argues that by allowing our 'ego' or 'mind self' to be caught up in dreams of how our life will be better at some time in the future – if only we can win the lottery, get that better job or house, move to that other place or find that special relationship – we yearn for external pleasures that, even if we gain them, will bring only temporary fulfillment. That is because they are immediately followed by a thirst for more, or by a high potential for emotional pain because things we have gained can just as easily be lost or taken away.[12] He emphasizes that real joy, by contrast, comes from within – from just 'being' in the now, and from recognizing the simple beauty of all other forms and our underlying unity with them. All this ties in with the Eastern doctrine of 'impermanence', which cautions us that nothing lasts forever, and that everything changes.

While most of us only obtain fleeting glimpses of this unity at best, Tolle insists that with practice we can learn to see life like this all the time – and to switch back into a time-mind-conditioned view only when it suits us, rather than allowing it to dominate our perceptions. Moreover, even though we will see later that most of his ideas can be found in Eastern scripture dating back several thousand years, he does practice what he preaches. After his sudden enlightenment he apparently spent several years with no home or possessions, living as a vagrant on a park bench. He describes every moment of this experience as being one of true, unadulterated bliss – indeed it was the constant stream of people coming up to him and saying 'we want some of what you have got' that convinced him to become active in life again and to share his message. So his advice is not to quote the Buddha, or to hope to achieve Buddha-like enlightenment at some point in the future, but just to *be* the Buddha, right here, right now.[13]

Another modern exponent of the power of now is Sydney Banks, a Scottish-born philosopher now resident in Canada who is best known for his 2001 novel *The Enlightened Gardener*. But he had summarized his simple philosophy three years earlier in *The Missing Link*, concentrating on the three principles of 'mind, consciousness and thought that enable us to acknowledge and respond to existence'. He suggests that we should strive to synchronize our 'personal mind' with the 'universal mind'.[14] He then adds the now familiar exhortation that to do this properly we need to live in the now, as well as recognize that we create our own reality with our thoughts – so that letting go of the negative is of vital importance.[15]

There are a number of other proponents of these ideas of cosmic consciousness and the power of now, most of them predating at least Tolle and Banks, but because they place them in a rather broader context we will come to them in due course.

Quantum Mysticism

The first half of the twentieth century witnessed a rapid expansion of our understanding of the physical and not-so-physical world, involving distinguished scientists such as Ernest Rutherford, Max Planck, Albert Einstein, Niels Bohr, Werner Heisenberg and Paul Dirac, among many others. The first important discoveries were that the supposed particles inside an atom sometimes behave like waves, and that atoms and even their nuclei mainly consist of empty space – that is, a vacuum. This paved the way for the traditional Newtonian view of fundamental 'building blocks of matter' to be shattered by the introduction of quantum theory, which proposed that protons, electrons and so on are fundamentally only 'probability waves'.

There remain many different interpretations of quantum theory, but one is that these waves only 'collapse' – that is become particle-like and, for example, take on a specific position – when they are observed; this in turn suggests that the 'observer' plays an integral role in the outcome of any quantum experiment. This idea of interconnectedness is taken a step further with the idea that spinning electrons appear to be able to 'communicate' with each other instantaneously over huge distances, or 'non-locally'.[16] It is these interpretations of quantum theory that have provided apparent scientific reinforcement for the principle of the unity of all things – with some taking the implications further and arguing not just that everything in the universe is connected, but also that it all works off a unified, underlying consciousness.

A number of prominent 'quantum mystics' have gained a considerable reputation in spiritual circles as a result of their efforts to tie all this in with traditional mystical approaches, especially from the East. But some of them are not averse to glossing over the fact that there are other interpretations.[17] For example there remains considerable disagreement about what constitutes an observer – especially about whether they have to be 'conscious', and if so how this is defined – and this has fundamental implications for what causes the quantum wave function to collapse, if indeed it does. Moreover some interpretations of quantum theory reject the idea of non-local communication.

The first such mystic to gain widespread prominence was the American Fritjof Capra, whose 1976 book *The Tao of Physics* continues to be hailed as one of the classics of the genre. More recently the cult documentary 'What the Bleep Do We Know?' made a significant breakthrough into the mainstream when it was released by Fox in 2005. Its primary aim was to use quantum theory to prove that we create our own reality, and it made stars of the two main physicists who appeared in it, again both American – Amit Goswami and Fred Alan Wolf. But the film and its main protagonists are not without their critics, who suggest that their science is not as foolproof or even scholarly as it might seem to the uninitiated.

One general criticism is that, however much the physical world might be described by theorists as 'illusory' and merely made up of patterns of energy, only the most advanced spiritual adepts are likely to possess the ability to manipulate it. And even then we might question how far they can really go. For example, they might be able to levitate or move objects, but could they really create them from scratch or make them disappear for good? They might be able to smash piles of bricks, walk on hot coals, lie on beds of nails and so on, but could they walk away unscathed from being hit head-on by a car doing fifty miles an hour?

Another criticism is that the quantum behavior of the microcosm does not necessarily reflect what happens in the hugely complex systems that make up our physical environment. The classical view still held by most physicists is that quantum indeterminacies are cancelled out – that is, they become far more deterministic – at the macro level. In other words, the almost limitless possibilities that might apply to the probability wave of a single electron are reduced by huge orders of magnitude each time we increase the complexity of the system it belongs to, from atom to molecule and so on.

In 'What the Bleep' a young boy teaches the main character to aim a basketball directly into the basket from distance. Admittedly we have no argument with the idea that we create our own reality, and this is a fine example of how total focus and belief can exert a massive influence. But is quantum theory playing any significant part? If we reject the interpretation that the wave function does not collapse at all but instead creates an unlimited number of parallel universes – which we will consider briefly in a moment – under more conventional interpretations the wave functions of all the quanta that make up the ball would have been collapsed by observation long before this point. So arguably a successful shot would not rely on the thrower managing to manifest the one quantum probability path for the ball as a whole whose trajectory led to the basket, but from an energetic focusing of consciousness that is underpinned by an entirely different process. Wolf also discusses the issue of creating our own reality, perhaps rather less than convincingly, in his 1999 book *The Spiritual Universe*.[18]

Of course any correlation of spiritual truths with proven scientific theory would provide massive support for a Rational Spiritual worldview. But the argument that these attempts at least are somewhat misguided is made in a deconstruction of 'What the Bleep' by Tom Huston, a founder member of the Integral Institute – of which more shortly:[19]

> Even the founding fathers of quantum physics/mechanics – Max Planck, Niels Bohr, Werner Heisenberg, Erwin Schrödinger, Sir Arthur Eddington, et al – *who were all self-proclaimed mystics*, strongly rejected the notion that mysticism and physics were describing the same realm. The attempt to unify them is, in the words of Planck, 'founded on a misunderstanding, or, more precisely, on a confusion of the images of religion with scientific statements. Needless to say, the result makes no sense at all.' Eddington was even more explicit: 'We should suspect an intention to reduce God to a system of differential equations. That fiasco at any rate must be avoided. However much the ramifications of physics may be extended by further scientific discovery, they cannot from their very nature [impinge upon] the background in which they have their being.'
>
> And there's the crux of the confusion. Quantum physics deals with the abstract, symbolic analysis of the physical world – space, time, matter, and energy – even down to the subtlest level, the quantum vacuum. Mysticism deals with the direct apprehension of the transcendent Source of all those things. The former is a mathematical system involving intensive intellectual study, and the latter is a spiritual discipline involving the transcendence of the intellectual mind altogether. It's apparently only a very loose interpretation of physics, and a looser interpretation of mysticism, that allows for their surprising convergence – and opens the door to the even wilder idea that by drinking some of this quantum mystical brew, you'll be able to create your own reality.

Although these attempts to correlate quantum theory with reality-creation may be misguided, we will see later that there may be other ways in which it supports a spiritual worldview – in which case some of these judgments may be unduly harsh.

For now we might usefully close this section by discussing Hugh Everett's 'many worlds' hypothesis, first put forward in 1955.[20] It too has proved popular in esoteric and mystical circles – it is not only supported by Wolf, for example, but as we saw in the previous chapter it is also a major plank of the Seth material. It is this interpretation of quantum theory that we rejected above and it suggests that, rather than living in a single, physical world created by a multitude of progressively collapsing quantum wave functions, in fact we live in a 'multiverse' in which entirely new, parallel worlds or universes are created out of every single possibility in every single wave. This would mean they do not collapse as such, but we think they do because from moment to moment our consciousness is only aware of the one possible universe that it is experiencing.

It is true that the world of modern theoretical physics does sometimes force us to accept theories that seem totally counter-intuitive. However if this one were to prove correct it would be completely at odds with everything we know about soul behavior and the whole idea of experience and growth. For example, it would surely imply that a new soul consciousness would effectively be created by, or would split off from the host soul at, each point on the wave function. Admittedly an essentially holographic soul consciousness would be quite capable of coping with this almost infinite diversification, but we never hear interlife subjects talking about their soul consciousness experiencing many worlds at the same time. Not only that, but there would be hugely diminishing returns in creating infinite numbers of universes from moment to moment, each one only minutely differentiated. From an experience perspective this would represent a huge waste of effort, and it seems inconceivable that Source would operate in such a philosophically inelegant way.

Finally, our research in *The Wisdom of the Soul* supports the idea that we live in a single, collectively created, non-illusory reality that is deliberately designed to be perceived as having dimensions of space and time – precisely in order to allow us to gain experience in the harsh environment of the physical world. This reality is not an illusion created separately by each of us, but rather a grand experiential stage that we co-create with our free will by *interacting* with each other.[21] And although our soul consciousnesses might be connected and all One on a fundamental level, they nevertheless remain independent of each other on another level. This is the crucial basis of the theory of the holographic soul, to which we will return shortly.

The Big Picture, Enlightenment and Types of Illusion

Despite the foregoing criticism of quantum mystics, let us be quite clear that the ideas that we are all one, that we should attempt to live fully in the now and that we create our own reality remain fundamental to this book. What we must beware of, however, is the overall context into which these key concepts are placed. They can of course be slotted into the broad framework of individual soul experience and growth that we have carefully built up from multiple sources of evidence – which from now on we will refer to as the 'Experience Model'. Indeed Pathwork, for example, does exactly this. However many of their modern exponents adopt, either implicitly or explicitly, a somewhat different view of their implications and of the broad context into which they should be placed. So it is time to apply the scalpel and dissect what they are really saying in terms of the 'big picture'.

Most of the commentators mentioned so far in this chapter love to use the word *illusion*, although in different contexts. If all they meant by this was that we should see through the illusion that only the material world exists or matters, and that we should all learn to become more spiritual, we could hardly disagree. But in fact only Goswami shares our support for the Experience Model, as he shows in his 2001 book *Physics of the Soul*.[22] The others can be split into various camps. On the one hand some do accept the concept of individual soul reincarnation, but insist that the physical world itself is effectively an illusion, so that the whole purpose of existence is to see through this and 'escape' from the cycle of karma by attaining the ultimate goal of enlightenment, or 'gnosis'. Others go further and completely reject any notion of individuality, whether of the human identity, soul, or anything else. They insist that in itself this is entirely illusory, so that when we die our soul energy automatically rejoins Source, and therefore they reject reincarnation as well. Others still accept the idea that we are individual souls attempting to gain experience on behalf of Source, but not that we reincarnate. And there are various other shades of grey between all these, which we might refer to as various 'Illusion Models'.

At this point we should briefly discuss the term *nondualism* that has become popular of late. It is used to suggest that, for example, matter and spirit are not really separate at all, although it can be extended to cover any pairing of supposed opposites. However it is confusing because all the approaches mentioned above – including that of the Experience Model,

once it is placed in its proper holographic context – can be described as
nondualist, even though they are fundamentally different. So while it is
certainly true that most of the modern commentators who use the term do
tend to subscribe to one or other of the Illusion Models, as we will see later
this is by no means a logical necessity of adopting a nondualist worldview.
That is why this term has not been used to describe these models.

So who supports which Illusion Model? If we start with the escape or
gnosis version we have, for example, Krishnamurti. He clearly accepts the
theory of reincarnation, although in the following passage from *The
Awakening of Intelligence* he is being typically forthright with his audience,
while his views on karma may not be to everyone's taste:[23]

> You believe in reincarnation as an idea, a comforting idea, but rather vague,
> so you don't care what you do now. You really don't believe in karma
> although you talk a great deal about it. If you really, actually, vitally
> believed in it, as you believe in earning money, in sexual experience, then
> every word, every gesture, every movement of your being would matter,
> because you are going to pay for it in the next life.

In fact Vedanta and most forms of Yoga go along with the idea of
individual soul reincarnation, but the main aim is usually to escape from
the cycle of *avidya-karma-samsara*. Meanwhile, as derivatives of
Buddhism it is difficult to judge exactly what it is that might or might not
reincarnate under Taoism and Zen – but again the overriding principle is
always the attainment of enlightenment or *nirvana*, so it does not really
matter what has gone on before. Of course to some extent we would agree
with this approach, but unless it is put into some sort of broader context one
is still entitled to ask, 'why do you even want to achieve this apparently
enlightened state?' The answer is unlikely to have anything to do with
individual souls attempting to grow by experience.

In *The Spiritual Universe* Wolf goes rather further, insisting that the
whole 'fall into matter' is a false compulsion on a quantum level and,
therefore, on a human and karmic level. Referring to the 'Dirac Sea', that is
the vacuum from which quantum waves emerge, he asserts:[24]

> I believe I can show that all suffering arises from the soul's addiction to
> substance, which in quantum physical terms means the vacuum's tendency
> to create light and energy, forming the basis of materiality. This addiction is
> the root cause of all suffering. I see this addiction as the fundamental
> mechanism by which spirit becomes matter...
> We need to grasp that desire for a material form is the root cause of any
> and all addictions. Once the soul falls into matter, it becomes addicted, and

it ultimately suffers seeing itself as the self. To relieve the soul's suffering, spirit must return to its nonmaterial state. In a way, the trapped soul must give up its most precious feeling, that it is real. We need to examine how this fall into matter occurs and why we suffer. The fall is necessary for a universe to arise and our sentient suffering ensues as night follows day.

Wolf even goes as far as to suggest that 'many spiritual practitioners believe that once God wakes up to all of the suffering being created by human beings, He/She will give up His/Her addiction to the material world'.[25] He later adds: 'At death you get a chance to awaken. Then all of this circle of suffering shows itself as an illusion, a dream of ignorance.'

Although he does not specifically mention them, Wolf's ideas seem to represent a modern take on the Gnostic texts, and while these are of similar provenance and age to the *Hermetica* their tone is entirely different. They are dominated by the idea that one particular 'lesser god' created the physical world and everything in it because of his arrogant assumption that he was the ultimate creative power, and due to his ignorance of the true power above him. Accordingly true Gnostics regard the whole physical world as a mistake, indeed an abomination that should never have arisen, and this oppressively negative view pervades the entire Gnostic corpus – even though it is of course the original source of the concept of 'gnosis'.[26] Of course this view itself might be regarded as somewhat abhorrent, and we will shortly return to why the 'fall into matter' was in no sense a mistake but all part of the big plan.

We cannot be entirely sure whether Wolf even accepts the idea of individual souls, because elsewhere he attempts to provide a logical proof – rather unconvincingly, it must be said – that there can only be one consciousness or 'mind of God', and that if there were more than one the manifested universe could not exist.[27] Certainly Banks seems to reject any notion of soul individuality, because in *The Missing Link* he briefly asserts:[28] 'Nature is a cosmic illusion suspended within the boundaries of time, space and matter. When one awakens from this illusory dream state, it is known as the *Great Awakening.*' Then on his website he makes his position rather clearer:[29] 'From nothingness, you came to the form, and when we die, we go from the form back to the nothingness again.'

Capra seems to adopt a similar stance. Admittedly most mainstream interpretations of quantum theory do accept that the observer is an involved participant in any experiment. But in *The Tao of Physics* he spends a great deal of time elucidating the apparent view of many Eastern approaches, which goes much further than mere involvement and suggests that the relationship between observer and observed is completely dissolved – so that they are 'not only inseparable but also become indistinguishable'.[30] Whether or not this is a correct interpretation of these approaches, we can only conclude that he supports it – and, of course, its implication that any notion of individuality on any level is entirely illusory. But we must maintain a clear head here, and remember that this is indubitably *not* what the science is saying.

The one person we have not yet discussed in this section is Tolle. Because his books are quite reasonably aimed at giving self-help advice rather than setting out his theoretical worldview, fathoming the latter is somewhat difficult. He repeatedly refers to the need to stop identifying ourselves with the 'dysfunctional egoic mind', which creates a sense of separateness instead of unity, and he refers to this as the 'illusory self'.[31] This could be interpreted that he believes there is no such thing as the separate, individual soul – an impression strengthened by his regularly referring to Buddhist, Taoist and Zen teachings – but in fact all he means by it is that our ego is primarily rooted in our thoughts, and these are at the heart of most of our problems. But even this can be misinterpreted if we are not careful, because he does not suggest that *all* thought is bad. He merely means that instead of allowing mindless, egoic thought to lead, rule and 'possess' our lives, we should let our underlying 'consciousness' or 'awareness' produce directed thought as appropriate – so thought becomes our servant not our master.

None of this necessarily ties him into any of the Illusion Models, but there is one brief passage in *The Power of Now* that seems to go rather further. It is a brief description of life after death, and in particular of the light or 'portal' described by near-death subjects:[32]

> This portal opens up only very briefly, and unless you have already encountered the dimension of the unmanifested in your lifetime, you will likely miss it. Most people carry too much residual resistance, too much fear, too much attachment to sensory experience, too much identification with the manifested world. So they see the portal, turn away in fear, and then lose consciousness. Most of what happens after that is involuntary and automatic. Eventually, there will be another round of birth and death. Their presence wasn't strong enough yet for conscious immortality.

From this it seems clear that he does accept the idea of individual soul reincarnation, but is suggesting that the primary aim is to reach a stage of enlightenment whereby the soul chooses the non-reincarnatory path after death. He is also suggesting that those who are insufficiently aware choose the reincarnatory path instead, in total ignorance, and only sleep between incarnations. Clearly this is completely at odds with the evidence for the interlife we have carefully collated in the previous chapters. So is he suggesting that the purpose of earthly life is not to experience but merely to achieve enlightenment so that we do not have to return?

Most of the broader context he discusses in *A New Earth* seems to support this conclusion.[33] He describes the purpose of humanity being to 'awaken', which he defines as 'a shift in consciousness in which thinking and awareness separate', and awareness is in turn defined as 'a conscious connection with universal intelligence', or 'presence', that is 'consciousness without thought'. However he does add that 'for most people awakening is not an event but a process'. Does he mean this happens over an extended period, even over many lives – and that perhaps a certain amount of multiple-life experience is required before this process can even commence? We will see shortly that this interpretation is supported by his view of the purpose of the universe as a whole. But what we can conclude is that the broader framework of his spiritual worldview is not always entirely clear.

The Case Against Illusion

It will be clear by now that, although the situation is not entirely black and white, we tend towards support of the Experience rather than the Illusion Models. Why is this? Of course we can begin by referring back to the huge weight of evidence we have amassed throughout this book, which suggests not only that we reincarnate as individual souls but that we do so to experience and grow. So any worldview that sees this process as illusory and whose main aim is merely to shortcut it, or that goes further and maintains we do not have individualized souls, is clearly at odds with this evidence.

Sri Aurobindo discusses 'illusionism' at some length, first indicating that it does not properly take account of the entire big picture and spectrum of evidence:[34]

> The theory of illusion cuts the knot of the world problem, it does not disentangle it; it is an escape, not a solution: a flight of the spirit is not a sufficient victory for the being embodied in this world of the becoming; it effects a separation from nature, not a liberation and fulfillment of our nature. This eventual outcome satisfies only one element, sublimates only one impulse of our being; it leaves the rest out in the cold to perish in the twilight of the unreal reality of *maya*. As in science, so in metaphysical

thought, that general and ultimate solution is likely to be the best which includes and accounts for all so that each truth of experience takes its place in the whole: that knowledge is likely to be the highest knowledge which illumines, integralizes, harmonizes the significance of all knowledge and accounts for, finds the basic and, one might almost say, the justifying reason of our ignorance and illusion while it cures them; this is the supreme experience which gathers together all experience in the truth of a supreme and all-reconciling Oneness.

Aurobindo continues that from a logical and philosophical perspective illusionism is inconsistent and even self-contradictory:

It is our first premise that the Absolute is the supreme reality; but the issue is whether all else we experience is real or unreal... The states of existence through which we approach and enter into the Absolute must have their truth, for the untrue and unreal cannot lead into the real: but also what issues from the Absolute, what the Eternal supports and informs and manifests in itself, must have a reality. There is the unmanifest and there is the manifestation, but a manifestation of the real must itself be real; there is the timeless and there is the process of things in time, but nothing can appear in time unless it has a basis in the timeless reality. If myself and spirit are real, my thoughts, feelings, powers of all kinds, which are its expressions, cannot be unreal; my body, which is the form it puts out in itself and which at the same time it inhabits, cannot be a nothing or a mere unsubstantial shadow. The only reconciling explanation is that timeless eternity and time eternity are two aspects of the Eternal and Absolute and both are real, but in a different order of reality: what is unmanifest in the timeless manifests itself in time; each thing that exists is real in its own degree of the manifestation and is so seen by the consciousness of the Infinite.

His basic message here seems to be, 'why would Source bother messing about with physical existence if there was no point to it?' This is a question rarely confronted by supporters of the Illusion Models, and it is one to which we will return. But elsewhere he reemphasizes that illusionism can only work by assuming some sort of major error in the big plan, which is in itself an impossibility:[35]

The existence of the individual is not an error in some self of the Absolute which that self afterwards discovers; for it is impossible that the absolute self-awareness or anything that is one with it should be ignorant of its own truth and its own capacities and be betrayed by that ignorance either into a false idea of itself which it has to correct or an impossible venture which it has to renounce.

He backs this up by completely dismissing the Gnostic view that the physical world is an abomination, instead assuring us that the descent of consciousness into materiality and ignorance of spirit is entirely deliberate:[36]

> Earth life is not a lapse into the mire of something undivine, vain and miserable, offered by some power to itself as a spectacle or to the embodied soul as a thing to be suffered and then cast away from it: it is the scene of the evolutionary unfolding of the being which moves towards the revelation of a supreme spiritual light and power and joy and oneness.

Finally Aurobindo emphasizes that the pursuit of unity to the exclusion of all else merely imposes an unnecessary limitation:[37]

> A self must be one in its being – otherwise we could not have this experience of unity – and yet must be capable in its very unity of cosmic differentiation and multiple individuality. The unity is its being, yes, but the cosmic differentiation and the multiple individuality are the power of its being which it is constantly displaying and which it is its delight and the nature of its consciousness to display. If then we arrive at unity with that, if we even become entirely and in every way that being, why should the power of its being be excised and why at all should we desire or labor to excise it? We should then only diminish the scope of our unity with it by an exclusive concentration accepting the Divine Being but not accepting our part in the power and consciousness and infinite delight of the Divine...
>
> We may plunge into the absorption of an exclusive unity, but to what end? For perfect union? But we do not forfeit that by accepting the differentiation any more than the Divine forfeits His oneness by accepting it. We have the perfect union in His being and can absorb ourselves in it at any time, but we have also this other differentiated unity and can emerge into it and act freely in it at any time without losing oneness.

This is a perfect prelude to the concept of the holographic soul, as we will shortly find out.

The American philosopher Ken Wilber takes a similar view. We briefly mentioned the Integral Institute above, and he set this up in 1998 to apply certain consistent, holistic, integrated models of analysis to any area of human activity – for example medicine, business, ecology and spirituality. But in his 2007 book *The Integral Vision* he suggests that those who think 'the entire world of material form is the fallen realm of illusion, and those who believe in it are lost in ignorance, sin, maya and samsara' are only considering one of the four quadrants of the integrated spiritual model, and are therefore 'quadrant absolutists'.[38] This should perhaps come as no great surprise given that his work seems to have been heavily influenced by Aurobindo, whose whole approach was to develop what he called 'integral knowledge' and 'integral yoga'.[39]

Pathwork too takes a dim view of any path to enlightenment that is attempted as a short-cut, without putting in the hard work of gaining experience:[40]

> Another law of great importance for this purpose is that the opening to the greater universal consciousness must not be approached in a spirit of magic that is supposed to eliminate the becoming, the growing, and the learning process. Now, in whatever way this ultimate of power is supposed to fill and sustain you, your outer mind must go through the steps of acquiring whatever knowledge and know-how are necessary. You all know this in the fields of arts and sciences. You cannot be inspired as a great artist, no matter how much genius you have, unless you learn the craft and the technical outer dexterity. If the childish lower self wants to use the channel to the greater universe in order to avoid the initial tedium of learning and becoming, the channel will remain closed. For this amounts to cheating, and God cannot be cheated. It is then that the personality may become seriously doubtful that anything beyond the mind exists because no inspirational response comes forth on the basis of using magic to coddle the sense of laziness and self-indulgence.

In fact the fundamental message of Pathwork is that you cannot achieve any sort of enlightenment unless you first put in the effort of sorting out your psyche:[41]

> You hear so much today about the concept of consciousness expansion. Often this is believed to be a magical process that suddenly occurs. It is not. To attain true spiritual consciousness, it is necessary to pay attention first to the material within you that you have not yet fully used, that you are not fully using right now... Often people go through various spiritual practices and wait for a miraculous manifestation of the greater consciousness, while their immediate mind and thought power is ensnarled in the same grooves of negative attitudes, feeling, thinking, and outlook. They must either be disappointed, or they experience delusions.

On top of all this, in *The Wisdom of the Soul* we deliberately asked our subjects to 'comment on the suggestion that the reincarnation cycle is just an illusion, and that when this is recognized a soul can return to Source'.[42] One responded 'that is *their* illusion, they have chosen, and they know within their energy, that they have come to earth to experience'; another said 'that is part of their learning process'; while a third insisted 'you can't reduce the lessons into one life'.

Another subject gave a wonderful response to a slightly different but related question about spiritual practice:

> There are many different ways of developing, and while a high level of spiritual enlightenment can be achieved through years of meditation, the same level can be achieved in a fraction of a second through laughter.

Picking up on this, what are we to make of the tendency towards asceticism displayed by some supporters of the Illusion Models? As previously suggested a degree of regular contemplation and meditation is surely necessary for any committed spiritual seeker, but to cut oneself off entirely from the regular activities of life is somewhat at odds with the idea of gaining experience. Indeed, various commentators specifically counsel against such an approach. Wilber warns:[43] 'Some spiritual practitioners focus only on meditative states, unaware or disdainful of developmental stages, which is unfortunate. Combining both is one of the main aims of an Integral Life Practice.' Similarly in his 2005 book *Lucid Living*, which contains familiarly titled sections such as 'all is one' and 'now is all you know', British author Timothy Freke insists:[44] 'Lucid living isn't withdrawing into some detached state of enlightenment. It is enjoying an exhilarating state of enlivenment!'

This message also comes through from Ruth Montgomery's channeling entities:[45]

> The Guides... directed attention to what they termed the 'wrong attitude of many Orientals, who try to escape the eternal wheel by withdrawing from life and living one of pure contemplation'. This, they said, 'defeats the very purpose of rebirth, for instead of helping others and doing all possible to make a real contribution to the betterment of mankind, they withdraw into themselves, thinking of their own salvation rather than helping others to achieve it'.

Again we find a similar distaste for asceticism in Pathwork:[46]

> The path is the finding of this center, this deep inner spiritual reality, and not some mystical, illusory, religious escape. Quite the contrary, it is immensely pragmatic, for the true spiritual life is never in contradiction to practical life on earth. There must be a harmony between the two aspects of the whole. The concept of forsaking everyday living is not true spirituality. In most cases, it is merely another kind of escape... The universe is abundant in its joys, pleasures, and bliss. Man is supposed to experience them, not forsake them.

The friction that arises out of relating with others is a sharp instrument of purification and self-recognition, if the self is so inclined. By withdrawing from this challenge and sacrificing the fulfillment that intimate contact gives, many aspects of inner problems are never called into play. The thus-resulting illusion of inner peace and unity has even led to concepts that spiritual growth is being furthered by isolation. Nothing could be further from the truth. However, my statement must not be confused with the fact that intervals of seclusion are a necessity for inner concentration and self-confrontation. But these periods should always alternate with contact, and the more intimate such contact is, the more it bespeaks of spiritual maturity.

The same idea comes through from Yogananda's guru who advises that a 'twofold existence' involves 'conscientiously engaging in earthly work while remaining immersed in an inward beatitude'.[47] This is echoed in what is arguably the finest and most quoted piece of Hindu scripture, the *Bhagavad Gita*, which forms part of the *Mahabharata* epic. This relatively short text combines philosophical depth with refreshing simplicity, and in it Krishna encourages us to actively engage in life:[48]

Not by refraining from action does man attain freedom from action. Not by mere renunciation does he attain supreme perfection. For not even for a moment can a man be without action. Helplessly are all driven to action by the forces of nature. He who withdraws himself from actions, but ponders on their pleasures in his heart, he is under a delusion and is a false follower of the path. But great is the man who, free from attachments, and with a mind ruling its powers in harmony, works on the path of karma yoga, the path of consecrated action. Action is greater than inaction: perform therefore thy task in life. Even the life of the body could not be if there were no action.

But to complete the broader picture of this text, later he explains exactly what he means by the 'path of consecrated action':[49]

The man who sees Brahman abides in Brahman: his reason is steady, gone is his delusion. When pleasure comes he is not shaken, and when pain comes he trembles not. He is not bound by things without, and within he finds inner gladness. His soul is one in Brahman and he attains everlasting joy. For the pleasures that come from the world bear in them sorrows to come. They come and they go, they are transient: not in them do the wise find joy. But he who on this earth, before his departure, can endure the storms of desire and wrath, this man is a Yogi, this man has joy.

This finding of inner peace and balance is exactly that proposed by modern commentators suggesting we should live in the now. But what does

Krishna mean by attaining 'freedom from action'? This clearly refers to no longer having to incarnate, but in the following passage we find that this 'striving for perfection' takes many lifetimes, because even the 'good' repeatedly 'fail in yoga':[50]

> Neither in this world nor in the world to come does ever this man pass away; for the man who does the good, my son, never treads the path of death. He dwells for innumerable years in the heaven of those who did good; and then this man who failed in yoga is born again in the house of the good and the great. He may even be born again into a family of yogis, where the wisdom of yoga shines; but to be born in such a family is a rare event in this world. And he begins his new life with the wisdom of a former life; and he begins to strive again, ever onwards towards perfection.

It is not difficult to place this in the context of an overall aim of experience and growth over many incarnations, rather than of achieving enlightenment suddenly and immediately releasing oneself from the karmic round of addiction.

To conclude this section, we are not suggesting that Krishnamurti, Banks, Capra, Wolf and others like them have not made hugely important contributions in pressing us all to adopt a more spiritual approach to life – to live more in the now, to recognize that we create our own reality, and to appreciate that we all form part of One, Unified, Divine Source. However it is important that these ideas be put into the proper broader context, and it is here that their tendency to support the various Illusion Models might be brought into question.

Holographic Theory and Consciousness Research

The idea of the hologram was first mooted in the 1940s, although it was not until the invention of the laser in 1960 that they could actually be produced. A basic hologram is created by shining a light beam through a 'splitter' angled at forty-five degrees. Some of the light carries straight on through as an 'illumination beam' that lights up all sides of an object, for example a book. An 'object beam' is then reflected off this at a forty-five-degree angle onto a 'photographic plate' placed at a similar angle. At the same time the light splitter produces a 'reference beam' that's bounced off a mirror angled at forty-five degrees, and then onto the plate, creating an interference pattern. Whenever the plate is subsequently illuminated by the original reference beam, a holographic, three-dimensional image of the original object is created in its original position, even when the object itself is no longer actually there.

But the crucial aspect for our purposes is that the photographic plate can be broken into increasingly small fragments, and each one will still reproduce the entire image – albeit with a slight loss of clarity at the extremes.[51] This is why holographic theory encapsulates ideas such as 'all the parts of the whole are fundamentally connected' and even 'the part contains the whole', and in turn why it has been applied to theories of the brain, of consciousness and of the universe. Potentially it also helps to explain non-local communication, because in a hologram the concept of location becomes redundant.

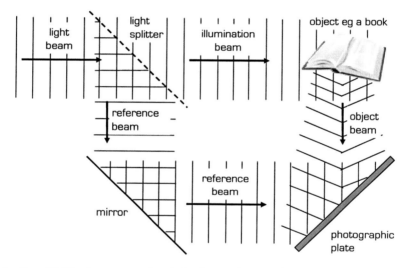

In the 1940s the neurophysiologist and consciousness researcher Karl Pribram made a name for himself with his pioneering research into the limbic system of the brain, conducted first at Stanford and then Yale Universities. But it is his development of the 'holonomic' model of the brain that most interests us here. He proposes that there is a 'primary reality' underlying our perception of the physical world, which is a 'frequency domain' that operates holographically and outside the normal constraints of space and time.[52] Nor was he slow to tie this in with the mysticism of the East:[53]

> As a way of looking at consciousness, holographic theory is much closer to mystical and Eastern philosophy. It will take a while for people to become comfortable with an order of reality other than the world of appearances.

But it seems to me that some of the mystical experiences people have described for millennia begin to make some scientific sense. They bespeak the possibility of tapping into that order of reality that is behind the world of appearances... Spiritual insights fit the descriptions of this domain. They're made perfectly plausible by the invention of the hologram.

The other main pioneer of holographic theory is the theoretical physicist David Bohm. Like Pribram he earned a growing reputation with his early research into plasma physics, conducted about the same time at Berkeley and then Princeton Universities. Indeed it even caught the eye of Einstein, with whom he collaborated briefly. But after falling foul of McCarthyism Bohm left the US, working for a time in Brazil before taking up a position as professor of theoretical physics at Birkbeck College in London. From the perspective of applying holographic theory he initially worked with Pribram on the brain model, but he then moved on to its broader application to the universe as a whole, as described in his 1980 book *Wholeness and the Implicate Order*.[54] Here he postulates that the quantum vacuum represents an underlying reality or 'implicate order' in which all quantum possibilities reside, but in which a 'hidden variable', the 'quantum potential', produces the 'explicate order' of the observable universe. Moreover there is an interactive series of 'enfoldings' and 'unfoldings' between the two orders, and it is to express this fundamental dynamism that he coins the term 'holomovement'. But he also asserts that consciousness and matter are interdependent and mutually enfolding projections of the underlying reality – in other words, that all matter and energy contains at least some element of consciousness. From a philosophical perspective this 'panpsychism' assumes that not only is there a universal consciousness underlying everything, but that it must have existed from the very beginning of the universe – of which more shortly.

A number of other consciousness researchers have recognized the importance of the hologram and attempted to build on the work of Pribram and Bohm. For example in his 1988 book *The Adventure of Self-Discovery* Grof describes his 'holotropic therapy', which is designed to promote altered states of consciousness without the need for hallucinogenic drugs. Meanwhile in *Stalking the Wild Pendulum*, published the same year, Itzhak Bentov discusses ideas such as that our bodies are mirrors of the whole universe, at every level, and that all knowledge that has ever been generated is potentially available to us.

Another key player who has developed this latter idea is the philosopher Ervin Laszlo. He spent a number of years lecturing and researching at several universities in the US, interspersed with secondments in which his expertise in systems theory formed part of various economic and humanitarian studies sponsored by the United Nations and other global bodies. Then in 1984 he moved to Tuscany, from where in 1993 he set up the international think-tank the Club of Budapest. But as he explains in his 2004 book *Science and the Akashic Field* his lifelong dream was to make sense of the world, and over many decades this developed into his positing an '*integrated* theory of everything'.[55] This, he suggests, is broader than the attempts of physicists and cosmologists to attain the Holy Grail of uniting the quantum theory of the microcosm with the relativity theory of the macrocosm – not least because they are not complete without a spiritual aspect.[56]

Laszlo concentrates on the unexplained 'coherence' or connectedness that is observed in several areas of modern research.[57] Needless to say the first of these is quantum theory, and the non-local communication or 'entanglement' posited by some versions of it. The second is cosmology, and the three dozen or so highly specific, finely tuned and apparently non-random rules that govern the observable universe and its evolution – indeed that allow it to exist at all. The third is evolutionary and quantum biology, and the apparent connectedness of and communication between cells both in simple organisms and in complex ones such as human beings, and also between organisms and their environments. And the fourth is transpersonal consciousness research and the telepathic and telesomatic connections between human beings, which he argues have been proved by controlled experiments with telepathy, remote viewing, dowsing, spiritual healing and directed prayer.

Laszlo's integrated solution to all this is to posit that the quantum vacuum is in fact a 'plenum' in which tiny vortices interact to produce and store unlimited information.[58] Referring to holographic theory he uses the metaphor of how ships' wakes leave interfering wave patterns on the surface of the ocean – and how, on a still day, these patterns can be used long afterwards to deduce the original speed and direction of any given vessel, and even its size. Under ideal conditions, this information would build up and up, containing a full record of every vessel that ever sailed on that stretch of water. But the crowning glory of his theory is to make the connection between this and the akashic records, and to postulate a new, universal, 'akashic field' – or 'A-field' for short. He is also professional enough to mention that the maverick scientist and inventor Nikola Tesla made the same connection in an unpublished paper back in 1907.

Of course we must remember that not all quantum theorists even accept the idea of non-local communication, so again these holographic theories of the brain, of consciousness and of the universe and are not without their detractors. Moreover the fact that Bohm was a great admirer of Krishnamurti, even though they had an on-off relationship in their later years, did not endear him to some in the scientific community.[59] Nevertheless it is probably fair to say that these holography-related quantum theories are generally regarded as rather more grounded than much of the material presented in, for example, 'What the Bleep'. Moreover Laszlo's concept of the A-field in particular has interesting implications for the overall Experience Model, as we will shortly see.

The Holographic Soul

The problem with these applications of holographic theory is that they are often used to support the Illusion Models. But again, just because certain phenomena suggest a fundamental *connection* between everything in the universe, in no sense does it automatically follow that either the physical world or any sense of individuality is an illusion.

This, of course, is where the simple yet philosophically elegant concept of the holographic soul comes into play, because it recognizes the fundamental interconnectedness and unity of the universe while simultaneously accepting the validity of our individual experiences of the physical world. So let us recap the definition first developed for *The Wisdom of the Soul*:[60]

> Soul consciousness is holographic. We are both individual aspects of Source, and full holographic representations of it, all at the same time. However this does not mean that soul individuality is in itself an illusion. The principle of the hologram is that the part contains the whole, and yet is clearly distinguishable from it.

Of course most of the spiritual commentators who support the Experience Model were trying to capture this concept, albeit hampered by the fact that the hologram had not been invented when they were writing. For example, Annie Besant describes how we are 'like unto the infinite Lord and one with Him, but with our own thread of memory'.[61] And Edgar Cayce talks about aiming for 'more and more at-onement' with God yet remaining 'conscious of being oneself'.[62] Similarly Silver Birch asserts:[63] 'The Great Spirit has provided you with part of Himself... You are the Great Spirit and the Great Spirit is you.' Then, when asked about a potential loss of individuality as different parts of consciousness are reunited, he responds: 'Does the stream lose itself when it flows into the mighty ocean, or is the ocean many streams?' This brings to mind the archetypal Buddhist discussion of whether, when one candle is used to light another, the flames are the same or different. This is now usually used to support the doctrine of *anatta*, which as we saw in the previous chapter effectively maintains that the individually identifiable soul does not survive and reincarnate. But perhaps we might dare to suggest that the example of the flames was originally supposed to have a nondualistic interpretation as 'one-*yet*-many' instead of the dualistic one now preferred of 'one-*not*-many'.

In Pathwork the Guide is, as usual, eloquent and specific on this topic:[64]

> Every individual consciousness is universal consciousness. It would not be correct to state that it is a part of it, for a part implies it is only a little of it, a fragment of a whole. Wherever consciousness exists at all, it is all of original consciousness... [Nevertheless] individualization is an integral aspect of the universal life power.

Meanwhile Aurobindo addresses himself to the 'difficulties of the normal mind when face to face with the experience of cosmic and transcendental *unity* by the *individual*'. And like all the more profound spiritual commentators he encourages us not to consider this from a fragmented, dualistic perspective, but to apply more unified, nondualist reasoning to the interplay of the concepts of individuality and unity themselves:[65]

> The individual exists though he exceeds the little separative ego; the Universal exists and is embraced by him but it does not absorb and abolish all individual differentiation, even though by his universalizing himself the limitation which we call the ego is overcome... All is in each and each is in all and all is in God and God in all... The individual exists in the Transcendent, but all the Transcendent is there concealed in the individual... So it is with the One and the many, the finite and the infinite, the transcendent and the cosmic, the individual and the universal; each is the other as well as itself and neither can be entirely known without the other and without exceeding their appearance of contrary positions... The infinite multiplicity of the One and the eternal unity of the many are the two realities or aspects of one reality.

In as much as the concept of the holographic soul properly takes into account all of the evidence now collated, both for individual soul reincarnation and the unity of all things, it does arguably represent the most all-encompassing, holistic and inclusive application of holographic theory. But we should acknowledge that this attempt to unify all the evidence merely follows the lead set by Aurobindo's integral approach:[66] 'The integral knowledge admits the valid truths of all views of existence, valid in their own field, but it seeks to get rid of their limitations and negations and to harmonize and reconcile these partial truths in a larger truth.'

Why Does Source Manifest At All?

At the beginning of the previous chapter we gave ourselves the objective of attempting to answer the key question of why we are here. But so far we have progressed no further than the two key words *experience* and *growth*, and to the enquiring mind this is surely not enough. Why do we have to experience and grow? For whose benefit, and in what context? To answer these further questions, the second part of the definition of the holographic soul simply states that the individual and collective aim is one and the same:

> The primary aim of Source, in diversifying into all the billions of holographic soul aspects of itself that operate in the various realms throughout the universe, is to experience all that is and can be. So as individualized aspects of Source who have chosen to reincarnate on this planet, we are merely fulfilling a small part of that objective by gaining a balance of the experiences available via this route.

This definition has been deliberately framed to recognize that Source does not only gain experience through life on earth. There is close to universal agreement from both scientific and spiritual sources that there are many different forms of advanced life, both physical and nonphysical, spread throughout the universe – even if the fascinating question of the number of physical planets inhabited by human-type forms as yet remains unanswered.[67]

We have already suggested that this ultimate question of why Source bothers to manifest the universe at all is the one that so often seems to confuse adherents of the Illusion Models, who either avoid it altogether or insist that mere humans should not presume to ask it. But in our research for *The Wisdom of the Soul* several of our subjects had no such qualms, and gave perfectly simple answers that corroborate the definition above:[68] 'It's this longing for balance, experience and growth.' 'To remain vibrant and strong. By growing through diverse creations, the consciousness expands.' 'Because of an overall desire to know and touch everything, to go to the limits of absolutely everything imaginable. It's all just infinite possibilities, infinite permutations.'

The idea that experience, self-exploration and simple joy in creation is the ultimate and sole motive of the Universal Consciousness is expressed in a number of our most profound sources that are not afraid to tackle the ultimate question. For example in Pathwork the Guide has this to say:[69] 'Since life is always moving, reaching out, expanding and contracting, finding new areas of experience and branching into new boundaries, creative life itself cannot be different. Thus it finds forever new forms to experience itself.' More recently near-death survivor Mellen-Thomas Benedict reports:[70] 'Creation is God exploring God's Self through every way imaginable. Through every piece of hair on your head, through every leaf on every tree, through every atom, God is exploring God's Self.' Meanwhile in *A New Earth* Tolle reports that at least the 'outer purpose of the universe is to create form and experience the interaction of forms – the play, the dream, the drama, or whatever you choose to call it'.[71] He also seems to accept that our individual awakenings all play their part in this broader drama, and it is this that suggests he may not be entirely in the illusion camp.

In fact in many respects Tolle's worldview seems to draw heavily on, or is at least closely related to, that of Aurobindo – who again provides the most detailed analysis of this topic, although it can be summarized in a few simple sentences.[72] He sees humanity's essential ignorance of its own divinity as being a condition of the original creative act, when the involution of the Divine Source produced 'divided forms of force and energy'. But by the gradual evolutionary and transformative process of reestablishing contact with its higher consciousness, humanity is helping to fulfill the universal intent, which is to experience the 'ultimate delight of being'.

A related question is whether God or Source or whatever we choose to call it is already 'perfect'. An interesting answer that is entirely consistent with Aurobindo's view is provided by the pioneering spiritual physicist Raynor Johnson in his 1953 book *The Imprisoned Splendour*:[73]

> Why should perfection exclude change? Why should perfection be thought of as static, not dynamic... We may conceive of the Infinite Artist in the joy of His artistry forever producing new forms; the Infinite Lover in the joy of His being forever creating new objects for His love. The exfoliation of the Infinite can have no limits... The creative activity of God includes embryonic spiritual beings, entities having simple consciousness, which is, however, infinite and eternal. The maturing of these so that they come to

know their divinity (which they already possess, but do not realize they possess) is perhaps the basis of the whole cycle of Becoming. How can they know their infinity if they do not know the finite? How can they know the meaning of immortality if they do not know mortality? How can they know omnipresence if they do not know limitation? This very special kind of knowledge of their own nature has to be won by an age-long process of descent into the prison of space and time and a gradual ascent therefrom, in which knowledge, and ultimately omniscience, is won.

This clearly suggests that experience and 'ascension' are not mutually exclusive but integrated aims, and this is an important topic to which we will return. Meanwhile what is true of us as holographic aspects of Source must be true of Source itself, so all this can be summed up neatly in one question: How can Source appreciate its own perfection if it has never experienced imperfection?

Origins, Cycles and the Metaverse

Let us now turn briefly to certain spiritual and scientific views of the origins of the universe, because these raise some interesting additional issues. The traditional Eastern model of universal cycles, described using the concept of 'days and nights' or even 'lives' of Brahma, is that over time periods that are unimaginably long to the human mind the Divine Source slumbers in its passive phase, even though it still retains the potential for unlimited creation within it. Then it suddenly bursts forth into manifestation of all the forms, both physical and nonphysical, that go on to populate the new universe. In fact this basic idea underlies all the most sacred origin texts and traditions of all ancient cultures right across the globe, once their masks of anthropomorphism are removed.[74]

So historically Big Bang has tended to be seen as just another 'dawn of Brahma', with cosmology having nothing to tell us about what happened before that, but this picture is now changing. As Laszlo points out the discovery of the incredible fine-tuning of the physical laws of our universe, which must have been in place from the outset, has demanded some sort of explanation.[75] On the one hand it has been suggested that during the Big Bang every possible type of universe was created simultaneously, and that ours happens to be probably the only one whose parameters allowed for any sort of physical life to develop, let alone complex life. On the other there might indeed be a cycle of creation, but one in which successive universes are created at random, and this one time out of many we got lucky. Yet surely these are philosophically inelegant solutions, similar to that of Everett's multiverse.

However there is a scientific theory that closely mirrors the Eastern model, and it involves the idea of a 'metaverse' that exists for all time and out of which successive universes spring. This model is gaining ground at least in part because any unsatisfying randomness can be overcome if, as Laszlo suggests, the original quantum field in the metaverse retains the knowledge and experience of all the universes that have been created previously – so that 'an entire series of sequentially and always more coherently evolving universes' are produced. Indeed he argues convincingly that the evolution-versus-creationism debate so beloved of Daniel Dennett, Richard Dawkins et al is a complete red-herring, and that what these materialists now have to explain in a convincing and philosophically satisfying way is why the universe as we know it exists *at all*:

> In the final count, the evolutionist/creationist controversy has no point. The question 'design or evolution?' poses a false alternative. Design and evolution do not exclude each other; indeed, they require one another. The metaverse is unlikely to have come into existence out of nothing, as a result of pure chance. And if it – more exactly, its primordial vacuum – was already 'in-formed', the metaverse was in a sense *designed* to give rise to a series of sequentially evolving universes. The bottom line is not 'design or evolution'. It is 'design *for* evolution'.

But is even this the end of the story? One further question we might consider is exactly how Source assimilates the experiences of all its myriad aspects. Simplistic, traditional views talk about souls escaping from the karmic cycle and 'reuniting' with Source.[76] Yet the concept of the holographic soul suggests that we never split off from it in the first place, and that it is always within us and us within it. This would suggest that it must assimilate and recycle all experience as it goes along, which is exactly what Laszlo's theory of the A-field also suggests, but from a different perspective.[77] On that basis we would never need to have any sort of formal, ultimate remerger with it. Nevertheless, there does seem to be a body of regression and other evidence that suggests we continue to evolve in other less physical planes after we have exhausted our growth potential on earth;[78] and it may even be that some sort of final remerger with Source awaits each of us when we realize full perfection on a soul level.[79]

Nevertheless this continual assimilation of experience would also seem to obviate the need for Source itself to engage in any sort of overall cycle of manifestation and complete reabsorption. Moreover it is generally accepted in both spiritual and scientific circles that in the underlying nonphysical realities there is no such thing as time – which merely provides a framework to allow conscious, thinking beings to make sense of their experiences while in the physical plane. This suggests that it is not appropriate to talk about universal *cycles* at all. In *A New Earth* Tolle uses the metaphor that although the sun rising and setting is very real to us, someone in space would just see it shining continuously, so that the idea of universal cycles is only a 'relative truth'.[80] Similarly Aurobindo refers to the idea that the universe 'disappears and reappears rhythmically in time' as 'the old belief', and further insists that 'integral Brahman possesses both the passivity and the activity simultaneously and does not pass alternately from one to the other'.[81] Not only that, but cosmologists are not even united that the universe will eventually collapse, some arguing that the data suggests it will keep on expanding ad infinitum.

Yet, despite all these objections, the idea of a metaverse that produces increasingly refined universes via some sort of process of cause and effect remains an elegant and attractive one – precisely because it would allow Source to experience entirely different universes with different underlying parameters.

Conscious Creation

We saw in the previous chapter that it is exactly because of the universal operation of cause and effect in our current lives, often referred to as the 'law of attraction', that we end up creating the reality that we experience. But what are the real implications of this idea? We have seen that most of the time we remain quite unaware of how our past choices have created the effects we are currently experiencing, especially if we are going through a difficult patch. But if the problem is major we should not forget to reflect on whether it might be something we deliberately incorporated into our life plan, while more minor problems might represent something we have attracted to ourselves because of past actions in *this* life. Either way this will encourage us to take complete responsibility for what is happening, and for seeing it as a challenge to be overcome or, better still, an opportunity for growth, rather than trying to hide from it and place the blame on other people, blind chance, karmic destiny or a higher power.

More than this, though, we also saw in the previous chapter that proactive, conscious creation requires us to look forward not backward, and to concentrate on how our choices in the present are affecting what happens to us in the future. This is the idea that a whole plethora of modern books on the power of positive thinking, visualization and more recently 'cosmic ordering' have tapped into. Of course anything that helps people to feel more in control of their lives and to take full personal responsibility is to be applauded, but some commentators have criticized supposedly spiritual approaches that seem to be targeted at some of our most shallow and materialist aspirations. For example, two of the most popular examples of this recent trend are Barbel Mohr's 2001 book *The Cosmic Ordering Service* and Rhonda Byrne's *The Secret* that came out as a book and a film in 2006. For all their good points they are somewhat simplistic and repetitive, and in both we find a rather single-minded concentration on popular, emotive issues such as health, wealth and weight. Also they both follow the trend of tying creation into quantum theory – with Wolf again appearing in the film of the latter.

More than this, though, do these books in their simplicity promise more than they can deliver? Is it really correct that *any* one of us can realize *anything* we want at *any* time, with no restrictions? A more balanced contribution is arguably made by the British astrologer Jonathan Cainer in his 2006 book *Cosmic Ordering*, in which he does acknowledge certain limits. For example he urges that our desired outcomes should not be too specific, nor should we be too impatient about when they happen, otherwise we give the universe no room for maneuver.[82] He warns about desires that might be in conflict with those of another person – which supports our earlier contention that we interactively co-create our physical reality.[83] And he emphasizes that there is usually a significant difference between what we want and what is best for us – of which more shortly.[84]

Tolle and Pathwork

Each of these two important sources add something new to the topic of creating our own reality, and their approaches are highly similar in some respects and yet very different in certain others, so comparison is instructive.

Although Tolle accepts that there is nothing wrong with attempting to direct our own future reality, his advice is that we should not pin all our hopes on this future, and obsess about it to such an extent that we miss out on the now and on just being. Moreover he emphasizes that we can concentrate on the now by being totally engaged in any activity we are currently performing as part of a plan for a better future. Therefore he advises that we give it our full attention, and perform it as something worthwhile in itself with no thought for the desired outcome. This, he says, is the path of inner peace and balance. But again we might add that being fully 'present' and connected is likely to ensure that we stay close to our life plan anyway – and this is probably rather more productive than endlessly speculating about whether or not we are 'on course'.

Let us now turn to Pathwork. We mentioned in the last chapter that it is not just our conscious thoughts that dictate our experiences but even more so our *unconscious* thoughts, emotions, attitudes and intentions. These are, of course, rather harder to examine and control, yet some approaches insist that it is absolutely crucial we tackle them, even though a great deal of self-discipline and analysis is required. This is one reason why we might concentrate on a specific outcome as much as we like only to find it still does not come to fruition – because we might be harboring subconscious attitudes and emotions that are blocking it. Some modern approaches do discuss this aspect; for example Mohr reports:[85] 'Problems are external signs that there is still programming in our subconscious that doesn't contain what we consciously desire.' However they tend to remain somewhat circumspect about the overall spiritual context, and especially the hard work that has to be put in. Not so Pathwork:[86]

> If you unconsciously want to cheat life by wanting more than you are willing to give, you violate another important cosmic law so that no matter how much you may try to believe in the possibility of life's abundance, it will not work. It will not 'take,' and your substance will refuse the impression until you remove this violation of law. Life cannot be cheated – and it is well that way. Another law is that you cannot skip a step. If you want a result, but this result depends on the elimination of obstructions which violate another law, the obstruction must first be dealt with. Therefore your meditative aim may have to be altered along the way. If you are not willing to correct what stands in the way, the result cannot come; creation in this area cannot take place.

All this again falls within the overall context that the main aim of incarnate life is grow to the point where we properly reconnect with our divine higher self. Nor is Pathwork alone in advising that to do this we need to uncover the undesirable, undeveloped character aspects of our lower selves, and the idealized self-image or 'mask' that we create in an attempt to hide these from ourselves and others.[87] As we might expect Aurobindo talks in very similar terms about making the effort to reject negative qualities, and about opening up to our inner spiritual force so that we move out of the ego and become unified with the world around us.[88] But few other spiritual approaches match the extent to which Pathwork explains just what is required, and in particular its integration of spirituality with basic psychology. Tolle, for example, merely suggests that we should work on being in the now without worrying too much about *why* each of our destructive mental patterns crops up in our thoughts. So both approaches broadly identify the same effect – that is negative thought patterns both conscious and unconscious that block real clarity and presence. But arguably for most people Tolle's will be more akin to repeatedly taking aspirins that only get rid of the effect for a limited period of time, whereas Pathwork insists that we reach down into the real, underlying cause for a long-lasting remedy.

It is also perhaps worth noting what the Guide has to say about the mind:[89]

> There are many spiritual movements which practice to discard and inactivate the mind altogether. This is undesirable because it creates split rather than unification... The practice of leaving the mind temporarily inactive is advisable. But to accuse the mind as if it were the devil and to oust it from man's life is missing the point.

Conscious Creation versus Life Planning and Divine Will

Apart from brief comments like Cainer's that what we want is not always what is best for us, generally speaking modern books about conscious creation tend to avoid any mention of the kind of difficult circumstances we regularly choose as part of our life plan in order to help us to learn and grow. In fact the whole idea of life planning is rarely if ever discussed in these books, yet it must have just as significant an influence on our life experience as a far-reaching but arguably not-unlimited ability to fashion our own reality as we go along. So if we find that we are consistently unsuccessful in manifesting a particular outcome, as we have just seen it may be that there are subconscious blockages related to it that we still need to work on. But it may equally mean that our higher self and guides are themselves attempting to block something that is well outside our life plan.

Not only that, but these modern books are merely tapping into a wisdom that has been around for a long time. And in the more profound, original sources we find rather more emphasis on the need for an element of selflessness, even of divine purpose, if our attempts to create our own reality are to be successful – even if this only involves the subtle switch from talking about a general 'law of attraction' to 'God's law'. For example Spiritism contains the suggestion that the 'quality of intention' is crucial, and that 'If man obeyed the law of God, he would not only spare himself much sorrow, but would also procure for himself all the felicity that is compatible with the grossness of earthly existence.'[90] Similarly Yogananda's guru describes a divine 'right course':[91]

> Human life is beset with sorrow until we know how to tune in with the Divine will, whose 'right course' is often baffling to the egoistic intelligence. God bears the burden of the cosmos; he alone can give unerring counsel.

Of course this is exactly the same as the 'right action' proposed by Taoists. Silver Birch echoes these thoughts when he discloses a 'great secret' – which rather suggests that he beat Byrne to the punch – because he emphasizes that to use it one has to 'live one's life right' and 'seek first the kingdom of God':[92]

> Life consists not only of the things you do, but of the things you say and the things you think. Do not imagine that only your deeds count. They do to a large extent, but your words and your thoughts are also part of you. It is sad that so many of you are slaves to your thoughts, instead of being their masters... The Great Spirit is infinite, and you are parts of the Great Spirit. If you have perfect faith and live your lives right, then you are able to participate in the bounty of the Great Spirit. If every person in your world had perfect faith, then he would receive. If a person were hungry and yet had perfect faith, then he would receive the answer. That is how the Law [of cause and effect] operates. If you learn to attune yourselves to the Law, the results must come. If the results do not come, that only proves that you are not in tune with the Law... Many people start with fear in their hearts. They are afraid they will not get results, and the element of fear disturbs the vibration. Perfect love casteth out fear! Seek ye first the kingdom of God and His righteousness, and all these things shall be added unto you... I have always told you that the Law is perfect in its operation. Sometimes you do not see the fulfillment, but I know that cause and effect always follow each other, because it is the Law.

For Cayce, too, creating our own reality in a constructive way requires us to be in tune with the 'Christ consciousness':[93]

> Will is that force that is compatible with, or against, the will of the All-Creative Energy. Call it nature, God, or whatnot – it is either with or against! Developing to or from... Know first that no urge, no influence, is greater than the will of the self to do what it determines to accomplish in any direction – whether physically, mentally or spiritually... For there is that within self that is creative; and it, that creative force, cooperating with

the divine without, will lead to the choice of that which is life... But each soul is given the birthright of the ability to choose – under any environment, any circumstance, any experience... For each entity makes a record upon time and space through the activities of that stylus, the mind... In the flesh and in the spirit, mind is the builder... Thoughts are things; the mind is as concrete as a post or tree.

Tolle backs up the idea of divine purpose with a slightly different slant:[94] 'Fulfilling your primary purpose is laying the foundation for a new reality, a new earth. Once that foundation is there, your external purpose becomes charged with spiritual power because your aims and intentions will be one with the evolutionary impulse of the universe.' He adds that through 'awakened doing' we 'become one with the outgoing purpose of the universe'.

So although we all have to live in the physical as well as the spiritual and, for example, the need for money cannot be ignored, the art of conscious creation was never designed to be applied to exclusively material aims. As long as it remains an egocentric, self-centered and inwardly focused approach it will bear only limited fruit. The real secret of the secret is to learn to turn it outward into a life of service to others.

Surrender

Although various spiritual sources urge us to follow a divine path of right action if our attempts at conscious creation are going to bear fruit, some go further and suggest we should actually move beyond conscious creation to a point where we just surrender to the divine will, or to the universe – or, perhaps more accurately, to our life plan itself. After all, this is a plan that our own higher self knows only too well, which will always be in accordance with the greater good of the whole. In other words they advise that we should let go of any and all outcomes we might desire, and merely surrender to what will automatically be the right path if we remain properly connected to our higher self via meditation and so on. Aurobindo, for example, urges us to be 'wholly possessed by the Divine Consciousness' and to 'live and act in a complete self-giving and surrender'.[95]

In practice it seems many people mix and match the two approaches, consciously creating when they seem to be in the flow and surrendering when they are not.

Transformation

We have seen that the one, fundamental message that consistently emerges from all the most reliable and profound sources of spiritual wisdom is that our primary aim should be to become more in touch with the divine element within ourselves. In fact so many sources contain this message, from all epochs and all areas of the globe, that to record them all would require another volume entirely.

So let us summarize everything we have learned about this evolutionary path of transformation from the perspective of the individual human soul. Our successions of lives are undertaken within an environment of increasing personal responsibility and free will. As we are exposed to the full gamut of human emotions, and as we start to listen to the increasingly strident spiritual urgings of our intuitive inner voice – which is the spokesperson for none other than our own higher self – we gradually learn to become more balanced and loving in our responses. We increasingly learn to transform our lower self so that we consciously rather than unconsciously create our own reality, although accepting that sometimes surrender is more appropriate. And sooner or later we also open our eyes to our unity with everything and everyone, and so become less selfish and more altruistic in our outlook. Finally the experience potential of incarnating on earth is exhausted when we attain that degree of inner development whereby everything we think, say and do comes from our higher self – that is to say we have achieved complete non-attachment and are fully present in the now. But all this will take many lives, and there are no short-cuts or quick fixes on this path of experience and growth. Not only that but the end of the physical reincarnation cycle only marks the beginning of a far lengthier cycle of further soul development in more nonphysical realms.

While this transformation starts with the self, the hope is that it will, indeed ultimately must, spread to humanity as a whole. So let us look at the visions of the long-term future provided by what have arguably proved our two most reliable and informative sources. The first is Pathwork, in which the Guide discusses the unified state of consciousness that is our ultimate objective:[96]

> In the unified plane of consciousness, there are no opposites. There is no good or bad, no right or wrong, no life or death. There is only good, only right, only life. Yet it is not the kind of good or the kind of right or the kind of life that comprises but one of the opposites of the dualistic planes. It

transcends it and is of a completely different nature. That good, or that right, or that life which exists on the unified plane of consciousness combines both aspects of the dualistic way of life. In the unified state of mind, no conflict exists because the dualism is combined and the opposites no longer conflict with one another. This is why to live in a unified state, in absolute reality, is the bliss, the unlimited freedom, the fulfillment, and the unlimited realization of potentials that religion calls heaven...

When the road to the unified principle is chosen, soon what first appeared as one good and one bad ceases to be so, and one inevitably encounters good and bad on both ends. And when this road is pursued still further, there no longer is any bad, but only good. The road leads deep inside into the real self, into truth that surpasses the fearful little ego interests. When this truth is sought deep inside of the self, the unified state of consciousness is approached...

What we call the real self, or the divine substance in man, or the divine principle, or the infinite intelligence, or any number of other names mankind has chosen for the deep inner live-center, exists in every human being. It contains all wisdom and truth that man can possibly envisage.

Of course this 'unified state' in which there are no longer any opposites is exactly what the term *nondualism* properly refers to, and the Guide is one of its finest exponents. But we can see clearly now that by no means does this require the simultaneous adoption of one of the Illusion Models.

The second of these sources is Aurobindo, who maintains that the path of transformation will culminate in the development of an ultimate 'truth consciousness', or what he calls 'supermind'.[97] And his message of hope is that, as increasing numbers of individuals go through this change, earth will witness the emergence of a new 'life divine' that fulfills the original intent of 'truth, delight and perfection'.

However long this process might take, and however bumpy the ride on the way, it appears that we are indeed heading for a new world in which humanity will increasingly operate from a different level of consciousness. But the advocates of this kind of transformation do not seem to be suggesting that as a result the earth experience will have outlived its usefulness. Instead it seems that the process of growing will continue here both individually and collectively. It also seems likely that souls with different levels of experience will still be incarnating on earth – even if there is good reason to suppose that any 'new' soul energies will support the general growth trend because they will already be programmed with the experiences of others, via the continuous recycling process we referred to earlier. So reaching this new plane of human evolution will most likely be gradual and not an end in itself, only a new beginning.

This is why arguably the use of words like *ascension, transcendence* and *enlightenment* is less than helpful, because they seem to suggest a static objective. Whereas in the most profound spiritual worldviews there is no dichotomy between *transformation* and experience, because they are both dynamic processes rather than ends in themselves. Indeed, ultimately, they are one and the same thing.

There is a simple message on which it is appropriate to end, and that is to remind ourselves that the Divine is *love*, pure and simple. So in opening up to our higher selves love matters above all else. And nobody is in a position to make this point more eloquently than our two near-death survivors, whose experiences of unity we discussed at the beginning of the chapter. So let us bring our journey to a close by allowing each of them to share their profound messages of love and hope, starting with Mellen-Thomas Benedict:[98]

> Then the Light turned into the most beautiful thing that I have ever seen: a mandala of human souls on this planet. I saw that we are the most beautiful creations – elegant, exotic – everything. I just cannot say enough about how it changed my opinion of human beings in an instant. I said/thought/felt, 'Oh, God, I didn't realize'. I was astonished to find that there was no evil in any soul. People may do terrible things out of ignorance and lack, but no soul is evil. What all people seek, what sustains them, is love, the Light told me. What distorts people is a lack of love. The revelations went on and on. I asked, 'Does this mean that humankind will be saved?' Like a trumpet blast with a shower of spiraling lights, the Light 'spoke', saying, 'You save, redeem and heal yourself. You always have and always will. You were created with the power to do so from before the beginning of the world.' In that instant I realized that *we have already been saved*; this is what the Second Coming is about...
>
> From what I have seen, I would be happy to be an atom in this universe. An atom. So to be the human part of God, this is the most fantastic blessing. It is a blessing beyond our wildest estimation of what blessing can be. For each and every one of us to be the human part of this experience is awesome, and magnificent. Each and every one of us, no matter where we are, screwed up or not, is a blessing to the planet, right where we are...
>
> I went over to the other side with a lot of fears about toxic waste, nuclear missiles, the population explosion, the rain forest. I came back loving every single problem. I love nuclear waste. I love the mushroom cloud; this is the holiest mandala that we have manifested to date, as an archetype. More than any religion or philosophy on earth, that terrible,

wonderful cloud brought us together all of a sudden, to a new level of consciousness. Knowing that maybe we can blow up the planet fifty times, or five hundred times, we finally realize that maybe we are all here together now. For a period they had to keep setting off more bombs to get it into us. Then we started saying, 'we do not need this any more'. Now we are actually in a safer world than we have ever been in, and it is going to get safer. So I came back loving toxic waste, because it brought us together. These things are so big. Clearing of the rain forest will slow down, and in fifty years there will be more trees on the planet than in a long time. If you are into ecology, go for it; you are that part of the system that is becoming aware. Go for it with all your might, but do not be depressed or disheartened. Earth is in the process of domesticating itself and we are cells on that Body. Population increase is getting very close to the optimal range of energy to cause a shift in consciousness, and that will change politics, money and energy.

And, finally, here is George Rodonaia:[99]

Anyone who has had such an experience of God, who has felt such a profound sense of connection with reality, knows that there is only one truly significant work to do in life, and that is to love; to love nature, to love people, to love animals, to love creation itself, just because it is. To serve God's creation with a warm and loving hand of generosity and compassion – that is the only meaningful existence.

THE TEN PROPOSITIONS OF RATIONAL SPIRITUALITY

- the soul survives independent of the physical body
- souls have many lives, not just one
- our many lives are not linked by a karmic law of action and reaction
- we reincarnate to gather experience so we can grow
- the only judgment after death comes from ourselves
- we are responsible for all aspects of our lives because we plan and choose them
- we always have free will to deviate from our life plan
- we are all One and all God
- soul consciousness is holographic, and represents the part and the whole all at the same time
- the aim of Source is to experience all that is and can be

SOURCE REFERENCES

Excerpts from *Between Death and Life* by Dolores Cannon reproduced by kind permission of Gateway, an imprint of Gill & Macmillan, and of Ozark Mountain Publishers. Excerpts from *Remarkable Healings* by Shakuntala Modi reproduced by kind permission of Hampton Roads Publishing Company. Excerpts from *Journey of Souls* and *Destiny of Souls* by Michael Newton reproduced by kind permission of Llewellyn Publications. Excerpts from *The Search for Lives Past* by Peter Ramster reproduced by kind permission of Somerset Film & Publishing. Excerpts from *Light and Death* by Michael Sabom reproduced by kind permission of Zondervan Publishing House, a division of HarperCollins Publishers. Excerpts from *Life Between Life* by Joel Whitton and Joe Fisher reproduced by kind permission of Doubleday & Company, an imprint of Random House.

Ellipses (…) in quotes indicate omitted elements are considered inconsequential, irrelevant or repetitive. All italics and rounded brackets in quotes are original, whereas any explanatory comments are in square brackets.

Although many of the professionals whose research is discussed in this book have doctorates in psychology, psychiatry or other disciplines, the title 'Dr' has not generally been used, merely to avoid laborious repetition.

Publication details for the books referenced below can be found in the bibliography.

Preface

[1]   Lawton, *The Book of the Soul*, chapter 9, p. 241.

Chapter 1: Near-Death and Out-of-Body Experiences

[1]   Sabom, *Light and Death*, chapter 3, pp. 43–6.

[2]   For example see Fenwick, *The Truth in the Light*, chapter 1, pp. 9–11 or Ring, *Life at Death*, chapters 3 and 4.

[3]   Formerly known as the Committee for Scientific Claims of the Paranormal, or CSICOP.

[4]   What follows is a summary of the arguments found in Fenwick, *The Truth in the Light*, chapters 14 and 15; Ring, *Life at Death*, chapter 11; and Sabom, *Light and Death*, chapter 10, pp. 175–84.

[5]   For further discussion of the after-effects of near-death experiences see Fenwick, *The Truth in the Light*, chapter 9 and Ring, *Life at Death*, chapters 8

and 9.

6   Ring, *Life at Death*, chapter 11, p. 212; he is referring to the study performed by Karlis Osis and Erlendur Haraldsson, reported in their 1977 book *At the Hour of Death*.

7   This idea was first put forward by Noyes and Kletti in 'Depersonalization in the Face of Life-Threatening Danger', *Psychiatry* 39 (1976), pp. 19–27.

8   For example see Fenwick, *The Truth in the Light*, chapter 3, p. 26 and chapter 9, p. 135.

9   Blackmore, *Dying to Live*, p. 85; the theory is based on the research of Tomasz Troscianko of the University of Bristol.

10   Fenwick, *The Truth in the Light*, Introduction, pp. 2–3.

11   Ibid., chapter 1, pp. 14–15.

12   Ring, *Life at Death*, chapter 10, p. 202.

13   Fenwick, *The Truth in the Light*, chapter 12, p. 171; he refers to the pioneering research into children's near-death experiences undertaken by Melvyn Morse, an American pediatrician, reported in 'Childhood Near-Death Experiences', *American Journal of Diseases of Children* 140 (Nov 1986), pp. 1110–14.

14   Ibid., chapter 11, pp. 159–66.

15   Ibid., Introduction, p. 2.

16   Ibid., chapter 4, p. 62 and chapter 9, pp. 133–4.

17   Sabom, *Light and Death*, chapter 7, pp. 134–41.

18   Ring, *Life at Death*, chapter 10, p. 201.

19   Ibid., chapter 11, pp. 216–17.

20   Sabom, *Light and Death*, chapter 3, pp. 41–2.

21   Ibid., chapter 10, pp. 184–5.

22   Ibid., chapter 3, p. 47.

23   Woerlee, 'An Anesthesiologist Examines the Pam Reynolds Story: Parts I & II', *The Skeptic* (UK edition) 18 (Spring and Summer 2005); further discussion can be found at www.near-death.com/experiences/articles009.html and at www.infidels.org/library/modern/keith_augustine/HNDEs.html.

24   Fenwick is at the forefront of such arguments; see *The Truth in the Light*, chapter 14, pp. 198–208.

25   Sabom, *Light and Death*, chapter 10, pp. 187–9.

26   See www.infidels.org/library/modern/keith_augustine/HNDEs.html.

27   It seems that Sabom's own confusion may stem from his being overly literal about what Pam meant by the 'top', because he talks about an 'overhanging edge' right at the very top of the saw *bit* itself. But the actual groove where the

bit clips into the handle could easily be casually described as at the top, especially when the entire length of the handle is also taken into account.

[28] van Lommel et al, 'Near-Death Experience in Survivors of Cardiac Arrest: A Prospective Study in the Netherlands', *The Lancet* 358 (Dec 2001), pp. 2039–45.

[29] For full details of the Rodonaia case in George's own words, minus the veridical aspect, see Berman, *The Journey Home*, chapter 2, pp. 31–7; this is reproduced in full at www.ianlawton.com/nde3.htm.

[30] The veridical aspect of the Rodonaia case is most reliably presented in Atwater, *Beyond the Light*, chapter 5, p. 81; for further analysis of certain confusion surrounding this see www.ianlawton.com/nde4.htm.

[31] Clark, 'Clinical Interventions with Near-Death Experiencers' in Greyson and Flynn, *The Near-Death Experience*, pp. 242–55.

[32] Ebbern, Mulligan and Beyerstein, 'Maria's Near-Death Experience: Waiting for the Other Shoe to Drop', *Skeptical Inquirer* 20:4 (1996), pp. 27–33.

[33] http://michaelprescott.typepad.com/michael_prescotts_blog/2007/07/page/2.

[34] Leading the way is the AWARE project led by Parnia from Southampton University. Although the eighteen-month pilot study only involved a few hospitals in the UK, in September 2008 it was extended to cover many more, not just in the UK but in mainland Europe and North America.

[35] See Ring, *Life at Death*, chapter 10, pp. 192–6; Sabom, *Light and Death*, chapter 9; and Fenwick, *The Truth in the Light*; chapter 13.

[36] Greyson and Bush, 'Distressing Near-Death Experiences', *Psychiatry* 55 (Feb 1992), pp. 95–110.

[37] Atwater, *Beyond the Light*, chapter 3, p. 41.

[38] Ibid., chapter 3, p. 42; Ring and Sabom also provide critiques of Rawlings' theories in their main chapters on unpleasant experiences referenced in the note above.

[39] Berman, *The Journey Home*, chapter 5, pp. 84–91.

[40] Ring, *Life at Death*, chapter 12, p. 249.

[41] Atwater, *Beyond the Light*, chapter 3, p. 45.

[42] For a fuller description of the different aspects of these planes, and a diagrammatic representation, see Lawton, *The Wisdom of the Soul*, under Question 2.4.

[43] In *Life at Death*, chapter 12, pp. 246–50 Ring similarly differentiates between the 'world of light' and a 'lower frequency domain', but he insists on referring to the former as the 'astral'. By contrast some people refer to the intermediate plane as the astral because it is only here that departed spirits might retain what is often referred to as the 'astral body' for any length of time. But when we

come later to the phenomenon of 'astral projection' we will find that it might encompass both planes. Arguably therefore it is better to use the word *intermediate* than *astral* wherever possible.

[44]   One of the most celebrated is recounted by the Northumbrian monk known as the Venerable Bede around the turn of the eighth century. In his *Ecclesiastical History of the English Nation*, Book 5, Chapter 12, he describes the experience of a man called Dritheim. After his 'death' he traveled through a 'vale' with souls jumping from 'dreadful flames' on one side into the 'violent hail and snow' on the other, and back again, with no respite. At the far end he came to the edge of a 'black pit' from which spewed 'black flames full of human souls' and an 'insufferable stench', while 'dark spirits' threatened him with 'burning tongs'. But they fled from the presence of a being with the 'brightness of a shining star' who conducted him into a 'clear and open light', and over a 'vast wall' into a 'delightful field full of fragrant flowers' in which there were 'innumerable assemblies of men in white' and 'many companies seated together rejoicing'. But further on they entered a 'much more beautiful light' with 'sweet voices' and a 'wonderful fragrancy' that made even the 'flowery field' seem 'mean and inconsiderable'. Of course he wanted to remain, but was escorted back, and spent the rest of his days as a monk.

[45]   Ring mentions this in *Life at Death*, chapter 12, p. 249; apparently the idea came from Itzhak Bentov in a personal communication (see p. 296, note 59).

[46]   Atwater, *Beyond the Light*, chapter 3, p. 50.

[47]   Monroe, *Journeys Out of the Body*, chapter 3, pp. 46–8.

[48]   Ibid., chapter 3, pp. 55–8.

[49]   Ibid., chapter 5, pp. 74–5.

[50]   Ibid., chapter 5, pp. 80–1.

[51]   Ibid., chapter 8, pp. 123–5.

[52]   Ibid., chapter 5, p. 78.

[53]   Ibid., chapter 8, pp. 120–1.

[54]   Blackmore, *Beyond the Body*, chapters 6 and 12.

[55]   Edwards, *Reincarnation*, chapter 11, pp. 141–55 and chapter 12.

[56]   Ibid., chapter 11, pp. 162–3.

[57]   Sabom, *Light and Death*, chapter 7, p. 135.

[58]   Edwards, *Reincarnation*, chapter 11, p. 150.

[59]   Ibid., chapter 9, pp. 127–31.

[60]   Ibid., chapter 17.

[61]   I had personal experience of this with my father in the early 1990s. While he might not even recognize that he was talking to his youngest son, he could quite

happily tell me exactly what main jet he had used in the carburetor of his works Norton in specific races in the early 1950s!

[62]   Huxley, *The Doors of Perception*, pp. 10–11.

Chapter 2: Children Who Remember Past Lives

[1]   Wes Milligan, 'The Past Life Memories of James Leininger', *Acadiana Profile*, Dec 2004; this is reproduced in full at www.ianlawton.com/cpl3.htm.

[2]   At http://abcnews.go.com/Primetime/Technology/story?id=894217&page=3.

[3]   See   http://skeptico.blogs.com/skeptico/2005/07/reincarnation_a.html;   the article is entitled 'Reincarnation All Over Again'.

[4]   See www.pittsburghlive.com/x/dailycourier/news/s_189477.html.

[5]   Note that in 2009 – that is, after this summary was originally written – James' parents released a book about his experiences called *Soul Survivor*. Skeptics would probably suggest this is an attempt to profit from the case that, coupled with the fact his memories have now disappeared, destroys its credibility. However, Bruce makes a telling point in correspondence with me dated 17 August 2009: 'This story is humbling in every way. If I was motivated by money I could have saved thousands by believing Andrea about a past life.'

[6]   Lenz, *Lifetimes*, 'Beyond Birth and Death', pp. 192–6.

[7]   See the Wikipedia article for the *USS Arizona*.

[8]   See Brownell, *Reincarnation*, 'He Knew Who He Was', pp. 9–12; Delanne, *Documents pour servir à l'Etude de Réeincarnation*, chapter 9, pp. 254–6; and Muller, *Reincarnation*, chapter 1.

[9]   The background information that follows is taken from an obituary at www.healthsystem.virginia.edu/internet/personalitystudies.

[10]   Stevenson, *Children Who Remember Previous Lives*, chapter 5, pp. 105–28.

[11]   Ibid., chapter 8, p. 175.

[12]   Ibid., chapter 10, p. 211–12.

[13]   Stevenson, *Twenty Cases Suggestive of Reincarnation*, chapter 2, pp. 67–91.

[14]   Stevenson, *Cases of the Reincarnation Type I*, pp. 70–106; for a summary see *Children Who Remember Previous Lives*, chapter 4, pp. 56–8.

[15]   Edwards, *Reincarnation*, chapter 16, p. 255.

[16]   Ibid., chapter 16, pp. 276–7. The 'Ransom Report' was originally referenced by the American parapsychologist and Stevenson critic D Scott Rogo in his 1985 book *The Search for Yesterday*, but he admitted he had not been able to obtain a copy and only went on hearsay. Nevertheless Edwards obtained a summary from Ransom after he saw an article on reincarnation by Edwards in *Free*

Inquiry magazine.

[17] Stevenson, *Children Who Remember Previous Lives*, p. 290, note 20.

[18] Correspondence with me, 5 February 2008.

[19] For Stevenson's own descriptions of his methodology and his attempts to remove potential weaknesses see *Children Who Remember Previous Lives*, chapter 6; *Twenty Cases Suggestive of Reincarnation*, Introduction; and *Cases of the Reincarnation Type I*, General Introduction, pp. 8–50.

[20] Angel, 'Empirical Evidence for Reincarnation? Examining Stevenson's Most Impressive Case', *Skeptical Inquirer* 18:5 (1994), pp. 481–7; note that various correspondence between Stevenson and Angel was published in subsequent issues. The full details of the Imad Elawar case can be found in *Twenty Cases Suggestive of Reincarnation*, chapter 6, pp. 274–320.

[21] See www.skepticreport.com/newage/stevensonbook.htm.

[22] Stevenson, *Twenty Cases Suggestive of Reincarnation*, chapter 4, p. 55.

[23] See, for example, his comments in ibid., chapter 4, p. 91.

[24] See http://skepdic.com/stevenson.html.

[25] Chari, 'Review of Twenty Cases Suggestive of Reincarnation', *International Journal of Parapsychology* 9 (1967), pp. 217–22.

[26] Stevenson, *Cases of the Reincarnation Type I*, General Introduction, pp. 18–20.

[27] See *Children Who Remember Previous Lives*, chapter 7, pp. 150–9 and *Twenty Cases Suggestive of Reincarnation*, chapter 8, pp. 331–43.

[28] See www.richardwiseman.com/research/research.html.

[29] Stevenson, *Children Who Remember Previous Lives*, chapter 7, p. 165.

[30] Stevenson, *Twenty Cases Suggestive of Reincarnation*, chapter 8, pp. 365–6.

[31] Nicol, 'Review of Cases of the Reincarnation Type I', *Parapsychology Review* 7:5 (1976), pp. 12–15; one case analyzed was that of Jagdish Chandra.

[32] Moore, *The Philosophical Possibilities Beyond Death*, chapter 23; the case was that of Sujith Lakmal Jayaratne.

[33] Pasricha and Barker, 'A Case of the Reincarnation Type in India', *European Journal of Parapsychology* 3:4 (May 1981), pp. 381–408.

[34] Pasricha, 'New information favoring a paranormal interpretation in the case of Rakesh Gaur', *European Journal of Parapsychology* 5:1 (Nov 1983), pp. 77–85.

[35] Wilson, *Mind Out of Time*, chapter 3, pp. 58–60 and *The After Death Experience*, chapter 3, pp. 34–6.

[36] Stevenson, *Cases of the Reincarnation Type I*, pp. 321–36; see in particular pp. 332–3.

[37] Ibid., pp. 281–311; see in particular pp. 310–11.

[38] Ibid., pp. 266–80; see in particular pp. 274 and 276–7.

[39] Ibid., pp. 107–43; see in particular p. 131.

[40] Stevenson, *Twenty Cases Suggestive of Reincarnation*, chapter 2, pp. 91–105; see in particular pp. 95 and 104, where he indicates that the father of the previous personality had not entirely given up hope of a prosecution long after he first started investigating the case.

[41] This is in his earlier book; in the later one he inexplicably narrows this twenty down to nine, and does not mention the other twenty-one.

[42] Stevenson, *Cases of the Reincarnation Type I*, General Introduction, p. 30.

[43] Ibid., p. 100.

[44] Ibid., General Introduction, pp. 29 and 32.

[45] Edwards, *Reincarnation*, chapter 16, p. 268.

[46] Wilson, *Mind Out of Time*, chapter 3, pp. 53–4.

[47] Stevenson, *Children Who Remember Previous Lives*, chapter 8, p. 175.

[48] For interval details in the former case see *Twenty Cases Suggestive of Reincarnation*, chapter 6, pp. 276 and 281; and in the latter *Children Who Remember Previous Lives*, chapter 4, p. 67.

[49] Wilson, *Mind Out of Time*, chapter 3, pp. 54–5.

[50] Stevenson, *Children Who Remember Previous Lives*, chapter 8, p. 174.

[51] Ibid., chapter 8, pp. 177–8.

[52] Ibid., chapter 8, p. 180.

[53] See ibid., chapter 7, pp. 159–62 and *Twenty Cases Suggestive of Reincarnation*, chapter 8, pp. 343–82.

[54] See Stevenson, *Children Who Remember Previous Lives*, chapter 5, pp. 111–12 and Muller, *Reincarnation*, chapter 1, pp. 72–5.

[55] Stevenson, *Cases of the Reincarnation Type I*, General Introduction, p. 33.

[56] Edwards, *Reincarnation*, chapter 10, pp. 136–8.

[57] Ibid., chapter 10, pp. 139–40. In his 'Irreverent Postscript' Edwards revisits the modus operandi problem, this time questioning how God as 'pure mind' could influence anything on earth, and in particular be involved in intelligent design; see ibid., pp. 301–3.

[58] Ibid., chapter 10, p. 138.

[59] Stevenson, *Where Reincarnation and Biology Intersect*, chapter 1, p. 12 and *Reincarnation and Biology*, chapter 1, pp. 14–16.

[60] Stevenson, *Where Reincarnation and Biology Intersect*, chapter 1, p. 4.

[61] Stevenson, *Reincarnation and Biology*, chapter 19, pp. 1562–3.

62 Stevenson, *Where Reincarnation and Biology Intersect*, chapter 10, p. 73.

63 Ibid., chapter 1, p. 3.

64 See ibid., chapter 5, pp. 38–41 and *Reincarnation and Biology*, chapter 5, pp. 300–23.

65 See ibid., chapter 10, pp. 74–5 and ibid., chapter 10, pp. 728–45 (see especially pp. 741–2 and 745).

66 See ibid., chapter 18, pp. 129–31 and ibid., chapter 18, pp. 1382–1403 (see especially pp. 1398 and 1400–1).

67 See ibid., chapter 19, pp. 137–9 and ibid., chapter 19, pp. 1553–65.

68 Stevenson, *Children Who Remember Previous Lives*, p. 289, note 19.

69 See, for example, Muller, *Reincarnation*, chapter 2 and Brownell, *Reincarnation*, 'Memories of Past Lives', pp. 13–30. Meanwhile two unusual cases that began in childhood but continued into adulthood, those of Katherine Bates and Laure Raynaud, are discussed in great detail in chapter 10 of Delanne's *Documents pour servir à l'Etude de Réeincarnation*. Also I have had a personal experience that may be of interest; see the paper *Finding Big Bill* at www.ianlawton.com/apl1.htm.

70 Lenz, *Lifetimes*, 'Introduction', pp. 13–18.

71 Ibid., 'The Experience of Reincarnation', pp. 47–68.

72 Ibid., 'Beyond Birth and Death', pp. 196–205.

Chapter 3: Past-Life Regression

1   Stevenson, *Children Who Remember Previous Lives*, chapter 3, p. 43.

2   Wambach, *Reliving Past Lives*, chapter 3, p. 37.

3   Wilson, *Mind Out of Time*, chapter 6, pp. 97–100.

4   For the background see Iverson, *More Lives Than One*, chapters 1 and 2.

5   Ibid., chapter 11.

6   Harris, *Investigating the Unexplained*, chapter 18, pp. 156–7.

7   Iverson, *More Lives Than One*, chapter 6.

8   Harris, *Investigating the Unexplained*, chapter 18, pp. 161–3; see also his article 'Are Past Life Regressions Evidence of Reincarnation?', *Free Inquiry* 6:4 (Autumn 1986).

9   Wilson, *The After Death Experience*, chapter 4, pp. 50–1.

10 For brief general summaries of cryptomnesia research see Harris, *Investigating the Unexplained*, chapter 17, pp. 150–3 and Edwards, *Reincarnation*, chapter 5, pp. 71–2; for a more detailed treatment see Wilson, *Mind Out of Time*, chapter 7.

[11] See Penfield, 'The Brain's Record of Auditory and Visual Experience: a Final Summary and Discussion', *Brain* 86:4 (1963), pp. 595–696 and his 1958 book *The Excitable Cortex in Conscious Man*.

[12] Zolik, 'An Experimental Investigation of the Psychodynamic Implications of the Hypnotic Previous Existence Fantasy', *Journal of Clinical Psychology* 14 (1958), pp. 179–83.

[13] See Kampman, 'Hypnotically Induced Multiple Personality', *Acta Ouluensis Universitatis Series D*, Medica 6 Psychiatrica 3 (1973), especially appendix 4; 'Hypnotically Induced Multiple Personality: an Experimental Study', *International Journal of Clinical and Experimental Hypnosis* 24:3 (Jul 1976), pp. 215–27; and 'Dynamic Relation of the Secondary Personality Induced by Hypnosis to the Present Personality' in Frankel, Fred and Zamansky, Harold (eds.), *Hypnosis at its Bicentennial* (Plenum, 1978), pp. 183–8.

[14] The details that follow come from Edwards, *Reincarnation*, chapter 5, pp. 60–6 and Wilson, *Mind Out of Time*, chapter 4, pp.72–9.

[15] Edwards, *Reincarnation*, chapter 5, pp. 66–7.

[16] This is irrespective of whether memory storage and retrieval mechanisms are fundamentally nonphysical for current as well as past lives, a topic to which we will return in the final chapter.

[17] Wilson, *Mind Out of Time*, chapter 4, p. 80.

[18] Ducasse, 'How the Case of "The Search for Bridey Murphy" Stands Today', *Journal of the American Society for Psychical Research* 54 (1960), pp. 3–22.

[19] Harris, *Investigating the Unexplained*, chapter 18, pp. 155–6.

[20] All information about this case comes from Wilson, *Mind Out of Time*, chapter 12 unless otherwise stated; a brief summary of it is provided in Keeton and Moss, *Encounters With the Past*, Prologue.

[21] For example the following two sources contain only brief summaries of the trial that concentrate more on the accusations themselves, which concern a cat called 'Sathan' that was supposed to be the devil incarnate: Russell, Jeffrey, *A History of Witchcraft* (Thames and Hudson, 1980), pp. 92–4; and Greenwood, Susan, *The History of Early Witchcraft* (Southwater, 2002), pp. 146–7.

[22] Morgan, Glyn, *Essex Witches* (Spurbooks, 1973), chapter 2.

[23] All three of the relatively recent sources listed in the notes above contain the correct date, as do the following: Hole, Christina, *Witchcraft in Britain* (Granada, 1977), pp. 41–3; Purkiss, Diane, *The Witch in History* (Routledge, 1996), p. 155; Martin, Lois, *The History of Witchcraft* (Pocket Essentials, 2007), p. 94. This is compared to Wilson's report of two books with the wrong date that were published in the 1920s. He correctly points out that the date in Keeton and Moss' own book is the wrong one, but of course this may just be because they used the date from the regression without thinking further about it.

It is also interesting to note that a general history of Chelmsford that I consulted refers to the original pamphlet in full as *The Examination and Confession of Certain Wytches at Chensford... before the Queens maiesties Judges, the xxvi day of July Anno 1566* – that is, with the correct date on it; see Grieve, Hilda, *The Sleepers and the Shadows* (Essex Record Office, 1988), Vol 1, p. 157.

24   Iverson, *More Lives Than One*, chapters 4–5.

25   Harris, *Investigating the Unexplained*, chapter 18, pp. 159–61.

26   In addition Wilson reports that his investigations revealed the vault was most likely seventeenth century; see *The After Death Experience*, chapter 4, p. 52,

27   Ibid., chapter 4, p. 51.

28   Although Brown's book was self-published and is therefore difficult to obtain, the material presented here comes from his summary of the case in an article of the same name in the *Journal of Regression Therapy* 5:1 (1991), pp. 62–71.

29   See www.csp.navy.mil/ww2boats/shark1.htm.

30   See the Wikipedia article for the *USS Shark*.

31   Snow, *Looking for Carroll Beckwith*, chapters 1–5.

32   The detailed descriptions of the two parts of the regression dealing with Beckwith's life are in ibid., chapters 3 and 5.

33   The details of these initial investigations are in ibid., chapters 6 and 7.

34   Ibid., chapters 8 and 9.

35   The details of these second-stage investigations are in ibid., chapters 10–12 and 14–16.

36   Ibid., chapter 13.

37   Bob's full tabulation can be found in ibid., chapter 11, pp. 109–11.

38   Ibid., chapter 10, pp. 96–7.

39   See Harris, *Investigating the Unexplained*, chapter 18, p. 156 and Wilson, *The After Death Experience*, chapter 4, p. 53.

40   Iverson, *More Lives Than One*, chapters 7–8.

41   All the factual details for the Alison case are taken from various Wikipedia articles unless otherwise stated.

42   Harris, *Investigating the Unexplained*, chapter 18, pp. 157–9.

43   Costain, *The Moneyman,* p. viii.

44   Wilson, *The After Death Experience*, chapter 4, pp. 52–3.

45   Costain, *The Moneyman*, pp. 25 and 106.

46   Ibid., p. 25.

47   Ibid., p. 18.

48 Ibid., p. 419.

49 Ibid., pp. vii and 14.

50 Ibid., p. 277.

51 Ibid., p. 497.

52 Tarazi's two earlier articles about this case are 'The Reincarnation of Antonia', *Fate Magazine*, Oct 1984, pp. 50–6 and 'An Unusual Case of Hypnotic Regression with Some Unexplained Contents', *Journal of the American Society for Psychical Research* 84:4 (Oct 1990), pp. 309–44.

53 The background information comes from *Under the Inquisition*, Introduction, pp. 11–19.

54 Indeed in *Under the Inquisition* she is clearly aware of Kampman's research and includes it in her references. It is therefore something of a shame that she did not attempt to regress Laurel in an attempt to establish any potential source of her information – even though such a thing is hard to imagine given the details of the case.

55 Tarazi, *Under the Inquisition*, Notes and References, pp. 659–79.

56 For the background to his initial research see Ramster, *The Truth about Reincarnation*, Preface and chapter 1.

57 For the background to his documentary see Ramster, *The Search for Lives Past*, Foreword and chapter 1.

58 See ibid., chapter 1, pp 29–30 and chapter 6, with additional details and some minor corrections from the documentary itself.

59 See ibid., chapters 2 and 3, with additional details and some minor corrections from the documentary itself.

60 I checked a number of modern maps and if it is on them at all it appears only as 'Stone' or 'Stone Lane'.

61 Although the word is listed in some modern dictionaries in England it is nevertheless obsolete and was only ever used in the southwest – and certainly not in Australia.

62 I was able to locate this building myself in the summer of 2008, but it is now in a serious state of disrepair. It is entirely overgrown inside and out, and now houses a rusting car and various other rubbish. I was not even able to enter to try to ascertain whether the floor slabs are still there.

63 Ramster insists that the correspondences were excellent and not well presented in the film; he also maintains that he has written a new book and that it will be accompanied by a new film, with new cases, information and analysis in both; however the release dates for these have still to be decided (correspondence with me, 3 June 2008).

64 Moreover, although both Laurel Dilmun and Linda Tarazi have now passed on,

Tarazi's daughter Laila has confirmed that she still has boxes of her mother's correspondence with university professors and others, and many of the notes from and tapes of the original sessions (correspondence with me, 29 April and 1 August 2008).

65 Wambach, *Reliving Past Lives*, chapter 1, pp. 1–5.

66 Ibid., chapter 6, p. 81.

67 The key results are all contained in ibid., chapter 8, while chapters 9–11 contain examples of individual data sheets. It is interesting to note that one particular subject living in Mesopotamia in 1700 BCE referred to teaching the 'code of Hammurabi', which Wambach rejected because her further research apparently indicated this code was not developed until 1300 BCE (see chapter 8, p. 113). But because I have some knowledge of this subject I can reveal that specialist sources available even at the time of her survey – as well as more modern ones – do indicate that Hammurabi ruled Babylon using his well-known law code in the first half of the eighteenth century BCE (see, for example, Georges Roux, *Ancient Iraq*, Chronological Table IV, p. 507).

68 Wilson, *Mind Out of Time*, chapter 2, pp. 29–35.

69 In a review of *Ancient Egypt Speaks* published in the *Journal of Egyptian Archaeology* 23 (1937), pp. 123–4.

70 Brownell, *Reincarnation*, 'An Arabian Incarnation', pp. 44–7.

71 Ramster, *The Truth about Reincarnation*, chapter 2; see especially pp. 24–5.

72 Ramster, *The Search for Lives Past*, chapter 6, pp. 226–8.

73 He reports that the film was edited by people who had little real knowledge of the subject matter (correspondence with me, 3 June 2008; see also note 63 above).

74 Stevenson, *Xenoglossy*, p. 58.

75 Wilson, *Mind Out of Time*, chapter 6, pp. 112–13.

76 Stevenson, *Unlearned Language*, pp. 73–153 and 205–9.

77 Thomason, 'Past Tongues Remembered', *Skeptical Inquirer* 11:4 (1987), pp. 367–75.

78 Stevenson, *Unlearned Language*, pp. 140–1.

79 Akolkar, 'Search for Sharada: Report of a Case and its Investigation', *Journal of the American Society for Psychical Research* 86 (1992), pp. 206–47; for possible normal sources see especially p. 215.

80 Stevenson, *Unlearned Language*, pp. 7–71.

81 Wilson, *Mind Out of Time*, chapter 6, p. 112.

82 Stevenson, *Unlearned Language*, pp. 169–203.

83 Wambach and Snow, 'Past-Life Therapy: The Experiences of Twenty-Six

Therapists', *Journal of Regression Therapy* 1:2 (1986), pp. 75–7.

[84] Ramster, *The Truth about Reincarnation*, chapter 3, pp. 89–91; a pictorial reproduction of some of the writing is included.

[85] Ibid., chapter 2, p. 21; again a pictorial reproduction of some of the writing is included.

[86] Whitton, *Life Between Life*, chapter 11, pp. 167–9.

Chapter 4: Past-Life Therapy

[1] The main bodies are, in the US, The International Association for Regression Research and Therapies, or IARRT (see www.iarrt.org), and the International Board for Regression Therapy, or IBRT (see www.ibrt.org); and in Europe the European Academy of Regression Therapy, or EARTh (see www.earth-network.org), and the Past Life Regression Academy (see www.regressionacademy.com).

[2] For an excellent summary of the earliest experiments see Muller, *Reincarnation*, chapter 3, pp. 138–44. In addition de Rochas himself provides extensive details of other cases known at the time in *Les Vies Successives*.

[3] See Muller, *Reincarnation*, Introduction, p. 27; apparently in many cases Björkhem was able to trace the past life to a real historical person.

[4] Cannon, *The Power Within*, chapter 16, p. 170.

[5] Grant and Kelsey, *Many Lifetimes*, chapter 6, pp. 133–4.

[6] Netherton, *Past Lives Therapy*, Introduction, pp. 6–7.

[7] Fiore, *You Have Been Here Before*, Introduction, pp. 4–5.

[8] Ibid., Introduction, p. 6.

[9] Whitton, *Life Between Life*, chapter 1, p. 4.

[10] Wilson, *Mind Out of Time*, chapter 2, pp. 43–5.

[11] Woolger, *Other Lives, Other Selves*, chapter 1, p. 15.

[12] Weiss, *Many Lives, Many Masters*, chapter 4, p. 54.

[13] Ibid., chapter 4, p. 57.

[14] See his book *Same Soul, Many Bodies* (Piatkus, 2004). This trend was begun by Helen Wambach and Chet Snow in *Mass Dreams of the Future* (McGraw-Hill, 1989) and by Bruce Goldberg in *Past Lives, Future Lives* (Newcastle Publishing, 1982). For a critique see Lawton, *Hypnotic Progression* (paper at www.ianlawton.com/bosextr2.htm) and *The Wisdom of the Soul*, Questions 4.2.3 and 4.2.4.

[15] This is the official journal of The International Association for Regression Research and Therapies, although this was originally known as the Association

for Past Life Research and Therapies.

[16] Cladder, 'Past-Life Therapy with Difficult Phobics', *Journal of Regression Therapy* 1:2 (1986), pp. 81–5.

[17] Denning, 'The Restoration of Health Through Hypnosis', *Journal of Regression Therapy* 2:1 (1987), pp. 52–4.

[18] Van der Maesen, 'Past-Life Therapy for Giles De La Tourette's Syndrome: A Research Study', *Journal of Regression Therapy* 12:1 (1998), pp. 97–104. The summary results in this paper are not the easiest to interpret properly, hence my representation of them in a table.

[19] Van der Maesen, 'Past-Life Therapy for People who Hallucinate Voices', *Journal of Regression Therapy* 13:1 (1999), pp. 39–42.

[20] Edwards, *Reincarnation*, chapter 6, p. 98.

[21] Tarazi, *Under the Inquisition*, Introduction, p. 13.

[22] See, for example, Lawton, *The Wisdom of the Soul*, Question 1.6.4. However this tends not to be the case with interlife memories; see Question 2.4.3.

[23] Woolger, *Other Lives, Other Selves*, chapter 10, pp. 265–71.

[24] Netherton, *Past Lives Therapy*, chapter 4.

[25] Whitton, *Life Between Life*, chapter 12.

[26] Fiore, *You Have Been Here Before*, Introduction, pp. 6–8.

Chapter 5: Interlife Regression

[1] Cannon, *The Power Within*, chapter 16, pp. 179–80. This report contains a number of other details of 'White Brothers' and 'Blue Sisters' and so on that seem likely to have been subjectively influenced by the subject's conscious knowledge.

[2] Bernstein, *The Search for Bridey Murphy*, pp. 145–84.

[3] Huffman, *Many Wonderful Things*, chapter 1, pp. 16–19.

[4] There is a less revealing interlife exchange with Catharine Warren-Browne in *Born Again*, chapter 7, pp. 230–4; and because Holzer was deliberately asking about it he may well have obtained useful information from other subjects that he does not mention in the book, which primarily concentrates on proof of past lives.

[5] Whitton, *Life Between Life*, chapter 3, pp. 19–21.

[6] Fiore, *You Have Been Here Before*, chapter 11, p. 216. I contacted her to check the status of this material; it seems that, unfortunately, certain tragic circumstances around that time prevented her from completing a book called *The Interim* that she was in the process of writing next; and now, even more

unfortunately, she no longer has all her drafts and case notes from that time (correspondence with me, 18 July 2004).

[7] Wambach's 750 subjects who could access and then recall their pre-birth experiences represented only about forty percent of her total volunteers, which is an extremely low proportion compared to most estimates. However hers was a unique group situation in which she was deliberately attempting to take everyone to the deepest state of hypnosis in which they *should* still have had conscious recall to allow them to then record their experiences; but in fact it would appear that this blanket level of deep hypnosis was probably just too deep for a significant proportion of her subjects to have any conscious recall. See *Life Before Life*, chapter 2, pp. 26–7.

[8] Cannon, *Between Death and Life*, chapter 1, pp. 3–4.

[9] Modi, *Remarkable Healings*, chapter 1, pp. 21–2.

[10] Ibid., chapter 3, p. 186.

[11] Considerable confusion has existed over the timings of Newton's research. He provided minimal biographical material in either of his first two books: for example in *Journey of Souls*, published in 1994, he merely states that 'the travels of souls... have come to me from a ten-year collection of clients' (Introduction, p. 5); while in *Destiny of Souls* he confirms that 'during the decade of the 1980s... I was formulating a working model of the world between lives' (Introduction, p. xii). Both statements suggest a starting point for his interlife research of the mid-1980s. However Newton queried this assumption in the original *Book of the Soul* in correspondence with me dated 16 February 2007, and provided the following biographical information on which the revised dates are based: 'I grew up in Southern California and eventually in 1956 established a practice in Los Angeles... I started working on LBL around 1968 and really began to specialize in the 1970s and 1980s. I did not publish until the early 1990s because I wanted thousands of cases to draw upon.' He provided further clarification on 14 February 2008: 'You are correct about my contributing to misunderstandings over my comments in an early edition of *Journey of Souls* about the "ten-year case collection". I have since corrected this because what I meant to say was that most of the cases in *Journey* were over the ten years prior to publication due to the fact that these cases were better researched and facilitated, with much more experience behind me from my work in the 1970s. Also, I had a much better map of the spirit world. That did not come across, but I hope the record is now straight.'

[12] Newton, *Journey of Souls*, Introduction, p. 2.

[13] Ibid., Introduction, p. 3.

[14] Ibid., Introduction, p. 6 and *Destiny of Souls*, chapter 1, p. 10.

[15] These were first categorized in this form in my introduction to *The Wisdom of the Soul*.

16 Weiss, *Many Lives, Many Masters*, chapter 3, pp. 39–40.

17 Modi, *Remarkable Healings*, chapter 3, pp. 107–10.

18 See Holzer, *Born Again*, chapter 3, p. 55 and Ramster, *The Search for Lives Past*, chapter 1, p. 25.

19 See Wambach, *Life Before Life*, chapter 2, p. 27 and Whitton, *Life Between Life*, chapter 3, p. 23.

20 Correspondence with me, 24 January 2005 and subsequent discussions.

21 Newton, *Destiny of* Souls, Introduction, p. xii.

22 Newton, *Journey of Souls*, Introduction, pp. 4–5.

Chapter 6: The Interlife Experience

1   See, for example, Tomlinson, *Healing the Eternal Soul*, chapter 7, p. 98. Newton refers to the 'superconscious', and Whitton and Wambach to the 'metaconscious', state.

2   To name names would be invidious and counter-productive. Suffice to say that such criticism is reasonably widespread.

3   Whitton, *Life Between Life*, chapter 4, pp. 30–1.

4   Ramster, *The Truth about Reincarnation*, chapter 2, p. 49 and chapter 6, p. 133.

5   Newton, *Journey of Souls*, chapter 1, p. 9.

6   Fiore, *You Have Been Here Before*, chapter 11, pp. 222–3.

7   Holzer, *Born Again*, chapter 5, p. 126.

8   Modi, *Remarkable Healings*, chapter 3, p. 115.

9   Cannon, *Between Death and Life*, chapter 1, pp. 8 and 16.

10 Holzer, *Born Again*, chapter 5, p. 125.

11 Whitton, *Life Between Life*, chapter 4, p. 30.

12 Newton, *Journey of Souls*, chapter 2, p. 25 and chapter 3, pp. 27 and 39.

13 Cannon, *Between Death and Life*, chapter 2, p. 19.

14 Modi, *Remarkable Healings*, chapter 3, pp. 115 and 117.

15 Ramster, *The Truth about Reincarnation*, chapter 6, p. 133.

16 Fiore, *You Have Been Here Before*, chapter 11, p. 223.

17 Newton, *Journey of Souls*, chapter 2, pp. 22 and 24.

18 Whitton, *Life Between Life*, chapter 4, p. 35.

19 Ramster, *The Truth about Reincarnation*, chapter 2, p. 49.

20 Cannon, *Between Death and Life*, chapter 2, p. 21.

21 Modi, *Remarkable Healings*, chapter 3, pp. 120–1.

22 Ring, *Life At Death*, chapter 12, pp. 236–7.

23 Ramster, *The Truth about Reincarnation*, chapter 6, p. 134.

24 See Weiss, *Many Lives, Many Masters*, chapter 10, p. 140 and Huffman, *Many Wonderful Things*, chapter 5, pp. 72–4.

25 Newton, *Destiny of Souls*, chapter 4, pp. 90–1.

26 Newton, *Journey of Souls*, chapter 5, pp. 54–5.

27 Whitton, *Life Between Life*, chapter 4, p. 33.

28 Cannon, *Between Death and Life*, chapter 2, p. 21 and chapter 5, pp. 62–5.

29 Ibid., chapter 1, p. 8.

30 Modi, *Remarkable Healings*, chapter 3, pp. 115–16 and 119.

31 For a discussion of soul energy fragmentation see Lawton, *Spirit Possession* (paper at www.ianlawton.com/bosextr3.htm) and *The Wisdom of the Soul*, Question 1.3.

32 This comes from his personal correspondence with Ring quoted in *Life At Death*, chapter 12, p. 238.

33 Tomlinson, *Exploring the Eternal Soul*, chapter 2, pp. 32–4, 37 and 39.

34 Fiore, *The Unquiet Dead*, chapter 4, p. 26.

35 Newton, *Destiny of Souls*, chapter 4, pp. 116 and 120–1.

36 Modi, *Remarkable Healings*, chapter 3, pp. 120–1.

37 Whitton, *Life Between Life*, chapter 4, p. 30.

38 Cannon, *Between Death and Life*, chapter 11, pp. 170–6.

39 For a discussion of earthbound or even supposedly demonic spirits, and of the extent to which they can possess still-living humans, see Lawton, *Spirit Possession* (paper at www.ianlawton.com/bosextr3.htm) and *The Wisdom of the Soul*, Questions 1.1 and 1.2.

40 Newton, *Journey of Souls*, chapter 4, p. 46 and *Destiny of Souls*, chapter 3, pp. 59–60.

41 Modi, *Remarkable Healings*, chapter 3, p. 115.

42 Cannon, *Between Death and Life*, chapter 2, pp. 20–1.

43 Ramster, *The Truth about Reincarnation*, chapter 4, p. 110.

44 Newton, *Journey of Souls*, chapter 4, p. 49 and *Destiny of Souls*, chapter 4, p. 93.

45 Holzer, *Born Again*, chapter 5, pp. 123–8.

46 Ramster, *The Truth about Reincarnation*, chapter 2, p. 56 and chapter 6, p. 134.

47 For example, see the translation of and commentary on the relatively late *Bhagavata Purana* 3.30 provided by AC Bhaktivedanta Swami Prabhupada, the

founder of the 'Hare Krishna' movement, in the best-selling *Laws of Nature* (Bhaktivedanta Book Trust, 1991), chapter 2 ('Bad Karma'). The description of the hellish torment suffered by the man who merely loves his wife and family is actually way beyond anything the other religions manage to conjure up, including being set on fire, being made to eat his own flesh, having his entrails pulled out and limbs torn off, and then being drowned. All this before having to reincarnate in every animal form before finally being given another chance at human incarnation.

[48]   Fiore, *The Unquiet Dead*, chapter 18, p. 160.

[49]   Newton, *Journey of Souls*, chapter 4, p. 49 and *Destiny of Souls*, chapter 3, pp. 66 and 74–5.

[50]   Woolger, *Other Lives, Other Selves*, chapter 11, pp. 298–9.

[51]   Cannon, *Between Death and Life*, chapter 6, pp. 105–8 and chapter 7, p. 115.

[52]   Newton, *Journey of Souls*, chapter 5, p. 56.

[53]   Newton, *Destiny of Souls*, chapter 5, pp. 156–7, 160–2 and 167.

[54]   Ramster, *The Search for Lives Past*, chapter 7, p. 269.

[55]   Ibid., chapter 2, p. 59.

[56]   Weiss, *Many Lives, Many Masters*, chapter 12, p. 171.

[57]   Fiore, *You Have Been Here Before*, chapter 12, pp. 240–1.

[58]   Whitton, *Life Between Life*, chapter 4, pp. 39–42.

[59]   Modi, *Remarkable Healings*, chapter 3, pp. 116–17.

[60]   Newton, *Journey of Souls*, chapter 6, pp. 85–6.

[61]   Newton, *Destiny of Souls*, chapter 6, pp. 222–3.

[62]   Cannon, *Between Death and Life*, chapter 13, pp. 195–6.

[63]   Fiore, *The Unquiet Dead*, chapter 4, p. 22.

[64]   Huffman, *Many Wonderful Things*, chapter 5, pp. 74–6.

[65]   Moody, *Life After Life*, chapter 2, pp. 64–5 and 67–8.

[66]   Ring, *Life at Death*, chapter 4, p. 67 and chapter 12, p. 240–1; see also chapter 10, pp. 196–8 where he discusses a 1977 paper by Noyes, R and Kletti, R, 'Panoramic Memory: A Response to the Threat of Death', *Omega* 8, pp. 181–93.

[67]   Fenwick, *The Truth in the Light*, chapter 8, pp. 114–15.

[68]   Lenz, *Lifetimes*, 'The Experience of Reincarnation', pp. 68–74.

[69]   See www.ibeginagain.org/articles/eric_taub.shtml.

[70]   Wambach, *Life Before Life*, chapter 5, p. 97.

[71]   Ramster, *The Search for Lives Past*, chapter 7, p. 264.

72 See Modi, *Remarkable Healings*, chapter 3, pp. 117 and 121 and Fiore, *You Have Been Here Before*, chapter 12, p. 241.

73 Holzer, *Born Again*, chapter 5, p. 128.

74 Newton, *Journey of Souls*, chapter 7, pp. 92–4 and 105–6 and *Destiny of Souls*, chapter 5, pp. 193–4.

75 Whitton, *Life Between Life*, chapter 4, pp. 44 and 48.

76 Cannon, *Between Death and Life*, chapter 4, pp. 36–9 and 43 and chapter 5, pp. 69–71.

77 Weiss, *Many Lives, Many Masters*, chapter 12, p. 171.

78 Ramster, *The Search for Lives Past*, chapter 7, p. 252.

79 See Huffman, *Many Wonderful Things*, chapter 5, p. 75, Cannon, *Between Death and Life*, chapter 13, p. 193 and Newton, *Journey of Souls*, chapter 7, pp. 87–8.

80 See Newton, *Journey of Souls*, chapter 12, p. 213 and *Destiny of Souls*, chapter 9, pp. 362 and 370–3.

81 Newton, *Journey of Souls*, chapter 12, pp. 219–20.

82 Whitton, *Life Between Life*, chapter 4, p. 43.

83 Cannon, *Between Death and Life*, chapter 16, p. 231.

84 Modi, *Remarkable Healings*, chapter 3, pp. 186–7 (see also pp. 121–2).

85 Weiss, *Many Lives, Many Masters*, chapter 10, p. 140 and chapter 12, pp. 172–3.

86 Huffman, *Many Wonderful Things*, chapter 5, pp. 76–7.

87 Newton, *Journey of Souls*, chapter 12, pp. 206–17.

88 Wambach, *Life Before Life*, chapter 2, p. 29 and chapter 3, p. 42.

89 Ramster, *The Search for Lives Past*, chapter 2, pp. 60–1.

90 Ramster, *The Truth about Reincarnation*, chapter 6, p. 135.

91 Cannon, *Between Death and Life*, chapter 4, p. 40.

92 Whitton, *Life Between Life*, chapter 4, p. 43.

93 Newton, Journey of Souls, chapter 14, p. 262.

94 Wambach, *Life Before Life*, chapter 3, pp. 42–56.

95 Fiore, *The Unquiet Dead*, chapter 4, p. 22.

96 Ramster, *The Search for Lives Past*, chapter 7, p. 265.

97 Newton, *Journey of Souls*, chapter 14, pp. 249–51 and 253–60.

98 Wambach, *Life Before Life*, chapter 3, pp. 42–56.

99 Modi, *Remarkable Healings*, chapter 3, p. 121.

100 Whitton, *Life Between Life*, chapter 4, p. 44.

Source References

101 Ramster, *The Truth about Reincarnation*, chapter 6, p. 135.

102 Cannon, *Between Death and Life*, chapter 12, pp. 181 and 184.

103 Newton, *Journey of Souls*, chapter 12, pp. 201 and 205.

104 Cannon, *Between Death and Life*, chapter 4, pp. 46 and 56–8.

105 Wambach, *Life Before Life*, chapter 3, pp. 47–60.

106 Ramster, *The Search for Lives Past*, chapter 7, p. 265.

107 Ramster, *The Truth about Reincarnation*, chapter 6, pp. 135–6.

108 Whitton, *Life Between Life*, chapter 4, pp. 43 and 45.

109 Ibid., chapter 4, pp. 30 and 51.

110 See Newton, *Journey of Souls*, chapter 12, p. 205 and Cannon, *Between Death and Life*, chapter 7, pp. 120–1.

111 Wambach, *Life Before Life*, chapter 3, pp. 46–7.

112 Lawton, *The Wisdom of the Soul*, under Question 2.4.

113 Newton, *Destiny of Souls*, chapter 4, pp. 116–18.

114 Tomlinson, *Exploring the Eternal Soul*, chapter 8, pp. 136 and 144–7.

115 Weiss, *Many Lives, Many Masters*, chapter 12, p. 172.

116 Newton, *Journey of Souls*, chapter 15, pp. 269–70 and *Destiny of Souls*, chapter 9, pp. 384–8.

117 Newton, *Journey of Souls*, chapter 15, p. 267.

118 Whitton, *Life Between Life*, chapter 4, p. 53.

119 Cannon, *Between Death and Life*, chapter 15, pp. 225–6.

120 Wambach, *Life Before Life*, chapter 6, pp. 99 and 116.

121 Modi, *Remarkable Healings*, chapter 2, p. 102.

122 See Wambach, *Life Before Life*, chapter 6, p. 120, Cannon, *Between Death and Life*, chapter 16, p. 233 and Modi, *Remarkable Healings*, chapter 2, p. 102.

123 Cannon, *Between Death and Life*, chapter 16, pp. 233–4.

124 Wambach, *Life Before Life*, chapter 7, pp. 122–3.

125 Ibid., chapter 6, p. 106.

126 Newton, *Journey of Souls*, chapter 15, pp. 268–71.

127 Cannon, *Between Death and Life*, chapter 15, p. 221 and chapter 16, pp. 229–30.

128 Newton, *Journey of Souls*, chapter 5, p. 67.

129 Whitton, *Life Between Life*, chapter 4, p. 53.

130 See Modi, *Remarkable Healings*, chapter 3, pp. 183–4 and Cannon, *Between Death and Life*, chapter 4, pp. 43–4.

[131] Cannon, *Between Death and Life*, chapter 15, p. 219.

[132] Note also that Jim Tucker found that 112 out of 1100 children with past-life memories mentioned spending time in another realm, sometimes meeting relatives or other figures identified as 'God', a 'king' or a 'holy man'; see *Life Before Life*, chapter 8, pp. 168 and 171–3.

[133] Joan Grant, who we met in chapter 4, reveals some amazing memories of the intricacy of her thought processes from as early as four months old, and of her indignance at being treated like a baby; see *Many Lifetimes*, chapter 7.

[134] Woolger, *Other Lives, Other Selves*, Chapter 11, pp. 295–6.

[135] Netherton, *Past Lives Therapy*, chapter 16, pp. 175–6.

[136] See Newton, *Journey of Souls*, chapter 5, p. 68 and Lawton, *The Wisdom of the Soul*, Question 2.4.2.

[137] Montgomery, *Here and Hereafter*, chapter 1, pp. 17–20.

[138] Ibid., chapter 3, p. 32.

[139] Ibid., chapter 5, p. 63 and chapter 6, pp. 69–75.

[140] Ibid., chapter 6, pp. 67–8.

[141] Lenz, *Lifetimes*, 'Death, Dying and Other Worlds', pp. 95–121.

[142] Lenz actually suggests that the idea of life planning and choice is included in 'Far Eastern doctrines of the rebirth process' and in 'Hindu philosophy'. However he gives no source references, and his suggested further reading only contains the Hindu *Bhagavad Gita*, the Buddhist *Dhammapada* and the *Tibetan Book of the Dead*, none of which contain this idea in any explicit sense. Nor do any other traditional Eastern texts as far as I am aware.

[143] For example because the library of life books is closely associated with more detailed life previews as well as reviews, as well as with ongoing learning with the soul group; because reviews with elders are almost certain to imply planning with them as well; and because any more detailed planning by definition suggests simple planning.

[144] Whitton, *Life Between Life*, chapter 4, p. 57.

[145] Cannon, *Between Death and Life*, chapter 16, p. 237.

Chapter 7: Experience and Growth

[1] In *The Life Divine* Sri Aurobindo, who we will meet properly shortly, devotes some time to discussing what he classifies as the four main approaches to life and their implications for day-to-day behavior; although he uses different language they are effectively the reincarnational experience model that he and we support, the illusion model that we will discuss properly in the final chapter, the single-life model and the materialist model; see book 2, chapter 16, pp.

695–702.

2   See note 47 to chapter 6.

3   See, for example, Lawton, *The Wisdom of the Soul*, Question 2.2. Not only does much channeled material tend to support this view, but none of the interlife pioneers mention any of their subjects having a choice to reincarnate as an animal. The only slight exception is Newton's suggestion that a human soul can experience anything it likes in a 'space of transformation', which includes what it is like to be any type of animal (see *Journey of Souls*, chapter 10, p. 168); and that some subjects have experienced being different life forms on other planets (ibid., chapter 11, pp. 192–3). But it seems highly likely that the group nature of animal soul energy itself precludes the possibility of any sort of process of reincarnation similar to that experienced by humans. This group nature is not only demonstrated by the way groups of animals react similarly and instantaneously without apparent communication, such as flocks of birds changing direction, but also by some intriguing research conducted in the late nineteenth century by A F Knudsen. He hypnotized individual horses to perform certain movements, and found that certain others in the field would react in the same way, with group sizes varying from anywhere between three and eighteen animals. He was also able to repeat the experiment although with less elaborations with cattle, who he felt were generally less intelligent and whose group sizes were correspondingly larger at between fifty and a hundred animals. These experiments worked even when the main animal subject was as much as five miles distant from the others (see TenDam, *Exploring Reincarnation*, chapter 12, pp. 259–60).

4   For a modern summary see Judy Hall's *The Way of Karma*, chapter 1, pp. 7–9. This is at least partly based on theosophical thinking.

5   This is taken from an article entitled 'Rebirth' in *Arya*, Nov 1915, reproduced at www.hinduwebsite.com/divinelife/auro/auro_rebirth.asp.

6   Aurobindo, *The Life Divine*, book 2, chapter 22, pp. 839 and 841–3.

7   Newton, *Journey of Souls*, chapter 4, pp. 50–1.

8   Weiss, *Many Lives, Many Masters*, chapter 12, p. 172.

9   Modi, *Remarkable Healings*, chapter 3, pp. 186–7.

10   For further discussion of emotional learning, and repetitive and progressive soul behavior, see Lawton, *The Wisdom of the Soul*, Questions 2.1 and 2.4.1.

11   Whitton, *Life Between Life*, chapter 4, p. 45.

12   Cannon, *Between Death and Life*, chapter 4, pp. 59 and 61.

13   Montgomery, *Here and Hereafter*, chapter 7, p. 79.

14   Newton, *Journey of Souls*, chapter 13, pp. 226–9.

15   Newton, *Destiny of Souls*, chapter 9, p. 364.

[16] This tends to suggest that homosexuality is not merely a 'nature versus nurture' issue, whatever modern geneticists might be discovering about selected DNA strands relating to emotional or other traits. Meanwhile, on a related topic, it seems likely that less experienced souls may tend to stick with one gender for their incarnations; so when they first decide to experiment with incarnating in the opposite sex they may experience gender identity problems.

[17] One of my older sisters was taken from our family in a car accident for which she was completely blameless many years ago, when she was only in her thirties with two young children. It was a major test for us all to accept what had happened – especially when, for example, several of us had deliberately risked our lives for many years, weekend in, weekend out, racing motorcycles. Above all we faced the major test of not blaming the other driver – a young man who made the mistake of overtaking before the brow of a hill, the sort of mistake we have all made as inexperienced drivers. Although of course her loss was painful, I am thankful for the time I spent with her – and for the fact that her death was one of the major triggers that prompted me to start thinking far more metaphysically, especially about what might happen after death.

[18] See Newton, *Journey of Souls*, chapter 12, pp. 219–20, Cannon, *Between Death and Life*, chapter 8, p. 140, Montgomery, *Here and Hereafter*, chapter 7, p. 79 and Huffman, *Many Wonderful Things*, chapter 5, p. 75.

[19] Newton, *Journey of Souls*, chapter 12, p. 220; see also *Destiny of Souls*, chapter 9, p. 373.

[20] The whole issue of whether World War II and its build-up could have been part of a major light-realms plan for humanity to try to teach itself never to repeat the events is, of course, highly controversial. Implicit in it is the idea that Hitler and his acolytes were not some of the most evil souls ever to incarnate, but highly experienced souls who took on a seriously demanding task. This idea has been expressed in a few places, and for what it is worth we had some confirmation of it in our research for *The Wisdom of the Soul*, but felt at the time that it was more diplomatic to leave this aspect out. However it has been apparently corroborated in research conducted in the US by Peter Jenkins with medium Toni Winninger, who claims to have channeled Hitler's soul; see *Talking with Leaders of the Past*, pp. 158–63.

[21] One of the most widely referenced modern translations into English was produced by Francesca Freemantle in 1975, and these interpretations of context come from her assistant and co-commentator Chögyam Trungpa; see *The Tibetan Book of the Dead*, Commentary, pp. 2–3 and 6.

[22] The Republic 10:614–21; see Lee, *Plato: The Republic*, pp. 361–8. My thanks go to Judy Hall for pointing out the references to Plato and the *Hermetica* in her 2001 book *The Way of Reincarnation*, chapter 1, p. 256; and to Steiner in her follow-up *The Way of Karma*, chapter 10, pp. 137–8.

23 Stobaeus 26; see Scott, *Hermetica*, pp. 200–1 (although note that this translation is not accepted by all authorities).

24 Besant, *The Ancient Wisdom*, chapter 7, p. 197.

25 Ibid., chapter 7, pp. 219–20.

26 Ibid., chapter 7, pp. 223–8.

27 These are some of the regular features of a series of lectures given in various European cities in 1912–13 and compiled in *Life Between Death and Rebirth*, first published in 1968; see, for example, pp. 14 and 41.

28 Ibid., Lecture 11 (Frankfurt, 1913), pp. 207–10.

29 For example with little apparent logic he insists that 'superficiality' in one incarnation will invariably lead to 'lying' in the next and 'incorrectly formed organs' in the third; see *Manifestations of Karma*, Lecture 3 (Hamburg, 1910), p. 67.

30 Ibid., Lecture 4 (Hamburg, 1910), p. 72.

31 Ibid., Lecture 3 (Hamburg, 1910), p. 65.

32 Steiner, *Reincarnation and Karma*, Lecture 4 (Stuttgart, 1912), p. 67.

33 Fortune, *The Cosmic Doctrine*, Introduction, p. 12.

34 Biographical information comes from www.spiritwritings.com/kardec.html.

35 Kardec, *The Spirits' Book*, book 2, chapter 7, p. 199.

36 Ibid., book 2, chapter 3, pp. 116–18.

37 Ibid., book 2, chapter 6, p. 177.

38 Ibid., book 2, chapter 7, p. 197 and chapter 1, pp. 92–3.

39 Ibid., book 2, chapter 6, pp. 163–4.

40 Ibid., book 2, chapter 6, p. 167 and chapter 7, pp. 183–4.

41 Ibid., book 2, chapter 7, pp. 183–6.

42 Ibid., book 2, chapter 4, p. 120, chapter 2, p. 107 and chapter 1, p. 102.

43 Lancelin, *La Vie Posthume*, chapter 2, p. 32. He is also admirably aware of the possibility that his own mental projections might telepathically influence his subjects (chapter 2, p. 40), although he still maintains that their corroboration of the main tenets of Spiritism is fascinating because in some smaller details he disagrees with these (chapter 9, pp. 268–9). As to specifics he reports that some of his subjects had to negotiate realms populated by terrifying beings – shades of the *Tibetan Book of the Dead* – before being guided to more sublime realms by protective light beings (chapter 2, p. 38); that some found themselves in realms so sublime that he had difficulty in persuading them to leave and come out of trance (chapter 6, pp. 193–4); and that generally, having spent time contemplating where they failed and where they did well in previous lives, they chose the new life tests that would be of most benefit to them, either alone or

with the aid of higher beings (chapter 12, p. 395).

44 Austen, *The Teachings of Silver Birch*, pp. 19–20.
45 Ibid., pp. 122 and 128.
46 Ibid., pp. 50, 61–2 and 226–7.
47 Ibid., pp. 127 and 130.
48 Ibid., p. 176.
49 Ibid., p. 110.
50 For a full discussion of Cayce's readings on Atlantis, the Great Pyramid and the Hall of Records see Lawton, *Giza: The Truth*, chapter 5, pp. 242–63.
51 Woodward, *Edgar Cayce's Story of Karma*, chapter 4, pp. 99–101 and chapter 5, p. 141.
52 Ibid., chapter 4, pp. 106–9.
53 Todeschi, *Edgar Cayce on the Akashic Records*, chapter 3, p. 49.
54 Woodward, *Scars of the Soul*, chapter 3, pp. 136–43.
55 See, for example, Woodward, *Edgar Cayce's Story of Karma*, chapter 7, pp. 219–23, and in particular reading 288:7 on p. 221.
56 Ibid., chapter 7, pp. 225–7.
57 See, for example, Todeschi, *Edgar Cayce on the Akashic Records*, chapter 1, p. 7, chapter 4, pp. 78–9 and chapter 6, pp. 100–2.
58 See, for example, Woodward, *Edgar Cayce's Story of Karma*, chapters 5 and 6 and Cerminara, *Many Mansions*, chapter 18.
59 Todeschi, *Edgar Cayce on the Akashic Records*, chapter 1, pp. 2–3.
60 Ibid., chapter 7, p. 122.
61 Ibid., chapter 7, pp. 130–1.
62 The 258 lectures can be downloaded individually, free of charge, from www.pathwork.org/lecturesObtainingUnedited.html. Alternatively for an albeit still lengthy summary, which includes most of the extracts cited in this chapter and the next, see Lawton, *Introduction to Pathwork* (paper at www.ianlawton.com/se6.htm).
63 Pathwork Lecture 12, 'Spirit at Work: Life in the Spirit World', pp. 3–4; see note 62 above.
64 Pathwork Lecture 3, 'The Spirit World: You Choose Your Destiny', pp. 1 and 9–10; see note 62 above.
65 Pathwork Lecture 249, 'Pain of Injustice: Cosmic Records of All Personal and Collective Events, Deeds, Expression', p. 4; see note 62 above.
66 For a full discussion see Lawton, *The Seth Material* (paper at www.ianlawton.com/se1.htm) and *The Wisdom of the Soul*, Question 4.2.

⁶⁷ Roberts, *Seth Speaks*, chapter 9, pp. 134–9 and 146 and chapter 11, pp. 179–80.

⁶⁸ Ibid., chapter 9, pp. 138 and 143 and chapter 11, pp. 174–5.

⁶⁹ Ibid., chapter 11, pp. 168 and 184–5.

⁷⁰ Ibid., chapter 4, p. 66, chapter 11, pp. 170–4 and 185, chapter 12, pp. 195–6 and chapter 13, p. 221.

⁷¹ Ibid., chapter 12, p. 203.

⁷² Ibid., chapter 4, pp. 65–6.

⁷³ Ibid., chapter 12, p. 205.

⁷⁴ Ibid., chapter 13, pp. 220–4.

⁷⁵ Aurobindo, *The Life Divine*, book 2, chapter 22, pp. 832–4.

⁷⁶ Ibid., book 2, chapter 22, pp. 834–6.

⁷⁷ Ibid., book 2, chapter 22, pp. 830 and 834.

Chapter 8: The Holographic Soul

¹ Extracted from Berman, *The Journey Home*, Chapter 2, pp. 34–5; his description of his experience is also reproduced in full at www.ianlawton.com/nde3.htm.

² See www.mellen-thomas.com; his description of his experience is also reproduced in full at www.ianlawton.com/nde1.htm.

³ Grof, *Realms of the Human Unconscious*, chapter 5, pp. 183 and 203–5.

⁴ Strassman, *DMT: The Spirit Molecule*, chapter 16, pp. 238 and 244.

⁵ Yogananda, *Autobiography of a Yogi*, chapter 14, pp. 143–8.

⁶ A prime source of transcripts of these is *The Awakening of Intelligence*, a compilation first published in 1973.

⁷ See, for example, ibid., part 2, chapter 1, pp. 65–9 and part 5, chapter 1, pp. 188 and 193–5.

⁸ See, for example, ibid., part 6, chapter 4, p. 291.

⁹ See, for example, ibid., part 2, chapter 3, pp. 95–8.

¹⁰ See, for example, prominent CSI member Martin Gardner's article 'David Bohm and Jiddu Krishnamurti', *Skeptical Inquirer* 24:4 (2000), pp. 20–3. It is perhaps both ironic and revealing that Krishnamurti himself stressed the need not to deceive oneself, be hypocritical or have delusions of grandeur; see *The Awakening of Intelligence*, part 7, chapter 5, p. 347.

¹¹ Tolle, *The Power of Now*, chapter 3, p. 41.

¹² Ibid., chapter 1, p. 24.

¹³ Ibid., chapter 1, p. 25.

[14] Banks, *The Missing Link*, pp. 21, 31.

[15] Ibid., pp. 99–108.

[16] Bell's theorem, which was only experimentally proved in 1982, runs as follows. Two 'entangled' electrons will always have opposing spin directions, although as long as those directions remain unobserved they remain unknown. But if one of them is taken to the moon, and the spin direction of the one remaining behind is measured about any selected axis, the other one will instantaneously be found to have the opposite spin about the same axis. Supporters of non-local communication argue that the electron on the moon is 'given' its spin at this point by the other one – and indeed by the measurer – because it had no means of knowing in advance what axis would be chosen.

[17] For an excellent summary see the Wikipedia article 'Quantum Interpretations'.

[18] Wolf, *The Spiritual Universe*, chapter 11, pp. 217–20. His assertion that the difference between success and failure in this task comes down to the extent of 'vigorous intent' does not hold up well against the more sophisticated arguments we will discuss at the end of the chapter. Indeed, as much as this book is full of references that appear to show massive erudition, it seems that Wolf is not averse to throwing random assumptions into his arguments or making huge, unsupported leaps of logic.

[19] Huston, 'Taking the Quantum Leap... Too Far?', *What Is Enlightenment* 27 (Winter 2004); see www.enlightennext.org/magazine/j27/what-the-bleep.asp.

[20] See note 17 above.

[21] Lawton, *The Wisdom of the Soul*, Question 4.2.1.

[22] See his description of the 'nine lives of the soul' in *Physics of the Soul*, Epilogue.

[23] Krishnamurti, *The Awakening of Intelligence*, part 5, chapter 2, p. 205.

[24] Wolf, *The Spiritual Universe*, chapter 9, pp. 159 and 162–3.

[25] Ibid., chapter 9, pp. 164–5 and 180.

[26] The main Gnostic texts that contain this basic message are the *Apocryphon of John*, the *Hypostasis of the Archons*, *On the Origin of the World* and the *Tripartite Tractate*; for a modern translation see Robinson, *The Nag Hammadi Library*.

[27] Wolf, *The Spiritual Universe*, chapter 12, pp. 228–40. As an example of his logical contortions he wonders why, if his assertion is correct, there is so little telepathy – and then concludes that natural selection must have bred it out of the human race because empathy would make us less able to compete.

[28] Banks, *The Missing Link*, p. 67.

[29] See the 'Philosophical Reflections' page at www.sydneybanks.org. This quote comes from 'The Salt Spring Island Conversations' under the heading 'It's All

Spiritual'.

[30] Capra, *The Tao of Physics*, chapter 10, p. 154; see also his summaries of mystical Hinduism, Buddhism, Chinese Thought, Taoism and Zen in chapters 5–9 respectively.

[31] See, for example, Tolle, *A New Earth*, chapter 1, pp. 14 and 21–2 and chapter 2, pp. 26–7.

[32] Tolle, *The Power of Now*, chapter 7, p. 118.

[33] Tolle, *A New Earth*, chapter 9, pp. 258–9.

[34] Aurobindo, *The Life Divine*, book 2, chapter 6, pp. 487 and 496.

[35] Ibid., book 2, chapter 3, p. 404.

[36] Ibid., book 2, chapter 16, p. 709.

[37] Ibid., book 2, chapter 3, pp. 386–8.

[38] Wilber, *The Integral Vision*, chapter 5, pp. 149–50.

[39] See, for example, *Ken Wilber and Sri Aurobindo: A Critical Perspective* at www.infinityfoundation.com/mandala/i_es/i_es_hemse_wilber.htm; this was written by Aurobindo supporter Rod Hemsell.

[40] From Pathwork Lecture 224, 'Creative Emptiness', p. 4; see note 62 to chapter 7.

[41] From Pathwork Lecture 189, 'Self-Identification Determined Through Stages of Consciousness', p. 7; see note 62 to chapter 7.

[42] Lawton, *The Wisdom of the Soul*, Question 2.1.2.

[43] Wilber, *The Integral Vision*, chapter 5, p. 147.

[44] Freke, *Lucid Living*, under the heading 'you are a paradox'.

[45] Montgomery, *Here and Hereafter*, chapter 1, p. 19.

[46] From Pathwork Lecture 204, 'What is the Path?', pp. 6–7 and Lecture 180, 'The Spiritual Significance of Human Relationship', p. 2; see note 62 to chapter 7.

[47] Yogananda, *Autobiography of a Yogi*, chapter 14, p. 148.

[48] Bhagavad Gita 3:4–8; see Mascaro, *The Bhagavad Gita*, pp. 17–18.

[49] Bhagavad Gita 5:20–3; see ibid., p. 29.

[50] Bhagavad Gita 6:40–3; see ibid., p. 35.

[51] This basic theory on holography can all be found in the Wikipedia article of the same name.

[52] Pribram wrote various books and articles about his theories but they are relatively hard going for the layperson. For an excellent overview see Michael Talbot's 1991 book *The Holographic Universe*, chapter 1.

[53] Taken from an interview with Pribram entitled 'Holographic Memory' in

Psychology Today 12 (Feb 1979), pp. 83–4.

[54] As with Pribram this book is hard going for the layperson, but again an excellent summary is provided in Talbot, *The Holographic Universe*, chapter 2.

[55] Autobiographical information on Laszlo comes from the second appendix to *Science and the Akashic Field*; see pp. 158–69.

[56] This view was reinforced by Laszlo having a mystical experience of unity in 1986, which he describes in the preface to his 1993 book *Creative Cosmos*.

[57] Laszlo, *Science and the Akashic Field*, chapter 3 and the first appendix.

[58] Ibid., chapter 4, pp. 66–77.

[59] See note 10 above.

[60] Lawton, *The Wisdom of the Soul*, under Question 2.1.3.

[61] Besant, *The Ancient Wisdom*, chapter 10, p. 305.

[62] Reading 2172:1; see Todeschi, *Edgar Cayce on the Akashic Records*, chapter 3, p. 47.

[63] Austen, *The Teachings of Silver Birch*, pp. 60–1 and 174.

[64] From Pathwork Lecture 152, 'Connection Between Ego and Universal Power', pp. 1 and 3; see note 62 to chapter 7.

[65] Aurobindo, *The Life Divine*, book 2, chapter 3, pp. 384, 387, 389, 391 and 403 and chapter 16, p. 689.

[66] Ibid., book 2, chapter 16, pp. 694–5.

[67] This is discussed in Lawton, *The Wisdom of the Soul*, Question 2.6 and for example, by most of the channeled sources quoted in the previous chapter. For a full, scientific discussion of the statistical likelihood of life on other planets see Laszlo, *Science and the Akashic Field*, chapter 5, pp. 94–8.

[68] Lawton, *The Wisdom of the Soul*, Question 2.1.3.

[69] From Pathwork Lecture 152, 'Connection Between Ego and Universal Power', p. 3; see note 62 to chapter 7.

[70] See www.mellen-thomas.com.

[71] Tolle, *A New Earth*, chapter 10, p. 280.

[72] This is broadly taken from the summary of *The Life Divine* in the Wikipedia article of the same name.

[73] Johnson, *The Imprisoned Splendour*, chapter 19, pp. 402–3.

[74] Arguably these were only pulled together and properly interpreted for the first time in *Genesis Unveiled*. The relevant chapter is reproduced in full at www.ianlawton.com\guextr3.htm.

[75] Laszlo, *Science and the Akashic Field*, chapter 5, pp. 82–93.

[76] As Aurobindo points out this very objective originally led to the development

of ideas of illusion; see *The Life Divine*, book 2, chapter 16, pp. 705–6.

[77] This idea also gained support from our subjects in *The Wisdom of the Soul*; see Question 2.3.1.

[78] See, for example, ibid., Question 2.5.

[79] See ibid., Question 2.3.1, under the heading 'Reuniting with Source'.

[80] Tolle, *A New Earth*, chapter 10, p. 281.

[81] Aurobindo, *The Life Divine*, book 2, chapter 3, p. 402 and chapter 12, p. 599.

[82] Cainer, *Cosmic Ordering*, Chapter 2, p. 36.

[83] Ibid., Chapter 1, p. 31.

[84] Ibid, chapter 9, p. 141.

[85] Mohr, *Cosmic Ordering for Beginners*, p. 77.

[86] From Pathwork Lecture 194, 'Meditation Laws and Approaches', p. 8; see note 62 to chapter 7.

[87] See the overview in Lawton, *Introduction to Pathwork* (paper at www.ianlawton.com/se6.htm).

[88] See the summary of *The Life Divine* in the Wikipedia article of the same name.

[89] From Pathwork Lecture 224, 'Creative Emptiness', p. 7; see note 62 to chapter 7.

[90] Kardec, *The Spirits' Book*, book 2, chapter 6, p. 168 and book 4, chapter 1, p. 368.

[91] Yogananda, *Autobiography of a Yogi*, chapter 14, p. 149.

[92] Austen, *The Teachings of Silver Birch*, pp. 49–52 and 59.

[93] Cerminara, *Many Mansions*, chapter 24, pp. 278–9.

[94] Tolle, *A New Earth*, chapter 9, p. 265 and chapter 10, p. 294.

[95] Aurobindo, *The Life Divine*, book 2, chapter 16, pp. 690–1.

[96] From Pathwork Lecture 143, 'Unity and Duality', pp. 1 and 4; see note 62 to chapter 7.

[97] See the summary of *The Life Divine* in the Wikipedia article of the same name.

[98] See www.mellen-thomas.com.

[99] Extracted from Berman, *The Journey Home*, Chapter 2, p. 36.

BIBLIOGRAPHY

This bibliography is limited to the books specifically referenced in this work. The details given below are for the imprint or edition consulted, although the original date of publication quoted in the main text may have been earlier.

Atwater, Phyllis, *Beyond the Light*, Thorsons, 1994.

Aurobindo, Sri, *The Life Divine*, Lotus Press, 1990.

Austen, A W (ed.), *The Teachings of Silver Birch*, Spiritualist Press, 1973.

Baker, Robert, *Hidden Memories*, Prometheus Books, 1992.

Banks, Sydney, *The Missing Link: Reflection on Philosophy and Spirit*, International Human Relations Consultants, 1998.

Banks, Sydney, *The Enlightened Gardener*, International Human Relations Consultants, 2001.

Bentov, Itzhak, *Stalking the Wild Pendulum: On the Mechanics of Consciousness*, Inner Traditions, 1988.

Bentov, Itzhak, *A Cosmic Book: On the Mechanics of Creation*, Inner Traditions, 1989.

Berman, Phillip, *The Journey Home*, Pocket Books, 1998.

Bernstein, Morey, *The Search for Bridey Murphy*, Pocketbooks, 1978.

Besant, Annie, *The Ancient Wisdom: An Outline of Theosophical Teachings*, Kessinger Publishing, 1998.

Blackmore, Susan, *Beyond the Body*, Heinemann, 1982.

Blackmore, Susan, *Dying to Live*, Grafton, 1993.

Blackmore, Susan, *Consciousness: A Very Short Introduction*, Oxford University Press, 2005.

Blavatsky, Helena, *Isis Unveiled* (2 volumes), Theosophical Publishing House, 1972.

Blavatsky, Helena, *The Secret Doctrine* (2 volumes), Theosophical University Press, 1988.

Bohm, David, *Wholeness and the Implicate Order*, Routledge, 1995 (first published 1980).

Bowman, Carol, *Children's Past Lives*, Bantam, 1997.

Brown, Rick, *The Reincarnation of James, The Submarine Man*, Rick Brown, 1989.

Brownell, George, *Reincarnation*, Aquarian Ministry, 1949.

Byrne, Rhonda, *The Secret*, Simon & Schuster, 2006.

Cainer, Jonathan, *Cosmic Ordering*, Collins, 2006.

Cannon, Alexander, *The Power of Karma in Relation to Destiny*, Rider, 1936.

Cannon, Alexander, *The Power Within*, Rider, 1954.

Cannon, Dolores, *Between Death and Life: Conversations With a Spirit*, Gateway,

2003.

Capra, Fritjof, *The Tao of Physics: An Exploration of the Parallels Between Modern Physics and Eastern Mysticism*, Flamingo, 1992.

Cayce, Edgar Evans, *Edgar Cayce on Atlantis*, Howard Baker, 1969.

Cerminara, Gina, *Many Mansions: The Edgar Cayce Story on Reincarnation*, Signet, 1999.

Clark, Rabia, *Past Life Therapy: The State of the Art*, Rising Star Press, 1995.

Costain, Thomas, *The Moneyman*, Permabook, 1961.

Crookall, Robert, *The Study and Practice of Astral Projection*, Aquarian Press, 1961.

Delanne, Gabriel, *Documents pour servir à l'Etude de Réeincarnation*, BPS, 1924.

Edwards, Paul (ed.), *Immortality*, Macmillan, 1992.

Edwards, Paul, *Reincarnation: A Critical Examination*, Prometheus Books, 2002.

Fenwick, Peter and Elizabeth, *The Truth in the Light: An Investigation of Over 300 Near-Death Experiences*, Berkley Books, 1997.

Fiore, Edith, *You Have Been Here Before: A Psychologist Looks at Past Lives*, Ballantine Books, 1979.

Fiore, Edith, *The Unquiet Dead: A Psychologist Treats Spirit Possession*, Ballantine Books, 1988.

Flammarion, Camille, *La Mort et son Mystère* (3 volumes including *Autour de la Mort* and *Aprés la Mort*), Paris, 1921–2.

Fortune, Dion, *The Cosmic Doctrine*, Samuel Weiser, 2000.

Freemantle, Francesca and Trungpa, Chögyam (trans.), *The Tibetan Book of the Dead: The Great Liberation through Hearing in the Bardo,* Shambhala Publications, 1992.

Freke, Timothy, *Lucid Living*, Books for Burning, 2005.

Goswami, Amit, *The Self-Aware Universe: How Consciousness Creates the Material World*, Simon & Schuster, 1993.

Goswami, Amit, *Physics of the Soul: The Quantum Book of Living, Dying, Reincarnation and Immortality*, Hampton Roads, 2001.

Grant, Joan, *Winged Pharaoh*, Harper, 1938.

Grant, Joan and Kelsey, Denys, *Many Lifetimes*, Ariel Press, 1997.

Greyson, Bruce and Flynn, Charles P (eds.), *The Near-Death Experience: Problems, Prospects, Perspectives*, Charles C Thomas, 1984.

Grof, Stanislav, *Realms of the Human Unconscious: Observations from LSD Research*, Souvenir Press, 1979.

Grof, Stanislav, *The Adventure of Self-Discovery*, State University of New York Press, 1988.

Hall, Judy, *The Way of Reincarnation*, Thorsons, 2001.

Hall, Judy, *The Way of Karma*, Thorsons, 2002.

Harris, Melvin, *Investigating the Unexplained*, Prometheus Books, 2003.

Holzer, Hans, *Born Again*, Doubleday, 1970.

Huffman, Robert and Specht, Irene, *Many Wonderful Things*, DeVorss & Co,

1988.

Huxley, Aldous, *The Doors of Perception*, Vintage Classics, 2004.

Iverson, Jeffrey, *More Lives Than One? The Evidence of the Remarkable Bloxham Tapes*, Pan, 1977.

Jenkins, Peter and Winninger, Toni, *Talking with Leaders of the Past*, Celestial Voices, 2008.

Johnson, Raynor, *The Imprisoned Splendour*, Hodder & Stoughton, 1953.

Kardec, Allan, *The Spirits' Book*, Cosimo Classics, 2006.

Keeton, Joe and Moss, Peter, *Encounters With the Past*, Sidgwick & Jackson, 1979.

Krishnamurti, Jiddu, *The Awakening of Intelligence*, Harper & Row, 1987.

Lancelin, Charles, *La Vie Posthume*, Sorlot & Lanore, 1990.

Laszlo, Ervin, *Creative Cosmos*, Floris Books, 1993.

Laszlo, Ervin, *Science and the Akashic Field: An Integral Theory of Everything*, Inner Traditions, 2007.

Lawton, Ian, *Genesis Unveiled: The Lost Wisdom of our Forgotten Ancestors*, Virgin, 2004.

Lawton, Ian, *The Wisdom of the Soul*, Rational Spirituality Press, 2007.

Lee, Desmond (trans.), *Plato: The Republic*, Penguin Classics, 2003.

Leininger, Bruce and Andrea, *Soul Survivor: The Reincarnation of a World War II Fighter Pilot*, Grand Central Publishing, 2009.

Lenz, Frederick, *Lifetimes*, Ballantine Books, 1979.

Mascaro, Juan (trans.), *The Bhagavad Gita*, Penguin Classics, 2003.

Modi, Shakuntala, *Remarkable Healings: A Psychiatrist Uncovers Unsuspected Roots of Mental and Physical Illness*, Hampton Roads, 1997.

Modi, Shakuntala, *Memories of God and Creation: Remembering from the Subconscious Mind*, Hampton Roads, 2000.

Mohr, Barbel, *The Cosmic Ordering Service*, Hampton Roads, 2001.

Monroe, Robert, *Journeys Out of the Body*, Broadway Books, 2001.

Montgomery, Ruth, *Here and Hereafter*, Fawcett Crest, 1968.

Moody, Raymond, *Life After Life*, Bantam, 1976.

Moore, Brooke Noel, *The Philosophical Possibilities Beyond Death*, Charles C Thomas, 1981.

Muldoon, Sylvan J and Carrington, Hereward, *The Projection of the Astral Body*, Rider, 1929.

Muldoon, Sylvan and Carrington, Hereward, *The Phenomena of Astral Projection*, Rider, 1951.

Muller, Karl, *Reincarnation: Based on Facts*, Psychic Press, 1970.

Netherton, Morris and Shiffrin, Nancy, *Past Lives Therapy*, Ace Books, 1979.

Newton, Michael, *Journey of Souls: Case Studies of Life Between Lives* (5th edition), Llewellyn, 2002.

Newton, Michael, *Destiny of Souls: New Case Studies of Life Between Lives*, Llewellyn, 2003.

Newton, Michael, *Life Between Lives: Hypnotherapy for Spiritual Regression*, Llewellyn, 2004.

Osis, Karlis and Haraldsson, Erlendur, *At the Hour of Death*, Avon, 1977.

Pasricha, Satwant: *Claims of Reincarnation: An Empirical Study of Cases in India*, Harman Publishing House, 1990.

Penfield, Wilder, *The Excitable Cortex in Conscious Man*, Charles C Thomas, 1958.

Pierrakos, Eva, *The Pathwork of Self-Transformation*, Bantam, 1990.

Ramster, Peter, *The Truth about Reincarnation*, Rigby, 1980.

Ramster, Peter, *The Search for Lives Past*, Somerset Film & Publishing, 1992.

Rawlings, Maurice, *Beyond Death's Door*, Thomas Nelson, 1978.

Ring, Kenneth, *Life At Death: A Scientific Investigation of the Near-Death Experience*, Quill, 1982.

Roberts, Jane, *The Seth Material*, Prentice Hall, 1970.

Roberts, Jane, *Seth Speaks*, Bantam, 1974.

Roberts, Jane, *The Nature of Personal Reality*, Prentice Hall, 1974.

Robinson, James, *The Nag Hammadi Library*, HarperCollins, 1990.

de Rochas, Albert, *Les Vies Successives*, Chacornac, 1911.

Rogo, D Scott, *The Search for Yesterday*, Prentice Hall, 1985.

Sabom, Michael, *Recollections of Death: A Medical Investigation*, Harper & Row, 1981.

Sabom, Michael, *Light and Death: One Doctor's Fascinating Account of Near-Death Experiences*, Zondervan, 1998.

Schwartz, Robert, *Courageous Souls: Do we Plan our Life Challenges Before Birth?* Whispering Winds Press, 2007 (re-released as *Your Soul's Plan* in 2009).

Scott, Walter, *Hermetica*, Solos Press, 1992.

Shroder, Tom, *Old Souls: The Scientific Evidence for Past Lives*, Simon & Schuster, 1999.

Snow, Robert, *Looking for Carroll Beckwith: The True Stories of a Detective's Search for His Past Life*, Daybreak Books, 1999.

Steiner, Rudolph, *Life Between Death and Rebirth*, Anthroposophic Press, 1968.

Steiner, Rudolph, *Reincarnation and Karma*, Anthroposophic Press, 1977.

Steiner, Rudolph, *Manifestations of Karma*, Rudolf Steiner Press, 2000.

Stevenson, Ian, *Twenty Cases Suggestive of Reincarnation* (2nd edition), University Press of Virginia, 1974.

Stevenson, Ian, *Xenoglossy: A Review and Report of a Case*, University Press of Virginia, 1974.

Stevenson, Ian, *Cases of the Reincarnation Type* (4 volumes: India, Sri Lanka, Lebanon/Turkey, Thailand/Burma), University Press of Virginia, 1975–1983.

Stevenson, Ian, *Unlearned Language: New Studies in Xenoglossy*, University Press of Virginia, 1984.

Stevenson, Ian, *Children Who Remember Previous Lives: A Question of*

Reincarnation (2nd edition), McFarland & Co, 2001.

Stevenson, Ian, *Reincarnation and Biology* (2 volumes), Praeger, 1997.

Stevenson, Ian, *Where Reincarnation and Biology Intersect*, Praeger, 1997.

Stevenson, Ian, *European Cases of the Reincarnation Type*, McFarland & Co, 2003.

Strassman, Rick, *DMT: The Spirit Molecule*, Park Street Press, 2001.

Talbot, Michael, *The Holographic Universe*, HarperCollins, 1996.

Tarazi, Linda, *Under the Inquisition: An Experience Relived*, Hampton Roads, 1997.

TenDam, Hans, *Deep Healing: A Practical Outline of Past-Life Therapy*, Tasso Publishing, 1996.

TenDam, Hans, *Exploring Reincarnation*, Rider, 2003.

Todeschi, Kevin, *Edgar Cayce on The Akashic Records*, ARE Press, 1998.

Tolle, Eckhart, *The Power of Now: A Guide to Spiritual Enlightenment*, Hodder & Stoughton, 2005.

Tolle, Eckhart, *A New Earth: Awakening to Your Life's Purpose*, Penguin, 2006.

Tomlinson, Andy, *Healing the Eternal Soul*, O Books, 2006.

Tomlinson, Andy, *Exploring the Eternal Soul*, O Books, 2007.

Tucker, Jim, *Life Before Life: A Scientific Investigation of Children's Memories of Previous Lives*, Piatkus, 2006.

Wambach, Helen, *Reliving Past Lives: The Evidence Under Hypnosis*, Hutchinson, 1979.

Wambach, Helen, *Life Before Life*, Bantam, 1979.

Weiss, Brian, *Many Lives, Many Masters*, Piatkus, 1994.

Whitton, Joel, and Fisher, Joe, *Life Between Life*, Warner Books, 1988.

Wilber, Ken, *The Integral Vision: A Very Short Introduction to the Revolutionary Integral Approach to Life, God, the Universe, and Everything*, Shambhala Publications, 2007.

Wilson, Ian, *Mind Out of Time? Reincarnation Investigated*, Gollancz, 1981.

Wilson, Ian, *The After Death Experience*, Corgi, 1989.

de Wohl, Louis, *The Living Wood*, Ignatius Press, 2008.

Wolf, Fred Alan, *The Spiritual Universe: One Physicist's Vision of Spirit, Soul, Matter and Self*, Moment Point Press, 2006.

Woodward, Mary, *Edgar Cayce's Story of Karma*, Berkley Books, 1972.

Woodward, Mary, *Scars of the Soul: Holistic Healing in the Edgar Cayce Readings*, Brindabella, 1985.

Woolger, Roger, *Other Lives, Other Selves: A Jungian Psychotherapist Discovers Past Lives*, Bantam, 1988.

Yogananda, Paramhansa, *Autobiography of a Yogi*, Crystal Clarity, 1995.

INDEX

THE WISDOM OF THE SOUL
profound insights from the life between lives

by Ian Lawton *with* Andy Tomlinson

Rational Spirituality Press, 2007
www.rspress.org

'This fine book provides much-needed information about everything from trapped spirits to demonic beings; from the purpose of incarnation to extraterrestrial realms; and from legends of Atlantis to global warming and humanity's future. I cannot recommend it highly enough.' Edith Fiore, pioneering regression therapist and author of *You Have Been Here Before*

'The research in this book poses questions that have rarely, if ever, been asked before.' Hans TenDam, pioneering regression therapist and author of *Exploring Reincarnation*

For thousands of years our view of the afterlife has been handed down to us by a variety of prophets and gurus

But in the last few decades thousands of ordinary people have been taken back into their 'life between lives' in the light realms

Their consistent reports form one of the most profound sources of spiritual wisdom ever available to humanity

And now two researchers have decided to push this source to its limits...

It is important enough that we should understand what happens to us between lives in the light realms: how we receive energy healing to lighten our vibrations; how we review our lives without judgment from higher beings; and how we choose and plan our next lives along with close soul mates, in order to face the lessons and experiences that will most allow us to grow.

But what if we could use the interlife experience to answer a host of more universal questions of spiritual, historical and philosophical importance? About everything from unusual soul behavior and soul development, through humanity's past and future, to the true nature of reality and time? What if multiple regression subjects came up with consistent answers? And what if they displayed wisdom so profound as to be way beyond any normal human capacity?

THE LITTLE BOOK OF THE SOUL
true stories that could change your life

by Ian Lawton

Rational Spirituality Press, 2007
www.rspress.org

'This is a wonderful collection of stories, which I very much enjoyed. I will keep a copy for myself and happily pass the others on.' Peter Fenwick, fellow of the Royal College of Psychiatrists and author of *The Truth in the Light*

'This is a very nice collection of intriguing cases. I hope it gets a lot of attention.' Jim Tucker, University of Virginia Division of Perceptual Studies and author of *Life Before Life*

'I like this little book a lot. It's a perfect hand-out for past-life clients, or especially skeptical friends.' Thelma Freedman, Secretary of the International Board for Regression Therapy

How did a Russian scientist left for dead in a mortuary for three days make contact with his neighbor's sick baby... and wake up with a cure that all the doctors had missed?

What about the Indian girl with memories of a past life... who astonished her former husband by reminding him how he had borrowed money from her just before she died?

Or the Australian woman who recalled past-life details of a carving on the stone floor of a small cottage... and was able to locate it under decades of chicken droppings when brought to England for the first time?

These amazing reports are not new age mumbo jumbo. They have been properly investigated by professionals. And they will make you think long and hard about who you are and what you are doing here.

[This is a short, simple pocket book, written in a storybook style. It contains a selection of the most interesting near-death and past-life cases that support Rational Spirituality, interspersed with simple summaries and analysis.]

YOUR HOLOGRAPHIC SOUL
and how to make it work for you

by Ian Lawton

Rational Spirituality Press, 2010
www.rspress.org

'I predict that the author's proposal of a holographic model of the soul will be one of the most important concepts of our time.' *Hans TenDam, pioneering regression therapist and author of Exploring Reincarnation*

'The idea of the holographic soul brilliantly solves many spiritual conundrums.' *Judy Hall, pioneering regression therapist and renowned spiritual author*

If you're a newcomer to spirituality, would you like to know about the evidence that your soul consciousness will survive without your physical body, and that you have many lives? Would you like to understand why you reincarnate, and what that means for how to approach your everyday life? And would you like to learn about your true relationship to God?

Or if you're a more experienced spiritual seeker, would you like to unravel the enigma of being part of All That Is and yet also an individual soul? And would you like to understand the oft-misunderstood interplay between experience and illusion, and between conscious creation and active surrender?

It's only now that we can finally answer all these questions and more using a spiritual framework that is logical, coherent and philosophically elegant. One that unites a modern scientific discovery with ageless spiritual wisdom in a simple yet revolutionary new concept... that of the holographic soul.

[This is a short, simple pocket book, written in a question-and-answer style. It tackles seven key questions to build a Rational Spiritual framework, and then offers ten suggestions for how we can use it to get the most out of our day-to-day lives.]

look out for

THE FUTURE OF THE SOUL and

THE HISTORY OF THE SOUL

coming soon from

Rational Spirituality Press

Ian Lawton was born in 1959. In his mid-thirties he became a writer-researcher specializing in ancient history, esoterica and spiritual

philosophy. His first two books, *Giza: The Truth* (1999) and *Genesis Unveiled* (2003), have sold over 30,000 copies worldwide. In *The Book of the Soul* (2004) he developed the idea of Rational Spirituality, also establishing himself as one of the world's leading authorities on the interlife. And in *The Wisdom of the Soul* (2007) he first introduced the idea of the holographic soul. His other books include *The Little Book of the Soul* (2007), *The Big Book of the Soul* (2008, a complete rewrite of the 2004 book), *Your Holographic Soul* (2010), *The Future of the Soul* (2010) and *The History of the Soul* (2010, a revision of the 2003 book). For further information see *www.ianlawton.com*.

LaVergne, TN USA
09 August 2010
192646LV00004B/57/P